# Abou K

'Heroic retrievals, digging ...ng the mists of memory, reveal the secret history of a Dublin band finding themselves, and the words and sounds of that city's emerging subterranean moment.'

**Iain Sinclair** (writer, psychogeographer and Dublin contemporary of the Strangelies)


'Adrian Whittaker has hacked through the undergrowth and rediscovered a forgotten wonderland of the weird folk underground. Rich in colourful half-memories and eccentric detail, this telling playfully re-animates a dormant British/Irish counterculture, with its dreams of the curiously curious and the abnormally odd.'

**Rob Young** (writer for *The Wire* and author of *Electric Eden: Unearthing Britain's Visionary Music* )


'This book creates the conviction that we were a band of some cultural significance, which runs contrary to my assessment that we were borderline frauds having a great time with our limited resources. It adds a bit of weight to what we did; maybe we could call it validation. It certainly makes an entertaining read.'

**Tim Goulding**, Dr Strangely Strange

# About Dr Strangely Strange

'The first two Strangely Strange albums testify to the existence of a fiercely creative and highly intelligent sensibility at large in Ireland at the dawn of the 1970s.'
**Gerry Smyth**, in *Beautiful Day – Forty Years Of Irish Rock*

'I have loved Dr Strangely Strange ever since my eyes were opened by a soup-stained copy of *Heavy Petting* sourced from Taboo Records, Stoke Newington, some 20 years ago. The shop has since closed but my eyes remain open. The LP features the psychedelic blues licks of Gary Moore, making for a cautious but compelling hybrid of fragile folk forms and more muscular rock moves. The lengthy Sign On My Mind is a slowly uncoiling acid-folk classic, rivalling Fairport's A Sailor's Life and Trees' Sally Free And Easy.'
**Stewart Lee**, stand-up comedian, writer and director

'The original Strangelies, Tim Goulding, Ivan and myself, had an appreciation of each other's talents and musical abilities – or lack of them – and had great patience and empathy for each other. We became a creative Gestalt.'
**Tim Booth**, founder-member

'I had strictly no idea who Dr Strangely Strange were. I bought their first album in 1969 when I was fourteen, based on the sleeve and because I bought (almost) anything Island released.

*Kip Of The Serenes* was a vital part of the soundtrack of my adolescence, possibly the most precious, as in the Paris rural suburb where I grew up no one, even remotely, knew about them. Why did the music of Dr Strangely Strange so profoundly echo with me? I suppose the elegiac melancholy of their Irish music blended with the bucolic landscapes of my teenage years, the woods and fields I walked to the station where I caught the train to school. The passing of the seasons, the loneliness too. Their psychedelic folk was possibly the most relevant expression of my emotions. To this day the sheer perfection of Strings In The Earth And Air still sends shivers down my spine.

Their first album is a blessed moment: it captures at its purest the timeless grace of those years, seen through the wide-open eyes of the idealist youth I was.'
**Olivier Assayas**, director of *Irma Vep, Personal Shopper, Something In The Air* and many other films

'Rifling through the racks in a tiny record store I came across *Heavy Petting*. The actual music turned out to be a treasure trove of acid folk extraordinaire! Thank goodness I am an obsessive-compulsive completist; if it hadn't been for the elaborate cover design, I might never have heard of them at all. As soon as I heard *Heavy Petting* I sought out and purchased *Kip Of The Serenes*, which remains my all-time favourite of their albums. The eccentric classic track that defines the strength and surrealism of 'Strangely' music is Strangely Strange But Oddly Normal. A transcendental Zen masterpiece with a bizarrely perfect chorus of what Lady Jaye affectionately called 'caterwauling,' extending the pop failsafe mechanism of 'la la's' into extra-terrestrial territories. The Strangelies blend absurdism with lyrical poetry, emotion with coarse pub humour, and sudden melodic changes with incongruous soloing. The Strangelies' songs swerve and dodge all over the place. Where the ISB is essentially pastoral, the Strangelies are more Chaucerian, bawdy in a noisy medieval Irish inn.

Dr Strangely Strange albums are that rarity of items, music that can uplift the most dour and maudlin moment. In the end, my addiction to Dr Strangely Strange is rooted in the stretching of poetry into epiphany. Philosophy and 'popular' music is a difficult marriage, but like all good Zen masters (one Strangely became a Zen monk!) humour illuminates as brightly as wisdom. I cannot imagine not having the twisting turning contradictions and malapropisms that litter this wonderful, wonder-full music with diamonds of hope. Dr Strangely Strange smiles at you and if you cannot smile back, oh goodness, we are lost...'

**Genesis Breyer P-Orridge**, performance artist, poet and musician


'As a devotee of the quirky, quixotic and quite wonderful Incredible String Band, I decided to search out other madcap artists of a similar vein. Such outfits, I soon discovered, were like hen's teeth because the ISB seemed to these ears by far the most innocently original psych-folkies to emerge from the patchouli-scented late Sixties.

My quest took me to Trees, Trader Horne, Mellow Candle, Mr Fox, Fresh Maggots – all sufficiently weird and worthy of attention, but none quite as endearingly eccentric. Then I heard *Kip Of The Serenes* by Dr Strangely Strange, clearly 'the next ISB' in the mind of producer Joe Boyd, who had welcomed them to his Witchseason stable. Aside from Boyd, the album's other immediate ISB connection was a sublime and encouraging rendition of Ivan Pawle's Strings In The Earth And Air, which I knew as a Robin Williamson cover version.

Now my mission was finally bearing fruit! Here was that elusive band yielding two massive tick boxes. Elsewhere, the Strangelies charted a suitably eclectic course, populating their songs with unlikely characters (for a folk band from this side of the Atlantic) such as cowboy Roy Rogers. Only in this case the same piece managed to squeeze in Lloyd George, Rupert Bear and the age-old problem facing most aspiring bands... a bank overdraft. Barmy but brilliant! Then there was the track called Strangely Strange But Oddly Normal which remains genuinely, er, strange, along with the unbridled joy of Donnybrook Fair and the overtly proggy (well, who wasn't in 1969?) Ship Of Fools.

Dr Strangely Strange were never able to scale the dizzying heights of *Kip*, although *Heavy Petting*, with flashes of guitar heroics from a fresh-faced Gary Moore, bears plenty to admire. After that, it was mostly a case of what might have been... but seeing the two Tims, Booth and Goulding, and Ivan Pawle reforming for a slightly shambolic but stirring gig at Camden's Jazz Cafe a few years ago was a joy to behold.'

**Simon Cosyns**, Deputy Editor, *The Sun*

Adrian Whittaker
with Tim Booth, Tim Goulding and Ivan Pawle

# Dr strangely strange
# FITTING PIECES TO THE JIGSAW

There are no facts, only versions *(old folk saying)*

# OZYMANDIAS BOOKS

First published in Great Britain in 2019 by Ozymandias Books

## OZYMANDIAS BOOKS

London E8 2HY
Book website/contact: *www.drstrangelystrange.co.uk*

British Library Cataloguing-in-Publication Data: a catalogue record for this book is available from the British Library.

ISBN 978-0-954780-81-4
Every effort has been made to contact copyright holders.
However, the publishers will be glad to rectify in future editions any inadvertent omissions brought to their attention.

IRELAND • UK • FRANCE • BELGIUM • HOLLAND • DENMARK • BERLIN • WALES • DALSTON
**This book is an EU product**

 Gomer

Printed in Wales by **Gwasg Gomer Cyf / Gomer Press Ltd, Llandysul. Diolch!**
Papers used by Gomer are from well-managed forests and other responsible sources.

In memory of the Orphans:

'Orphan Annie' Mohan

Annie Christmas

Phil Lynott

Gary Moore

Frank Murray

and Anthea Joseph

# Visuals

. . . . . . . . . . .

DESIGN, LAYOUT AND GRAPHICS

**Mychael Gerstenberger**
Malbuch
Berlin | Alt-Mariendorf | Germany
www.malbuch.wordpress.com


TYPESETTING

The text is set in 10-point Swift,
designed by Gerard Unger. The lines of the characters aim to follow
the sweeping motions of the similarly named bird.


PHOTOGRAPHY

Special thanks to our three featured photographers:

The late **Annie Goulding** (*Kip* photos, Mount Street Orphanage era)

**Johanna** (cover photo, Sandymount Orphanage garden and
Sandymount Strand photoshoot; Dargle Cottage photoshoot)

**Jay Myrdal** (from Dalston to Hampstead Heath, 1970 photoshoot)


THANKS ALSO:

To **Iain Sinclair** for photos from his archive,
to **Jeffa Gill** for photo research
and all the other individually credited photographers.

**Barrie Wentzell** photo in Part Three used by permission.

All other photos are from the Dr Strange archives.


Thanks to **Tim Goulding** and **Tim Booth**
for permission to use their artwork.

# CONTENTS

# Dr Strangely Strange: Fitting Pieces To The Jigsaw

Most fans of Sixties music will know a little about Dr Strangely Strange: that they were Irish, that they were psychedelic folkies, that their most famous song was Strangely Strange But Oddly Normal. Rock fans will have heard something about the two Orphanages, the Dublin communal houses where they lived on and off from 1966 to 1970, from references by Thin Lizzy and by Gary Moore. Incredible String Band cognoscenti will know Ivan Pawle guested on *Changing Horses*, and that Robin Williamson covered his song Strings In The Earth And Air. And in most cases that's probably it.

The Strangelies had no hits, virtually no-one covered any of their songs, they only recorded two albums, and they were around on the British music scene for rather less than three years. So what kind of book is this, anyway? It certainly isn't a traditional music biography; after much deliberation, I decided Ivan's line about 'fitting pieces to the jigsaw' sums up the approach nicely.

A large section of the book aims to give a picture of the emergent counterculture in Dublin. After some scene-setting in Part One, Part Two is thematic rather than chronological, focussing on the Strangelies' Dublin milieu, then on the cusp of a beatnik into hippy transformation, and what it was like living and playing weird music in Ireland in the Sixties.

This book features lengthy contributions from Ivan Pawle and the two Tims, Booth and Goulding; all three Strangelies are fluent and articulate interviewees and emailers, and this to some extent dictated the format. I have always liked using interviews, but something that shifted me further away from the 'insert quote here' approach to biography was a 2003 visit to my local theatre, the Arcola in Dalston, where I saw a performance of *Come Out Eli*. Director Alecky Blythe had researched the infamous Hackney police siege of gunman Eli Hall, taping interviews with just about everyone involved (apart from Eli, who killed himself at the end of the siege). In her play, the actors wore headsets and reduplicated verbatim her collage of voices of the interviewees. It was a great success, both funny and moving.

So, the book is mostly a collage of oral and written history, drawn from the three key band members – but we are talking events of fifty years ago. This poses many challenges to the biographer relying on missing, conflicting or downright erroneous memories. Did Ivan Pawle really become a cleaning obsessive whilst on an acid trip, prefiguring a later career as a laundrette operator? Was their (unfinished) third album going to be called *Rabbits Wet My Sack*, or was it *A Rabbit Wet My Sleeping Bag*? Did Phil Lynott co-write Tim Booth's Donnybrook

Fair? Did Tim Goulding actually become a Buddhist monk? Did Tim Booth convince a gullible American dope dealer that Ivan was a failed Kamikaze pilot who would be only too happy to bring in a planeload of Afghan hash? And why oh why is this the sole detail Goulding remembers about a particularly scary series of encounters with paramilitaries and Provos on a Northern Ireland tour: 'Helpless hysterics in a Chinese restaurant where the waiter spent a lot of the time on the phone remonstrating with a dry cleaner who had stolen his trousers.'

I came to see my role as like an old-style record producer – going for new takes, suggesting overdubs, trying a different arrangement, mixing and sequencing tracks. I abandoned any lingering obsession with exact dates, facts and info and took to heart what Joe Boyd had said to me about memory when I was quizzing him about some nagging detail for a book about the Incredible String Band: 'Let there be Rashomon!' *Rashomon* is a famous 1950 film by Akira Kurosawa in which a murder is described in four mutually contradictory ways by its four witnesses. Not that there are any murders in the History Of Strange. I think...

The band members had a useful take on memory, proving surprisingly tolerant of each other's fanciful embroideries or even inventions. Tim Booth: 'An old friend, Martin Kelleher, came by recently and over a glass of wine we got to discussing the nature of memory and how it might be that different individuals remember an established event from the past in totally different ways. He came up with an elegant conceit: think of the event itself and the a priori establishing evidence as to its authenticity (posters, whatever) as a Maypole. Now take the memories of the participants and allow them to tie their stories to the pole and let them dance. Sometimes the dance may occlude the pole, other times reveal it, but the onlooker is the better for the spectacle.'

Goulding also came up with a useful angle on this, from John Le Carré's *Pigeon Tunnel*: 'Was there ever such a thing as pure memory? I doubt it. Even when we convince ourselves that we are being dispassionate, sticking to the bald facts with no self-serving decorations or omissions, pure memory remains as elusive as a bar of wet soap.'

Were they 'an Irish Band'? Strangelies both were and were not very 'Irish' in terms of Sixties British stereotypes. Ivan was an English runaway from Suffolk; Tim Goulding and Tim Booth, the two other Strangelies, were from what could be loosely termed the 'Anglo-Irish' classes, with a deep mistrust of the prevailing austere nationalism. But all three were steeped in Irish culture, Irish mythology and the patterns and vocabulary of everyday spoken Irish English. There is a parallel with their friends and allies Sweeney's Men, who came out of the same Dublin scene and also didn't fit into 'Irish' stereotypes: Terry Woods was into country-and-western songs and Americana, Andy Irvine was English and liked British folk and the music of the Balkans, and Johnny Moynihan was steeped in modal tunings and played the Greek bouzouki.

Part Three of the book – recording sessions, album releases and life on the road – is approximately chronological and perhaps more akin to a traditional biography. But unlike, say, Ian Hunter's *Diary of a Rock 'n' Roll Star*, the Strangelies touring days were remarkably eclectic. They developed a convoluted routine called 'Tessie', which involved, en route to a gig, a volunteer knocking at the doors of random strangers and saying: 'I'm sorry I'm here, I'll leave immediately. But – I may be back.' As well as the student circuit, gigs included appearances at an Irish agricultural fair and Belgian village halls, as well as a week's run in a Dublin cabaret revue. Along the way there were encounters with Ivor Cutler and with Joni Mitchell, who set some of Goulding's lyrics to her own music, and a run-in with the Edgar Broughton Band, not to forget a pre-planned onstage custard pie attack on Terry Woods. They recorded and played with some great musicians, too, including Gary Moore and Dave Mattacks, and, at different points, all of Sweeney's Men. The band never really split up, but moved into an extremely part-time mode from around 1972 onwards, so Part Three ends there.

The final part brings the story briefly up to date; the last decade has seen something of a Strangelies renaissance, bringing the band critical acceptance from some unlikely quarters. Iain Sinclair has always carried a torch for them, but other admirers range from Genesis Breyer P-Orridge to film director Olivier Assayas, Stewart Lee, Richard Herring, Scritti Politti's Green Gartside and Simon Cosyns of *The Sun* newspaper. As well as playing Dublin's plush Sugar Club, in recent years they have appeared at The Barbican in London and, in October 2011, played a well-received *Heavy Petting* gig at Camden's Jazz Café.

The viewpoints in this book are predominantly male, and so it is a matter of great regret that I couldn't talk to two of the key women in Strangelies history, the late 'Orphan Annie' Mohan and the late Annie Christmas, who headed up the second Orphanage in Sandymount. Linus, who was in and out of the band around 1969, declined requests for an interview, as did a couple of other key female figures from the Dublin era and beyond. My especial thanks, then, are due to Jeffa Gill for her memories of the Mount Street Orphanage, and to the one and only Mary McSweeney for recalling life at Glen Row and beyond.

Huge thanks to Ivan and the two Tims for signing up to this project with such alacrity. I think the reader will begin to distinguish their individual voices as the book progresses: Ivan, precise, occasionally pedantic, with a bookish tinge but a keen eye for the absurd; Booth, one for both extravagant descriptions, acerbic analysis and mordant comments; Goulding, off-beat, associative, tangential, with an eye for odd surreal details and an underlying Zen acceptance. They are all very funny, too.

Adrian Whittaker, Autumn 2018

**Footnote: Names**

A note on Irish name spellings: I have stuck to the spellings that the band used at the time – so Ashling and not Aisling, Patrick rather than Padraig, but Eiléan (and not Eileen) Ní Chuilleanáin. Though I've tended to use first names in the book, I distinguish Tim Booth from Tim Goulding, as the band do, by use of their surnames. All the Strangelies loved bestowing nicknames on their mates (and each other), and you'll find these cropping up here and there.

# PART 1
## Early Days

. . . . . . . . .

# CHAPTER 1

# 'A world that has vanished' Dublin in the early Sixties

Dublin was the birthplace of Dr Strangely Strange. In the early Sixties, it embodied a weird mixture of age-old tradition and the first stirrings of some kind of counterculture. The consensus is that the spirit of the Sixties only really swept Dublin the following decade.

It was still a place where many pubs had no women's toilets, where women would only be served half-pints, and where they would often not be served at all if they wore short skirts. It was also common for men with long hair to be banned. Contraception was illegal, although there was a small black market in condoms, run by Northerners. The Catholic Church was so powerful that it came very close to getting the government to impose a ban on all women under 18 from leaving the country, to prevent possible pregnancy. It was a place where the showbands had a stranglehold on the pop music scene and had an enforced break for the whole of Lent, where black people were objects of curiosity at best, where the gay scene was restricted to one bar, and where Catholics would be excommunicated for attending Trinity College (unless they were dentists).

In the introduction to a book of Dublin photos from 1966, Brian Leyden evokes the atmosphere in the streets:

'It is hard to appreciate the silence that fell over Dublin on long hot summer Sundays in the 60s. The population at rest after Sunday Mass and the midday Sunday dinner. No shopping. Everything closed. No cattle herded to the boat. No traffic congestion. Just the sun-struck glass of closed shop windows. The pub doors bolted. The Holy Hour in force across Ireland. The photos show Dublin's streets are almost empty of traffic, with more bicycles in evidence than cars. Men wear trilbies in bars. A woman holds a clay pipe between her teeth. Cows are herded down streets. Horses and carts act as lorries, hauling loads. A woman walks up the steps towards what looks like a derelict building; it's one of the tenements that were still in existence then. People look poor. It's a compelling insight into a world that has vanished.'

The political party in power, Fianna Fáil, had an unchanging remit of austere nationalism, strongly influenced by the Catholic Church, and the overall political climate in Dublin was little different. The local Holy Hour, introduced under pressure from the right-wing Archbishop of Dublin, John Charles McQuaid, was a piece of law that forced Dublin pubs to close, not just on Sunday afternoons, but from 2.30 till 3.30 in the weekday afternoons. It was created so working men, who were paid weekly on a Friday morning, would have to leave the pub, go home to their wives and thus avoid spending all their wages there.

Homeless families in Sixties Dublin

Most housing in Dublin was severely overcrowded and many working-class people still lived in the old tenements, with no piped water and with outside, shared toilets. Turf fires were the normal heating, even in shops and bars. Council house construction was at the lowest rate in Europe, and those living privately in newer conversions were not protected by rent control, which meant ever-spiralling rents. A 1969 housing report states: 'Housing is a form of poverty which affects every member of a family. And the pattern of crime, desertion and alcoholism in [Irish] major towns can be traced to a large degree to a policy of making people live in conditions which are unbearable.' A growing squatting scene and the adoption of shared houses (like the one most of the band lived in from 1965 onwards) were part of the response to the housing crisis.

There is a fascinating TV documentary by literary historian Anthony Cronin, compiling footage from the beginning of this era, largely filmed in melancholy, spartan pubs, profiling the Dublin writers Patrick Kavanagh, Brendan Behan and Flann O'Brien. The literary greats, like Yeats, Joyce and Beckett are long gone from the city, which is portrayed as isolated and self-regarding, narrow and puritanical, a provincial place from which the creatives like Joyce and Beckett needed to escape or became, like Brendan Behan and Flann O'Brien, trapped by drink and the negativity of their peers.

But there were some islands of otherness.

Dr Strangely Strange grew organically out of the early Sixties scene around Trinity College, Dublin, where founder members Ivan Pawle and his friend Tim Booth had both been students. Like the band members themselves, TCD was in no way typically Irish. It was effectively a Protestant university, for a start. It had been created in 1592, at a time when the English state was strengthening its control over the kingdom and when Dublin was beginning to function as a capital city. Politically, the plan had been to bring Ireland into the mainstream of European learning and strengthen the Protestant Reformation within the country.

In the Sixties, Trinity retained a strong Protestant tradition. Around the time Ivan and Tim Booth (and the two brothers of Tim Goulding, the eventual third Strangely) studied there, Trinity had 3,000 students, of whom only 800 were Catholics. Most were English Catholics; hardly any Irish Catholics enrolled as undergraduates as the Catholic Church still effectively banned attendance. An Irish Catholic who enrolled without the permission of Archbishop McQuaid was committing a mortal sin. A case had to be made directly to him to obtain the necessary dispensation: studying dentistry, a course not available on Catholic premises, was usually deemed acceptable. To boost falling student numbers, TCD had increased its enrolment of students from Britain and the United States. At this point, nearly half the student body came from outside the island of Ireland, making it an unusual, even unique institution – a small, multicultural, mainly Protestant university, curiously cut off from, but also part of an old Catholic city. One writer described it as 'an eccentric little world.'

The public perception of TCD was that all the students were sons of well-off (Protestant) farmers, but the truth was far from that. It was certainly predominantly male, and women were not permitted to live on campus: they had to leave the premises by early evening. The student body, though, was a cosmopolitan mix of visiting Americans and Africans, posh boys, proto-hippies and ascetic Beckettians. The college had strong connections with modern Irish literature: Samuel Beckett had both studied and taught at Trinity, and the novelist JP Donleavy, part of the vanguard of modern Irish literature in the Fifties, had come over from New York to study science at Trinity and stayed on in Ireland since then.

There was no real pop or rock music scene at Trinity; it had a folk club and sometimes a Jazz And Blues Society (mostly for listening to records). The singer Ian Whitcomb, in the charts in 1965 with You Turn Me On, writes about his time there in *Rock Odyssey*. 'The campus was a haven for oddities: obscure Scottish peers, eccentric offspring of ancient British families, an Egyptian count, a Mauritanian Teddy Boy, and a couple of African tribal chiefs.' His band, Bluesville Manufacturing, found themselves slotted into the showband circuit: 'The showbands were pretty dreary affairs of enervating ballads and wet-rock, accompanied by demure high-kicking and the swinging of instruments from right to left in strict unison.' Writer Damian Corless sums up the ballroom scene in a recent memoir: 'The showbands ruled the roost of the Irish ballroom circuit... they were highly paid to be human jukeboxes, faithfully reproducing the hits of the day... listening in to the Radio Luxembourg Top Twenty in the hope of catching the gist of the new entries. They were just about the only show in town.'

The 'haven for oddities' was a fertile breeding ground for all kinds of plans and projects. Another Trinity student, Iain Sinclair, notes that the countercultural aspects of Trinity were affected by the visiting Americans, like Ivan's friend Tony Lowes (q.v.): 'They brought a degree of Lower East Side energy (and reference and drugs). And money. They liked to get things done. Against the local inertia.' It was where many of the people in this book first came across each other, where Tim Booth ran into Ivan Pawle and where, eventually, the first ever Dr Strangely Strange concert was performed.

The other island of otherness was the geographical centre of the embryonic counterculture, sometimes known as Baggotonia. In the late 18th century the Dublin aristocracy had moved southwards across the Liffey, building elegant Georgian streets in a previously unfashionable area around Baggot Street and Merrion Square. Meanwhile, the northern part of central Dublin became decrepit and was slowly transformed into one of the worst slums in Europe. There's a line in Roddy Doyle's *The Commitments* which sums up the position of people from the Northside: 'Do you not get it, lads? The Irish are the blacks of Europe. And Dubliners are the blacks of Ireland. And the Northside Dubliners are the blacks of Dublin.'

South of the Liffey, much of the Georgian new build had itself become dilapidated and ramshackle by the Sixties and the richer residents had moved on, though there were still some living links with its more illustrious past – for example, WB Yeats' daughter Anne still lived on Upper Mount Street. Some parts of Baggotonia were hurriedly demolished by the government before anyone could intervene. The writer John Banville, who also lived on Upper Mount Street, has a convincing rationale for this in his Dublin memoir, *Time Pieces*: 'The ultra-nationalists who ran the country then had scant regard for the delights of Georgian architecture, and indeed many of them would have seen Georgian Dublin as a despised monument to our British conquerors...' Later in the Sixties, opposition to the demolitions started to coalesce around The Dublin Housing Action Committee, inspiring at least one Dr Strangely Strange song.

The decaying houses that were left were soon bought up by landlords on the make, and the area was home both to Dublin working-class families and a mixture of artists, poets, musicians and beatnik types. Banville recalls that Ireland in this era was 'a hard, mean-spirited place for anyone with artistic ambitions,' but small informal groups and cliques of like-minded individuals developed across a spectrum which ran from 'heads' to 'straights.' One of these cells was based, from 1965, in a decaying house in Lower Mount Street, inhabited by Ivan Pawle and an ever-changing supporting cast. There was little interaction and no sense of an overarching network; each group had its own preferred hangouts, routines and bars. Though John Banville is exactly the same age as Ivan and the Tims, and lived round the corner from them in the same period, they never met. Their worlds didn't overlap at all – the pubs, and even the Dublin poets they liked, are quite different.

Later chapters will look in more detail at the particular esoteric Dublin subculture the band inhabited, but first Ivan, Tim Booth and Tim Goulding will tell us how they ended up there.

# CHAPTER 2

# Three pre-meds – by the band

## Ivan Pawle: 'I was caught trying to practise Rebel Rouser by Duane Eddy in the back row during a maths class'

My father, Ivan Peter Pawle, was born in 1921. He and his elder brother, Kenneth, grew up in Brightlingsea, a seaside town near Clacton, in Essex. Their father was a fisherman and sailor, and the lads crewed for him, crossing over to Brittany on fishing trips. My Dad attended Colchester High School but I think he spent as much time as possible on the water, gathering gulls' eggs, sailing and fishing. He went into the Merchant Navy and served on various Atlantic convoys as a merchant seaman. He spent about 18 months on the Falklands at one stage, which, as an ornithologist, he enjoyed.

My mother had been adopted by Emily and Joe Henry Clegg, mill owners up in Rochdale, and sent to boarding school at Polham Hall, Darlington. She had previously been married to a man called Peter Grant, who lived in Sussex and was a serious musician, highly involved in folk music.

After the war, she and Ivan bought a small mixed, arable farm in Suffolk, probably with some financial aid from Joe Henry and Emily. A lot of young couples did the same thing, but I think most of the menfolk had been officer class. My father was a born naturalist and also had 'green fingers,' but the farming was financially gruelling.

I was born in 1943 in Cambridge General Hospital. My father was away at sea and my mother was working as a librarian in Thaxted, Essex. My late sister Rosemary was a couple of years older than me, and Pippa, my younger sister, came along in 1948. After

Ivan at Fairfield prep school, 1949 (FAR LEFT)

Ivan grooms his dog on wheels

primary school we all went off to boarding schools, which my parents could ill afford: they thought to give us the best advantages in life thereby.

In the school holidays I enjoyed running around with the Chaplins, a family living on a similar farm four or five fields away. We would cycle everywhere and fish for rudd, roach and sticklebacks. Tony Chaplin had met Paula in the Spanish civil war, and they had a Spanish guitar we used to have a go on, and a piano. It was there I heard Johnny B Goode on 208 Radio Luxembourg – what a sound! When not trying to make music their son Christopher and I built crystal sets: he graduated to valve radios and he went off to work in the BBC after grammar school. His younger brother Giles was good on piano and another brother, Oliver, made an album in 1974 called *Standing Stone* which is highly rated by cognoscenti. Their mother got a job at Summerhill progressive school, a different kettle of fish from my preparatory school!

We had my mother's grand piano at home and we all took piano lessons at school. I stopped at about Grade 5 or 6, just wanting to play by ear. My mother had danced – ballet and American tap. She showed me the rudiments of boogie-woogie in the key of F. I bought the sheet music for Rock Around The Clock. An Irishman came to our prep school to teach Latin and play harmonium for hymns, and I persuaded him to help me to parse the sheet music, but it still didn't bear much resemblance to Bill & The Comets' record.

There was a wind-up gramophone and a few records. Specifically I enjoyed a single by Nellie Lutcher, with Fine Brown Frame on one side and Hurry On Down on the other. There was also some boogie-woogie by Albert Ammons and Meade Lux Lewis. On the classical side there was a good deal of ballet music, and I liked the *L'Arlésienne* suite by Bizet. The nearest thing to 'folk' would have been The Foggy Dew by Peter Pears and Benjamin Britten.

My mum met Alistair Chisholm, a shy but charming gentleman living on a farm a few miles away and they fell in love. She left home when I was around 14 and eventually married him, becoming Madam Chisholm of Chisholm. In the holidays from boarding school the three of us children stayed with Nana, my father's mother, in Brightlingsea. After my mother left, we had a Texan family from Bentwaters airbase lodging with us. They had a guitar on which I learnt I Guess Things Happen That Way by Johnny Cash. I bought a Jew's harp, which was confiscated when I was caught trying to practise Rebel Rouser by Duane Eddy in the back row during a maths class.

Age 14 I went off to Haileybury public school. Stirling Moss had been expelled for taking a parent's car for a spin one Speech Day. I am quite proud to have been to the same school as Clement Attlee and Erskine Childers. It was a decent school, not too snobby in fairness.

My first day there I met Carl Hallam; it was 1957, but he already had a single of Dimples by John Lee Hooker (on 78rpm mind you). We auditioned to join the choir – unfortunately our voices were breaking and we were summarily dismissed. Once my voice had broken I joined the choir as a second bass, and loved singing in the school chapel: hymns, carols, Verdi's Requiem and Fauré's Requiem.

Some cultural highlights included a performance of *Waiting for Godot*: I saw this during my first term, and was astounded (it was 1957 – I was just 14 years old). On Saturday nights we would usually have a film or a concert or a talk. We had a concert by Julian Bream, the percussionist James Blades another time, and a man demonstrating the Theremin.

Carl Hallam and I collaborated in a couple of musical ensembles, he on bass, me on guitar or piano. Our rock 'n' roll band, The Virtues, was loosely modelled on The Ventures and The Shadows. One Saturday the lead guitarist was playing an away cricket match, so when he failed to turn up in time for our concert, I put down my rhythm guitar and moved over to the piano. A few weeks earlier we had formed a jazz appreciation society and gone to the Hammersmith Odeon to attend a Count Basie concert in which Jo Jones the drummer had performed an extended drum solo. Inspired by this, I announced the piece as 'Like Exodus,' starting with a drum roll and an enthusiastic approximation of the opening chords of Grieg's piano concerto in A minor. I then vamped away to the best of my ability around those basic chords. Once I started running out of inspiration, Carl did a short bass solo, whereafter Martin Wonfor hit the skins; he was doing a pretty good solo – think Sandy Nelson's Let There Be Drums plus. As he became more involved, possibly louder and faster as well, a master in the front row rose to his feet and bellowed for him to stop. Not a hope! Eventually the drum solo died down and we wrapped up the piece with some of the opening chords. One of the true highlights of my musical career.

I started flute lessons, but I was too impatient and switched to fife and bugle to play in the Combined Cadet Force military band – anything to get out of drill. I joined the RAF section and we went on a summer camp to Little Rissington airbase, to which I brought my guitar. A lad from another school also had a guitar, and we had a kind of joust as champions for our schools. I have to say that he had more chops than me, but I had more songs, and we played together fairly well: bits of Buddy Holly, Eddie Cochran, and Lonnie Donegan.

Eisenhower came to visit England, and we all went up in a big plane to escort Airforce One down to British soil. Later I was to walk on about three Aldermaston marches, on which music played an integral part, probably starting an interest in folk and protest music.

We formed a small jazz group at school. Most of our material was fairly mainstream – Satin Doll was one of our best numbers. Charles Warlow on acoustic guitar composed a piece entitled 'For Four' – Carl played bass, I played flute, and Tony Skinner played drums. We entered the school quartets competition and were Highly Commended by the external examiner. We were surprised and pleased!

I had a friend, Robert Kirk, who played oboe, and we tried playing our own compositions along the lines of Jimmy Giuffre's Train And The River. One Christmas holiday he formed a dance band in which I played piano (chancing my arm). We played three or four gigs around Birmingham in 1960 or 1961.

During my last terms at school I would sometimes take records out of the school record library. I became hooked on Sibelius: there was an LP conducted by Colin Davis with the LSO with the Second Symphony on one side and the 7th on the other.

My father sold the farm and went off to start a new life in Paris – he would only have been about 40 years of age. When he first moved, Pippa and I stayed a couple of times. Two musical highlights there – one was attending *Daphnis et Chloé* with sets by Marc Chagall. Another was Bud Powell at the Blue Note with J.J. Johnson and Kenny Clarke.

Looking moody at Frinton-on-Sea, 1962 (LEFT) (Photo: Charles Warlow)

On piano at Brightlingsea (BELOW)

When I left school, and inspired by Jack Kerouac spending some time as a forest watchman, I got a job as a watchman on an oil tanker on the River Colne. I stayed with my grandmother in Brightlingsea and attended Colchester Tech, with a view to getting better at German to matriculate at Trinity College Dublin for an Honours degree. I didn't get brilliant A levels (French and German) so that automatically ruled out Oxbridge. I wanted a third level university as it gave me a chance to take a step back and see what life might hold. A bunch of new universities, like Sussex, had just started up. Dublin was more exotic, and furthermore had a four-year under-graduate course. I knew nothing about Ireland, apart from knowing some Irish boys at school. The rich literary tradition had some bearing, I guess, but it was more an instinctive thing.

In the event I didn't get into the Honours class, and did General Studies, qualifying for a grant from Essex County Council. Doing General Studies actually gave me more time to pursue extra-curricular activities. At Trinity I embarked on a degree course commencing in 1962, graduating in 1966. I made friends immediately with Tom Baker, with whom I shared digs at 181 Rathgar Road. Tom was doing Business Studies and had a great interest in and knowledge of film. He had been friends at school with Mike Reeves, who was to make *Witchfinder General.* Tom soon introduced me to like-minded souls Chris Bamford and Iain Sinclair, who had met sharing digs in Sandymount. Iain had just done a year at the London School of Film Technique in Brixton. We became stalwarts of the Dublin University Film Society; it was an exciting time for film, with Bergman, Godard and Fellini. We would also go off to the suburbs to catch rare gems. Chris and Iain and Tom wrote a couple of plays and films (Super 8 and 16mm) in which I was privileged to act. With these lads I also got involved in helping to produce *Icarus*, the poetry magazine, for which Tim Booth did the artwork.

I had not done much acting at school, but decided to join Players, the Trinity drama society, and acted in a couple of plays: I had a small part in JP Donleavy's *Fairytales Of New York*. Iain directed Samuel Beckett's *Krapp's Last Tape*, with Tom doing the lighting. It had originally been a radio play, but they wanted to incorporate a film element. Old Krapp was played by Frank Wilcox, with me on stage and film as the young Krapp. I was staying at the Orphanage that time with Orphan Annie, and we filmed a short sequence down by the pier at Sandycove, in which Krapp is reminiscing about his brief halcyon fling with Effi on the Baltic. Annie and I acted, dressed as Edwardians. 'Ivan Pawle handled [his] part in a pleasing, restrained manner,' said *The Irish Times*.

We had a party after the play at the Orphanage, attended by Robin Williamson who was staying there at the time.

Not long after I came to Dublin, late 1962 or early 1963, I was in The Bailey, a favourite city centre watering hole, catering for every caste and class, in the company of a pair of fellow students. I was up at the bar ordering a pint of stout in my best British accent when a glass of vodka hurtled past my head. It was an L-shaped bar, and the glass had been thrown from across the other side. Brendan Behan had taken exception to the sight and sound of me, and, in fairness, I can well understand where he would have been coming from. I was a little bit shaken, but everything soon went back to normal. I had quite long hair, and one bystander said I might have slightly resembled Garech Browne, founder of Claddagh Records, with whom Brendan had some disagreement at the time.

In summer 1964 I went with some friends via Italy to Turkey, where I bought a saz in the bazaar. A couple of new friends entered my life around then. Tony Lowes had come to TCD in 1963 from Westchester, a smart Manhattan suburb. The family money came from the Reader's Digest, and Tony seemed quite urbane compared with us lot. I bought some grass off him. He was practising to be a writer and studied English. Tony had a flat in Fitzwilliam Square but was moving into the Mill House at Brackenstown, outside Swords (just north of Dublin).

I spent summer 1965 working at the Birdseye peavining station, Great Yarmouth, saved money, then went on a holiday to Brittany with Chris and Iain and

## T.C.D. plays by Beckett and Sartre

"KRAPP'S LAST TAPE" is not quite one of my top ten plays as entertainment, though this is probably due to its depressing quality and an incurable feeling that there is enough "sord and sick" in the world already. It is a difficult solo test-piece and therefore a *tour de force* when successful.

When I heard that D.U. Players had put Krapp Younger on the stage in person, along with Krapp Elder and the now dumb tape-recorder, I was a bit dubious as to the result, but in fact it paid off: impact was gained by the visual element and Ivan Pawle handled this new part in a pleasing, restrained manner.

The slick relation between the lighting and the script thus rendered necessary went like clockwork (unusual for a first night) and Tom Baker is to be congratulated. Another successful device of the producer, Ian Sinclair, was the use of silent ciné-projection for one sequence, though perhaps for slightly too long, and the tear in the parasol was given such prominence that one was left wondering whether it had some deep meaning or not.

Frank Wilcox's Krapp Elder was excellent, though he should be careful in the early clowning sequences not to draw more laughter than he can kill when he wants to. Make-up and costume by Orphan Annie (that's what it says) were just right.

In Sartre's "In Camera," the Players showed their aptitude for demonstrating the familiar thesis that Hell is other people. Few adverse criticisms are possible; congratulations to the producer, Meredith Yates; to Ian Milton (Valet), Garcon (David Watson) and especially to Mirabel Walker for her vicious study of Inez, and Ann McFerran for her Estelle, which was a superb performance on several planes, a superficial Betty Boop with several layers of evil underneath. Keith Hornby's set design was apt and striking, and the efficient stage management was by Jennie Holmes and Claire Gaynor. **G.H.D.**

A beatnik in Paris (Iain Sinclair)

Anna. That autumn I moved into the Orphanage at 55 Lower Mount Street with Annie Mohan and Likky McKechnie. Robin Williamson came over to visit Likky, and then that Christmas she went back to Scotland. My first encounter with LSD was a tab Robin and Likky gave me around that time. I didn't take it immediately. When I came to take it I more or less enjoyed the trip and took quite a few trips after that.

(ABOVE) Trinity Vampires do wacky

(BELOW) Trinity Vampires do moody – Ivan back right

I met Tim Goulding around that time – he had returned from studying weaving in Sweden. Tim was friends from school in the UK with Laurence Bicknell, an artist living in Upper Mount Street. At a time when he was besotted with Italy and Italian friends, he wanted to change his identity. His pals called him Lorenchi, which soon became shortened to Renchi. He did some artwork for *Icarus* when not working in a small film animation studio.

I think I would have met Tim Booth through doing *Icarus*, on the campus at Trinity and in one or two of the favourite watering holes like The Pike, which was an after-pub coffee shop where singers and strummers sang folksongs. He also did some set designs for Players. I helped Booth out in Co Kildare one day when he was decorating a house for a 21st birthday party. There was an Everly Brothers' single there, and we discovered that we could sing good harmonies together on When Will I Be Loved? After The Pike closed down, Smokie Joe (Joe Cogan), an antique dealer, opened the Studio Club above his photographic studio.

When I first came to Dublin I had bought a Spanish guitar from a graduate who was heading off to Australia. Two girls, Kate Nesbitt and Sue Shepherd, sang folk songs (Joan Baez etc) with an engineering student, Jerry Harrington, accompanying on guitar. The engineering course was particularly intensive, so he had to concentrate on studies – I stepped into his shoes in The Idlers. I enjoyed the challenge of learning the material, and standing next to two very attractive young women!

There was a rock'n'roll band in Trinity called The Vampires (different from a contemporary Dublin band of the same name, which featured Tony Kenny). Parallel with The Idlers' situation, the rhythm guitar/ main vocalist Dennis Kelly was an engineering student who had to do some hard studying to get the exams. Thus I joined that band, with Edwin Evans and Charlie Fay on drums and lead guitar, and Neill O'Callaghan on bass.

We played the usual canon of four-piece material of the time, with special emphasis on the Shadows etc. Dennis had been a more visceral showman than I, and could even do Chuck Berry songs pretty well: I was better on the Buddy Holly side of things.

There was some good music at the Trinity Jazz Club – I saw there people like Fiachra Trench (Brian Trench's brother and later string arranger for Van Morrison and the Pogues), Bill Somerville-Large (later recording engineer for Kate Bush, inter alia), Ian Whitcomb and Barry Richardson (later in Bees Make Honey). I bought a soprano saxophone off Ruan O'Lochlainn (also later in Bees Make Honey), hoping to transfer my flute and penny whistle skills, but to no avail. My friend Maurice Conlan was a good alto saxophonist – we used to listen to Willis Conover's Jazz Hour in his flat on Baggot Street on Wednesday nights.

One pub Chris Bamford and I used to frequent in the early evening was The Brazen Head. The woman of the house was Miss Cooney, who served stout in bottles – they had none on draught. There was a piano there, and after a bottle or two I would pluck up the courage to have a go on it. In fairness, the clientele consisted of a handful of old codgers. I was trying to work out a few Irish airs.

After University I moved to London, where I briefly tried a spot of supply teaching, but my heart was not in it – plus I have no natural talent in that area. I knocked around Portobello Road for a few months, getting odd jobs through the Manpower agency. I met Jay Myrdal (who guested on *Kip Of The Serenes*) when he was working as a photographer at a corporate event and I was helping on the catering side. Jay had an old Borgward Isabella estate car with a broken front spring, but it brought us on some expeditions around London. Iain and his wife, Anna, had moved over to Dalston, Hackney, as had Renchi with Judith, his wife. I met various members of the Exploding Galaxy and various other creative personalities.

1967 was a strangely episodic year for me. There was a foot and mouth epidemic in the United Kingdom and one was discouraged from travelling between rural UK and rural ROI. London became too frantic, and early in 1967 I moved back to Ireland, staying for a while with Tony Lowes at the Mill House.

Around this time, in about June 1967, I met Mary McSweeney, though we didn't get together until some months later. We only started to cohabit in earnest at the beginning of 1969, when our daughter Niamh would have been about one year old.

Later in summer 1967 I was back in London to score LSD for friends from the Mill House scene. It was very hot, with a preponderance of bad acid and several of my acquaintances falling prey to methedrine and worse. I had a bad trip, possibly something known as STP. I thought to find God in the Buddhist Society off Kensington High Street. Eventually I somehow got on an Aer Lingus flight back to Ireland and returned to Swords, where I could breathe. [Ivan's verbatim account of this horrific episode features in Iain Sinclair's *Kodak Mantra Diaries*, based around Allen Ginsberg's visit to London in July 1967.] After that experience I felt somewhat delicate, chastened even. I took little acid thereafter, favoured mushrooms if anything.

Back in Swords I met Humphrey Weightman, a guitar player who was staying out at Castletown House. Iain was making a documentary film of Allen Ginsberg's visit to Europe for a German TV company: he asked me to put William Blake's Ah, Sunflower! to music. I had no technical knowhow and no equipment, saving my saz and my penny whistle, but I think Humphrey owned a cassette recorder, which would have been fairly 'state-of-the-art' at the time. We repaired to Tim Goulding's painting studio out at his parents' place in Co Wicklow and recorded a fragment of chanting with an open-tuned acoustic guitar, finger cymbals, possibly my saz, maybe recorder or tin whistle. Basically we just chanted 'Ah, sunflower, aaah sunflower' to a mesmeric drone. I was disappointed in myself that I was not capable of producing a more robust piece. It didn't get used in the end.

Then, in autumn 1967, came the offer of a gig with Tim Booth for the Dublin University Folk Club...

## Tim Booth: 'I was a pretentious child... full of hippy shit'

My mother came from a family of English Quakers. Her full maiden name was Eileen Constance Peet. I think she was born in England, but moved to Ireland when she was very young. She had trained as a painter in the late Twenties in various London art schools – a very adventurous thing to do – and was a beautiful draftswoman.

My father was Church of Ireland. His family came over to Ireland as followers of Cromwell's army, when his branch of the family went by the name of Ploughman. Over the years this transmogrified to Pluman and I have distant cousins of that name living near Athy. He only found out about his Cromwellian antecedents during the war, when as a young Captain in the Irish Army taking over command of a section of the Curragh camp (where Brendan Behan was interned for IRA activities) he found that a fellow officer refused to shake his hand, stating that as an Irishman he would not shake the hand of 'any fucking Cromwellian.'

When my parents married, they went on a painting honeymoon on bicycles to the west of Ireland. My father – although never taught – was a considerable draftsman as well, but when children came along, they both stopped painting. My mother continued to sketch and draw whenever she could, but my father, by now a director of motor assemblers Booth Brothers, took up farming, a love he continued to lose money on until his death at the age of 70 in 1976. My mother lived on until 2000 and died at the age of 94, but, sadly, her last years were filled by memory loss and dementia.

My parents had 4 children: my elder sister Jane, followed by me in 1943, my younger sister Susan and my younger brother Peter, who succumbed to Hodgkin's disease on his 18th birthday. My parents never got over his death. Strangelies were about to take the

The young Booth, 1948

stage in Mothers Club, Birmingham when the news came down the line, and even though I thought we should do the gig, Ivan and Tim thought otherwise and whisked me off to London to catch an early morning flight back to Dublin.

All four of us kids were educated at Newtown School, Waterford, a co-educational Quaker school where we boarded. When I was 12, my mother – an accomplished pianist – wanted me to take piano lessons but the piano did not have the required coolness factor, so after a decent amount of negotiation she took me to McCollough Pigott's on Dublin's Dawson Street and for six old Pounds bought me a steel-strung acoustic guitar. And that's where my troubles began.

No. Not really. They began much earlier, dribbling out of the big valve radio in my parents living room, *Music While You Work*, *The Billy Cotton Band Show*, *Dick Barton Special Agent*, with its 'da diddle dah diddle dah' refrain and one fateful Sunday afternoon, *Riders of the Range* on the BBC Light Programme. This was a western adventure series about a cowboy gunslinger Texas Ranger called Jeff Arnold and was written by Charles Chilton (before he went on to write *Journey into Space*). Best of all, to alleviate the drama and extend the plot, there were musical interludes. These – supplied by a proto country swing band who called themselves The Sons Of The Saddle – featured somewhere in their line-up an instrument so awesomely nifty, so silvery smooth as to chill the spine. I had never heard the like. My mother played Chopin and Debussy, my father sang gustily flat in church, my elder sister seemed to like Fats Waller, but this sound I was hearing in the gaps between the singing Sons was like a needle of ice inserted into my tiny brain, the music of the spheres, silver notes twanging and sliding, turning the cosmos… I was a pretentious child… full of hippy shit even then, but you know what I mean because it was a steel guitar.

There was little or no music in national school, but boarding school – to which my parents sent me when I was two days past my 10th birthday – was very different. The senior boys were so very cool: to my cultchie eye they looked as if they had stepped fully formed from the pages of *Life* magazine and the senior girls… wow oh wow… the girls all looked like young film stars and the music they played on the record player in the mixed common room in the evenings was so revolutionary. I should explain that 'cultchie' is a Dublin slang word for a being from the country, as in 'agricultural.'

The school, being one of the only co-educational schools in the country, was very advanced for its time – that's the main reason I was sent there – and held dances for its pupils every couple of weeks. We shuffled around the parquet floor of the classroom under the eagle eye of the headmaster – no indiscreet touching or fondling among the senior pupils was tolerated – to the music of Bill Haley and the Comets, Marvin Rainwater, Perry Como, and later, Cliff Richard, Elvis, The Shadows and Joe Brown and the Bruvvers.

With my new guitar, I was about to buy into this golden circle of coolness, but I had overlooked one vital fact. I needed to learn how to play it, and this proved difficult. Firstly, you had to tune it. Mmm. Then, there were things called chords to be mastered and then… you had to learn how to pitch your voice to the key you had chosen to play within. So much stuff. And then Denis Kelly with his Groucho Marx hair style and walk arrived in from Sligo and he could play Three Steps To Heaven and Diana with a very cool finger flick which, after hours of practising, I finally mastered. So we became a junior band and when fellow pupil Brian Trench revealed how musically talented he was, there was no holding us.

17 years old, developing a taste for freedom
and the open road... Summer Breeze

By my final year, we were doing a spot in the school's dances, calling ourselves The Romans, playing Everly Brothers, early Elvis and some of our own stuff. Our signature tune was Roaming In The Gloaming – see what we did there? – with a massive off-beat and a sort of Sir Douglas Quintet attempted vibe.

School over, University began. Trinity College Dublin in the early 60s was a total mind fuck for a seventeen-year-old from Kildare. The grant aided English students were not only older, but so much hipper and worldly wise; some had just finished National Service and they knew everything there was to know about music and there was a jazz society where you could also hear Ian Whitcomb lash out his stride piano style or Ruan O'Lochlainn play an electric guitar with a tone so gently round and sustained that the first time I heard him I thought it was a clarinet.

My father wanted me to do engineering, but I persuaded him to let me attempt geology – which, having a problem with numbers, later diagnosed as dyscalculia – I managed to fail, achieving 38.9% of the required 40% pass mark. All, however, was not lost. I was allowed to change courses without losing a year and slotted bemusedly into something then called General Studies where I undertook English, Philosophy and History and, having now only nine hours of lectures a week, my pipe was truly loaded.

## Ian Whitcomb and the fake 'Bluesville'

When Ian Whitcomb, in 1965 still a Trinity College student, had a surprise American hit with You Turn Me On, his label Tower Records demanded a promo photo urgently. He hastily assembled a group of mates who had nothing to do with Bluesville, the Trinity R&B band who backed him on the single, but vaguely looked the part, including Tim Booth (FAR LEFT) and Ivan Pawle (THIRD LEFT). Ian is on the far right. The fake photo was widely reproduced in the States as the record rose to No 10 in the Billboard charts – and, Ivan informs us, to No 1 in Seattle.

Mick Colbert taught me how to fingerpick. He was a tall brooding man with an alcohol problem, but could sing and play with great passion and delicacy. He was resident in The Pike folk club for many years and went on to run Slattery's downstairs, where we often played for and with him. In later life he became a television commercials director and was very good at it. He became violent when drunk, mostly in defence of his friends when he thought they had been insulted (he had been a very good boxer as a youth). He once saved my life and this is that story:

## LOVE IS PLEASING

Mick was singing, eyes closed, fingerpicking his guitar when the fight started. I hadn't noticed the men in the far corner of the club, dockers awash from an evening's drinking. Now one, a spivvy whippet, was on his feet, a chair held in the air.

'Fuckin' Bollix.' He shattered the chair on his companion's head. Chaos. Bodies falling, women screaming, fists thumping in the confined space. The mill subsided as the dockers legged it down the stairs into the night. We followed, but they were gone. We followed anyway, into Baggot Street and in the confusion I'd got separated from the others. That's when Mr Whippet stepped out from a doorway, a blade shimmering.

'Come on ye little cunt,' he said and I didn't know what to do. He ran at me. I froze.

Mick Colbert in the Paris snow, 1988

Someone pushed me aside and sidestepping the knife, hit him once. Mr Whippet fell, head cracking off the iron railings, weapon flying. Mick stood over him a moment then kicked him concisely.

'Just fuck off. Next time I'll kill you.' Stooping to pick up the fallen weapon, then turning to me. 'You all right?'

'Yeah – where'd you learn to do that?'

'I was Inter University flyweight champion.'

In the club again, Mick, in his corner, tuned his guitar, closed his eyes and resumed.

Booth's student card, 1964

'Love is pleasing, love is teasing...' his voice lilting, the knuckles of his fingerpicking right hand swollen and bruised.

This is where Denis Kelly comes back into the picture. He was a blue-jeaned engineering student, but was taking time from his studies to play rhythm guitar with a Trinity beat group called The Vampires. I sometimes dropped into their rehearsals, perhaps with a vague notion that I might join in. By this time I had improved enough on guitar to spend time in the emerging Dublin folk circuit, playing a few 'ballads' and a bit of American folk – learnt from the recordings of Alan Lomax – and some early fingerpicked Bob Dylan. And I think that's where I first came across Ivan Pawle – rehearsing to become a Vampire.

Denis was finding it hard to take time from his engineering studies to play that old timer rock 'n' roll, so Ivan was roped in as a potential replacement. I had seen him around. He sometimes played

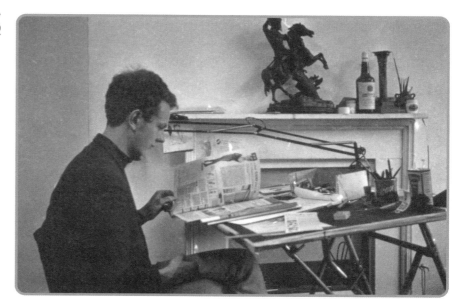

Booth, age 21, working as a 'Junior Visualiser'
in Arks advertising, Dublin, 1964 (Photo: Tony Pattison)

guitar for two fabulously voluptuous fellow students who undertook a folkish kumbaya type of thing and I was a tad envious. Those girls were so beautiful. How had he managed to inveigle his way into such a threesome? I had also seen his energetic performance with The Vampires and was greatly impressed by his version of Twist And Shout. He knew his chops for sure, so I don't know how it happened, but your riverboat captain... we started to play together.

My school friend Stephen Pearce could play guitar a bit. He had a semi-acoustic, might have been an Epiphone, during our last years in boarding school. When I was a student I would occasionally drop down to Shanagarry in Co Cork, where his family pottery was based, and bring a guitar. The Irish traditional/parlour singer Seán O Sé was booked to appear in the Shanagarry village hall, and somehow Steve persuaded the committee to allow us to open for him. We met Seán and his wife backstage. He was in a tux. We were proto-hippies, postbeatnik in our apparel. We went on and were very well received, a mixture of Buddy Holly, Lonnie Donegan, Steve's party piece Ain't Misbehavin' (chords supplied and taught by Brian Trench), topped with a rousing version of The Jolly Tinker. Imagine our surprise when on coming off stage we were confronted by a very angry Seán and his wife. Had we stolen his thunder, upstaged him? No. The Jolly Tinker was the culprit – the words were deemed obscene by the moral guardians of Ireland, including the O Sé tribe. Seán raged at us. We were nonplussed. The wife had to restrain the irate singer. As we made a dignified retreat, we heard her say to him: "Seán, Seán, don't go down to their dir-tee level!" And this became a catchphrase during our later Strangelies partnership.

## House Of David Jugband

At that time I was living in a basement flat in 28 Waterloo Road which I shared with a banjo-playing Welsh student, Jake Harries, and Brian Trench. Brian and I had a friend in common, the late Trevor Crozier. He claimed to be from Bridgewater in Devon, spoke with a Devonshire burr, but may very well have been South African. He was of piratical mien and walked with a limp, resultant of childhood polio. He knew hundreds of songs – from music hall to blues by way of Ewan MacColl – and had a girlfriend, Margie. She was a really good blues singer and together they performed in various folk clubs such as The Pike. I had but recently come across the Jim Kweskin Jug Band and Trevor, Brian and I were very taken with the singing of Maria Muldaur, who was at the time married to Kweskin. We thought we could do that – or at least Margie could – and under the tutelage of Trench (now our washboard player), licked a few of their tunes into shape. After a few false starts we were joined by Richard (The Hawk) Hawkins on 5-string tenor banjo (he was also my TCD history professor), Jake Harries on autoharp and Annie Christmas on jug. We called ourselves The House Of David Jugband and performed in various guises in and around Dublin in places such as the Neptune Rowing Club. The height of our fame was being engaged to perform at the fabled Trinity Ball, which we did to considerable acclaim. It was all downhill after that.

Some time in 1966 I walked into O'Donoghue's pub on Dublin's Merrion Row to borrow a fiver from Paddy O'Donoghue – the very best publican in the known universe – against a freelance cheque I was expecting and during the course of the evening met Jenny Richardson. She was – and still is – serenely, wonderfully beautiful, from Edinburgh and had recently graduated from the art college there and she spun me golden-tongued, silver-eyed stories of how wonderful the scene was in Scotland and would I like to visit her and of course I would and I did and discovered that she ran – with her friend, another Jenny with flaming hair and an impeccable eye – a shop the like of which I had never seen before – or since.

It was called 'The Incredible Here Today Gone Tomorrow Shop' and was at least a decade before its time. The shop specialised in second hand items: furniture, and most essentially, beautiful clothes, many bought by weight from the Edinburgh rag stores. I seem to remember she paid a shilling a pound weight to the rag man, no matter what the item might be: old leather, wonderful tweed suits – cut for the gentry with lead weights in the hems to make them hang correctly – silk scarves and wonderful 1920s shoes.

Because of what it sold, the shop attracted a clientele. As did the area – Rose Street – full of tough pubs and humans of uncertain virtue. And to the shop willowed in some incredible young men like Nicky Walton, tall and as elegant as his whippet Leaf, with an eye for a good suit and linkage to a tailor who could take it in or up, so as our skinnier frames could display the necessary ragamuffin elegance. And he had a friend with a limp, a touch taciturn, tough, take-no-shit-from-anyone, called Clive Palmer who apparently played the banjo. I confess, I was a touch scared of him, but Jenny had his measure and told me of the band he sometimes played with and when the first Incredible String Band record came out, I was so impressed with myself and Jenny to think that we were acquainted with these Gods.

I never heard the band play in Edinburgh at that time, but I did meet up with many of their influences – all through Jenny – the likes of Owen Hand, whose wife Ruth ran a secondhand shop (Madam Doubtfire's in Leith) who had a very neat clawhammer guitar style that complemented my own. Many others, such as Hamish Imlach, too numerous to mention with any degree of verisimilitude.

Back in Dublin in 1967, the offer of a Freshers' Week gig came up...

# Tim Goulding: 'The weirdy son of Sir Basil'

15th May 1945, a week after Victory in Europe Day, I was born in a nursing home in Hatch Street, Dublin. Soon afterwards I was christened in a bombed-out church in London, where my grandmother lived. The English connection comes from my mother's side. Her father was Sir Walter Monckton, a college friend of Edward VIII and his personal lawyer, who once said: 'My daughter was fined for speeding in Hyde Park in the Thirties; she was doing 25 miles per hour. When asked why, she replied that she was bound for Windsor Castle and the abdication papers were on the back seat.'

I grew up in Ireland. My earliest memory is lighting a bonfire in my bedroom in one half of a tin globe, shades of the fires to come (a large series of paintings I did later, of night fires in West Cork, where the gorse is burnt off on the mountains in the springtime).

My parents were wealthy and high-profile people in Dublin society. My mother, Lady Valerie Goulding, founded the Central Remedial Clinic in Pembroke Street in Dublin. It catered for children with polio, which was endemic in the early Fifties. Later in my life, I worked there briefly. Today it caters for 4,000 disabled people with many conditions but not one Polio patient, thanks to widespread inoculation campaigns.

My dad, Sir Basil Goulding, was a wacky genius, a touch of the Renaissance man. To live in his shadow is a hard act to follow. He was captain of football at Oxford, Irish squash champion, played cricket for Ireland and was also an ace skier and tennis player. Apart from that he was a master gardener, and I grew up in a magic woodland garden beside the valley of the river Dargle, which flowed through it in a deep ravine (hence Ballad Of The Wasps). The house was perched high above the ravine and was an old cottage with a regency extension; in the Sixties my dad added another large extension in Modernist vein. It included my mother's bedroom that flew out towards the river on a heavily reinforced pillar. We posed for the cover of *Heavy Petting* on the balcony.

My dad had trained as an architect but abandoned this to take over his father's business, Goulding Fertilisers. When asked what he did he replied 'manure magnate.' He was also a superb cabinet maker and carpenter. He was well known in Ireland as a collector of contemporary art, mostly Irish plus some international names. In 1962 he became the founding Chairperson of the Contemporary Irish Art Society, which led to the development of many important art collections in Ireland. Its aims were to encourage a greater level of patronage of living Irish artists which, at the time, was extremely low. The Society raised funds to purchase contemporary artworks, which were then donated to public collections.

I never went to art school, preferring to plough my own furrow, but my Dad was my real teacher. We spent hours leafing through catalogues, rehanging paintings and absorbing the works of Sam Beckett. He used to write his chairman's report in Beckettese. In fact, the word 'Basilese' was bandied about: dense and almost indecipherable prose. He could read piano music and used to play Forties and Fifties show tunes and boogie-woogie with a really loose and enthusiastic touch. Dad took up roller skating at the age of seventy and appeared on the Mike Murphy show on RTÉ.

Many well-known people visited our house from the theatre world: Bob Hope, Rock Hudson, James Cagney, Peter Ustinov and the dreaded Jimmy Savile too. Louis Armstrong came round for drinks when I was about seven, the first black man I'd ever met. Artistic stars from the Irish contemporary scene became my teachers as well as many international artists, such as Barnett Newman and Henry Moore (to whom I remember showing my studio). So, life at Dargle Cottage, Enniskerry was a continuous stage for unusual gatherings and events, which probably equipped me well for life in the Strangelies.

I remember the Irish Army band playing on the lawn above the river, an all-night party with ballet dancers performing on a grassy steppe, an opera singer singing from the high balcony and a lady dressed as a mermaid languishing on a rock in the river, while above her a tightrope walker traversed the ravine. On the river itself a bandstand had been built which the band had to row out to.

As a boy and young man my main interest was the wild glen and the river, the mystery of nature and also the mystery of being alive. I have been a lifelong 'Spiritual Detective.' I was what was called a delicate and sensitive child, but occasionally prone to violent tempers. At the age of seven I contracted primary TB and spent some weeks in bed and was not allowed to ride a bike for a year. This was by far the worst part of it.

Timmy & Hammy, 1950

My poor younger brother Ham was at the receiving end of my theories. I taught him how to walk two inches above the ground (a failure) and when he asked me to demonstrate this I was mysteriously 'too tired.' I also taught him to fly by jumping off a first-floor balcony with an umbrella. He landed heavily in the flower bed but went on in later life to become an ace pilot. A successful student.

My first best friend was a very neurotic youth who was prone to 'fits' and with whom I planned archaeological investigations into a parallel universe which was dominated by espionage. It turned out he lived in a stately home with a mother who wrapped herself in cold wet sheets when ill (regularly) and a Canaletto hanging in the breakfast room.

As was the norm amongst my parents' class, the Anglo-Irish, we were sent off to school in the UK. I was shipped off by mail boat, The Queen Maud, to an alien land with a wooden tuck box full of sweets to meet fellow spindly youths in grey flannel short-trousered suits who were equally scared shitless. From the age of seven I went to two British establishments: Ludgrove School in Berkshire and Winchester College in Hampshire. Before managing to squeak into Winchester I was dragged up to the austere Gordonstoun College in northern Scotland, a bleak spot. The ethos was 'outward bound' and scared the hell out of me. On returning from the assault course 'entrance exam' I was arduous in my studies for Winchester.

There I led the life of an outsider with a handful of friends, Renchi Bicknell, the filmmaker and artist, being the closest. We read poetry and played musical instruments at dawn in the shunting yards of the nearby railway, organised banana eating competitions, printed and illustrated handmade books, edited an art and literary magazine and composed alternatives to the classical regime. I played the cello, with difficulty, and learnt to play classical piano up to the age of twelve. Then it became too much like maths, with the result that to this day I cannot read the dots. My particular diet of music included Bartók, Shostakovich, Charlie Mingus, The Modern Jazz Quartet, Dave Brubeck and Gabriel Fauré, so I missed out on popular music until I was nearly 18. The first concert I attended was at the Albert Hall, with Sir Adrian Boult conducting the London Symphony Orchestra with Maura Lympany playing Greig's First Piano Concerto. The first record I bought, though, was Long Tall Sally by Little Richard, 'the man who put funk in rock 'n' roll.' My reward for all this was holding the record

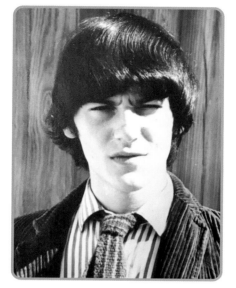

for being the most beaten boy in my house. The usual pretext for these beatings was 'bad attitude.'

My first sexual experience was a grope in a broom cupboard with a horsey girl; my first evening out was with a silent girl, with whom the mode of communication was finally agreed to be through the medium of Japanese poetry.

Despite this very challenging existence – strangers in a strange land, loneliness – we survived. But it maybe spawned the outsider mentality which most artists thrive on. On my entering a gala ball with my parents, the Prime Minister of the day, Jack Lynch, remarked: 'There goes the weirdy son of Sir Basil.' Maybe he was spurred by my dress of black tights and purple velvet tabard with gull wing sleeves lined with turquoise blue silk, crowned by a large triangular jewel-encrusted Afghan necklace. Two-tone hand-painted jesters' shoes stood out amongst the tuxedos. How dull we have become.

Tim in the early Sixties

After leaving secondary school I landed a two-year Scholarship to Konstfackskolan, the state school of art in Stockholm. I was studying textile design and was in a class of 19 girls doing embroidery, amongst other things. I had a flat in central Stockholm. Across the courtyard was a brothel, but I was the one in trouble with the janitor for holding séances. The pull of wanting to be a painter made me leave after a few months and I returned to Ireland in disgrace.

For a few years I lived at Dargle Cottage and had a studio there. I also spent time in the Dublin art 'ghetto', and it was at this time that I started to make friends with Trinity students (both my brothers were studying there) and in particular Ivan and Tim Booth.

Tim at a Dublin Hunt Ball, 1963, with friends Mark and Di

My one friend from Winchester, Renchi, came to live in Dublin. Our set congregated at Toners Pub in Merrion Row. Alec Finn (later of De Dannan) auditioned me for a rock 'n' roll band but it turned out to be too big a challenge for me. After all, I was coming from playing Mozart and Beethoven at school, though later I meandered on my parents' Bechstein Boudoir and played 'by ear.' Around the end of 1965 I moved into the Orphanage and lived there with Orphan Annie, Ivan Pawle, Jeffa Gill and many other floating voters.

# Part 2
## Strange World – pubs, clubs, Orphanages and Orphans

The emerging Dublin counterculture inhabited
by the band and their peers, 1966 – 1968

# CHAPTER 1

# Mount Street: The first Orphanage

We have to start with Annie. She was actually christened Patricia Mohan, but had been baptised 'Orphan Annie' by Ivan, and so the large flat she rented at 55 Lower Mount Street soon became known as 'The Orphanage.'

She had grown up in Emor Street, on the southern outskirts of Dublin, with four siblings. Her parents were from the country and her father was a tailor from Co Wexford. She ran away from home and went off to Scotland when she was about sixteen, where she met Ian McCullough, with whom she travelled to Morocco for a few months. She then started studying weaving in Edinburgh, where on the crafts scene she met Christina (Likky) McKechnie (later of the Incredible String Band) who had left school to work as a ceramic artist in the Buchan Potteries, painting some of their best-selling designs involving a thistle with a bluebell and heather.

Ivan had first met Annie on one of her visits back to Ireland in the summer of 1963, when she was seventeen. She had come over for the All Ireland Fleadh Cheoil in Mullingar, a very popular Irish traditional music competition. Ivan: 'Back in Scotland, she moved between Glasgow, Edinburgh and Mull with a cohort of Beats. In 1965, the next time she came back, she brought Likky with her.'

In autumn that year, Annie decided to rent a flat for them both and invited Ivan to move in; he assumed the persona of a sort of butler/valet/batman. The three settled into the new place. Ivan: 'We were a happy, harmonious trio.'

Mount Street was a slightly decaying Georgian townhouse. Booth: 'Beneath the gombeen conversion into flats undertaken in the 1950s, it still was a very dignified building.' [A 'gombeen' is a shady, small-time wheeler-dealer].

Ivan: 'There was another flat up on the third floor – a young, very quiet couple lived there. Annie's flat was on two floors, plus a basement. The small kitchen was straight ahead, and this was where visitors would mostly hang out. A small bedroom on the landing, where Likky slept, and later Jeffa Gill. Above, the bathroom and a large room, which was a sitting room and also served as Annie's bedroom. Goulding: 'I soon moved in to live with Orphan Annie. Our bedroom on the first floor was large and freezing cold. It was decorated in a trashy

Tim and Annie by the Orphanage front door. All photos in this section by 'Orphan Annie' Mohan.

Edwardian style but I do remember the beautiful irises in a windowsill vase.' Jeffa, too, remembers Annie's 'elegant purple irises in vases.'

A priest would collect the rent on behalf of the old lady who had previously lived there and was now in hospital; he eventually inherited the house when she died. Jeffa: 'The rooms overlooking the front were locked up, with the old lady's furniture inside (you could peer in through the keyholes!). Our rooms overlooked the back, and my room, previously Likky's, had a cold green lino floor. These days, I think you would call the décor shabby chic – old mirrors, stained glass, mahogany stairs, and a little kitchen with a leather chaise longue which Humphrey Weightman used to sleep on.'

Ivan: 'Annie always put food on the table. She was a wonderful self-taught cook – we would get the cheapest cuts of meat and leftover vegetables from the markets. Butter beans were a great staple.' Jeffa also recalls Annie's 'elegant meals.' Goulding: 'Breakfast was always a surprise. This was not because of the cuisine, which was always of the first water despite being constructed from meagre ingredients, but who you might meet sleeping on the kitchen floor or on the chaise longue, accompanied by the house cat Orpheus. There was also a small animal called Virginia Waters who sadly got suffocated down the back of a chair.'

Shopping was mostly local. Jeffa: 'We would go out through the back garden and through the old coach house to the canal, where there were some tiny, smelly shops run by old ladies. If money was tight Annie and I would get half a pound of margarine, a tin of butter beans and 2 cigarettes.' Goulding: 'Opposite, a few doors down, was a small grocery shop called Cullens, and above this lived a budding poet called Rosemary Rowley. She's well-known in literary circles these days.'

Jeffa on the landing outside her room

Annie was right at the centre of things for the four years or so that the Orphanage existed. What got her through the unending stream of both wanted and unwanted visitors was a fundamental sympathy for outsiders, coupled with an underlying forcefulness. Ivan: 'Annie had finished formal schooling at an early age, but she was intellectually inquiring and loved to read and debate. She read a lot of the mystics Gurdjieff and Ouspensky, trying to formulate a cosmology far removed from the Roman Catholic dogma she had grown up with. The flat soon became a home for like-minded souls passing through.'

Annie in the Orphanage era

Goulding: 'Annie had a real "Irish mother" streak. She loved to welcome and cook for people and had a strong caring streak, born of adversity in her teenage years. In those days she ran the Orphanage with open arms. She coupled a great sense of humour with an enquiring mind, ever an avid reader of serious literature. She loved to party, too.'

Booth: 'She was generous and at that time saw very little bad in people, so she welcomed waifs, strays and Bandidos, all with the same magnanimity. She was quite forceful when she needed to be, but kept that determination well sheathed within the velvet glove of her humour and cooking.'

Likky was there for a few months. Though she had already met Robin Williamson by that point and they had what Robin has called an 'on-off relationship,' she was on the run after her intended marriage to Bert Jansch had been called off. After seeing the banns posted in the local registry office, Likky's family had warned Bert off, feeling the marriage was 'unsuitable.' Bert, by all accounts fairly philosophical about this, had taken off for London and fame without her. Before they broke up, Bert had taught Likky how to play Anji, a notoriously tricky rite-of-passage finger-picking piece with a descending bass line, written by Davy Graham. Ivan: 'She tried to teach me how to play Anji, but I totally lacked the dexterity! Later in my life I once met Davy Graham in a pub in Ladbroke Grove, and we went back to my flat in Tavistock Crescent, where he graciously gave me a rendition.'

As Likky was now an Orphanage resident, she and Annie had a conceptual link-up in mind. Ivan: 'She tried to get a job in Bewley's cafe in Grafton Street. Bewley's, a Quaker family, only employed orphans, but she didn't technically qualify as an orphan, so she got a job as a model in the School of Art. Annie got a few odd jobs, like one day a week she would do the accounts for Louis Clear who had a small printing works called Clearprint. Then she got taken on as a photographer's assistant at Creation, which was a publishing group on Grafton Street. She excelled there and later became an excellent photographer.'

Relationships in the house were complicated, though. After a brief affair with Likky, Ivan 'foolishly fancied Annie and moved to her room.' In Robin Williamson's autobiographical *Mirrorman Sequences*, he describes setting off for Dublin in search of Likky. Not knowing the number of the house, he ended up conversing with a night watchman next to a hole in the Mount Street tarmac. After a few hours, Likky happened to walk by, 'wearing a

The Happening (ABOVE) • Jeffa making clothes in her room (BELOW)

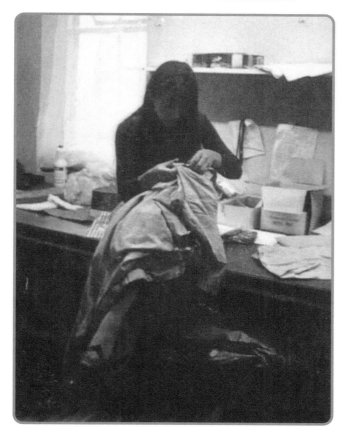

black and white op-art beret,' and the scene shifts to the Orphanage for a tender reconciliation: 'They made love as though nothing had changed.' Likky went back to Scotland with Robin that Christmas and Jeffa moved into Likky's old room.

Then Annie and Tim Goulding fell in love. Ivan: 'Their eyes met across a crowded room and I exited stage left, forlorn. I slept in the kitchen for a while then moved out.' Though Goulding soon moved in, Ivan remained a very regular visitor.

Beating the Strangelies to it, Jeffa Gill arrived at the Orphanage with her own nickname (she was actually christened Jennifer). Having grown up in a farming background in Worcestershire, she says she was 'a rebellious kid' who had left home for art college in Birmingham, studying design. Through being involved in a fashion show in Dublin, she met a man who had just returned from New York, where he had come across 'happenings.' The plan was to set up something similar in Dublin – not just a boutique but a hangout place and café.

Goulding: 'Jeffa started what was probably the first boutique in Dublin. It was situated on Morehampton Road and was called "The Happening." It was to be more than a clothes shop and offered coffee and some artistic exhibits.' Jeffa: 'There was not much fashionable clothing available in those days – you had to make your own trends! It went well for a while but then I moved into making clothes for individual people.'

Jeffa moved in after Likky left. She had first met Annie at The Happening, and remembers her as 'a voracious reader.' They became good friends and 'shared' Annie's pair of Russian brown leather boots, rare then.

By 1968 Jeffa had started to help Goulding making large felt banners for a planned exhibition, and would travel in his Dodge with him up to his parents' house to

The Dodge in Mount Street

work there in his studio. Perhaps in contrast to the Orphanage, she found Dargle Cottage very comfortable, even though it felt slightly surreal sitting around the ancient mahogany round table with Goulding's parents and other guests, being served by the family butler.

Back in Mount Street, Goulding recalls: 'Ivan, of course, was around a lot. He was the most tuned-in guy we had ever met, in a Taoist / Zen sort of way. If a horn hooted outside, he would notice that it was in tune with the whistle of the kettle and a song might ensue in the same key. He was conversant with the I Ching and would consult it using the 49-yarrow stick method.' [Yarrow sticks are a mathematically complex means of I Ching divination.] Jeffa also remembers Ivan patiently doing endless I Ching readings for her. Goulding: 'We often wandered Dublin in bare feet and sported unusually long hair. I remember calls from lorry drivers shouting "get your hair cut" to which the reply was "get your throat cut." The house became the hub of a small Dublin hippy community, although none of us would accept such nomenclature.'

'Around this time Ivan and I painted my Dodge Sedan, a seven-seater airport limousine with a flat six engine; it weighed about two tons and was festooned in chrome. The speedometer changed colour the faster you went, and it took a lot of manpower to slow it down. It also consumed about 12 miles to the gallon. We covered it in murals featuring, amongst others, an intricate Chinese dragon on the roof. An inscription saying "himmelhoch jauchzend, zu Tode betrübt" (heavenly joy, deadly sorrow) ran the length of one side. This was from Goethe (of course), a line often quoted by European intellectuals as characteristic of the Romantic soul. We can hold Ivan responsible for that one. There was also an electric hash pipe with battery painted on. On the other side was "No man is good enough to be another man's master." It being too expensive to run, I ended up selling it to Robbie McMillan (later to become Robbie Coltrane, the actor) for £1. He brought it to Edinburgh and drove American tourists around in it.' This is probably a good point to note that you could then get an Irish driving licence (valid in most of the world) simply by handing over one pound at the GPO. No test – or indeed lessons – was required.

# Acid

Goulding: 'At one point, *Time* magazine reported that the Orphanage was a crash pad for hippies. The cast of characters passing through included musicians, poets, alcoholics and travellers from Europe. We hosted a Latvian man who had read about us and came into Ireland with acid hidden in his socks. I referenced his visit later in my song I Will Lift Up Mine Eyes: "Deep in a Latvian thicket, there's a slough I'll leave behind."

LSD was very much a part of life at Mount Street. Ivan's first supplies had come from Edinburgh, possibly via Clive Palmer. If Clive was a source, that all ended in December 1966, when Clive and his friend Ian Ferguson were raided and charged with possession of a quantity of cannabis and of LSD. Following the recording of the first ISB album, Clive had taken off for Afghanistan and brought some hash back with him, strapped to his gammy leg to get it through customs, which he and Ian were then busy retailing. The police also found five LSD-impregnated sugar cubes; these were actually just for personal use and probably acquired before September 1966, when it was still legal. Clive thus became the first person in Scotland to be charged with possession of LSD, even though he thought the drug was 'rubbish,' preferring marijuana, and was remanded in Glasgow's Barlinnie prison. He was eventually released with a £100 fine, which he told biographer Grahame Hood 'took forever to pay off!'

Scoring acid for the Orphans usually involved either sending Ivan over to London, or a well-established mail-order system. Humphrey Weightman, an early band member who was resident in Notting Hill after leaving Dublin in 1967, was close to the web of drug connections involving his friend Howard Marks, and had introduced Goulding to Graham Plinston. Plinston was a shadowy figure who worked at one point as the news editor at the *International Times*, and went on to figure in Marks' bigger dope importing exploits until he was busted in 1970. He also had connections with Harley Street dentist John Riley, a notorious acquaintance of John and Cynthia Lennon who had first dosed John, George Harrison and their partners with acid in mid-1965 by slipping it into their coffee after a meal at his house.

Goulding: 'Much acid was sent to me in the post by Graham, who disguised it in a 28-day blister pack of oral contraceptives, which were illegal in Ireland at the time. We conjured up a scenario of a customs officer confiscating them and bringing them home to his wife.'

Plinston disappeared from the scene once he came out of prison. Humphrey Weightman: 'The last I heard of Graham – some 40 years ago – was that he was undergoing gender reassignment surgery in California. As you do.'

Oddly, both Mount Street and Sandymount Orphanages escaped any kind of police attention. 1967 saw the establishment of the Garda Dublin Drugs Squad, led by Inspector Denis Mullins; in January 1968, after six months of surveillance and detective work, police raided several private houses in south Dublin where they found heroin, LSD and marijuana. Not the Orphanages, though. Ivan: 'Dealing did not go on there, and Dinny Mullins knew that.' Booth reckons all involved were discreet, and Goulding even has a fond memory of Mullins.

Goulding: 'Dinny Mullins contacted us after a show at Liberty Hall. Loads of roaches were found in the hall, but none backstage. He reassured us that we were in the clear. The impression was that he was lenient with folk who had drugs "for their own use." I don't think either Orphanage ever had significant supplies of dope of any kind.'

## Acid rituals

Acid taking, especially in the early days of the Orphanage, had a strong ritualistic quality. One's mindset before starting the trip, as well as the setting itself, were important. As various texts prescribed, there would always be a 'straight' minder (or 'trip sitter') around in case things got tricky or scary. Psychedelic guides, who would actually guide you through and help enhance the trip, were also favoured, as encouraged by Timothy Leary in *The Psychedelic Experience: A Manual Based on the Tibetan Book of the Dead*. Goulding was Booth's minder on his first trip. Booth: 'He had told me to try it, as he thought I might enjoy acid – and he was right!' According to Ivan's friend Tony Lowes, Goulding even had a set of LPs that were supposed to guide you through your eight-hour trip, though Goulding disputes this: 'I think Tony's fevered imagination has taken over here.'

In Iain Sinclair's *Kodak Mantra Diaries*, Tony Lowes described the end of a particularly protracted trip taken near Swords in July 1967 with Ivan, Goulding and others. After tripping all night, 'we each rolled a magnificent reefer and went out with candles through the Brackenstown Estate to the top of the quarry… We sat there cross-legged on this summer's very early morning, and we knew from a corner of light in the sky it was going to be dawn very shortly. We lit up our reefers… It was light… this absolute sea of light. I sat up and looked at the forest that rolled away into the distance and it began to flash; neon, red and green… and just then a jet took off from the [nearby] airport and there was the most incredible ROAR of power and modern society… All I did was yell "Fucking Jesus H Christ!" as I tried to convey some idea of the power of this one moment. And that was it.'

## Visitors

Jeffa also recalls the many Orphanage visitors, including Robin Williamson, who once arrived in a (rented) horse and trap. Mike Heron and photographer Dave Robinson also passed by.

Booth: 'When I lived in Waterloo Road, our next-door neighbour was musician Peter Adler, son of har-monica-playing Larry Adler. Peter had a band called The Next In Line and Dave was often in attendance, so we met and before long, Dave was often a guest in our basement. He moved in mysteriously sophisticated ways, knew no fear, a tall angular figure with a neck like the finest titanium and a head of outrageously wild black hair. He had returned to Dublin from a stay in England some time in the mid-Sixties with two motorised Nikon 35 MM stills cameras, and was soon cutting a swathe through the photographic establishment. This led to work within the entertainment sector and in turn presented him with business opportunities. These included running some of the early Dublin beat clubs and managing a group called The Eire Apparent, featuring Henry McCul-lough on lead guitar (or Harvey, as I nicknamed him).

'Perhaps I introduced him to the Orphanage, or perhaps he met the Orphans in Toners pub. Before long he too became a regular visitor. Then he would vanish for periods, off on tour with his band to Majorca, the

States, then back in Dublin, reeling off his adventures, sharply dressed in a velvet suit, cigarette burns on the fabric the only evidence of another, deeper existence. In 1969 Linus and I, broke in London, ran into him in Shaftesbury Avenue and we went for a pint. He was back from touring the States supporting Hendrix and seemed to be loaded, the velvet suit of a better cut. Realising our penury, he fished in his pants pocket, peeled two twenty-pound notes off a roll and insisted I should take it – what then was a considerable wedge – in lieu of rent for all his sojourns in Waterloo Road.'

Goulding: 'There was a very erudite philosophy student called Robin Beresford Evans who was always tightly encased in black and was prone to use three words where one would do. These words tended to be technical philosophical words that few understood. Another denizen of the house for a wee while was Jenny Richardson, the Scottish painter, and her then boyfriend Andy Anderson, a self-proclaimed spiritual detective

Jenny (RIGHT) and Tim near Allihies

and wizard: every psychedelic folk band worth its salt had one then. It was the same Andy who, later in life, burst through the glass doors of the Brighton Bookshop with an axe, proclaiming he was an angel of light. In fact, he was.'

Goulding: 'Andy and Jenny lived in the derelict basement that you wouldn't leave a dog in.'

Booth: 'I never lived in, but I did stay in the basement – which I think used to be the kitchen – when I was moving from my flat in Ranelagh to what would become the second Orphanage. The basement had a stone-flagged floor and I remember Hayden Murphy's wedding party held down there, when a wigged-out Hayden danced barefoot among broken bottles without a scratch. I stayed down there a few nights on a sleeping bag on the springs of an old iron bed frame, to the great surprise of a nubile student nurse I managed to inveigle back one sultry evening.'

Goulding: 'Another visitor was a dear friend Julian Reeves, who was a psychologist and worked for the Eastern Health Board. When not attending to his duties he would be designing psychedelic drugs and inventing 3D cardboard mathematical structures. He was a devotee of iridology and would inspect our eyes and pronounce remedies. The pupils were often dilated. He also tried to persuade me to take up smoking cigarettes while tripping on top of the Little Sugar Loaf (apt) mountain in Co Wicklow. Alas the story ends tragically. He had terrible family troubles and ended up in the lock-up ward of the same hospital where he had been the doctor. I think we tried to spring him at one point, although I remember visiting him in his cell where, worryingly, he had a picture of the band on the wall with red crosses marked over our hearts. On leaving Ireland he worked for the drug charity Release in London. Before I went to India in 1972 I visited him there; he took a stone out of a pouch that he wore around his neck and asked me to place it in the holiest place I could find in India. I placed it on the altar of a Hindu temple. When I returned through London I called to the house to let him know, only to be told that he had taken an overdose a few days before. RIP Julian.'

Booth recalls 'numerous comings and goings, not the least being MaGoo, who looked like he should be able to rock and roll, but didn't have a note in his head.' He didn't like their music at all, either. [MaGoo is probably an anglicized version of the Gaelic name mac Eochadha.]

'He did however have an insouciant ageing Teddy Boy style, a curled and Brylcreemed pompadour, tight jeans and velvet collared walking-out jacket. MaGoo worked on the docks. A freelance docker, picked for work of a morning by a "button man" and assigned a ship to unload. He was rough but he loved Orphan Annie, Annie Christmas and Jeffa and would do anything for them.

'Jeffa made clothes. One Saturday noontime, as we were upstairs in the kitchen sitting down to an early breakfast, there was a loud knock on the front door. Investigation revealed several rolls of cotton duck leaning against the doorpost, each one clearly stencilled "Property of the Royal Dublin Society." MaGoo came by later to inquire whether she had received his gift and "iffen it was of any use as lining material for an auld suit, like?" He had a few friends who would also come by: Dykie, Mixo and Stab the Rasher. The latter travelled with a lethal docking hook – used to snag bales of goods into and out of ships' holds – sharpened to a killing point and hung snugly over his shoulder beneath his jacket.

'A body with stab wounds had been pulled from the water, resultant of a North Side/South Side dockers' dispute. I ran into MaGoo in O'Donoghue's, where he told me that one of his cronies was the prime suspect and was on the run in England. That's when he showed me the docking hook under his jacket. He was tooled up, just in case. The paranoia levels were very high with MaGoo and pals at that time; hooks were carried partly for work, but mostly for defence.

'Another time, he was barred from Toners and stumped off into the night, to return twenty minutes later with a huge truck and a heavy chain cable which he was attempting to wrap around the support pillar by the front door that held the entire building in place. The other end was attached to the truck and his notion was to drive away at speed, thus pulling the vital pillar out from its foundations and collapsing the building on Mr Toner's balding pate. Needless to say, there was drink taken – the reason for the barring in the first place. We talked him out of it.

'There were also musicians, Robin Williamson, a seventeen-year-old Phil Lynott – Annie Christmas saw him first – Ashtar, who ran a light show, poets, painters, nobs, dealers, journalists, chancers, gougers, horse-Irish and a lot more, but MaGoo stands out in my memory. There was a whiff of sulphur when he walked in the room. This was unusual and refreshing in days drenched with patchouli oil, incense and marijuana smoke.

'Last time I saw him, he was living quietly in the Corporation housing area at the back of Scruffy Murphy's pub [in the Waste Land]. He was dapper in an expensive Columbo trench coat; we went to the pub and I bought him a coffee as he had given up the jar. He asked fondly to be remembered to the women who made the Mount Street Orphanage such a haven. Shelter from the storm.'

Another regular visitor was sax player Steve Bullock: 'I had moved to Dublin from Somerset in 1967 to attend Trinity College and got to know all three Strangelies. The Orphanage was an open house and all kinds of musicians and hippies thronged the place. Johnny Moynihan, Luke Kelly and Gary Moore were regular visitors, and jams would go on late into the small hours. When I lived off Fitzwilliam Square, Ivan used to come round with his guitar and we would play free form for hours on end, me mostly on the flute because the sax was too loud. Once Ivan remarked that we had travelled from England and Ireland to the Middle East and North Africa in the space of an hour! I used to hang out with Booth since he was selling second-hand clothes, hippy stuff and records. Tim Goulding visited me to chat and smoke various substances, so we all got along together.'

Ivan and Renchi, Dublin 1967 (Iain Sinclair)

Ivan claims to remember 'a young couple of unknown teenage actors from England, Leonard Whiting and Olivia Hussey, staying a couple of days. They had just got the star parts in Zeffirelli's film of *Romeo & Juliet*. I think they were trying to get away from media attention in the UK. Very young and sweet.' However, Booth and Goulding do not recall this at all, and neither does Leonard Whiting. Funny old stuff, acid.

Lorraine Sufrin, who crops up a few times later in this book, came to stay at both Orphanages. On her first visit to Mount Street, she was accompanied by a banjo player from Manchester called Black Stan, who Ivan says was making a sociological documentary on the artistic scene in Dublin. Except for his hair and full beard, Stan was not actually black at all. He had arranged the tune Blackwaterside for guitar for Anne Briggs and later had a tune credited on her album. Ivan: 'I think Lorraine had just broken up with Roy Harper. She was a lovely, lively and engaging girl, not very tall with a head of tight curls. I think her ethnicity was half Jewish and half Lebanese. She was part of our group of friends and also knew the ISB.'

David Ambrose was another visitor: 'In the late Sixties I had decided, as you did then, to go and live in a cottage in the West of Ireland. As I was boarding the ferry in Liverpool, a striking hippy girl with long red hair

Scruffy Murphy's, the Waste Land

was getting off, and almost in passing she said, 'If you're in Dublin, go and stay at 55 Lower Mount Street.' Of course, I went there and knocked on the door. An upstairs window opened and a tangled mass of blonde hair and glasses leaned out. "Hey man, come on up!" Ivan, who'd never seen me before in his life.' David kept in touch and in 1970 booked the band to do a spot of mumming, of which more later.

Daily life in the Orphanage acquired a certain routine. Ivan: 'I can see and hear Jeffa in the kitchen with her sewing machine. The core "orphans" included Juniper Heron, a shy gentle girl who lived with her father

Annie snaps the band
at Sandymount Strand,
early 1969 (Photo: Johanna)

and stepmother in Celbridge and was Goulding's first girlfriend; I think he had met her through the weaving. Iain Sinclair would come by and Renchi, another regular visitor, lived in Upper Mount Street and was working at an animation studio just over the Mount Street Bridge.'

Goulding: 'The two Mount Streets were connected by the Waste Land, an empty lot at the back, named after the T.S. Eliot poem. By then Annie had become a good photographer and took quite a few photos in that location, some of them being used for Thin Lizzy publicity shots. The pub there, Scruffy [Sean] Murphy's, had very much local patronage.'

Ivan: 'The soundtrack at the time included My Generation, which we envisaged singing together in an old folks' home 50 years later. Positively 4th Street was out at the time. Renchi's only album was a Mingus LP, *Tijuana Moods*, which captured our imagination. One lunchtime Renchi and I worked out a version of Good King Wenceslas backwards, of which we were inordinately proud.'

There were other, more local visitors. Jeffa: 'We did have a regular visitation from a gang of children who lived around the flats at the back of the Waste Land. They became a standard item and would stay to listen to music or draw pictures.' Ivan: 'Annie would often give them something to eat. I remember one day they were fairly shaken as they had had a run-in with the toughest bunch of kids, those from the flats in Oliver Bond Street. I think they had accidentally strayed into their territory.'

The Waste Land kids
with Orphanage residents
and Ashtar (with headband)

Posing in Dublin, 1967 (FROM LEFT): Tim Goulding, Annie, Jeffa, Muriel Fleming, Louis Clear, Juniper Heron (with back to camera), John Fleming, Tim Booth, unknown (Photo: Iain Sinclair collection)

Another, older group of visiting lads was headed up by a teenage Phil Lynott. Jeffa: 'He was often around. He always arrived with a group of mates such as Paul Scully, never on his own. Sometimes a gang of us would all go out dancing in a basement club.'

Mostly, the evenings involved staying in playing music, the pub, or the odd artistic event. Jeffa: 'There was always music, often the sounds of Ivan's gentle practising chords.' Goulding: 'After dinner most nights there would be a walk across the Waste Land and on to Toners pub. Sometimes there might be a gig or an opening.' Ivan: 'We couldn't afford to do much drinking, but might spend a couple of hours chatting over a pint of the black stuff.' Jeffa: 'I had been barred from O'Donoghue's for wearing a skirt which, at only just above the knee, was considered too short! Toners was the hangout place.'

Goulding: 'The exhibition openings in those days were very generous with their free drink. By 1969 I had my first exhibition in The David Hendriks Gallery, St Stephens Green. This was a landmark psychedelic show

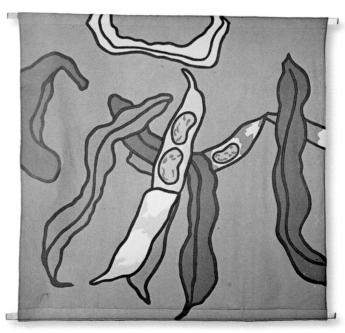

One of the banners produced by Tim and Jeffa (ABOVE)

Jeffa and friend Mole: painting by Jenny Richardson circa 1969 (LEFT)

that sported a mixture of the pop art style felt banners I had been making with Jeffa, and other acid-induced visions such as extremely close up views of blackberries, coffee beans, tea leaves and blades of grass.

'I had insisted on lassi, the Indian yoghurt drink, being served to complement the incense that was burning. By this time, I was not drinking and was more interested in meditation and Indian culture, but nonetheless the traditional generous portions of booze were on hand. One couple arrived fresh from the pond in St Stephen's Green and rubbed shoulders with the haute bourgeoisie in their dripping clothes. Later they were found in my art dealer's bed upstairs.'

Everyone had to move out by 1970, when the house was sold and knocked down. Jeffa: 'It was a good place, there was a sense of playfulness there. I "grew up" at the Orphanage – I was only around 18 when I moved in. In 1969, I had my 21st birthday party down in the basement!'

Goulding: 'The Orphanage really had open doors and with the enthusiasm of youth, and before serious pairing and babies took hold, and in line with the zeitgeist, we welcomed most who would turn up.'

Forty years later, Ivan looked back on the Orphanage in the song Halcyon Days:

**'Back in the Orphanage
Down by the Mount Street Bridge
Sure we never had a care:
And in the long dark nights of winter
Playing music round the fire,
Chasing our dreams and learning to share.'**

After the Orphanage: (FROM LEFT) Annie, her sister Finola, Jenny Richardson in 1973 in Tim's house near Allihies

# A Tale Of Two Orphans:
# Philo

Originally from Manchester's Moss Side, Phil Lynott arrived in Dublin in 1957 to live in Crumlin with his grandmother Sarah. As a mixed-race boy (his father was Guyanese) Phil sometimes came up against racism or at best, incomprehension; at the time there were only 4 indigenous black children in the entire city. His biographer, Graeme Thomson, comments that Lynott 'quickly seemed to become more Irish, more Dublin, than those who had been born and raised there.' He was also an enthusiastic student of Irish history and mythology.

From 1963 to 1967 he was lead singer in the Black Eagles, playing chart covers at teenage dances while still at school. By 1965 Lynott was 16 years old, out of school, nominally studying woodwork and metalwork but in reality, steeping himself in music and cinema – he loved films. Thomson's biography, *Cowboy Song*, tells us he was also developing eclectic tastes in music.

The time was right, then, for him to visit the Mount Street Orphanage. No-one can quite remember how his first visit came about, but certainly by early 1966 he was a frequent presence, sometimes with his friends Frank Murray (later manager of The Pogues) and Paul Scully (later sound engineer for The Pogues and producer of the Strangelies' third album in 1997).

Scully remembers going round to Mount Street around Christmas 1965 and being asked to be quiet, as Robin Williamson was meditating upstairs. He'd never heard of meditation. When Robin eventually emerged, he played Phil October Song, which he had just written. It spurred him into writing his own first song. Ivan says: 'After this, I remember young Phil singing a song for Robin, one he had freshly composed, called Death Of A Faun.' It was 'one of those Incredible String Band-y kind of things,' Frank Murray told Graeme Thomson, 'and bad!' True to form, the Strangelies thought it showed some promise.

The band kept an almost fatherly eye on Phil and he picked up a lot from them, including the customary Strangelies' nickname: 'Philo'. Tim Goulding, after talking about this period with Paul Scully, feels that 'Philo would have been attracted to us hippies as we were "Artistic cool" rather than "Street cool." Also we had connections in the art world.'

Philip in 1967 (Photo: Michael O'Flanagan)

In September 1967, Brendan 'The Brush' Shiels, an ambitious Dublin-based bass player, recruited Phil as vocalist in his new band, Skid Row. Conceived as a progressive band, Skid Row started off playing covers of songs such as I Am The Walrus and Hendrix's If Six Was Nine. Murray and Scully were brought in as roadies, local promoter Ted Carroll became the manager, and the band rapidly acquired a big following.

But alongside his rock career, Phil was still exploring other kinds of music, art and literature with the Strangelies at both Mount Street and the second Orphanage, Sandymount. He and Annie Christmas had a brief affair around this time, and he would often end up there after nights out in the town. When Gary Moore was recruited to Skid Row in early 1968, Phil arranged for him to live at Sandymount and, as Thomson writes, 'the bond [with] Dr Strangely Strange grew ever tighter.'

Phil was very ambitious, and here he had an entrée into another world he was keen to explore. In his book on Thin Lizzy, Martin Popoff comments: '[At the Orphanages] Phil's mind was opened to wider possibilities, well beyond the strict guidance Brush had kept him under as part of the almost showband-like early incarnation of Skid Row. It was here that Phil discovered both fashion and soft drugs, along with a world of music from folk to world and beyond.'

Ivan: 'Phil had a gentle, romantic side. Although he always walked with a jaunty swagger, he was not aggressive. His later stage persona demanded a "hard man" image and, good actor that he was, he was able to project that front. Facile to say, but his later espousal of heroin would have made that role easier to perform.

'I can't pretend to have known Philip well: I was nine years older than him, but I was a late starter and he an early developer: his musical talent was immediately obvious. In fact, early on he showed me a simple chord shape I hadn't previously sussed (the regular A major shape played with the barre, not sounding the top string). Phil was fond of Simon and Garfunkel, but I confess I found them a bit wet at the time!'

'One day Annie Christmas came by Mount Street, having borrowed her Dad's car, and brought Orphan Annie, me and Philip out to Finglas in North Dublin to visit John and Jessica Buckley. They were a young American couple, friends of Philip, totally untrendy, but very literary. Jessica roasted some lamb and we drank beer. It was a smoke-free evening and we just sat around chatting amicably about everything under the sun. I did say "smoke-free", but actually, as far as I can remember, the meat caught fire – I think the stove was fairly crock. We managed to salvage things without having to call the Fire Brigade. I just remember everybody being so laid-back. I bumped into John a few years later – I think he became an academic. It's sad to think that both Annies and Phil are long gone now, but I always fondly recall that evening, and the earnest literary side of young Philip.'

Skid row flyer by Booth (courtesy of Terry O'Neill)

The first Skid Row single, although written by Shiels, definitely bears a Strangelies' influence: it's a folky track called New Places, Old Faces, featuring tin whistle by Sweeney's Man Johnny Moynihan and produced by Donal Lunny. Booth: 'I designed the poster for the single. I remember the band cranking out a version of I Am The Walrus in the Dixon Hall, TCD, and being very impressed. To my untutored ears it sounded just like the record, only louder and even more complex.'

Phil would hang out with the Strangelies in Toners, often before heading across the road to Zhivago's discotheque (as featured in Goulding's song Dr Dim And Dr Strange). They would often take him along to Sinnott's, and although he never read his poetry there – it was probably a bit too high-powered a bill – he also tagged along to their Slattery's gigs, where Ivan remembers him reading some of his work. At Slattery's he also befriended the band Tara Telephone, who arranged for him to do an acoustic set and read at a Trinity College gig they had planned.

In June 1969 Phil was dropped from Skid Row (Brush claimed there were problems with the vocals) – and

Philip at Smileys Club, 1968 (Photo: Michael O'Flanagan)

he embarked on a new and more esoteric project, Orphanage. It was a fairly loose arrangement, including his old school friend Brian Downey, whose previous band, Sugar Shack, had broken up. The name was both a tip of the hat to Strangelies, and also to the fact that most band members were, as Phil said, 'a gang of bloody [musical] orphans!' Terry Woods, Paddy Moloney of the Chieftains, and various Strangelies also all took part in Orphanage gigs at one point or other. Eamonn Carr of Tara Telephone told Thomson: 'It would have been like the softer side of Lizzy. West Coast and dreamy, that's how I remember it… loose, slightly whimsical and meandering, with a pastoral feel.'

Orphanage material ranged from Dylan to the Beatles, Sam and Dave and the Lovin' Spoonful's Daydream. They even rehearsed a version of Booth's Donnybrook Fair, which Phil apparently told one band member he had co-written. He hadn't. 'Phil was always a man for saying what you want to hear,' says Goulding. Booth: 'I wrote Donnybrook Fair on my tod and there was never any co-writing with Phil. Linus contributed the "cloak of feathers" line at the end.'

By early 1970, Orphanage had morphed into Thin Lizzy and a distinctly more rock oriented approach, though the first album retains elements of what Thomson describes as 'a music that combined the dream-like lyricism of Astral Weeks, drawing powerfully on the pull of memory and place…' Phil always talked fondly of the Strangelies, and Thin Lizzy's 1972 Brought Down, a song about loss, namechecks them in the outro: 'God, it's a shame there's no more Dr Strangely Strange!' It's on *Shades Of A Blue Orphanage*.

Though the Strangelies were no longer a regular part of Phil's life, Booth in particular kept in contact. Booth: 'Ted Carroll was managing Thin Lizzy in London and I spent a lot of time in his small bedsit in Belsize Park, listening to music and smoking funny cigarettes. He asked me to design a logo and posters for the band. Then, when Whisky In The Jar was about to be released, he commissioned me to do the publicity posters in the form of a comic strip written around the lyric. We also produced a small noggin of whiskey with a Thin Lizzy label and this went out to record pluggers. The single was a success, so I was also asked to do the follow up single, Randolph's Tango, which also turned the lyrics into a cartoon strip.

'About this time, Phil had met Jim Fitzpatrick, a fellow Irish artist, and had asked him to become involved in their image and branding. Jim asked for permission to use my logo design, which I gladly gave. I did not totally finish working with Phil however. Along with Jim, I provided illustrations for two books of his poetry and lyrics, including *Songs For While I'm Away* in 1974, and other graphic work.

Phil died tragically young, in January 1986. Booth: 'Our paths diverged, but we would occasionally run into each other. The last time was in The Dockers pub in Dublin, one lunch time. I had been doing some film editing in Windmill Lane studios – just around the corner – and was having a light repast in the snug when I heard a bit of a commotion out in the main bar. Phil and entourage. I went out to say hello.

'It took him several moments to recognise me. I was shocked by his appearance. His face was puffy, the whites of his eyes yellow against his skin which was an unhealthy purple shade of brown. It was not a good moment for either of us. I think he was embarrassed that I should see him so obviously out of it. After a few awkward pleasantries, I left him to his sycophantic support team. A month or so later he was buried on Howth Hill.

'That last meeting really disturbed me. On our 1997 CD *Alternative Medicine* we recorded the song Epilog, which I wrote about him and for him, and for myself to lay his ghost.'

Booth's book illustration for Phil's Cowboy Song, a Thin Lizzy staple

**'Dragons in the air tonight, behind the moon I hear their bitter wings
There is no need to lie tonight, the time has come to face the faceless things...'**

## CHAPTER 2

# Toners – a home from home

Two Dublin pubs, Toners and O'Donoghue's, are important in early Strangelies' history.

O'Donoghue's was a Tim Booth hangout. In Merrion Row, near Saint Stephen's Green and built as a grocery store, it began operating full-time as a pub when purchased by the O'Donoghue family in 1934. Ivan says the pub 'was the undisputed home of traditional music;' the Dubliners had first established the music connection there after asking Paddy O'Donoghue if they could use the back room as a rehearsal space, and it was where they began performing in the early 1960s. Many other notable Irish musicians – including Séamus Ennis, Joe Heaney, Andy Irvine, Christy Moore, The Fureys and Phil Lynott – played at O'Donoghue's, and their photos are still displayed in the pub alongside pictures of the five founding Dubliners themselves: Ronnie Drew, Luke Kelly, Ciarán Bourke, John Sheahan and Barney McKenna. Strangelies' friend Pat Carroll wrote in a recent blog that it was not only a pub for musicians, 'but also an office, employment bureau and poste restante.' Andy Irvine composed a tribute song, O'Donoghue's, in which he reminisces about his early days in Dublin when he first started frequenting the pub in August 1962.

Booth: 'Paddy O'Donoghue was the proprietor. He and his wife ran an establishment catering for the serious pint drinker. The pour was the thing and the barmen had it down. There were always four or five pints under construction below the counter by the beer pulls and when a customer shouted for a pint, the one nearest completion was topped with porter and allowed to settle, reducing the wait from shout to presentation to a matter of minutes rather than the quarter of an hour required in less practised premises.

'Maureen ran the kitchen and looked after the dietary – "You'll have a sandwich?" – and emotional affairs of the numerous love-struck folk musicians who had made the pub their second home. I got to know the Dubliners reasonably well and enjoyed their bravado. Any hour of the day or night there was a session in O'D's and all you had to do to join in was join in. Musical ability had little to do with it, but when from time to time a genuine musician crossed the threshold, an appreciative silence fell.

'Paddy also acted as a bank for many. Clearing out old drawers a few years ago, I came across a Munster and Leinster Bank cheque book from the time and every second cheque stub was made out to Paddy. You could have the quiet word with him at the end of the bar and he would either cash your cheque or lend you a few quid until you were in funds again. A mighty man. But the town was full of mighty men in those days, back before the Celtic Fucktard and The Free Market when the only things that trickled down were to be found in the Gents…'

Goulding: 'O'Donoghue's was for more seasoned musos of the traditional variety and I felt unwelcome mainly because the length of my hair (down to the belly button). I was cautious as I had already been barred from the pub across the road, Doheny and Nesbitt's, for the locks.'

O'Donoghue's was also the birthplace of Sweeney's Men. The nucleus of the band, all of whom would later go on to play a part in the Strangelies' career, were Johnny Moynihan (Greek bouzouki) and Andy Irvine (mandolin), who were joined in 1967 by Terry Woods (guitar). At the time they were the most original Irish acoustic band around. Writer Colin Harper describes them as 'drawing uniquely from hillbilly music, the English folk tradition and the then still cobwebbed Irish tradition, all glued together with bohemian zest.' In May 1968, Andy left to live in the Balkans for 18 months. Former Eire Apparent electric guitarist Henry McCullough replaced him for a few months, until he was poached by Joe Cocker for The Grease Band. Sweeney's Men, after some considerable success, petered out late in 1969.

Toners in Baggot Street became a home from home for all the band members. Established in 1818, it is one of Dublin's oldest and best-known pubs and has been frequented over the years by some of Ireland's literary greats; rumour has it that Toners was the only pub that Yeats ever drank in. It had no licence for live music, and so was more conducive to conversation.

Booth: 'When not at the Orphanage, we hung out in Toners pub of an evening, partly because it was a bit old fashioned and quiet, but mainly because the Mister Toners, old and young, were true fine gentlemen and, along with little Charlie the genial barman, ran an establishment that was way beyond reproach and were also known to subsidise their impoverished clientele betimes. Here were to be found the cream of Dublin's avant-garde, writers, artists, musicians, poets, all still friends – or at least talking to each other. Totally far out man... and it was.'

'Most nights it was a pleasant watering hole with an indifferent pint. On Friday night it was heaving. When we first attended, Old Mr Toner – then in his late 70s – presided, his son, Young Mr Toner working behind the bar when Charlie the barman had a night off. Old Mr Toner wore a wing collar and stood straight and severe over considerable girth. We made him (Jeffa Gill mostly) an elaborate set of aprons with the word Toners appliquéd in felt across the bib, but they proved too flash and were never worn. When he died, it is rumoured his last words were: "Time gentlemen. Please." I'd like to think so. Charlie, on the other hand, had a wife and a pet poodle, fancied the horses and his closing time shout was a softly spoken, "Aw lads, it's gone the time – have ye no homes to go to?"

Toners, around 1969: note pillar on the right-hand corner, utilised in MaGoos's demolition attempt

Ivan: 'Toners had a snug, as most public houses did in those days. The snug was traditionally the domain of the fair sex. When we started frequenting, old Mr Toner would have frowned on serving females in the public bar, but he buckled under pressure. In those days the Gents was downstairs beside the cellar. Ladies had to go upstairs to the living quarters, which were guarded by an old English sheepdog called Whoopsie.'

Goulding: 'Young Mr Toner presciently sported a third eye, some sort of skin eruption. This seemed appropriate for the budding Buddhas in attendance: the Latvian with acid in his socks, and the military strategist who took to exposing himself as the evening wore on to shouts of "Put it away." There would be the occasional "dolly bird" hot from a showband gig, tanking up before making a dive for Zhivago's night club across the road where Phil Lynott would be on the prowl after a few drinks with us. Basically, it catered for artists and musicians. The atmosphere was homely and non-threatening. Some of the regulars were Bobby Ballagh, who was playing bass in a showband at the time and went on to be a set designer for Riverdance, amongst other things. I also remember Mick O'Sullivan and Brian King, who taught sculpture at the National College of Art, Dublin. Mick became professor of sculpture there eventually. Occasionally the poet Hayden Murphy.'

In Toners: (FROM LEFT) Orphan Annie, Dave Robinson, Betty Ballagh, Ken Dolan, Tim Goulding, Young Mr Toner, Philip "Lord" Margidale, Robert Ballagh and Jeffa. (Photo, with a self-timer: Dave Robinson)

Ivan: 'Donal Lunny was there a lot – he was an art student at the time, and had made a single, Mary From Dungloe, with Emmet Spiceland, but, to be honest, l didn't realise he was to be such a musical giant (Planxty, Moving Hearts etc). He was normally sat up at the counter with Vincent, a fellow art student.'

Booth: 'When young Mr Toner took over little changed, but we developed a more intimate relationship and – some time in the mid-Sixties – Orphan Annie invited him and Charlie to the Mount Street Orphanage for Christmas dinner. They could not attend, but sent around a crate of stout and a bottle or two of spirits and this became a tradition. There was even – one year – a few hundredweight of coal. Gentlemen Landlords of the first order.'

# Anthea Joseph

· · · · · · · · · · · · · · · · · · · · · · · · · · · · · · · · · · · · · · · · · · · · · · · · · · · · · · ·

At some point in late 1967 or 1968, Tim Booth and Ivan met an aspiring songwriter from New York called Patrick Carroll. He was a PG Wodehouse fan, able to quote vast chunks of the oeuvre, and a big aficionado of

Lord Buckley. His main songwriting partner was Jim McCann, but his claim to fame was a co-write with Andy Irvine called Old Woman In Cotton, recorded as the B-side of the Sweeneys' Waxies' Dargle single, which in 1968 reached number 5 in the Irish charts. Tim Booth and Ivan also co-wrote a song with him, a tongue-in-cheek country number called You'll Recognise The Feelin', which they sometimes featured in the Brian Trench-era Strangelies set:

> 'When you see my empty chair / Right across the table there,
> And everything you see / Reminds you of me,
> Don't believe I didn't care / I just couldn't stand the wear and tear,
> You would never let my heart be free / You'll recognise the feeling
> When it comes on you stealing / You'll recognise the feeling,
> When I'm gone.'

As Booth says, poignant or what?

Booth: 'Like us, Pat hung out of an evening in Toners, and that's where he introduced me to Anthea Joseph, his girlfriend at the time. At the time she was working as a record-plugger for EMI in Dublin. Her boss at EMI was a man called Harry Christmas, father of the late great Annie Christmas, the presiding presence in the Sandymount Orphanage. Anthea was also friends with Johanna Hudson and Orphan Annie. It was a very small world back then. She was a mighty woman with a true love of music, the arts and the creative individuals

Anthea with Humphrey Weightman, Dublin 1968. (Photo: Patrick Carroll)

who made stuff happen. She admired our attempts to find and follow our own furrow, so to help us out, she placed her considerable influence and reputation at our disposal.'

Anthea used to run the Tuesday night sessions in the cellar at the Troubadour folk club in Earls Court. In 1962, she saw a pair of cowboy boots and skinny jeans coming down the stairs, and recognised a man she'd seen on the cover of *Sing Out* magazine. It was Bob Dylan, on his first visit to London to perform in the TV play *Madhouse On Castle Street*. It is said that his only guide was a piece of paper from Pete Seeger bearing the words, 'Troubadour Folk Club, London, ask for Anthea.'

The writer Andrew Greig met Anthea later in the Sixties, during his brief musical career, and remembers: 'She let Dylan in for free on the understanding he'd come back to play there, for £5 I think, so she was the first person to offer Dylan a gig in the UK. They became friends, and throughout her life he would suddenly phone her from whatever part of the world he was in, at any time of the day or night. From that era, she also knew Tom Paxton, Paul Simon, Pete Seeger – this all added to her mythos and standing as a passionate ally and supporter of musicians. So for the proto-Strangelies to meet her and gain her friendship and advocacy was a big deal and very helpful.'

Through her time at the Troubadour, Anthea knew Joe Boyd. She played an important part in encouraging him to eventually sign up the band and returned to London at some point in late 1968 to work for him at Witchseason.

# CHAPTER 3

# Sandymount Orphanage

Booth: 'Rental property and landlordism in Dublin then were just as bad as now. Cold water bedsits in old Georgian houses where beautiful rooms had been divided and then subdivided again, water pipes bored through gracious stucco work, dirty black wiring and meters clipped along dado rails, shilling-in-the-slot gas meters jemmied into under-stair cupboards. All for extortionist rents, with greaseball landlords double-jobbing as politicians. As a student, I was rented a 12-foot by 8-foot sub-division of a once spacious Georgian room for four quid a week.

'Annie Christmas and a few friends had rented a 1950s 3-bedroom semi-detached house of little architectural merit, close to Sandymount Strand. This was a different type of set-up entirely. To enhance the overall feel of the place, they had sanded the floors and removed the staircase banisters. When two residents moved out, Annie invited me to move in, luring me with the offer of the front downstairs room. I accepted.

'We lived at 26A Newgrove Avenue from around late 1967: Annie Christmas, upstairs front, Anita Treweeke, a beautiful Australian with some great Four Tops records, in the upstairs back and myself downstairs. I had installed a zigzag of rope, floor to ceiling, to replace the missing stair banisters. Guests were accommodated in the small box room or on the couch or floor of the sitting room at the back of the house beside the meagre kitchen. There was a decent back garden and a greenhouse.'

Annie Christmas at the back of Mount Street Orphanage, with Goulding just visible at the bottom window

Goulding: 'I remember the house being furnished with exotic bric-a-brac. It was a treasure trove of found objects and Tim's surreal paintings, many of military subject matter. In June 1969 he was in the 'Young Irish Artists' show at the Brown Thomas Gallery and exhibited a painting of Rupert Bear in Vietnam. Rupert, in his usual yellow-checked trousers, was bleeding, a powerful anti-war statement.'

Ivan: 'Annie was working as a copywriter for an advertising agency, Booth was freelancing as a graphic designer, and I think Anita was also in advertising; she had two other Australian friends called Roger and Streg, and Tim Goulding's harmonium came from Roger, who had bought it in an auction room on the quays in Dublin. Tim had a wonderful Egyptian wall-hanging in his room, which he and Linus had picked up in the markets, up and down which their two cats, Mistress Mouse and Mr Puppup, would scurry frantically on occasion. Mr Puppup was named after a Patagonian Indian in a book Booth was reading at the time.'

Ivan at Booth's harmonium

Booth: 'Anita had a few different boyfriends, including the drummer from Rory Gallagher's band. Annie occasionally stepped out with Jim Duncan who referred to the unusual as "strangely strange... but oddly normal." Cue for a song. I of course was chaste as a nun, using the downstairs room as a studio from which I freelanced, produced paintings and began to show one or two in the annual Irish Living Art Exhibition. Gradually the dynamic changed. Ivan and Goulding dropped by to practise. Later on, I found an elaborate American harmonium in the Iveagh Market and brought it home. Phil Lynott would call by to visit Annie or to chat about a poster design for Skid Row. Word got out, and waifs and strays descended, some to stay a few days, some to go further out.' There was usually plenty of dope around; Michael O'Flanagan, a friend of Phil's, called round one day to film Brush Shiels playing the harmonium, and was impressed to see a block of cannabis resin sitting on the mantlepiece 'bigger than a bar of Sunlight soap.'

Booth: 'I first met Humphrey Weightman on Sandymount Strand, where he loomed out of the sea fog like a David Lean wet dream, laughing maniacally. He had recently been rusticated from Oxbridge and was exploring Ireland with girlfriend Mary in a grey minivan, and they stayed for a while. Then there was Australian actor Leon Lissek, who was filming *Where's Jack?* in the Wicklow mountains and really liked Annie. We all worked as extras and crowd directors on this movie and made lots of dosh, coming home too tired to even go to the pub, Ivan, Humphrey and myself boogying across the Sally Gap road in Wicklow at dawn in Humphrey's minivan, the ISB on the 8-track, for a 5 o'clock call.

'A London photographer arrived in a streamlined white sports car. He was tall with medium length blond hair which fell over his forehead and did a natty line in suits. Later while he was down the country, his cameras were stolen from the boot of the car, but he got them back later. An intelligent Garda – this is not an oxymoron, they do exist, though rare – spotted a gouger [criminal type] attempting to use one on the street, became suspicious of a knacker [tinker, now traveller] with a Hasselblad and, on asking about the camera, a chase ensued. Linus was recently back from the States with beautiful attitude, measuring me up for a shirt which she then made for me.

Tim in the Sandymount garden (Photo: Iain Sinclair)

'The dynamic slowly shifted towards music. Phil asked if Gary Moore could stay with us and he painted the interior of the house with his incredible sound. Strangelies began to use the front room as a rehearsal space and I moved my Iveagh Market Victorian bed up to the box room. Sandymount always had many visitors. I remember coming back from tour to find complete strangers in the house, but as they had been vetted by the formidable Annie Christmas, all was good. Ivan was always around for continual practice, especially when Gary was staying between gigs.'

The photo shows Tim in the back garden with Orphan Annie, wearing a Hendrix wig he'd bought in Carnaby Street. Goulding: 'I also wore the wig with the purple velvet tabard, homemade two-tone wizard's shoes with bells on the end and black tights to a high society wedding in rural Hampshire. The groom had told me to come as I liked. I was more than surprised to find all other male attendees wearing morning suits. It was not appreciated by the families.'

In 1968, Steve Peacock and his girlfriend Jenny made a pilgrimage to the Orphanage, which he thinks he had already heard about from Robin Williamson. Steve: 'We got the ferry to Cork, then hitched a lift to Dublin in a car full of fishermen.' They attended one of the front room rehearsals before a pub gig. A year or so later, he recalled the visit for a *Sounds* article: 'The house was littered with musical instruments – drums, guitars, whistles, a harmonium and percussive devices of many kinds – and an atmosphere of gentle, musical, vaguely insane happiness hung over the place.' It was a couple of years later when he worked out the identity of the shy young electric guitarist who was sitting in on the session. Steve: 'They gave me much pleasure, live and on record, and they were very kind and welcoming to me and Jenny when we turned up on their doorstep, probably smelling of second-hand fish!'

Booth: 'I had met the elusive Johanna, so she moved in with her two children, and yet again the dynamic evolved. She had a different set of friends and acquaintances, different musical tastes. The 8-track of her green VW Beetle pumped out Spirit, Straight Arrow on the eight-track. Spirit was grown-up stuff, but it wasn't long before Gary had their moves down, teaching Ivan and myself how to play Darling If, a song I still love to play.'

Booth: 'About this time, the mysterious Lee, an American hippy chick – she looked like a Robert Crumb drawing – arrived in from the States on a big motorbike (I like to think it was a Harley, but it was a Triumph Bonneville) and we gave her the front room to sleep in.'

Goulding: 'Lee interrupted Ivan whilst having his bath to ask If she could sit down on the loo beside him and have a dump. "Mind if I dump" became a catchphrase at the time.'

Booth: 'I walked in on her one morning while she was doing yoga. Some sort of a headstand, legs in the lotus position, naked, undercarriage exposed. She ate copious amounts of chocolate and worried that she might "break out." We worried as well, wondering how we would explain the resultant damage to the front room to our exasperated landlord, Mr Greene. But she only meant that the chocolate might cause her skin to erupt in a fresh set of pimples. She would come and go. I always liked to think she was undercover.'

Ivan: 'After Anita moved out the rentpayers graciously let Mary, me and little Niamh stay for a couple of months, after the lease had expired on our flat down the road. We moved in during the summer of 1969, possibly July or August. We were definitely there at the end of September at the time of Mary's birthday. I remember Jay Myrdal coming by one day when I was on my own and dying of flu. He lit a fire and made me a hot drink. Sandymount Strand was just down at the end of the road and at low tide Mary, Niamh and I would walk there. Of an evening, twenty minutes walking down Londonbridge Road would bring us to Toners Bar.'

Booth: 'It may all have been too much for Marymac; she, Niamh and Ivan stayed a few months, then moved to a flat on Pembroke Road.'

Iain Sinclair, who had relocated from Dublin to Walthamstow Tech to work as a film lecturer, came over from Dalston in 1969 with his Bolex to shoot some trial footage for a proposed documentary about the Orphanage. The surviving clips show 'the Egyptians hanging on my wall' in Tim Booth's room there, with Tim Goulding and Orphan Annie enacting an extract from Samuel Beckett's poem Whoroscope: 'What's that? An egg? By the brother Boot it stinks fresh. Give it to Gillot.'

Sinclair's proposal, backed by a shooting script, stills taken at the Orphanage and several rolls of trial footage, was sent to the Beatles company Apple, who, he says, 'had made encouraging noises about encouraging innovative independent production.' They turned it down. 'The mix was irresistible,' he writes in his book *Hackney, That Rose-Red Empire*, '...the hippie spirit, its paradoxes and the search for a breakaway band member, lumberjack-shirted Angus Airlie, rumoured to be living in Hamburg and associating with the cadre who later became the Red Army Faction.' 'Angus Airlie,' actually the name of a Scottish standing stone, is clearly lumberjack-shirted Brian Trench, but Ivan's erroneous notion that he had 'split to make revolution in France' had clearly become further mythologised over the years. After Apple, the proposal was sent to Jean-Luc Godard, who never replied, and the film idea was dropped.

Stan Schnier, later of the Incredible String Band, passed by the Orphanage in December 1970: 'In those days I was a roadie with Muddy Waters, and our last date on the tour was Dublin. During the show, a very beau-tiful woman appeared, dressed in denims, battered Nikons around her neck, long blonde hair trailing down her back. My partner roadie Bruce and myself were smitten in that way that only another roadie would appreciate. After the show, as we were packing up, this woman was still hanging out, taking photos of the band backstage; eventually, Bruce and I started chatting with her. She was Tim's girlfriend, Johanna.

Johanna outside Sandymount Orphanage

'Johanna started telling us about the world of Dublin's pubs, the parties, the roll-ups, buckets of stout. I only knew about shots of Wild Turkey, big fat joints and Hendrix. I knew nothing about the Irish folk scene. Nothing. By the end of the evening, phone numbers were exchanged and Johanna offered us a floor to sleep on at Sandymount if we wanted to hang back in Dublin for a day or two.

'The next day, we took Muddy and band to the airport and said our goodbyes. Bruce and I holed up for a few glorious days at the Orphanage, exploring the Irish Coast around Dublin, thanks to a resident who had con-veniently left their Triumph Bonneville in the yard. Everyone knew of Johanna and we went out every evening, to pubs, parties, events. I recall Phil Lynott selling mimeos of his poems on the street outside the pubs.

'It was Christmas Eve and Strangely Strange were on their way back from their last gig of their UK tour. Although I had a giant crush on Johanna, we were nothing more than close friends. That said, I wondered how her fella would react if he walked into his home and found two Yankee Urban Cowboys sitting by his fire, drink-ing his tea, trading tales with his lady. Bruce and I decided to take the evening boat to Liverpool and then train it to London. So, I did not meet Tim, but knew a bit about him and his band.

'Fast forward two mere months and I was working for a folk band I had met in London in Joe Boyd's office, the Incredible String Band. My first assignment was to pick up a Ford Transit and head up to the Scottish Borders in cover of night, through endless fog, over winding two-lane roads, with a highly detailed set of direc-tions eventually taking me literally through the middle of a farm yard, up a rutted dirt road and finally to a row of cottages. I stayed with a wonderful young lady that evening, if in fact I ever fell asleep on her tiny sofa.

'In the morning, the next-door neighbour stopped by for a cup of tea and it was none other than Johanna. Crazy. She, Tim and her two young sons lived next door!'

Booth: 'There were others, too numerous to mention, some bad, some strange, some who would prove friends. Annie Christmas in turn moved on, her father having received a posting by EMI to South Africa. She moved there and worked as a producer in the film industry. She was a much-loved, generous woman with a laugh that came up from the soles of her feet to pause the turning world. I loved her dearly and when she moved on, the Sandymount Orphanage succumbed to external forces such as rent problems. When Johanna upped

Annie Christmas filming an edition of the Ground Force gardening programme with Nelson Mandela in South Africa, 1999

sticks to Glen Row in early 1971 and I was still on the road, we reluctantly closed its doors.

'The Orphanages – although not deliberately set up as such – offered a viable alternative to the rental sector. We did pay rent, but it was shared and visitors were asked to either contribute or to pay by some form of kind. When they were abandoned, it was also a sign of the times. Dublin had become more affluent, and half of Mount Street was torn down and replaced with "modern" low rise. Where the graceful Georgian architecture of the Orphanage once stood, a squat Modernist bunker now houses the IDA (Irish Industrial Development Association), beloved of politicians, bankers and, you guessed it, landlords.

'They were such good times in the Orphanages, very little quarrelling or bullshit, very little money, lots of creativity and tons of loving, both physical and mental.'

## A Tale of Two Orphanages (Tim Booth)

Mistress Mouse and Mister Puppup sit outside the bar-room door
Their youngest son's in Jerusalem reporting on the war
And three blind master plumbers have just got back from the moon
And Harvey and the Grease Band singing words that have no tune

Hogarth's on the beach-head looking for another home
Leaving naught behind him but a photograph of Rome
The Egyptians hanging on my wall have nothing more to fear
And Harvey and his brass band singing words they learnt by ear

Orpheus the rambler was seen last night in France
By the orphans of the lighthouse at a Pentecostal dance
And meanwhile back on Mount Street oh the sun comes shining down
And Harvey and his pretties singing words which have no sound

Cloud bringers and go-getters get and bring what you can find
And nobody shouts or stumbles or has any axe to grind
Oh the priestly rent collector says his mind is on the bend
And Harvey and his brass band make their song come to its end
Well there ain't no point in kicking up a row,
There's nobody here but me...

# A Tale Of Two Orphans:
# Garo

Born in 1952 to a Protestant family in East Belfast, Gary Moore was already a proficient lead guitarist by the age of 15. Peter Green was his biggest hero, and he could soon also turn in note-perfect renditions of Hendrix and Clapton solos. After playing in a variety of local bands, Gary was talent-spotted by a well-established Belfast blues band, The Method. Their regular lead guitarist had been injured in a car crash, and so they asked Gary to stand in on a three-week tour of the Irish Republic in summer 1968. Frank Murray caught a set by The Method at Dublin's Club A Go Go, and was impressed by their 'brilliant' sixteen-year-old guitarist. He scurried down the road to the club where Skid Row were playing, and dragged Brush Shiels and Phil Lynott over to catch a second set. Brush, always with an eye for talent and for the main chance, immediately offered Gary a place in Skid Row. Brush told Moore's biographer, Harry Shapiro: 'I was lost for words. He was doing the whole [John Mayall's] Blues Breakers set – every single track off that album.' Paul Scully also saw Gary play early on, and told Shapiro: 'Seeing Gary was absolutely gobsmacking. It was Clapton, B.B. King, the riffs... everything.'

In an interview for the *Heavy Petting* re-release on Hux Records, Gary told me: 'I was playing with The Method and Brush came over to see me one night and asked me to join Skid Row as their guitarist was leaving – they didn't play blues at the time so I wasn't really that keen – but I joined the band and it all worked out really cool.'

Harry Shapiro's forthcoming official biography of Gary Moore, *I Can't Wait Until Tomorrow*, has provided invaluable detail for this following section.

As Gary says, swapping the blues he loved for Skid Row's embryonic prog was a difficult decision to make, but he was keen to escape Belfast. After Brush had been up to see Mr Moore senior and solemnly promised he would take care of his new band member, Gary was allowed to make the move to Dublin. Phil Lynott rapidly ensured that he was adopted by the tolerant Strangelies rather than the super-strict Brush. Tim Booth looked back at their first meeting in a piece for the Irish music magazine, *Hot Press*, after Gary's death.

Booth: 'I am in The Bailey, Dublin's then trendiest bar, when I become aware of this skinny boy from Belfast sitting by my side, dark hair falling over his eyes, a few pimples, nervous, shy and a bit twitchy, his left hand making shapes on an invisible guitar, a brown corduroy coat too tight across the shoulders and Philip says: "This is Gary, man, our new guitar player, needs a place to crash..."'

Gary and Brush in Skid Row

Gary: 'I met Tim in a bar one night and he said I could move in, so I moved in with Tim in 26A Newgrove Avenue in Donnybrook and stayed there for quite a while – we got on really well, me and Tim. I really enjoyed that time because when I wasn't playing with Skid Row I'd go and play with Strangelies with my sitar in bars.'

Booth: 'Gary moved into Sandymount for what became the very best of days, even though money and the times were tight. When Gary was not out and about working, he would augment the Strangelies, sometimes on guitar, other times, mandolin or fiddle, even banjo – he could play very passable bluegrass on any of these – and once he brought a sitar back, there was no holding us. We never used one subsequently, but we allowed Gary to sit in with it in Slatterys for the added hippy cachet. We would go off down to Slattery's basement of a Sunday night for a spot of poetry and... er... music, with or without the aid of fashionable pharma.

'Because there were drugs... a lot of cannabis and a touch or two of Dr Leary's fabled turn-on, and we knew that was preferable to the nasty speedy pills Gary favoured when first we met. There were also laughs, rib-shifting and profound, especially when Tim Goulding came by and inevitably when we played music all to-gether. One Sunday Gary and myself took our guitars down to Slattery's, there to perform a guest spot, but somewhere along the day I had ingested a healthy whack of lysergic and this came upon me as we took the stage, so it made for an interesting set. Gary towed me along in the wake of his guitar and the audience were none the wiser. Gary, however, sussed me. All it took was for him to look me in the eye. The gig was in the base-ment of the pub, down narrow fire-trap stairs, at the bottom of which was a broom cupboard fitted flush with the beauty-boarded wall. So, when we made our exit: "Let's take the lift, man..." he said, taking hold of my arm.

"Lift...? Erm... Gar... I don't think there's a...."

"Come on, man, course there is," and he ushered me into the cupboard, pulling the door open onto inter-esting lavender-fragrant darkness. "Bulb seems to have gone. What floor, man? Going up... Ladies' lingerie... Household... Haberdashery... and.... the roof garden!" Sweeping the door open onto the dingy basement again, where the last stragglers were leaving. I thought it fabulous, in the true sense of the word, that a roof garden could be below ground like this and so very very like the basement.

'Other times Gary would arrive back with either some new album he was into, or – because he had a phe-nomenal memory – he would take his guitar and play us something he thought we ought to know about, perhaps a new Zappa offering, and he could not only do all the guitar parts but the voices as well and remember all the stage announcements and laughter would split the seams of the house.' The 1968 Spirit album, *The Family That Plays Together*, was the first LP he owned and another particular favourite.

'In Sandymount one day came a knock on the front door, insistent and officious, and I opened it to find a tall, well-set and groomed man, hair a curly Brylcreemed wave, fawn camel hair coat with a black velvet collar – Gary's dad, down from Belfast to check on his errant son, and we must have passed muster. Looking at Gary's recent photos, I can see the father in the son...'

Gary was a musical perfectionist, and set himself demanding goals. He'd been given the sitar Booth men-tions by ex-Strangely Humphrey Weightman, passing back through Dublin some time in late 1968. Humphrey: 'I was with Brush Shiels and Gary one evening and gave it to Brush, because at least he could get some class of a sound out of it, but Gary walked away with it. As you do.' Booth felt he was 'a better sitarist than most' and

Gary, Ivan and Marymac in the
Sandymount garden, early 1969
(Photos: Mick Slattery)

Ivan remembers: 'He brought it down to the Pembroke pub when we were doing a gig in there and played along with us. It was grand; I think he played a solo on Sign On My Mind.' However, Sylvia Keogh, Gary's girlfriend in that era, remembers the sitar era differently. She told Harry Shapiro: 'He was getting very impatient with the sitar – after an evening in the pub we walked back across the park and when we got to the flat, the first thing he did was smash the sitar to bits.'

Gary could be very funny, but in those days he was fundamentally a shy person who lived for playing guitar, in any context and at virtually any opportunity. Once Strangelies began to use the front room at Sandymount as a practice space, he came to know their material so well that, when he came along to Eamonn Andrews Studios to play lead guitar on the 1970 *Heavy Petting* sessions, he needed no real rehearsal. Tim Booth told Shapiro: 'We fancied ourselves as being able to play, but we were in awe of his abilities. Ivan wrote very pretty songs and very good melodies, and that really interested Gary, so he loved to come and play with us. He didn't mind that we didn't play very well, because when we played with Gary he made us good.'

Ivan: 'I had one particular instrumental tune Gary and I used to play on the floor in Marymac's flat in Sydenham Road. It was inspired by the pair of starlings nesting in the cordyline tree in the garden. I had a light set of strings on Linus' guitar, which she kindly gave me for a long-term loan. I had an unusual tuning for that piece, a kind of a modal $6^{th}$ chord. Gary used to extemporise over it in a delightful manner.' Though Gary's customary Strangelies nickname was the bog standard 'Garo,' Ivan took to calling him 'Garibaldi Moorhen,' which he did not approve of.

The band were all protective of Gary, and when they realised early on that he'd taken to ingesting large quantities of amphetamine sulphate, they 'had a word with him,' says Booth. The Orphanage scene revolved very much around soft drugs – dope and acid – and Ivan accompanied Gary on his first trip, one May day in 1969. He told Shapiro: 'We had a great playful time. We went on the bus to Killiney Head on the south side of Dublin Bay. We went down to the beach and collected stones.' Unlike Phil Lynott, Gary never went on to develop any kind of major drug problem in his later career, so perhaps the Strangelies' early tutelage had some effect. Brush, who was not only anti-drugs but teetotal, possibly also played a role in this, though he had clearly had no great influence over Phil Lynott.

It's hard to say that the Strangelies had any direct musical influence on Gary, apart from that early single recorded by the Phil Lynott version of Skid Row. Gary: 'I think that track, which Brush wrote, New Faces Old Places, was sort of influenced by them – it was like a folk song almost.'

Booth: 'There was always a two-way influence going on between Gary and the Strangelies. His musical abilities clearly influenced us. He taught me some simple guitar lines which I attempted to use whenever I had to add in a sort of solo to one of Ivan's or Tim's compositions. Conversely, we opened his ears to other musical forms, and his eyes to the possibilities of visual art, as well as tampering with his consciousness...'

Once the Strangelies got their record deal and started touring in earnest, they saw less of Gary on a day-to-day basis, and even less when Skid Row relocated to the UK in 1970. He reappears later, though, on many occasions in band history, and they remained in regular contact. He always spoke highly of them. Looking back in 2010, he told me: 'The Strangelies are very special people and they were very good to me... they were the guys to hang out with then – the coolest people in town, very arty and bohemian. We'd go out to these large pubs on the outskirts of Dublin with a little stage... I really enjoyed going out and playing with them.'

# CHAPTER 4

# The debut gigs: 'We were received with a stunned silence by the student body'

A lot of confused memories surround the first ever Strangelies gig. Who was actually in the band? What was in the repertoire? Did *The Irish Times* print a review of it or not? How did the audience react? Was it any good?

According to Booth, after playing that summer in a hotel in Kerry, entertaining tourists with a selection of Irish and American folk songs, he had been offered a gig at the Dublin University Folk Club as part of the 1967 Freshers' Reception. The Ur-Strangelies came into being: 'Ivan had moved near me in a top floor flat near Baggot Street Bridge, so he was just around the corner. Somehow or other, we started to make music together and Cambridge dropout, Al Pacino lookalike Humphrey Weightman added his considerable guitar skills to our first gig in the Trinity Exam Hall.' Ivan: 'Humphrey was a tasty guitar player and had learnt some guitar from John Renbourn.'

Humphrey Weightman

A band name was needed. Ivan: 'Admittedly the name is a mouthful. Obviously Marvel Comics' Dr Strange was a major inspiration. Adverbs were rife at the time (Dylan song titles, for example). Even the Beach Boys had an album out called *Smiley Smile*. Our friend Jim Duncan was constantly heard to say, "Now that's strangely strange, but oddly normal," though he attributed the phrase to someone else whom I never met.'

In October the embryonic Strangelies made their debut. Ivan: 'I cringe to remember some moments. We cobbled together an acoustic melange. Booth had a version of Bobbie Gentry's Ode To Billy Joe with different words, including references to the Mamas And Papas jumping off Dublin's Ha'penny Bridge. As well as Hey Joe, some esoteric instrumentals and Wild Thing with me on ocarina and saz, we also did a couple of Dylan/New Lost City Ramblers songs.'

Booth: 'We were received with a stunned silence by the student body. Humphrey broke all the strings on his guitar... but the jazz critic of *The Irish Times*, George Hodnett, regarded it as our best gig ever.' However, despite several diligent searches in *The Irish Times* archive, no one has been able to find Hoddy's piece.

This particular line-up didn't endure for long. Ivan: 'Humphrey only did that one gig with Tim and me. And he insists it was Dr Strangely Strange *with* Humphrey Weightman. Then some time after that he and Annie Briggs went down to Allihies.' Humphrey: 'I've known Annie Briggs since we were both seventeen, when we'd listen to Chopin Nocturnes and out-there free jazz. Annie to me is the very finest stylist of the late 20th century. Alas, I have no recollection whatsoever of this Trinity gig. I do have a vague memory of attempting to (very badly) play the sitar solo on another occasion in Trinity, but I think we can draw a veil over that particular unpleasantness!'

By the end of the year Humphrey had left his sitar behind and headed for London, where he crops up in Howard Marks' memoir, *Mr Nice*. Humphrey: 'I knew him from Oxford University and I'd shared a flat in Notting Hill with him some time previously (before it became, ah, Notting Hill).' Marks writes: 'Humphrey had just come into some money, bought a new expensive stereo, and wanted to leave it, along with his extensive record collection, with us for safe keeping. We set it up, rolled some joints, and played the latest albums. It was great. Tensions began unwinding.' Humphrey: 'We bought a Monster Sound System, making bass speakers out of drainage pipes, and grooved on a ton of old-school soul.'

Brian Trench

Humphrey reappears in band history later on, but a replacement was needed. The impetus came from an upcoming January 1968 booking to support the Incredible String Band at two Dublin gigs in Liberty Hall, probably down to Ivan's connections with Robin Williamson and lobbying by Anthea Joseph. After a year studying in Berlin, Tim Booth's schoolfriend Brian Trench was back in Dublin and fitted the bill. Booth: 'Brian joined in and whipped us into harmonic shape.'

Brian Trench: 'My earliest musical experience had been as a keyboard player with two beat groups, BV5 and The Boomerangs, which featured singer Jon Ledingham, later a solo artist as Jonathan Kelly. He was a childhood friend of mine from Drogheda. In 1966 The Boomerangs recorded a double-sided single, Dream World / Upgraded, with myself on keyboards. I was also washboard player alongside Tim Booth in the House Of David Jug Band, which played folk music venues in Dublin, and appeared on Irish television in early 1966.

'I was studying French and German at Trinity, and when I joined the Strangelies in late 1967 I had just returned from a year abroad at the Free University Berlin. I played keyboards in a local band there, The Ones, who were support to the Jimi Hendrix Experience in Berlin in May 1967 at the Neue Welt club. Hey Joe had been released earlier that month, as well as the first Experience LP, *Are You Experienced?* Hendrix was well on the way to legendary status but the travelling Experience had to borrow amplification and drum kit from the Berlin beat bands who provided the support

programme. The Ones opened the afternoon concert. The guitarist in our band, Edgar Froese, went on to form psychedelic outfit Tangerine Dream. In a 1980 interview, Froese remembered fondly: "The Ones were a band of shitty idiots. We were absolute amateurs." The sleeve of The Ones' only single shows your humble shitty idiot far left and Froese second from right.

'So, I brought to Dr Strangely Strange a mixed experience and some formal musical knowledge: 10 years of classical piano. I wrote a half-dozen songs that became part of the group's repertoire, including one based on the Tristan and Isolde legend, and another called Old Dublin's Falling Down. I was probably more organised, though less adventurous musically, than Ivan and Tim, and may have taken it on myself to act as some kind of musical director, though Ivan and Tim gave the group its fey, folksy feel.'

## Liberty Hall

There was some excitement about the Liberty Hall gigs (an early show and a late show), a sort of summit meeting of the 'new' acoustic scene which also featured Jon Ledingham and Sweeney's Men. *Trinity News* was enthusiastic: 'Anyone who wants something different shouldn't miss the Incredible String Band concert this evening. With the addition of Jon Ledingham and an experimental new group, Dr Strangely Strange, the concert should be interesting and varied. If you miss it, don't say you didn't know about it.'

The (anonymous) reviewer in the following week's *News* turned in what reads like a very accurate impression of the 'group': 'Dr Strangely Strange opened the concert and surprised everyone by being a good deal better than their former publicity would have had us believe. This was their first public performance with this line up, and the extent of their triumph can be judged by the unanimous encore they received at the end of their act. Their songs have all been written by members of the group (for want of a better word) and apart from the completely original sequence and harmonies, contain many amusing references to other people, places and songs. They were obviously, and quite understandably, nervous, but with this excellent first performance behind them, they should have no difficulty in confi-

On stage at Liberty Hall

dently and fully exploring their varied talents. Their refreshing and original music can only be good for Dublin and one can only hope that they will achieve the success they deserve.'

In *The Irish Times*, 'Hoddy' was upbeat: '...another unorthodox group, well-rehearsed and featuring mild satire along Temperance Seven lines and other material, both straight and send-up; I predict a future for them.' He was cautious, though, to avoid saying what sort of future...

Brian Trench: 'That perhaps surprising reference to the Temperance Seven may relate to the few trad-jazz / blues numbers we used to play: I recall that I sang a version of Sweet Lorraine. I don't remember the atmosphere of the gig, but the photo does suggest to me that we were fairly relaxed.'

Booth: 'Trench had us tightly drilled. Quite rightly so. Don't remember the actual gig, but Trench and I remember the promoter never paid us for playing, or me for the poster I had designed. To judge by the black eye he was sporting when I ran into him on Grafton Street a week later, we were not the only act to have been ripped off. Same old same old.'

Oddly, despite the personal connections and similarities of genre, this was the only occasion the Strangelies and the ISB shared a bill. Was it perhaps seen as Too Much Of A Good Thing? No, says Ivan, they just had different booking agencies.

# The Trench era

As the review implies, Tim and Ivan had started to write their own material, of which more later. What did Brian Trench bring to the setlist? Sweet Lorraine, written in 1928 by Cliff Burwell and Mitchell Parish, has been recorded by many artists, including Teddy Wilson in 1935 and Nat King Cole in 1940, and Brian thinks 'we may have had a few more in that genre.' Ivan recalls that 'we rehearsed harmonies quite a lot with Brian. Honey What You Want Me To Do by Jimmy Reed was one of our regular numbers.' Brian also introduced some spoken word elements which no-one remembers too much about, though possibly a variant of one of these surfaced during recordings for the first album.

Brian brought along some original compositions, including 'a world-weary complaint, Life Is A Bucketful,' another called Sidetracked and 'a mild protest about Dublin Corporation's neglect of historic buildings' which they performed on their first TV slot on the *Late Late Show*. Though Ivan told the music press at the time that this was a 'disastrous choice,' Booth says it was 'topical as fuck, so we gained instant recognition and notoriety.' Brian: 'My song about the housing crisis, Old Dublin's Falling Down, was one of the few commentaries on social realities in the repertoire and was a risky choice, but hardly disastrous.' Ivan does remember that 'we got a very nice letter from the Dublin Housing Action Committee thanking us.'

Brian was much more politically engaged than the others, which Ivan found intriguing and possibly worrying, remembering 'we used to get heckled by Maoists because Brian was a socialist.' Though Brian did join the International Socialists a year or so after leaving the band, this isn't quite right. Brian: 'In 67-68 as part of my involvement in radical student politics I was for a time in an "academic freedom" campaign in which the Maoists were dominant. I was not a member of their group, The Internationalists. I don't remember that they

cared about my musical activities but I can well imagine
that they regarded Dr SS as irredeemably petit-bourgeois.
We performed very rarely within Trinity, and I would have
thought the Maoists were too busy organising the masses
to attend a gig. If Ivan's memory relates to an actual incident, I suspect it might have been an individual voice at an
individual event.'

Irish music press piece from April 1968

April, 1968

Dr. Strangely Strange are
Tim Booth, Brian Trench and
Ivan Pawle. They made their
debut at Liberty Hall on a bill
headed by the Incredible
String Band and since then
their name has been on the
lips of those who were, for
example, among the first to
appreciate the talent of Dylan,
Hardin, Tim Rose, and so on.

Anthea Joseph, EMI's ever-
aware information officer, describes them as "the only
group in Ireland to be part of
the Underground movement
that produced the Incredible
String Band, Pink Floyd,
Arthur Brown, etc. They write
their own songs, which are a
mixture of cynicism and
spool."

Ivan is the only Englishman
in the group. He's from
Peasenhall, Suffolk. Brian
Trench is brother of "Fee"
Trench, an exceptional pianist
noted for his work with Ian
Whitcomb. Tim Booth is a
freelance commercial artist,
among whose credits are the
Incredible String Band Dublin
concert posters and those for
Jon Ledingham's discs.

11·

# CHAPTER 5

# 'Reporting from experience and a large dollop of imagination' – early songs

The band developed a unique style combining folk, psychedelic, blues and baroque elements with the spoken word and started to gig at small Dublin venues, including a Sweeney's Men support slot in a Stephen's Green pub and Skid Row support in a Parnell Square cellar beat club, when Brian dared to use Brush's bass guitar. Ivan's songs Sign On My Mind and Strangely Strange But Oddly Normal were set staples, as well as an early version of Donnybrook Fair, but Brian says 'the repertoire had turned over fairly fully by the time the first album was recorded.' Another early song was the Tim Booth and Ivan co-write with Patrick Carroll, You'll Recognise The Feelin'.

The stability of the three-piece line-up with Brian Trench, coupled with the move to the first and then second Orphanages and lots of late-night jamming, led Ivan and Tim Booth to begin to write their own material. Ivan's early songs 'came out of the Mount Street Orphanage,' he says. Some dated back a few years, at least in embryonic form.

Ivan: 'I had bought a saz in the bazaar in Turkey. I could not master the microtuning and simply tuned it to DAD (a tuning I was to use three or four years later on the bouzouki). Dark-haired Lady was composed on the saz. On the way to Turkey we stopped off in Florence and stayed with a friend of a friend, a Brazilian singer called Heloisa Buarque de Hollanda. We went busking together, and she showed me the Brazilian [bossa nova] chords I used at the intro to the Goldenhair section of the song (Goldenhair is by James Joyce, although I failed to credit him at the time). Heloisa went on to become a Professor in Cultural Studies at the University of Rio De Janeiro, specialising in the Sixties.' Syd Barrett also set this poem to music, for his 1969 solo album *The Madcap Laughs*, but went for a haunted, spectral treatment diametrically opposed to Ivan's.

Ivan: 'Strangely Strange But Oddly Normal came out of a little tin whistle tune I played on the same trip, while hitchhiking in Italy. Though I didn't realise it at the time, the chord sequence is very similar to both Pachelbel's Canon and Ralph McTell's Streets Of London! I suppose it's become our signature tune. Strings in the Earth and Air – sometimes words come first, sometimes a melody. Sometimes they both come at the same time: I had a song without words and a friend put a copy of Joyce's *Chamber Music* before me. It was literally weird how well the words fitted the tune!

'Sign On My Mind and Frosty Mornings came out of the Orphanage. Frosty Mornings is about wintertime in the city. The Cmin to Dmaj chords have always fascinated me since we sang some Hungarian folksongs arranged by Matyas Seiber at school. The words of the first verse of Sign On My Mind arrived with the chord sequence, and I couldn't quite figure which key it would resolve into. The lyrics reflect where I was "at" at the time: missing boats, studying the I Ching, going barefoot, eating macrobiotic, keeping it all simple as can be. I was fairly self-contained and unencumbered, traipsing around between Marsh's Library, the Royal Dublin Society Library and the old Chester Beatty art gallery, and sleeping on friends' floors... (thank you – you all know who you are, or were!).

'When I wrote Mirror Mirror I was trying to study a bit of amateur cosmology, reading late Renaissance and early Enlightenment texts in Marsh's Library and looking at the world through Stephen Strange's eyes. Also, in retrospect, I detect nuances of our friend the Catman, Andy Anderson, in some of the spoken lines. I used a closing quote about the universe: 'How immense then does this universe appear. Indeed it must be either infinity, or infinitely near it.' That's from Charles Hutton's *Mathematical And Philosophical Dictionary* (1795).'

Tim Booth's early material included A Tale Of Two Orphanages (see Orphanages chapters). It was originally called £68 In The Red for autobiographical reasons. His other early song, Donnybrook Fair, is undoubtedly his magnum opus. Written in early 1968, it had already been extensively road-tested by the time the band came to record it. Musically it is reminiscent of the Incredible String Band's habit of stringing musically unconnected pieces together to form one collage-like song. The musicological term for this is 'durchkomponiert' ('through-composed'). In terms of psych-folk, the ISB's A Very Cellular Song, released in April 1968, will probably be the best-known example of this to readers. It wasn't released when Booth started writing Donnybrook, though he would have been familiar with earlier ISB tracks like Robin Williamson's The Mad Hatter's Song or The Eyes Of Fate, on the 1967 *5,000 Spirits Or The Layers Of The Onion* LP, which also share this approach.

Booth: 'The arrangement for Donnybrook grew organically as we performed it and realised how to build in elements to work an audience. Donnybrook Fair was from late medieval times a famed horse fair and carnival type get-together on the edge of Dublin and existed until quite recently. It was probably the origin of the usage of the word 'Donnybrook' to describe a bit of a barney with fisticuffs and the like. I wanted to make a potted history of Ireland from the perspective of the creative outsider and the Unicorn fit the bill. Ireland in the late Sixties – despite the arrival of a toddler counter-culture – was still in the grips of a bleak De Valera-based intro-spective nationalism and fun was hard to find, so you had to make your own. The song grew and grew and was an integral part of our live act. Still is.'

The 50th anniversary of the Easter Rising, in 1966, was still fresh in Booth's mind at this point; though the band (even Ivan) were steeped in Irish mythology, they had a visceral loathing for the austerity of the pre-vailing political climate. Most of the characters in the song are well-known figures in the history of the Irish in-dependence movement such as Patrick Pearse, Joseph Mary Plunkett and Henry Grattan, whose statue is still 'standing in the rain' outside Trinity College. The Number Ten bus stop is close by. Patrick Pearse was a poet and member of the Irish Volunteers who played a key part in the Easter Uprising. Tim had a mild obsession with Pearse's squint, which caused him only to be photographed in profile. Joseph Mary Plunkett, like Patrick Pearse, was a poet who played a key role in the Easter Rising and was subsequently executed. Tim reckons he was in the wrong place at the wrong time. Tim's mum felt that history had been unfair to Thomas Wentworth,

The Mighty Cretins Showband in Tim Booth's cartoon strip

a seventeenth-century Brit very much on the other side of the political divide, and christened her son Timothy Thomas Wentworth Booth as an act of reparation.

Muircheartach ('the leather cloakéd king') was a tenth-century Irish prince who set off on a tour of Ireland at the head of a thousand heroes, conquering all and 'feasting his hostages with knightly courtesy.' Deirdre of the Sorrows represents Ireland; she is a tragic heroine in Irish mythology, known for her great beauty. The Mighty Cretins Showband featured in a short-lived Strangelies cartoon strip by Tim (see illustration) and epitomise the stranglehold that showbands like The Mighty Avon Showband held on the Irish music scene in the late Sixties.

On the recorded version, starting with a little recorder tune, a mandolin briefly plays a jig (not trad, but written by Booth, as far as we can tell) and then goes into the main series of verses, after which there's a funfair organ section in which you can just about discern a few stallholders' shouts. Tim Booth tells us the band were thinking of Dublin's Moore Street market, where a familiar cry was 'cheap mechanical toys and balloons.'

The 'King Of Love My Shepherd Is' section towards the end is first sung to the tune of Waxies' Dargle, a Top Ten hit for Sweeney's Men in February 1968. The song is steeped in Dublin history. In the 19th century, during the summer, the gentry of Dublin would travel out to Bray and Enniskerry to picnic on the banks of the River Dargle; the name in Dublin slang became synonymous with 'holiday ' or outing. The cobblers in Dublin were known as waxies, because they used wax to waterproof the thread they used in stitching the shoes. The original Waxies' Dargle was said to be part of the Donnybrook Fair. Sweeney's had augmented the original two verses with a chorus, which Tim used in Donnybrook:

'What will ye have, will ye have a pint?
I'll have a pint with you sor
And if somebody doesn't order soon
We'll be thrown out of the boozer'

The King Of Love re-emerges, sung to its original hymn tune, to conclude the song (and, eventually, the album) with a rousing 'Amen.'

## Songwriting approach and influences

Tim Goulding sums up the Strangelies' overall approach to songwriting very well: 'Definitely tongue in cheek but nonetheless reporting from experience and a large dollop of imagination.' Ivan and Tim tended to write about aspects of their own lives and people they knew (later on, Goulding too), and their songs are littered with a panoply of 'characters.' The Incredible String Band didn't really take a similar approach, but, along with LSD, they are somewhere in the mix of influences.

Ivan: 'The String Band was undoubtedly an influence – even to the extent of "Sure, I can give this a go..." – the same spirit that was to inform the punk ethos ten years later. When Robin Williamson came over to Dublin,

I heard some superlative singing and playing, October Song, Womankind and the Smoke-Shovelling Song for example. Robin and Licorice left me some LSD, to take when I would feel ready for it, and obviously, acid was a huge life-changing eye-opener.' Shirley Collins worked with Robin a couple of years later, on some of the *Hangman's Beautiful Daughter* tracks, and told writer Rob Young that Williamson was something of an acid evangelist: 'You've never seen a tree until you've taken LSD.'

Ivan: 'In terms of musical creativity, it was the grass and hashish that got one going. No doubt about it. I found the music of the Incredible String Band perfectly wonderful, and unprecedented. I was inspired by it and thereby influenced, especially insofar as modes and modalities were opened up and explored as never before.

'When I left school I had made a few faltering attempts at songwriting; early influences would have been skiffle and Buddy Holly, then Bob Dylan, I guess. I used to like to go to a late-night coffee shop at the Pike Theatre, where I heard some good singers and pickers such as Booth's friend Mick Colbert.

'I have always maintained that I try to write my own stuff as I'm so bad at learning other people's songs, especially in the canon of folk music. I have always enjoyed listening to jazz, but realised from the start that technique, or at least a proficient command of one's instrument, is a prerequisite. Likewise classical. Rock 'n' roll demands a determined attitude plus "chops" – which I take to mean the correct grammar, syntax, and vocabulary. I idly mulled over these considerations as I tried to find my own role as a musical practitioner.'

Booth: 'The old Lysergic did have a bit of an influence in the songwriting, still does. The ISB much less so. I was always aware of the ISB and their capers, but when they gambolled off into Hubbardism like lambs to the slaughter, my interest waned. I was interested in rhythm and timing, enjoyed good flatpicking and rock 'n' roll music and these elements, coupled with harmony singing and hallucination, floated my boat. The other major influence on my limited songwriting was – of course – Bob Dylan.'

Goulding: 'I was never consciously inspired by the ISB but they were very strongly part of our musical scenario. LSD definitely gave a sneak preview to the 'awakened state' that many mystics alluded to. Hence the ISB's quotation of Thomas Traherne and friendship with Advaita [one-ness, see below] sage, Douglas Harding. I think the Strangelies were less philosophically explicit than the ISB. Definitely more tongue-in-cheek but nonetheless reporting from experience and a large dollop of imagination. Tim Booth's lyrics in particular are bulletins from a fevered frontline view of an alternative universe. Ivan's are beautiful and honest depictions of a psychedelic world view. My early songs were to some extent laced with an underlying sense of one-ness – the Buddhist concept of non-dualism. Ivan too refers to this in a later song: "The path exists but not the traveller on it." I explored this more consciously in later work.'

In February 1968, *The Irish Times* announced: 'Dr Strangely Strange and the Sugar Shack ought to be only some of the odd characters at a formal dance and supper at the Old Shieling, Raheny, from 11pm to 3am.' The Old Shieling Hotel was a popular music venue owned by a wealthy Kerryman, Bill Fuller, rumoured to be an IRA supporter, and so it also served as a refuge for IRA volunteers taking a break from their war in the North, hence the coded reference to 'odd characters.' The Republican band Wolfe Tones often played there.

Ivan recalls it was a launch for Sugar Shack's first and only single, a 'heavy' version of Walk Me Out In The Morning Dew. They featured Phil Lynott's old friend Brian Downey on drums. The Strangelies played support.

Robin Williamson and Anthea Joseph eventually prevailed on Joe Boyd to come over to Ireland and see the band live, opening for Skid Row. Brian Trench: 'My understanding is that Phil Lynott made the case to Skid Row that Dr SS should be included as special guests. As it happens, I met Brush Shiels recently and he recalled this gig, and Joe Boyd's presence. My memory of Boyd is that he wore a fleece coat (Astrakhan?) and stood at the back of the hall.'

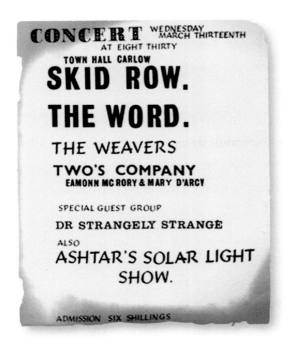

Joe travelled with Robin to Carlow, near Dublin, in March 1968 to see the band and three other acts including local psychedelic rock band, The Word. Leo O'Kelly of The Word: 'I was really chuffed to chat with Robin in the dressing room afterwards, as I was a big fan of The Incredible String Band.'

Booth: 'Skid Row was pre-Gary Moore, and still had Phil Lynott as lead singer. They played through Marshall amps at white noise volume, prancing around the stage like stallions. The gig was in the Town Hall, and for some reason the three of us sat on a school bench, all in a row like the wise monkeys (the other bands were rock bands, man, and stood). We played acoustically, singing into a single mic, performing heartily such epics as Life Is A Bucketful and Sidetracked, both from the Pen Of Trench, as well as some early songs of mine and Ivan's. We used Skid Row's PA and this flummoxed us as we had zero mic technique.'

## Ashtar's Light show

Ashtar, an acid-head friend from the Mount Street Orphanage, brought his Solar Light Show along. Ivan: 'In our bigger Dublin shows we often worked with Ashtar From Mars (Gregory Brown) who did amazing light shows. He was a friend of Phil Lynott's and also worked for Skid Row; he did light shows every chance he got. He'd also worked with Krishna Lights in London.' Tim Goulding says 'Ashtar was convinced that he had come from another planet,' though Ivan thinks this 'may have been in a parallel universe, rather than our own familiar solar system.'

Ivan: 'His lightshows were undoubtedly world class, up there with those at UFO. He would use back projections, like the Velvet Underground did, and oils to get that floating globule effect. Ashtar grew some pot plants in one of the borders in St Stephen's Green – I never heard of anyone else doing that before or since. The last time we met him he was doing the lights with Thin Lizzy and Horslips. We went over to the Town Hall

Killarney to see them in about 1974 – Ted Carroll was managing the Lizzy at the time and Gary was playing with them.'

Despite all the effort that had gone into setting up this showpiece gig, Joe wasn't impressed enough to start brandishing contracts, but clearly saw some potential and eventually sent the band a stalling letter. Meanwhile, there was a brief feature in the Irish press which made much of Joe's attendance at Carlow and had a reasonable stab at quantifying the band: 'The only real "underground" group in Dublin... their material is neither pop nor folk, but, like a lot of the most interesting groups around, is impossible to label... Someone has described it as trans-media.' Not sure who that 'someone' was, though it could have been Bernard Stollman of ESP-Disk (q.v.).

In May 1968 the band took part in an unusual gig at the Gresham Hotel in which Tiffany Scales (Miss Ireland) drew a raffle 'with style' and 'senior models... executed country dance routines' while displaying 'young sophisticate fashions from Dublin boutiques,' (all this from *The Irish Times*). Music was by the New Cottonmill Boys and 'The Dr Strangely Strange group, who suffered from a thin and tinny sound.' Jon Ledingham also played and 'got the scream treatment.' Jon had a few singles out in the Sixties but, as Jonathan Kelly, became a bona fide star with the 1972 album *Twice Around The Houses*. Goulding comments that the sound was pre-destined to be 'thin and tinny' because they didn't yet have him playing harmonium.

Around this time, Brian Trench left the band: 'I was studying for my finals, and was active in radical student politics, so I probably did not give as much effort and time to Dr SS as Ivan and Tim. Among the events that took my attention was the furore that followed the forceful breaking-up by police of a May 1968 protest against the presence in Trinity College of the Belgian King and Queen. I was involved in rallies and demonstrations inside and outside the college, and also writing for student publications, including articles about the May 1968 'events' in Paris. I must have left Dr SS soon after the Carlow gig, as by the summer of 1968 I was living in a cottage in the countryside, studying for my finals.

'Soon after my exams, I left Ireland for Bordeaux to pursue postgraduate studies in the sociology of literature. En route through England, I visited my musician brother and his wife and baby son in Devon. I ran through a (mistakenly locked) glass door in Marks and Spencer while I was with them, narrowly escaping very serious injury when the glass cut my chest. That incident was the basis of a paragraph in a 1970 Karl Dallas Strangelies feature in *Melody Maker*, which reported that I'd 'split to make revolution in France' and referred to me 'walking through a glass door in Bordeaux.'

Tim and Ivan stayed in touch, and in 1971 Brian played with them again, albeit very briefly, at a band recording session.

# CHAPTER 6

# 'Tim Goulding was dragged from his easel'

The band did not have to look far for Brian's replacement. Booth: 'Tim Goulding was dragged from his easel to become the vital transfiguring third member of the band.' Living at the Mount Street Orphanage with Ivan and Annie, Goulding was already both a good friend and familiar with the general Strangelies approach to life and music – and, probably most importantly, another acid head. He'd also recently bought a harmonium.

Tim Goulding at Mount Street

Goulding: 'They had an eye on my harmonium. I had an eye on Tim Booth's Japanese ping pong bats. I'm sure they rued the day that they set eyes on the harmonium as they carried it up and down stairs all over England and Ireland.'

The harmonium became a bit of a millstone. Dr SS were the first band to take a harmonium on tour – and probably the only one, right up to The Low Anthem, who recently toured with two! They had a team of roadies, though. This recalcitrant instrument, coupled with Goulding's highly individual take on 'jazz recorder,' made their sound even more distinctive. The ping pong bats got added later. Before Hoppy joined the band to play kit in late 1970, a variety of band members played percussion on a variety of instruments. The bats, usually played by Goulding, were hollow and created a percussive sound vaguely akin to bongos. Joe Boyd managed to keep them off the first LP sessions, though they were pressed into service in an unreleased 1970 recording.

Goulding was classically trained on the piano, and at his first gigs with them he struggled to learn to play by intuition: 'Joining the band was an exciting challenge as I was totally unfit for following other players. Typically they might say "This is in A and goes to E via D." That was fine, but what to do in A and E and D? I am still trying to puzzle that out.'

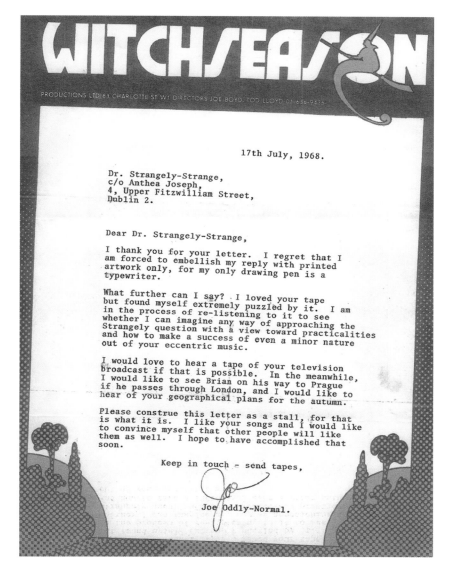

He settled in quickly though, bringing both suitably quirky songs and a new sound to the band. Ivan and Tim never progressed very far with a nickname for him, though occasionally he was referred to as Sir Basil and, says Goulding, 'unfortunately, Gelding.'

Booth: 'The harmonium gave us a unique sound and was a great instrument on which to write songs, because when you played a basic chord sequence and then pulled the top and bottom harmonic couplers out, you could hear the harmonic notes and get ideas as to where to pitch the melody.'

The band still had their sights set on signing a record deal with Joe Boyd, now a force to be reckoned with on the growing psych-folk scene, but had heard nothing very definite from him since the Carlow gig. Booth: 'Ivan and I decided to send him a tape and demoed two songs, Tale Of Two Orphanages and Mirror Mirror, playing them in one room in Sandymount while Liam Saurin recorded our efforts onto a Nagra reel-to-reel in the adjacent kitchen. He did a great job – he was the sound engineer in Ardmore Film Studios, who I had met while working as Art Director on a film called *Paddy*. We grouped around a single vocal mic to sing, but he put another mic out to catch the guitars. He did a great job and both Joe Boyd and Bernard Stollman complimented us on the quality of the recording.'

Goulding may possibly have played on this session too, but no-one is very sure and the tape has gone missing. In July Boyd wrote them a letter, signed 'Joe Oddly-Normal,' explaining that he liked their songs but wasn't sure if they were marketable.

The tape was also sent to Bernard Stollman, boss of ESP-Disk in New York (who typically released left-field artists, such as Pearls Before Swine, The Holy Modal Rounders and The Fugs). The ESP of the company name stood for Esperanto, a Stollman hobby-horse. He liked the two tracks and flew over to meet the band. Eventually he offered them recording time and a promise to release the resultant album; intriguingly, he also offered a studio slot and a separate deal to Humphrey Weightman, who he had possibly met in Dublin. Humphrey wanted to call his album 'Noh Flies On The Sea.'

The November 1968 letter from ESP-Disk makes mention of a 'four-dimensional idea,' though Stollman concedes this may be 'premature musings on an age that perhaps hasn't yet arrived.' This indeed sounds intriguingly well ahead of its time, but the band now have not a clue about it. Ivan: 'I simply can't recall what the four-dimensional project would have entailed; I suspect it must have been inspired by a synthesis of Marvel Comics' Doctor Strange, ingestion of hallucinogenic substances, and some putative soundscapes. It may have involved the feeling that "All things are possible." Humphrey surely has a better and more rational explanation!' (He didn't have any). Booth thinks: 'There was probably none. It was the Sixties.'

Booth: 'We continued to gig, practise and write songs and were joined in this endeavour by the beautiful Caroline Greville, who sang backing vocals and played various percussive instruments as well as being perhaps the most tolerant woman on the planet. And – as anyone who saw the revue we were later part of at the Gate Theatre will attest – a dab hand at the cartwheel.' Yet another ex-Trinity student and Tim Booth's girlfriend at the time, Caroline Greville was always known by the last syllable of her first name – 'Linus.'

November 18, 1968

Dear Tim and Ivan,

Please jointly sign one copy and return it to me. You should each retain one copy!

The enclosed letter to Mr. O'Donovan should be self explanatory.

This 4 dimension idea is not mandatory, since it may impede you in doing what you want to do. If it should happen to work out, do it...otherwise, consider it my prehaps premature musings on k an era that hasn't yet arrived.

Your duo may use as much as $250. worth of studio time, but I have officially allocated one half of that amount to you. You may show this letter to Mr. O'Donovan if need be to confirm that understanding.

This will mean that Humphrey and his crew have an identical sum to work with.

Some very wild things are being produced here at the amount by a new ESP group called CROMAGNON. Another new ESP group called OCTOPUS is developing into a fine blues-jazz-new music fusion.

Philips Undistries of Baarn, Holland has just confirmed by cable that they will distribute ESP all over Europe, so your album will be released as quickly as it is completed. Hoorah!

Cordially,

BERNARD STOLLMAN

E S P - D I S K'
156 5th Avenue      New York 10010
(212) 255-4800      Cable ESPDISK

Early PR photo of the four-piece with Linus, late 1968

Taping early rehearsals at Ham Goulding's flat in Monkstown, Co. Dublin (Photos: Ham Goulding)

(ABOVE) Tuning; next to harmonium is Keith Westmacott

(LEFT) Rehearsal with (FROM LEFT): Tape op Peter Waugh, Linus, Ivan

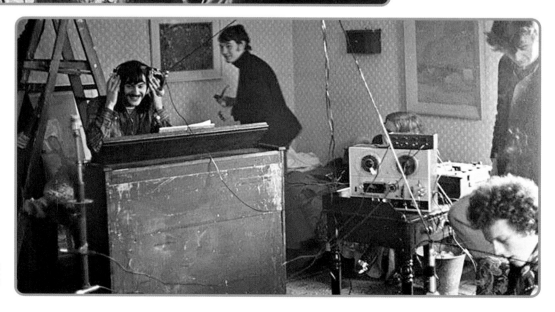

Goulding gets the headphones working; Booth far right

*Monte Carlo* still – Peter Cook in foreground, Ivan (in uniform) visible over his left shoulder

In summer 1968, restless again and perhaps losing patience in the wait for a deal, Ivan took off, heading to Rome for work at Cinecitta as an extra in a film called *Monte Carlo Or Bust*, a comedy caper starring various international luminaries including Peter Cook and Dudley Moore, for which Jeffa Gill and her colleague Janice were doing wardrobe. Ivan played a small role as a border guard who took and returned Gert Froebe's passport.

His next stop was Penwern farmhouse, near Fishguard in Pembrokeshire. After the break-up of David Medalla's Exploding Galaxy dance/mime/street theatre group, members Malcolm Le Maistre and Rakis had travelled to Paris to meet an heiress and patron of the hippy arts called Silvina, who granted them £5,000 to set up a new group called Stone Monkey. The plan was to work in various ways with the Incredible String Band, with whom Malcolm and Rakis had already performed as a duo in June that year at the Fillmore East, New York.

Stone Monkey performed at various ISB concerts in the late Sixties, and their biggest ISB collaboration came in 1970, with 'U'. This was an ambitious multimedia show, featuring music, back projections, striking costumes, dance and mime, which ran for 14 performances at the Roundhouse, Camden in 1970.

Preparations for filming being made in the Penwern farmyard, Peter Neal on the far right
(Photo: Peter Saunders)

Their series of ISB collaborations really took off when ex-Galaxy members John Schofield, Ishy, Rakis, Malcolm and Malenie Schofield moved into Penwern in July 1968, and were joined there by Robin and Likky. By the time Ivan turned up, they had already completed work on Peter Neal's *Be Glad* film, to which Stone Monkey contributed a 'fable' called The Pirate And The Crystal Ball. Mike Heron and Robin had cameos as Gods. The next joint project was a big concert at the Albert Hall, in November 1968, where Stone Monkey were to join the ISB on stage for the finale.

Ivan: 'When I arrived, Robin was writing Creation.' Robin had been reading a tract by Robert Graves titled *Adam's Rib*, which attempted a reconstruction of a pagan version of the seven days of creation. Using some of Graves' text as a centrepiece, Williamson had woven in other arcane references and his own poetry, with enigmatic lines such as: 'the archetypal postman delivering your seed letters, whose eyes are black eggs really.' The result was a lengthy and ambitious spoken word and music concoction, which eventually appeared on the ISB's *Changing Horses* LP. Ivan played piano on the recorded version.

Ivan: 'The plan was that we would all play and dance when the ISB performed it. We were on a macrobiotic regime at the time, and had picked some *Amanita muscaria* [Fly agaric or magic mushrooms] and fasted for a week. At one stage I went to Dublin and Linus came back with me to Penwern, so she was part of it as well. At the gig I played a keyboard. It was a small electric organ, very basic, a kid's toy that Robin had picked up somewhere. The late Nicky Walton [the friend of Robin's who appears on the sleeve of *Hangman's Beautiful Daughter*] was Neptune.'

The Albert Hall audience appeared to like it and gave them all a five-minute ovation. The music press, however, was baffled. A journalist named only as 'Keef' reported: 'The finale was a poem (unintelligible unfortunately) set to music. During its performance, the company was swelled by assorted dance-mime characters including Neptune and several nebulous nymphs.' The ISB spurned encores in this era, seeing them as an artificial construct (they soon changed their minds), so Keef reported glumly that 'the only result was to have two more glimpses of the weirdy dancers. Rather a let-down after an original, overwhelming, incredible concert.'

Rose Simpson (ISB): 'I remember we were quite committed to Creation as a serious idea and that encouraged the refusal to do an encore because it shouldn't be regarded as a piece you could just treat like another set of miscellaneous songs. However, as usual, some of Robin's songs just rambled on too long. Because it did have an important theme, and it was early days for that multimedia venture, and because we were still quite idealistic and believed in it and each other, the performance was a bit hypnotic for us too.'

However, things were finally moving on the Strangely Strange front. Later that November, after reporting that 'Ivan Pawle played with the Incredible String Band last Saturday at their Albert Hall concert,' *Trinity News* had an exciting announcement to make: 'Dr Strangely Strange, the Dublin group of interchanging musicians – Ivan Pawle, Tim Booth, Brian Trench, Tim Goulding, Caroline Greville, etc – is rumoured to be making it in London with contracts in the air.'

## Gigging in Dublin Clubs

Gigs had now started to be slightly larger events, though in 1968 and early 1969 they were largely restricted to the growing Dublin club scene. With the exception of Cork, where the band was also popular, gigs outside the capital were largely met with incomprehension or requests for some familiar material. Even in Dublin, it could be tough. One 1968 appearance was at The Embankment in Dublin, a regular gig for The Dubliners. Tim Booth: 'They [the audience] were completely open-mouthed. They didn't dislike it; they just didn't know what was happening. There was an American tourist sitting below me. He kept telling me to get my hair cut. Sean, who ran the place, had said he wanted to fill the place with people having a good time and hearing songs they knew. Then we got up and it was totally unfamiliar. Another time we were playing in a Dublin pub and an old woman came up and put her hand over my guitar strings and said "Why don't you play something we bloody know?" I suppose they thought we weren't doing songs like The Holy Ground because we couldn't, but we could if we wanted.'

Ivan: 'We played folk clubs rather than beat clubs because we were acoustic rather than electric, although our repertoire only contained snatches of folk material. It was music for sitting down, rather than music for dancing.'

There were three Dublin venues where the band played regularly and were assured of a receptive audience: The Neptune Rowing Club, Slattery's and Sinott's.

## Dublin haunts

Because of its club status, the Neptune allowed performers and friends an extra pint or two after the gig on Friday nights. 'One night,' says Tim Goulding, 'a vicious fight broke out and pints of Guinness flew and tables were upturned. The wee Strangelies remained glued by fright to their stage and emulated the band on the Titanic.'

It was run by Jimmy Corrigan, says Tim Booth, 'a lovely man who took great pride in the folk musicians who performed on the tiny stage. The club was held every Friday night in a green-painted corrugated iron club house on the banks of the Liffey just outside Dublin. There was a single microphone, an old cage Shure, and we performed alongside Sweeney's Men, Mick Colbert, Johnny Moynihan, The Press Gang, Gay and Terry Woods, The Fureys, The Cotton Mill Boys and the late great Frank Harte.'

Slattery's, in Capel Street, was a regular Sunday night gig. Tim Booth: 'It was run by Mick Colbert, a beautiful guitarist and singer. Whatever limited clawhammer technique I have is down to his teaching. Our gigs there entailed loading the harmonium – wrapped in plastic to protect it from the elements – onto the roof rack of Goulding's Renault 4, Gosport Lil, driving across town and then unloading same and manoeuvring it down a steep flight of stairs into the basement bar. The staircase had a right-angled turn and it took considerable deftness of touch to get the harmonium down without damage, either to the instrument or our backs. We also had to mule it back up the stairs, wrap it in plastic in the street and heave it back onto the roof rack post-gig. There were a couple of mics which we used for vocals, hoping the guitars would be picked up by them a bit as well, but the club was so small that acoustic instruments could be heard and the audience – all hardened drinkers and thus fans of the esoteric – gave us their total attention, as was the fashion betimes in Sixties folk clubs. We honed our act. Not really, but it was good practice for facing larger hostile audiences on the subsequent English university circuit a few months later.'

Slattery's was the scene of a showdown about Donnybrook Fair's reference to Patrick Pearse. Booth's mention of the Pearse squint in song caused him to be threatened with physical violence, he tells us, 'by a centrally-cast drunken Irish poet' named Ernie Bates who explained forcefully that he was 'sensitive to Pearse's sensitivity.'

Booth: 'Occasionally Gary Moore would join us on sitar and that added a touch of credibility to our act. We would try to do the gig totally straight, but I do recall that time with Gary when the broom closet at the foot of the stairs transmogrified into a lift and we spent some time in it travelling between floors and realities...

'We would play a set, 4 or 5 songs and the chat between for about half an hour, take a break when maybe there would be other acts or guests, and then finish off the night with another 4 or 5 numbers. As it was of a Sunday, the pub closed at 10, so we were often back in the Orphanage quite early – certainly before dawn.'

There was an intriguing group of Slattery's regulars, many of whom went on to greater things over the years. The Cana Band was a blues-based outfit featuring singer Rick Ward from the north of England with 'a fine gravelly voice.' Niall Fennell played French Horn with them, adding a soulful backing to Rick's interpretation of early Rolling Stones slow numbers such as Connection. Alec Finn (later in eclectic folkies De Dannan) played bouzouki; alongside Johnny Moynihan of Sweeney's Men, he was responsible for introducing the first trichordo Greek bouzouki into Irish music. The Cana Band took their name from a pub called the 'Canal Inn' – the 'l' had fallen off 'Canal.'

Phil Lynott's mates The Tara Telephone Company performed poetry and music and were, says Ivan, 'a strange outfit. They – like us – were very much of the times. Peter Fallon, the brother of the rock publicist BP Fallon, read his poems whilst various muses added sound effects.' Declan Sinnott, later briefly a member of Celtic rock band Horslips, played guitar and also read his poems. Eamon Carr, later the drummer in Horslips, played bongos. Other regulars included The Press Gang, a four-piece a cappella band whose repertoire was primarily English country songs and sea shanties. They were the first Irish group of this kind. Niall Fennell also added French Horn to the mix which, says Ivan, 'hugely enhanced their aural palette.' Niall would also guest with Tara Telephone.


Over their formative years, Strangelies played many gigs at Sinnott's in South King Street. The weekly gig 'Poetry and Music' was run in the first-floor lounge there by poet and writer Leland Bardwell. Tim Booth: 'It had a long narrow ascent, so we developed muscles humping the harmonium up and down which worked to our benefit later on tour, when we had to lift the fucker up on to Goulding's roof rack.' The trials of touring with a harmonium are a recurrent theme in Strangelies history.

'There was no amplification at all, but as poetry was involved, the audience was raptly silent and there were some among their number who felt that the good Doctor got in the way of the Art. I think we were paid ten shillings each for these gigs, but then, a pint of stout was less than two shillings and the audiences were generous, placing pints before us as we worked, to encourage brevity.

'The gig featured various Irish poets such as Eiléan Ní Chuilleanáin, Pearse Hutchinson, Macdara Woods and Hayden Murphy, interspersed with music and songs from the likes of Luke Kelly, Mick Colbert, Ronnie Drew, Johnny Moynihan and ourselves. There were no mics, so everything was acoustic. In my memory, the poetry far outshone our offerings and I have an image of the late John Jordan, dressed in a dinner-jacket suit and standing trembling behind a lectern as he wrestled down his astonishing poetry, and wrestled also whatever hallucinations his DTs caused him to experience, sweat on his brow, reading his work with ruined dignity. May he and the other poets and musicians – many now dead – who graced this wonderful event find contentment in their rest.

'Leland Bardwell was a legend. Poet, novelist, scarlet woman… you name it. Her best-known book is *Girl on a Bicycle*. Despite living a wild life, she died only a few years back, well into her nineties. A great woman. Eiléan Ní Chuilleanáin is still with us, along with her longtime partner, poet Macdara Woods. Before I moved into the Orphanage, she used to be my landlady, and after a Sinnott's session her party would often overflow into my downstairs flat. On one late night occasion, we tried a very drunken Luke Kelly of Dubliners fame for crimes against literature and found him guilty as charged. The sentence was summary removal of his nether garments and expulsion into the street… where nobody noticed, it being three am. After his assault on the front door nearly tore it from its hinges, we readmitted him into the cosy arms of poesy.'

Tim Goulding: 'I was always unsettled by the ubiquitous dialect that the poets used. Their everyday voices vanished and a strange "up on their hind legs" accent took its place.'

Ivan: 'Hayden Murphy was our age, and editor of the fabled *Broadsheet*, a poetry magazine – to which Linus and I contributed poems and Booth, illustrations – which came out three times a year. Pearse Hutchinson would read his poetry using the de rigueur declamatory voice which so unnerved Goulding!'

# Strangelies' 1968 Dublin

A lot of the Strangelies' old haunts have been demolished or have changed use, but there are enough left for a short constitutional. Once you've been to Trinity College, alma mater to Ivan and Booth, you can walk down Dawson Street and check out whether the Number 10 still goes down there. You'll find Henry Grattan standing in the rain (weather permitting) at the far end on St Stephen's Green. Continuing on down Harcourt Street, you'll pass the building which housed the Number 5 Club, scene of an embarrassing early gig. Also at the top end of Harcourt Street was the Eamonn Andrews Studio, where parts of *Heavy Petting* were recorded. The building is an office block now.

The next bit involves walking east and past 55 Lower Mount Street, site of the first Orphanage. The building has been replaced by a newish office block, but you can still see the Mount Street Bridge referred to in Ivan's song Halcyon Days. Toners, still a great pub, is nearby in Baggot Street. O'Donoghue's (traddy) and Sinnott's (touristy) are further along the same street, in Merrion Row and King Street respectively.

You could get the Dart from Barrow Dock station out to Sandymount, from whence it's a short walk to the second Orphanage at 26A Newgrove Avenue; just beyond that is Sandymount Strand, scene of the 1969 Dr SS photoshoot. The James Joyce Tower and Museum at Sandycove is a few stops further down the same train line. If you visit the GPO in O'Connell Street, Henry Street, at the side of the building, will take you to Capel Street and Slattery's Bar at number 29. Dr SS had a late Sixties Sunday night residency in the basement bar there which entailed a lot of lugging the harmonium up and down a steep flight of stairs. Slattery's has since been given a make-over and transformed into a 'sophisticated' haunt for clubbers.

And Donnybrook Fair? It used to be held on a flat green besides the River Dodder, probably now the site of the Dublin Bus Depot in Donnybrook Road, to the south-east of the centre. The fair was infamous for riotous behaviour, so much so that 'a donnybrook' is Irish slang for a brawl and general mayhem. It was 'suppressed' by the council in 1855.

Map: Deena Benjamin Omar • Graphics: Mychael Gerstenberger

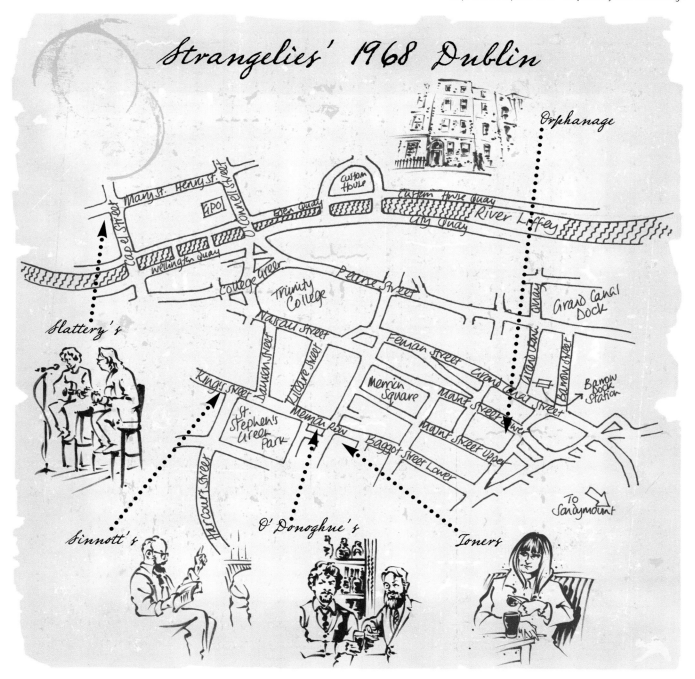

## Goulding's songs for *Kip Of The Serenes*

The band now had some solid experience of live performance and Stollman's offer had finally tipped Joe Boyd into action. Plans were formulated for the band to travel to London to record their first album for Witch-season. Spurred on by the record contract, Goulding had also started writing songs. Though notably more doomy than Tim's or Ivan's, they also feature the Strangelies' trademark array of characters, many of them friends.

The first song Tim ever wrote was Riding The West Cork Hack, very loosely based around an acid trip with some friends out in the hills near Allihies, which was interrupted by a policeman who had climbed up the hill to see what was going on.

Goulding: 'Riding the West Cork Hack involved visits to a parallel universe where all was plainly alive and shining, moment to moment. The Waking Dream was self-evident; my friends and I were tripping and I was clutching a rotten old bucket which was my new best friend. We were slightly threatened by the arrival of a local police sergeant, who explained he'd come up in plain clothes because he "didn't like to upset you." Still riding, we invited him back for tea (as you did) and it was decided that I should entertain him with a harpsichord recital. As I played, I could see the hairs on his chin growing. What were we thinking? Probably weren't, thank God.'

Dr Dim And Dr Strange provides little cameos for all four of the band and features an intriguing array of characters from the Orphanage and beyond. Goulding: 'It is a romp through the mindfields of Dr Strange's Dublin of the late Sixties. It owes more than a nod to the prelate Robert Burton, who wrote *The Anatomy of Melancholy*. The poor man suffered from 'a heavy heart and hatchling in my head' and 'was very desirous to be unladen of it.' No doubt he was also troubled by 'dry throat and hard stool.' The 'baker in Ferrara' is one of Burton's case studies. Catman the Minotaur refers to Andy Anderson, the sometime inhabitant of the Orphanage. We made a horror film in the deserted salt mines near my house in Allihies, West Cork, starring Andy as a Catman who committed heinous crimes underground wearing white gloves and painted whiskers. 'Martin's lawyer' was a particular discredit to this unloved profession, famous for his considered response to our friend Tony Lowes: 'You have nothing in writing – you can go fuck yourself.' 'Projectionist Zhivago' is a reference to Phil Lynott's favourite nightclub and also the Carlton Cinema where late night horror films were given added spice by an intoxicated projectionist. He would get the sequence of spools wrong

Film still of Andy as Catman

to a chorus of disapproval from the audience who assumed he was showing only edited highlights. 'Clip, Clip!' they would shout. The 'mad March steamer' is a reference to a John Masefield poem, Cargoes. The closing refrain, 'There's nothing there at all,' refers to the Advaita Vedantist view of life. This is also succinctly expressed in Ivan's chorus: "No matter what you do, don't forget it isn't you," in Frosty Mornings.'

The final *Kip* song, Ship Of Fools, is Goulding at his most apocalyptic and has a strong 'we're all doomed, I tell you' vibe (things improved for him gradually over the years). Goulding: 'It's a weird one. The first few lines refer to the four things King Solomon could never understand, and come from the Book of Proverbs. The child tenor and baby crooner are going at the crisis pipe as if there is no tomorrow (which in fact there isn't). Overall, the lyrics suggest an attack of extreme paranoia and displacement. There must be a syndrome for this state of mind, possibly DIJA... Drug Induced Juvenile Angst.'

Booth had another new song, Roy Rogers: 'I had discovered open tunings and these broadened my limited capabilities, and because the open D tuning I favoured was modal, it led – for me anyway – to uncharted areas. Roy Rogers featured a claw hammer pick on an open D tuning and the words just vectored in from that fabulous place – somewhere in the ether apparently – where words are stored. I have always had a thing for romanticised Western images and these came from a Zane Grey moment with a touch of Rupert Bear origami.'

The Strangelies were now played in, had more than an album's worth of material and had a stable core line-up of Ivan and the two Tims which was to last them a couple of years. By the end of the year, however, Linus and Booth had drifted apart, so at this point she wasn't part of the band or the recording sessions. In January 1969 the trio took the ferry from Dun Laoghaire to Holyhead and drove down in Gosport Lil to Joe Boyd's flat in Lots Road, Chelsea, where they were to stay whilst recording the first album.

# PART 3
## Of Transits and Transitions

Touring, recording and touring again – from psych-folk to 'folk-rock'

# CHAPTER 1

# 'Everybody sit in a circle and make a record'
## *Kip Of The Serenes*

In early January 1969 the trio arrived in London to stay with Joe Boyd in Lots Road, at the unfashionable end of Chelsea. Before the first studio session, there was time for a quick bit of instrument shopping: Goulding

acquired a Stylophone and in Portobello Road market Booth bought a Howson Phonofiddle, a strange, horned one-string instrument.

Sessions for *Kip Of The Serenes*, at John Wood's Sound Techniques studio in Chelsea, started on 4th January. Some of the first songs to be recorded were Roy Rogers, an early version of Mirror Mirror, and Strings In The Earth And Air, where the Phonofiddle gives a primitive, Harry Partch edge to the piece. The Stylophone made a one-off appearance on Dark Eyed Lady before it was nicked the same evening, when Anthea had arranged a gig at Les Cousins. This was the first of their many appearances at the club, and seems to have been a

AT LES COUSINS, 49 Greek Street, London's Folk & Blues Centre. 7.30-11.30.
### JOHN MARTYN
Singer-Songwriter Contemporary
### DOCTOR STRANGELY STRANGE
from Ireland there came Three, singing their music now for you infinity

success. Booth: 'Andy, who ran Cousins, was always very kind to us and liked to put us on to open for better-known acts, such as John Martyn or Al Stewart.' John Martyn was present that evening, together with Robin Williamson and Likky, who showed up to give their support.

The studio sessions settled down well, after some initial nerves which ST engineer Roger Mayer recalls as a 'deer-in-the-headlights routine.' Joe Boyd produced, though after the first session studio boss John Wood quickly handed over engineering duties to staffer Vic Gamm. At first, Tim Goulding felt slightly in awe of Joe: 'He was a cool dude who seemed to be at the centre of things and we were the country cousins come to town. But we were immensely grateful for his support, which went as far as letting us stay in his house. We wanted to credit Eric Clapton on the back cover, for passing by in a taxi. He was God at the time. There was a Hammond in the studio that was enticing…' Booth: 'A daunting yet enjoyable experience. We were studio novices and, before the days of electronic tuners, a lot of time was spent caressing machine heads, with Joe making comments like: "Ivan… that B string still sounds sharp!" over the foldback.' Ivan: 'Joe was also recording with Nick Drake and Chris McGregor's Brotherhood of Breath and we got slotted in at odd hours. There was a stimulating vibe there. It was our first time in a proper studio, and an awesome experience.'

Joe Boyd: 'I liked the fact that we could go into a studio without a drumkit, without taking rock 'n' roll time frames – go into Sound Techniques, everybody sit in a circle and make a record. I warned them that we couldn't spend a lot of time, and so the cheap and cheerful aspect of it was part of the appeal, I have to admit! We got the album done very quickly.'

The multi-track tapes reveal a pretty focussed approach by all concerned, probably helped by the relaxed atmosphere for which Sound Techniques was well known amongst musicians; to Fairport Convention's Dave Pegg, Sound Techniques 'was like coming home.'

After the first couple of days of recording, Ivan headed off to Penwern, where he spent a lot of time attending geology lectures in nearby Nevern, and the Tims went back to Ireland. In Dublin, Tim Booth showed two paintings in the exhibition 'Three Young Artists.' *The Irish Times* seemed to like them: 'One is entirely of felts, the other is in felts and Perspex. In both cases the subjects involve organic shapes… Mr Booth shows the clash and vibration of colour, and when black Perspex is used, light and shade interchanging gives an effect of movement and dazzling light.' Or maybe it was just the drugs? To cut down on harmonium transport, Booth bought another one at a Dublin market. It was installed in the music room at Sandymount.

Goulding bought himself and Annie a house-cum-studio near Allihies, West Cork: 'It was the old School House, last used in 1955. I was robbed. It cost £150.'

In February the band reconvened in Dublin in time for Andy Irvine's wedding. Booth: 'I remember the party afterwards in Mespil Road. Mick Colbert got a little overly refreshed and was ejected. He retaliated by kicking in the front door, a dignified Victorian number with brass knocker and accoutrements, took it right off its hinges. I left.'

As well as playing the usual haunts such as the Rowing Club, Slattery's and Sinnott's, they appeared at a Famine Relief benefit and at Dublin University Folk Society. Booth: 'I was a founder member of the society, so it was probably a fix.' There were also several gigs for Brush Shiels' weekly Ghetto Club, which usually featured many of the other Sinnott's regulars such as The Press Gang, The Cana Band and Terry Woods. Booth: 'It was Dublin's answer to Liverpool's Cavern Club, under the street in old brick-vaulted Georgian cellars at No 5 Harcourt Street. In 1967 or 1968 I met two absolutely identical twin sisters here and when we went out together, I was never sure which one I was with because they liked to swap around. They were lovely young women, Mary Quant haircuts, white lipstick and dark painted eyes. I see them still. Our first gig there was organised by either Phil Lynott or BP Fallon. We played acoustically, but all had vocal mics and went down quite well with the Dublin Mods whose turf we were stepping on.'

Another gig at No 5 was a disastrous support slot for Granny's Intentions, a beat/psych band from Limerick who were already hardened pros. Ivan: 'Their keyboard player, John Ryan, graciously offered Goulding the use of his keyboard, which saved us lugging the harmonium down there. Unfortunately, the instrument, a Vox Continental, had black keys for white and vice versa, like a harpsichord, and the lighting was poor. Tim was used to pumping the harmonium with his feet, whereas the pedal on John's machine was for controlling the volume, so the effect was inadvertently psychedelic. We learned more than we needed to know about dynamics and sudden key changes. It was a slightly mortifying experience at the time, but quite amusing in retrospect.'

Goulding: 'Further confusion occurred as my ultra-tight star-spangled trousers split at the seams. A flow of bum chords accompanied my fellow Strangelies' endeavours.'

There was a second television appearance. Irish TV, known confusingly as Raidió *Teilifís Éireann*, broadcast a 'popular music series' called *Like Now!* A March appearance by the 'Dublin folk/rock group' revealed a visually disparate bunch: Ivan rocking a cardy, Booth in a groovy leather jacket and Goulding in a Portobello Road kaftan. They played Mirror Mirror and did a short interview, but the tapes, sadly, have been wiped.

In Renchi's basement: Goulding sheltering from a mind storm.

The band returned to London at the end of the month. Linus had become close to Goulding and was now in the band again. Her one documented comment on this period is that she 'drifted in and out of the band.' This time they based themselves with Goulding's schoolfriend Renchi Bicknell in Dalston; living around the corner was the old Trinity friend of Ivan's, film-maker and writer Iain Sinclair, who shot some (silent) footage of the band rehearsing for the new album and listening to a playback at Sound Techniques.

Iain Sinclair: 'We had started to do a film diary of this loosely structured community living around us in Hackney. My wife Anna and I were living in Albion Drive, Renchi and his wife Judith were living just round the corner in Albion Square, but there was a constant floating population of other people staying here, there, backwards and forwards between the two all this time – a remnant of people who we'd known in Dublin and others from all sorts of places. Because I was just beginning to publish stuff around that period with a small press, poets and writers were always staying here

Renchi, Ivan and Goulding playing a mind game with a stuffed reptile and various sundries.

as well. It was a creative time; the Strangelies arriving here and staying over in Albion Square was very much part of the mood of that moment – it didn't seem at all out of the way.'

More studio sessions on 31st March and 1st April included Strangely Strange But Oddly Normal, Ship Of Fools, West Coast Hack and Donnybrook Fair. Ivan's friend Jay Myrdal was brought in to play glockenspiel on three songs. Jay: 'My main qualification for playing on the album was that I owned a glockenspiel! I couldn't really play it but Ivan said he only wanted a few notes and it would be OK... Though we did rehearse Frosty Mornings a bit, really we just busked it! I had met Ivan in 1966 when I was a photographer's assistant and got a private job covering a company picnic in Ruislip. The Manpower agency had provided the catering staff, who turned out to be a flamboyant guy called Desmond – and Ivan. After the picnic I gave them a lift back to London – there was a lamb carcass left over which they wanted to deliver to a friend. After a very long, involved journey and lugging it up five flights of stairs, we discovered he was a vegetarian.'

On the final day the band also recorded two tracks which didn't make it to the album, HMS Avenger and Ivan's work-in-progress, Cock-A-Doodle-Doo. He had written the first verse in Dublin, and the second in London. Ivan: 'It's about leaving Dublin with the band to seek our

Jay Myrdal, 1969

fortune in the wide world. I was using the open tuning chord of E major. I worked on the song in Renchi and Judith's basement at about the same time as we did the lost song, West Indian Drinking Chocolate Blues.' The band came back to Cock-A-Doodle-Doo the following year, after Ivan had written a final verse.

The loss of HMS Steam Frigate Avenger, by C.P. Williams (courtesy of National Maritime Museum and Hux Records).

## HMS Avenger

In the Brian Trench era, the band would often incorporate spoken-word pieces into their set. HMS Avenger is the only surviving recording of this side of their work. Someone, possibly Brian, had been reading an 1850 tome titled *Narratives Of Shipwrecks Of The Royal Navy; between 1793 and 1849*, by William O.S. Gilly. One section of the book documents the sinking of the steam frigate HMS Avenger, wrecked off the Algerian coast with heavy loss of life in 1847.

The Strangelies' version of the tale was recorded at the end of the final *Kip* session and there is an air of muffled, stoned hilarity to the 4-track session tapes. It begins with Booth, barely restraining giggles, intoning: 'It was a dark and stormy night, with high and windswept seas. Off the coast of Algeria, a steam frigate, HMS Avenger. She was running at eight knots with reefed sails, and bearing a crew of 250 souls and six heavy guns. She struck the rocks...'

In the course of the narrative, the Avenger morphs from a Royal Navy frigate to a sort of Titanic cruise ship, with party scenes in the 'first-class passenger lounge' cutting to Lieutenant Marryat announcing the sinking – 'Women and children first, cried the women and children.' There's a Booth ballroom song, as well: 'Come and do the tango with Dr Strangely Strange.' Linus claims her seat in the lounge is reserved, Ivan shrieks 'The rats!' more than once, and Goulding gets to drop in his current catchphrase, 'kip of the serenes.' Ivan's 'Fresh pears, bananas and chocolate' was the call of street vendors in Dublin city and at racecourses. Various Strangelies mates pop up in the stoned chatter – Annie Christmas, Jeffa Gill, Mole and Orphan Annie – and there is the obligatory reference to Patrick Pearse, who 'may have had a squint but he was sensitive about it.' In the end, Booth tells us, 'all were lost save four hardy souls.' Goulding: 'That was Sir Basil, Jeffa Gill, Mole and Orphan Annie.'

Joe Boyd probably threw up his hands in horror at the prospect of making anything coherent out of this track, though the band had clearly planned it for the LP. The ship (with some of the first-class passengers) features in Booth's graphic on the *Kip* sleeve, flying what looks to be a pirate flag featuring a man with an eye-patch. Pearse.

The verdict now? Booth: 'We used to do this live and it always went down well, so we began adding to it in a spontaneous manner until it became the great unwieldy beast on the recording. We found it funny.' Ivan: 'I suppose the Goon Show would spring to mind.'

HMS Avenger remained in the vaults until the wreck was salvaged in 2007, when the track was mixed for the *Halcyon Days* archive CD.

*Kip* was completed and mastered on 1st April, though Mirror Mirror, which had been up for consideration, was left off the album as the keyboard solo had drifted out of tempo. Right up to the last minute, the band were toying with a name change to 'Dr Strange L'Éstrange,' as you can see on the production master.

A few weeks later, Ivan repaid a favour to Robin Williamson by popping back to ST on 23rd April to play piano on Creation (released on the ISB's *Changing Horses*). The *Kip* masters were licensed to Island Records, and the album was released on 4th July 1969. Strangelies were the first of all the Irish 'progressive' bands to get a UK album release, beating Skid Row and Granny's Intentions to it by around a year.

Boyd's masterplan for *Kip* worked out pretty well – though the Strangelies lacked the musical chops of his regular clients Heron and Williamson, they usually nailed a song within a few takes. However, Linus thought Joe saw them 'as a challenge.' Interviewed for the book *101 Iconic Underground Rock Albums*, Ivan told author Richard Morton Jack: 'Joe was a very positive influence, and if he'd known our material better I think he might have suggested some judicious editing, like our habit of repeating choruses ad infinitum. He was very patient and encouraging, and knew how to get a good sound with the engineers, but left the musical arrangements to us. Overall we were thrilled with the album.'

The Island tape box label for Side A, where Booth's Roy Rogers is still down as £68 In The Red.

At the time, Joe saw the band as an Irish version of the Incredible String Band. He says: 'I liked them a lot, I thought they were fun, though there was a slight feeling that they were "ISB junior." It's hard to be really clear about my mental state at the time... Witchseason's books were not balancing and my response – which in hindsight was not exactly full of wisdom – was that if Island was giving me a certain amount of money every month, and if I could release more records without spending a lot of money, then one of them might do well and generally help the picture. The ISB were doing very, very well at the time, spending a lot of time in America; I had the idea that this Irish group that was ploughing a similar furrow might build up a big following in Ireland and England and be ISB junior and sell well. The ISB's sales didn't come through Witchseason, it was a straight Elektra deal, although I got royalties as producer. So that was part of it... Obviously at the time you couldn't see that this model of acoustic, folky, hippy music didn't have very long to live (*laughter*) – it was a burgeoning thing at the time! I thought that they were really nice guys and wrote some clever songs.'

There were some more London gigs in March, including a couple at Les Cousins and a Release benefit presented by John Peel at West Ham College, with Peel favourites The Occasional Word, Mike Hart and Bridget St John. There was also a late-night gig at the Electric Cinema, Portobello Road, before the main film started at midnight. Booth: 'I remember lifting the harmonium on to the stage in a lather of sweat and then being surprised at how much the Portobello hippies liked us.' Goulding: 'I think the stage was halfway up the wall.'

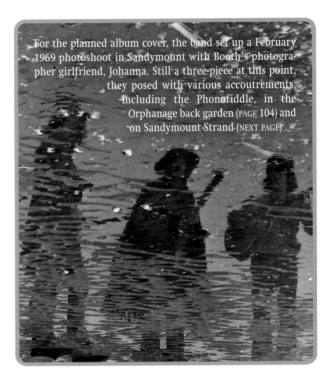

For the planned album cover, the band set up a February 1969 photoshoot in Sandymount with Booth's photographer girlfriend, Johanna. Still a three-piece at this point, they posed with various accoutrements, including the Phonofiddle, in the Orphanage back garden (PAGE 104) and on Sandymount Strand (NEXT PAGE).

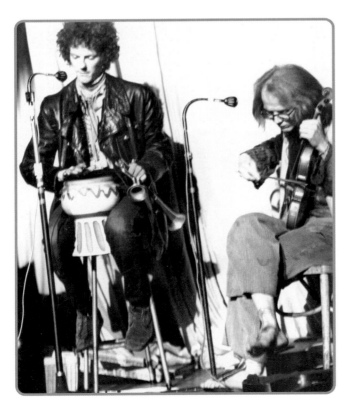

On the West Cork Hack, live in 1969.

Booking agent Julia Creasey had worked with the folk music promoter Roy Guest, arranging gigs for bands like the ISB and Pentangle, and was to play a major role in the Strangelies' live career for the next couple of years. Now based at NEMS Enterprises, she added them to her roster, and with a view to a possible joint tour, she organised an 'audition' for them with Ivor Cutler.

Ivan: 'Ivor Cutler was wonderful, no question. The idea was that we might be a good fit for a tour together, but there wasn't any palpable chemistry.' Booth: 'Ivor wore an embroidered smoking hat of the type now favoured by Goulding and I think we were invited to attend a gig because we had the harmonium – which he

borrowed. I remember he did a sketch about "Egg Meat" which ended with the protagonists watching eggs being fed with the aforementioned egg meat and ended with the line – spoken in Ivor's soft Scottish accent – "Look Mammy, see how they gobble it up!" I found him a bit tedious, if a touch lovely.'

In April the band were in Ireland again. With Linus back in the band, they needed some new album cover photos as a four-piece, so Orphan Annie took a sequence of colour pictures in the Dargle Valley and sent the best off to Witchseason. One was used for the *Kip* cover, and nearly 40 years later Joe Boyd turned up another two during a clear-out. In the cover shot, Booth is wearing a weird chicken mask from a theatrical costumier's: 'I wore it partly to hide from my bank manager and partly because I was uninterested in publicity – that day, at least.'

Booth provided a rear cover graphic featuring some of the characters and events in the songs, so the listener could while away stoned hours spotting them. That's Muircheartach on the horse, and the ship at the centre of the picture puzzlingly refers to the then unreleased HMS Avenger. The faces of the band appear floating in a cloud, top right. We have reproduced Booth's artwork on the back cover of this book.

There was another round of Dublin gigs at the usual haunts, but on 28th May Strangelies moved up the pecking order with a gig at the Adelphi Cinema supporting Fleetwood Mac. Goulding: 'We arrived at the stage door of the venue in a taxi in our medieval clothes, beads, and trinkets. I was wearing my Jimi Hendrix wig. There was a mob of young groupies swarming at the door and we thought, "This is it!" As we stepped out, we were met by a shout of "Don't look at them, they're horrible!"'

Booth: 'We were a three-piece for this gig: Goulding, Ivan and myself. Johanna took pictures. To satisfy some weird union requirement, we had to join the Irish Federation of Musicians. This meant we had to undergo a musical competence test, which we faced into with some trepidation. Would we be asked to sight read? Sharps

Precariously perched in front of Fleetwood Mac's equipment, the band essay West Cork Hack. Ivan's clay drum was potted by Booth's friend Stephen Pearce.

and flats?? On the day, a besuited Fed official asked me what were the relative minors if you were playing in the key of C. We passed with flying hallucinogenic colours and the Dublin audience gave us a rousing welcome.'

They were still in Ireland when *Kip Of The Serenes* was released in July.

Booth: 'A proud day for us all. We thought we must surely now be the very Bee's Knees. I remember an acquaintance called around to the Sandymount Orphanage looking for Gary Moore, and I made him listen to the entire album, which he did, becoming more and more restless as I plied him with enthusiasm, coffee and spliffs. I can still see the look on his face as he left, exhausted: a look more of pity than the admiration I had hoped for. He was a musician of considerable note who played in the showbands.'

Goulding: 'I showed it to my dad, who hoped it might be my last venture into music and that I would stick to painting. Unsaid but understood.'

Booth: 'Steve Pearce's father Philip loved classical music and had a super-duper stereo system with a Quad amp and speakers installed in their sitting room. I played him early Bob Dylan, Beatles and other stuff and he listened, smiling tolerantly. *Kip Of The Serenes* did however produce a comment: "Sounds a bit like Monteverdi." A man of impeccable taste. As is the son.'

The album was quickly adopted by the 'heads' it was aimed at, and became part of the standard hippy record library for stoned evenings in. However, Tony Lowes, Ivan's friend from the Orphanage milieu, first heard the album in particularly unusual circumstances. This is the piece he wrote about it.

## How I first heard *Kip Of The Serenes* – Tony Lowes

It was late in 1969 that I realised my return to London after 18 months travelling through the East was not working. Everybody was engaged, and I seemed to have lost the ability to engage. A feeling of unreality wouldn't leave me as I sat in the garden on Albion Square with the sun shining down and a slice of lemon in the water jug. Nothing had changed and the searing poverty and dirt and violence I had seen didn't exist. Ivan and Tim were about to make Strangely Strange's first album – Iain was travelling the hellish motorways of

England in a mini-van trying to sell copies of our works to down-at-heel bookshops – people were starting communes. I couldn't handle it. I had one travel dream left – to hitch-hike across the Sahara. So I set off again.

I had my heart set on coming in at the southern end of Morocco and following the caravan trail across the Sahara to the walled city of Kano in northern Nigeria. It didn't work. When I finally got to the border, the Atlas Mountains were permanently closed – border troubles. I had to backtrack all the way to the Mediterranean and along to Algiers, where it was only on the third day of waiting in the visa office when they called me in and gave me a visa. 'And how would they treat me in your country?' the official asked, stamping the visa at last. Heading down into the Sahara was easy enough at first – tourists crossed parallel to the coast in the relatively lush low mountains; old men played dominos in the cafes. But as you headed south – perched on a lorry with a Bedouin scarf across the face to filter the dust – villages vanished and there was nothing but a few barrels shading giant lizards to mark the way across the endless rubble-like land.

I met Sven, a Swede who was also hitching alone across the Sahara, and we travelled together to Messad, an oasis with running water and public baths and wheelbarrows of lettuce and tomatoes. It was just after we arrived that we came across two Europeans loading a Land Rover with crates of beer. We offered to help. They accepted and invited us to the gathering of teachers and aid workers they were having that evening. I don't remember the party, but I do remember being stretched out on the floor in our sleeping bags afterwards, Sven and I and our two hosts.

One of them asked what music we wanted – 'Whatever you want,' we said.

'There's this new band from Ireland,' he said, and the sounds of Ivan and Tim's voices and Strangely Strange But Oddly Normal floated across the room.

The finished album has a very nice flow to it, probably down to Joe Boyd. During the sessions for the ISB's *Wee Tam & The Big Huge* the previous year, he'd evolved a system of juggling possible track sequences using columns of paper cut in proportional length to the timings. The original Side One opens perkily with the Strangelies' theme song and Dr Dim And Dr Strange provides little cameos for all the band. After Booth's chipper Roy Rogers, there's a short extract from the Strangelies' 'medieval' repertoire in Dark-Haired Lady. The band had a few more pieces in this vein and even worked up a mummers' play, of which more later. But DHL doesn't remain medieval for long: after a jazzy, contrapuntal recorder solo and a Stylophone solo, it veers off sideways into a bossa nova lick. Then West Cork Hack takes us on a scary voyage into the Goulding interior. Side Two opens with Tale Of Two Orphanages, featuring a motley crew of characters including Tim Booth's two cats, this time drawn from the milieu of the band's two communal houses. Next is Ivan's treatment of Joyce's poem Strings In The Earth and Air, Goulding's favourite of all the Strangelies' songs. Following on, Ship Of Fools has an epic feel, but Frosty Mornings lightens the mood with a poppy shooby-doo coda and then it's the album's star track, Donnybrook Fair.

One of the things that made *Kip* sound distinctive was the use of the harmonium. It wasn't exactly new in pop and rock music. In 1965 John Lennon had been an early harmonium adopter, playing it on the Beatles' We Can Work It Out. *Sgt Pepper*'s Mr Kite also used a harmonium, and Pink Floyd had used one sparingly on Chapter 24, on their first album.

On *Kip*, though, its wheezing tones, combined with squeaks and clunks and rattles from the foot-operated bellows, gave the album a strange kind of unity. The harmonium's links with the church somehow chimed with the album's vein of acid mysticism, as well.

DSS were probably the first band to feature a harmonium consistently, certainly within their genre. Within a couple of years other acoustic bands followed suit, including Clive Palmer's COB, Trees and Planxty, where Christy Moore employed it to add simple chords and drones.

The band's old friend, publicist BP Fallon, neatly summed up the sound of the album for a 2006 book on Irish rock: 'Weaving tapestries of sound on

wheezing organic instruments that, when they weren't entirely in tune or in time, were entirely in tune with the times.'

## 'Certainly an acquired taste' – *Kip Of The Serenes* and the music press

Out in the mainstream world, *Kip* did not exactly hit the ground running, and was greeted with some baf-flement by most of the music press. *Record Mirror* loved it: 'First LP from an Irish folk-based underground group. Mellow sounds with clever and often amusing lyrics (Roy Rogers especially), and their literary heritage is certainly not ignored – viz the Joycean Strings In The Earth And Air. Beautifully fascinating back cover design, and altogether a listenable and worthwhile LP.'

**KIP OF THE SERENES. DR. STRANGELY STRANGE. Island ILPS 9106.**

Island have really released some quite exhilerat-ing stuff this month, including Nick Drake (reviewed last week) and the Fairport and Dr. Strangely Strange things we're having a go at this week. It's all part of a vicious plan to allow hard, nay, over, worked Island executives to have a well earned holiday over August, when no new albums are to be released. (I think that's what's written on the back of this fiver anyway).

Dr. Strangely Strange are a group from Ire-land but despite this they are utterly delightful if not vaguely similar to the Incredible String Band and Forest. As you probably haven't heard of Forest thanks to amazing disinterest and fast talking/copping out on behalf of a fair proportion of the ent. biz., the Incredibles are the only comparison you'll probably make.

Strangely Strange's music is a lot more per-sonal than the ISBs, they sing songs about each other, about the group and they have a nice rapp-ort with you — the listening audience, which is very engaging. Their songs are tinkling and often contrapuntal, just like the ISB but they have more form than those of Heron and Williamson. Both styles have their own appeal and the music of DSS is just another pleasant exercise in musi-cal fantasy. Actually it's not totally surprising that one is reminded of Elektra's dynamic duo on hearing this album, as it was produced by Witchseason's Joe Boyd.

Ivan Pawle, Tim Goulding, Tim Booth and a chick called Linus are the members of the group and they've written all the tracks on the album but one. They play an amazing number of instruments including Glockenspiel, violin, assorted guitars, thumb piano and organ and they play them well. Put the pieces together, the simple countrified ideas and the tremulous voices and melodies and you have a happy little album.

However, the rest of the reviewers were at best dubious: 'Hippy poetry often sounds suspiciously like barely-remembered fragments of stories told in primary school...' said *Melody Maker*, '... and as this charming quartet beat their tambourines and blow their recorders, creeping ennui sets in with numbing effect.' It got worse in *NME*: '[They] specialise in self-compositions, which are whimsical and humorous, not unlike the Incredible String Band... Unhappily, what starts off interesting begins to get intensely boring and irri-tating as the record drags on.' Finally, *Disc & Music Echo* found it: 'Strange indeed. They appear to be deadly serious about their music, but we found ourselves laughing at their incongruous sound, which comes from guitar, whistle, fiddle, percussion, harmonium and other instruments. It cannot be classified easily, but is certainly an acquired taste.'

The 'heads' at *International Times* were predictably much more in tune, although the idea of pleasing the reviewer 'despite' being Irish is surprisingly unreconstructed. Here's the uncredited *IT* review:

'Island have really released some quite exhilarating stuff this month... Dr Strangely Strange are a group from Ireland but despite this they are utterly delightful if not vaguely similar to the Incredible String Band and Forest. As you probably haven't heard of Forest thanks to amazing disinterest and fast talking/copping out on behalf of a fair proportion of the ent. biz. the Incredibles are the only comparison you'll probably make. Strangely Strange's music is a lot more personal than the ISB's, they sing songs about each other, about the group and they have a nice rapport with you, the listening audience, which is very engaging. Their songs are tinkling and often contrapuntal, just like the ISB but they have more form than those of Heron and Williamson. Both styles have their own appeal and the music of DSS is just another pleasant exercise in musical fantasy. Actually it's not totally surprising that one is reminded of Elektra's dynamic duo on hearing this album, as it was produced by Witchseason's Joe Boyd.

'Ivan Pawle, Tim Goulding, Tim Booth and a chick called Linus are the members of the group and they've written all the tracks on the album but one. They play an amazing number of instruments... and they play them well. Put the pieces together, the simple countrified ideas and the tremulous voices and melodies, and you have a happy little album.'

To end this section, French film director Olivier Assayas recalls the soundtrack of his adolescence.

## 1969, not far from Paris - Olivier Assayas

I had strictly no idea who Dr Strangely Strange were. I suppose I bought their first album in 1969 when I was fourteen, based on the sleeve and because I bought (almost) anything Island released, including the first album by a virtually unknown singer-songwriter, Nick Drake, released the same year.

*Five Leaves Left* and *Kip Of The Serenes* were a vital part of the soundtrack of my adolescence, possibly the most precious, as in the Paris rural suburb where I grew up no one, even remotely, knew about them. And they didn't particularly like them either, whenever I tried to share my feelings. You didn't hear them on the radio – I'm not even talking about French radio, I'm talking about my only tenuous connection to the English music scene: Radio One was out of reach, but for some reason you could tune in to Radio Luxembourg. The music press ignored them, both sides of the channel. And we were light years before any information, about even the most obscure of bands, was two clicks away.

Why did the music of Dr Strangely Strange so profoundly echo with me? I suppose the elegiac melancholy of their Irish music (I had no idea they were Irish, to the best of my knowledge they were four generic hippies, three guys and a girl) blended with the bucolic landscapes of my teenage years, the woods and fields I walked to the station where I caught the train to school. The passing of the seasons, the loneliness too. Their psychedelic folk was possibly the most relevant expression of my emotions. And even now, years later, every time I listen to that first album it is images of nature and spring in my countryside that come to me, and a form of nostalgia that was already there in the first place. To this day the sheer perfection of Strings In The Earth And Air still sends shivers down my spine. Of course, it resonated with another James Joyce poem, Golden Hair, set to music with equal grace by Syd Barrett on his first solo album that same year.

Years later, by the time Nick Drake had become a household name, Dr Strangely Strange had yet to resurface. They seemed to be a lost cause, a lost fragment of times gone by. And no one else seemed to care. I only gradually realised that their album had become a prized collectors' item. That, if one checked on the internet, you could see mentions of the band popping up here and there: so I hadn't been hallucinating after all, it wasn't just me, there were actual other people who felt the same about their music. I felt a sense of personal vindication when gradually the Dr Strangely Strange comeback took shape, first with the disastrous release of a badly mastered CD, then with the reappearance in 2005 of their second album, and finally in 2009, when forty years had passed, came the CD release *Kip Of The Serenes* deserved.

In the meanwhile, I had become aware of The Incredible String Band. It didn't take me that long but still, I was a pretty late convert; and when punk rock came, changed the world I lived in, and initiated a revolution I wholeheartedly embraced, *The Hangman's Beautiful Daughter* was never too far from my turntable. It made me think – had I been listening to their music in the Sixties, would I have been as impressed by Dr Strangely Strange? After all, by 1969, the ISB's best work was already behind them. Were the Strangelies only an offshoot, their Irish cousins, as I have heard mentioned? I don't think so. Their first album is a blessed moment: it captures at its purest the timeless grace of those years, seen through the wide-open eyes of the idealist youth I was. And when I made a semi-autobiographical movie about my coming of age, I couldn't imagine, to express teenage love, and the freedom of a summer in Italy, a better illustration than the music that had stayed in my heart all those years.

# CHAPTER 2

# From a cabaret season to a Dalston basement

Oddly, the band did no UK gigs at all to promote their album but remained in Ireland, playing the old Dublin haunts and having a bit of a holiday. Goulding worked on his art career, which had been given a boost when his paintings were featured in a May New York exhibition, 'Young Artists From Around The World.'

An unexpected and footsore visitor turned up at the School House one day that summer. It was Tim's friend Renchi Bicknell, a psychogeographer before the concept was even popularised, who had gone out of the front door of his house in Dalston and decided to walk to Allihies, possibly carrying with him the Howson Phonofiddle as a sort of talisman (though Goulding thinks it might actually have been a mechanical part for a car). He'd been inspired by the July 1969 moon landing and the subsequent moon walk.

Iain Sinclair: 'I think Renchi took off from Hackney without much preparation. He followed the Thames, then stayed in Gloucester, Forest of Dean, Brecon Beacons, boat from Swansea. A real rite of passage – now re-minding me of John Clare, or Van Gogh's walk from Ramsgate to Canterbury, Chatham, Lewisham, Welwyn. Renchi's walk was unmapped and instinctive.'

A post-lysergic Goulding at an exhibition from this era with his painting of tea leaves, Lapsang Souchong.

Renchi followed bridle paths and made sketches and paintings along the way which Iain still has, including a 'starry night' of the first day's walk, somewhere around Richmond, and another coming over the Brecon Beacons. Iain: 'Renchi's own little book, *Relations*, published by my Albion Village Press in 1973, includes 'School House Vision' drawings, the reference being to Tim's house, and the chemically induced (and very significant) vision attained by Renchi at the end of this epic tramp.'

After that, Goulding went off on what he calls 'an acid-laden holiday.' Marymac: 'At the end of summer 1969 Ivan was down in Allihies visiting Tim. Niamh and I got the train down to Killarney, were met by Ivan and Tim and headed back to Allihies through the seasonal mist and rain. I have strong memories of how vibrant the hedgerows were, even in the mist, with a profusion of montbretia and fuchsia. We spent a few days there, all of us staying at our friend Norman Steele's cottage. Linus was there too and then we all piled into Gosport Lil and went on a magical mystery tour of the peninsulas, camping in Goleen and Ahakista before making our way to Cork city just in time for the formal opening of that year's Living Art exhibition. We were, by that stage, a fairly scruffy, bedraggled-looking bunch, and I remember Tim wearing a chunky woollen sweater with half of one sleeve unravelling. He had one of his works on show there and was warmly greeted by the notables of the art world. After the opening, we continued our journey back to Dublin that night, having to stop at very frequent intervals because the engine was overheating. We arrived back after what seemed like a never-ending journey. Occasionally, while rummaging in the attic, I come across parts of a set of Happy Families cards that we drew and played when camping out on the peninsula.'

Goulding: 'Gosport always overheated, even on the motorways in England. I think we were fairly overheated as well by the thrill of the magical adventure – it was an acid-laden holiday. I remember that I had assumed the very stoned alter ego of Captain Boudhain Trips Thomorrowitz. The catchphrase of the time was: "These knives aren't very sharp." The whole tour was not unlike a mix between *Alice in Wonderland* and *The Hobbit*.'

Tim's postcards home to the Orphanage.

## 'We leapt at the chance of a few bob' – Strangelies do a week in cabaret

In September 1969 *The Irish Times* had an exciting announcement to make about a new revue which 'will feature the songs of the Dr Strangely Strange pop group.' The four-piece band, plus Marymac, were appearing in a week's run of a cabaret revue called *One Over The Eight* at The Gate Theatre, Dublin. One of the stars, John Molloy, who was a well-known comic and character actor, had fallen ill at the last moment. Ivan was friendly with Seamus Byrne, who worked in the fledgling Irish film industry, knew the director and had offered to help fill the casting gap. The Strangelies agreed to step in. Ivan: 'The pay wasn't great, but we leapt at the chance of a few bob.'

From *The Irish Times*

Ann O'Dwyer, who appears in the revue "One Over the Eight" which opens at the Gate theatre tonight after a week at Castletown House. The revue, which will include a number of new sketches, will also feature the songs and music of the "Doctor Strangely Strange" pop group. It is directed by John Lynch.

The co-stars of the show were John Keogh, who directed and had written the script, singer Ann O'Dwyer and Anne Bushnell, a popular Irish cabaret artiste. Before the run, the band had to do a crash course in dance with Desmond Domican, who ran a dance school in Parnell Square, practising routines such as 'If We Talked To The Animals.' However, the well-planned choreography did not go quite as planned. Booth: 'Linus and Marymac cartwheeled in from the wings during our opening number. This had never been attempted on the Gate stage before and has never been equalled since. Linus was an athletic young one and graceful as a swan.' However, Ivan remembers that 'Marymac totally fluffed her carefully choreographed steps. She hastily decided a dancing career was not for her.'

Booth: 'Audrey Corr, who was a professional actor and dancer, took pity on us and helped with some of the steps. She was also a friend of Leland Bardwell from the Poetry and Music gig in Sinnott's. Strangelies did a version of Donnybrook Fair and had a bit of a dance routine with Linus and Marymac dressed as Romanies, to the tune of Chérie je t'aime, Chérie je t'adore... But that segment got axed. We had to interact with Anne Bushnell on a couple of numbers; one was Hey, Big Spender!'

Goulding recalls that 'Ivan sat on a sofa in this scene while Ann Bushnell draped herself over him from behind making seductive noises, Booth and I watching from the wings and enjoying the sight of Ivan going rigid... she tickled him under the chin during their turn together and made purring noises. It was sensational.'

Ivan preparing himself (and a spliff) in the wings at The Gate

(LEFT) Anne Bushnell in a cabaret scene from the era

The band also appeared with Bushnell doing a three-part harmony ditty about Onassis and Jackie Kennedy, a version of The Isle Of Capri with refashioned lyrics:

It was to the Isle of Capri that he brought her,
For to start there a new family tree,
He placed a large diamond ring on her finger,
And she said 'Darling boy, you're for me.'

One night the show was enlivened by the presence in the audience of a Dutch beat poet of some repute, Harry Hoogstraaten. Ivan recalls that he 'had brought along a tin whistle and was very keen to encourage audience participation. We weren't comfortable with the idea at the time!'

'It was good fun but hard work,' says Ivan, but Goulding remembers: 'The whole thing was beyond kitsch. I don't think that the Doctors were appreciated by the theatre buffs.' Booth has better memories: 'It was a class show; it was indeed beyond kitsch... an excellent place for Strangelies to inhabit. I remember going over to Grooms Hotel after the show for a few highly illegal late-night pints. The whole of bohemian Dublin hung out there and as it was an hotel, you only had to claim to be a resident, should the Garda show up. I can remember no more. The dressing room was small, smelly and draughty, as was – I suppose – the show, but we had such a laff.'

The 'theatre buffs' were not won over. The 'Doctor Strangely Strange pop group' did 'little' for Seamus Kelly, The Irish Times theatre critic. '[He] opened the show with the In-Sound and a trio of girls, two-thirds of which bounced as if they were on the hockey field. His later spot with only one girl and a way-out number [Donnybrook Fair] about Robert Emmet and a unicorn, did even less.' Kelly left at the interval, pleading 'other engagements.'

## Project Gallery: poetry and music

Just after the revue at The Gate Theatre, there was an October gig at the Project Gallery, the opening of a six-day season of poetry and music. The poets on the first night were Eiléan Ní Chuilleanáin, David John, David J Henry Jones (a sound poet) and Michael Horowitz. Booth: 'It would have been connected with the Sinnott's upstairs poetry and music gigs, which Eiléan was involved in.'

Strangelies opened and closed the show. Their friend Hayden Murphy reviewed the event for The Irish Times, writing that 'music played second role to the muse,' but that 'music was splendidly represented by Dr Strangely Strange, an eccentric composer of erratic genius... A most enjoyable evening,' he continued, mentioning the 'gentle merriment of all,' and said that the band 'opened with an apocryphal tale of "rain, hail, sleet, snow," then improved and created a climate which communicated itself to the poets.' Everyone was stoned, in other words.

Ivan: 'The Project was located on the quays quite near to the Abbey. Someone had a video recorder, which was a rarity in those days – don't ask me who! Apart from Ballad Of The Wasps, we performed Sign On My Mind, Donnybrook Fair, Existence Now and Forty Men After Brown, which was a sort of cowboy song by Booth.'

Booth: 'That song only had one outing, I think. I have no recall of it, or the gig. It is as if the performance caused permanent erasure in our memory and – hopefully – the audience's.'

Goulding had introduced two new songs at the concert: 'Ballad Of The Wasps is set beside the Dargle river. It is an apocryphal tale of my friends Jeffa, Mole and Dave ingesting the sacrament of the Sixties and, whilst in a swoon of Olympian proportions, imagining they had transmogrified into wasps. When they awoke they ascended to the landmark rock, The Lover's Leap, and took off for eternity. Luckily they *had* turned into wasps, so no harm done. We introduced this song as a City and Eastern number whilst adding that it is a cautionary tale, the moral being "don't mess with your brain cells (if possible)." Dave, originally known as Tripper Dave, moved away to work on a chicken farm and became known as Chicken Dave. Existence Now deals with the human condition. We are all in this together, playing diverse roles and burdened with thought, angst and ego. Unaffected by these charades, life moves on from Now to Now. I like the line "caged in a city and sitting by a poisoned stream." This gloomy characterisation caused merriment to Tim and Ivan; the song was considered a bit of a joke by the band, but it was written in all seriousness, partly with Linus in mind.'

For some months, the band had clearly been suffering from a lack of direction, which was coupled with conflicting demands on their time. Ivan, now a father, was making a go of things with Marymac and their daughter Niamh, Goulding was ensconced in his new painting studio, and Booth was back as a jobbing commercial artist. Developing a musical career was made harder by the fact that they had no manager; Joe's deal with them was for recording and publishing only. Booth was the main spokesman, Goulding the chief driver, and roadie duties were shared.

In autumn 1969, three developments occurred which helped to propel them into their natural UK home on the college and club circuit. Agent Julia Creasey joined Blackhill Enterprises, bringing her 'contemporary folk artists' with her. This meant that, as well as doing gigs in their own right, the Strangelies became the go-to support act for a broad variety of Blackhill outfits, from Kevin Ayers to Edgar Broughton, Roy Harper, Bridget St John and the Third Ear Band. Second, Booth, probably the most career-oriented of the three, took the decision to appoint his old friend Steve Pearce as band manager (of whom more later). Finally, fate played a role: in November Island put Strangely Strange But Oddly Normal on the mega-selling 14/6d (77p) sampler album *Nice Enough To Eat*, along with tracks by successful acts Free, Traffic and Blodwyn Pig.

The upshot was a vast increase in gigs, leading by the end of the year to a fairly hectic touring schedule, now towing a pig trailer behind Gosport Lil containing the rudimentary PA equipment.

The band also started to get a picture of their audience, who were not restricted to 'heads' and students. Goulding: 'We assumed they were mostly intellectuals, but actually, a lot were schoolboys! We learned this fact after studying the audience at a gig in Limerick, where the average age was about fifteen.'

Later in October they were back in London, joined by Orphan Annie. They stayed with Renchi in Dalston. Iain Sinclair sensed a lot of positivity and creativity in the air: 'I think they were on a pretty good roll then. As you can see in my film, there was a lot of interaction with Renchi, doing the kitchen, playing the harmonium in the front garden… Tim was painting in this ground floor room which had bare boards; you can see the canvas spread out on the floor and he's kneeling over it doing these detailed paintings.

'I can remember Tim Goulding found himself in this little park in the middle of Albion Square which I'd never really looked at; I could see him doing these very precise paintings of the trees in that square, so suddenly I looked at those trees with another eye. Later on, they were working on a mummers' play. I don't know if it actually went anywhere, but it was part of that general ambience of this interest in medievalism, cooking strange macrobiotic foods, dressing up in funny clothes, going into the park and summoning earth spirits; the whole thing cooks up into a nice package.

'The thing you never had was structure. You had ideas, infinite ideas, a soup of ideas but luckily, you didn't really have to come up with hard-nosed structures. At that time, anything could be attempted, that's how it was. People could do an awful lot themselves without having to be sponsored or patronised or taken up by big organisations.

Goulding at work, a still from the film. He says: 'It was a psychedelic picture of kettles in circles with orange background. It was called "DON'T" and was in stock for several years in the David Hendriks Gallery, Dublin. When I eventually collected it, unsold, from the framer's assistant, she said, "Nobody did."'

Stills from Iain's film. Thanks to Simon Ryan/Hux

'I don't know if they thought they would be the next Incredible String Band, but they were excited about it, obviously. All kinds of different groupings come together and create, but this lot sparked off each other in a good way in that they were complete multi-spectrum artists – they tended to write, they played music... Tim Booth had drawn the cover for a magazine I edited in Dublin called *Icarus*, which I'd got a piece from William Burroughs for. It was a very traditional, slightly starchy university magazine and suddenly it had a comic strip-type cover based on a Batman theme, which Tim drew, and he also drew portraits of William Burroughs and various other people that went inside it – so I knew him as an artist as well as a musician. Tim Goulding had been a long-term friend of Renchi's – they'd been to school together, Winchester of all places – and they'd both been painters, essentially, before Tim came across into music. Ivan had been involved in a lot of film things I'd done, and he'd acted in *Krapp's Last Tape*, which was quite a hilarious experience – and this was a moment when all of that underground activity may have felt it could go public.'

## Dalston days

On their days off, the band explored their new habitat. Dalston, on the western side of the inner London borough of Hackney, probably reminded them of The Waste Land near Mount Street, with many crumbling old houses and a general air of decay. Unlike Dublin, it was a really cosmopolitan place where the white working classes lived alongside extended Caribbean families, Turkish Cypriots, East End Jews and post-1945 European refugees. It was an incredibly cheap area to live, which led in the late Sixties to a growing infiltration by impoverished teachers, social workers, writers and artists. Iain Sinclair provides an excellent 'fictionalised documentary' of the era in his book *Hackney, That Rose-Red Empire*.

The Balls Pond Road, north of Renchi's house, was already familiar to Ivan from his 1967

Goulding, Annie and Ivan heading off to Balls Pond Road.
Gosport Lil co-stars on the right (Photo: Iain Sinclair)

visits to the Exploding Galaxy's communal house there. (Exploder Malcolm Le Maistre remembers Ivan accompanying the Galaxy to an event at the Roundhouse, dressed in a tutu.)

Ivan led the Tims on forays up to a favourite Balls Pond hangout, a Turkish café with a great (Turkish) jukebox. South of Albion Square, near the Regent's Canal, was a scruffy bohemian pub named The Island Queen, also adopted as a hangout by Booth and Ivan because of its impressive jukebox. One afternoon's drinking in there inspired an eponymous baroque instrumental by Ivan, which cropped up in later setlists.

Perseverance works (Photo: Adrian Whittaker)

The Kingsland Road runs down the western edge of Dalston, with a street market called The Waste – which is more or less what it used to sell. Iain Sinclair had bought an ancient bike there. One day Goulding took a stroll down past The Waste in a new pair of shoes. Perhaps because Ivan and he tended to go barefoot most of the time, though this could get you banned from some establishments, it was a painful experience. This gave rise to a new song which combined the pinching shoes with a memorable acid trip from which, allegedly, he 'never came down again.' Goulding: 'Round there is an old factory named Perseverance Works, which we quickly adopted as a band motto.'

The 'R & JJ West Indian Restaurant' in Sandringham Road was another Dalston haunt. Ivan: 'That may well be the place we first tried West Indian drinking chocolate, and then improvised a blues in its honour.'

## Subterranean homesick blues

The band hung out and made music in Renchi's basement, sleeping upstairs in a half-completed room, plaster peeling from the outside wall. Booth: 'Funds were low and not improved by one of us adding a small bag of quick-drying cement into a soup he was preparing on the stove, mistaking it for flour. The soup thickened nicely but we did not deign to eat it. These were the days when we paid ourselves a pound a day and then had to make the decision: food or dope? Of course, food won out... occasionally.' As well as West Indian Drinking Chocolate Blues, another basement composition was The Dramamine Blues, inspired by the tablets Goulding used to take to ease his seasickness on the frequent ferry crossings over from Ireland. Ivan recalls that the well-worn line 'Woke up this morning' was replaced by 'Dozed off this morning.' Goulding: 'The song got slower and slower, to replicate the effects of the travel sickness drug coming on.'

Ivan's Kilmanoyadd Stomp was also finalised at Renchi's house, where in Iain Sinclair's film he is seen performing it at the harmonium. Ivan: 'Mary and I and little Niamh went to visit our great friends Stone Monkey at their cottage in Wales where they had moved after Penwern. They had a French organ there on which I wrote the song; I think a French organ draws the air through the reeds whereas a harmonium pushes it. There was quite a lot of interest in Dianetics at the time, hence my riposte at the end.' Ivan, perhaps encouraged by the ISB, had undergone the Scientology 'personality test' at their Tottenham Court Road office, conveniently situated near Witchseason, but had hurriedly moved on. As he implies in the final line, the song is a bit of a fun, throwaway composition: 'There's no meaning to this song and if you found one you'd be wrong.'

Linus in Renchi's basement (still from Iain Sinclair's film).

Kilmanoyadd – Ivan and Mary on a visit, with Niamh in the foreground and Mal's daughter Sarah Schofield (with hat).

# CHAPTER 3

# Playing the college circuit

Julia Creasey had set up a string of university gigs, starting in mid-October. It was a challenge to play the support slots the band were usually allocated, as the student audiences, there to see the headliners, could often get impatient or dismissive. To start with, the band missed the intimacy of the old Dublin haunts, though as time went by they evolved ways of winning sceptical audiences over. One memorable concert the following year involved handing out spliffs to those in the front row, the theory being that the good vibes thus engendered would slowly seep backwards to the rest.

After an unmemorable start in Sheffield, an Essex University gig supporting Michael Chapman epitomised how much the band had still to learn. Booth: 'I think this may have been our worst ever show, performance-wise. Our recent move on to the university circuit now meant we often shared the bill with lots of different types of acts. At the Essex gig, we played in a lecture theatre and the college supplied the PA, which we had no idea how to use, having been gigging with an old Vortexion 30-watt amp and two mics. The act before us – Brett Marvin And The Thunderbolts, with a very loud rhythm stick – were extremely proficient. When we went on, tuning problems, amplification difficulties and general panic caused us to spiral downward, each number being worse than the preceding. We did not have the stagecraft to know what to do and it was not pleasant, either for the audience or for us. 'Nuff said.'

After dates at Cardiff Institute of Science and Technology and Birmingham University, the band were loading in at Mother's Club, Birmingham when they got a call from Witchseason. Booth: 'My younger brother Peter had died, laid low by Hodgkin's disease. I thought the show should go on. I had discussed it with Peter when I went to say goodbye to him in Saint Luke's cancer hospital before the commencement of the tour – what if you die before I get back? He had laughed and said he probably would not be able to sustain his life much longer, but on no account was I to cancel a gig on his account. So, I was prepared to go on stage, but Tim and Ivan thought otherwise and they drove me back through the night to catch an early morning flight back to Dublin. Peter died on his eighteenth birthday.'

The tour picked up again in Redhill with a psychedelic gig supporting prog outfit Egg in, of all places, Saint John's Church. It featured a light show by 'Moonglum,' an outfit who had worked at David Bowie's Arts Lab in the Three Tuns, Beckenham. Goulding: 'Mont Campbell, Egg's singer and bass player, used the pulpit. I was shocked by the profanity of such a move, and was raging that we had not thought of it first.'

After another appearance at Les Cousins, where Renchi projected a trippy backdrop of his films and slides, there were two days of recording at Sound Techniques for *Heavy Petting*, their second album, with Jay Myrdal again guesting on glockenspiel. As well as Existence Now, for which Goulding had actually written Linus a small vocal cameo, her first and only, the band had another crack at Ivan's Mirror Mirror. It was a remarkable performance. Even though it was one of Ivan's best songs, featured on their original demo for Joe Boyd and ESP-Disk, it had slipped through the net so far. Ivan, despite suffering from a cold, taps into the vein of ennui he revisited so brilliantly on the later recording of Sign On My Mind. Even the deployment of the dreaded Japanese ping pong bats and a late entry on the second line just add to the song's underlying feeling of mortal vulnerability and fragility. Ivan can do fey and he can do cosmic: it's not always a successful recipe, but here these two ingredients combine into a real tour de force. It got left off the eventual album, of course, a rare case of Joe Boyd missing a trick. Why? The keyboard solo speeded up (again), nothing that a quick bit of editing couldn't have resolved.

Some more new songs were recorded, including Booth's Ashling and Going To Poulaphouca, as well as Ivan's Jove Was At Home, a song that really is little over-heavy on the feyness quotient. Poulaphouca is something of a throwaway number, a live staple at this point, with an a cappella section at the end which could continue for some time. Poulaphouca means 'pond of the pooka' and it's a place near Kildare, where Booth grew up. He ran a music club there in the Seventies, putting on one of the first gigs by the Boomtown Rats. Booth: 'It came from a Hofmann experience Tim, Ivan, Linus and I underwent on Baltinglass mountain, Co Wicklow, one autumn day in 1969. The low point for Goulding was looking over at me on the mountain top beside him and finding me to be six inches tall. This necessitated the emergency use of a heavy tranquiliser. In the lyrics, Sammy's Bar is the title of an old Cyril Tawney song.'

'Ashling also has a hallucinatory genesis. It is the Irish word for dream. Irish verse has a genre of ashling poems [aisling in Gaelic] where the poet trucks afield all alone and runs into a beautiful young one who is pale and atremble, and after endless alliterated interrogation it turns out the reason for her pallid shivering is because she has been ravaged and savagely used by a dark and sinister stranger, much as Celtic Catholic Ireland had been subdued by wicked England. Fine and subtle symbolism. After a deal of admiring the shape of her neck, breasts and thighs the poet vows to avenge her, and if the reader was still on the page, that was most likely what – eventually – took place. I thought I would turn the form on its head. This was recorded when Linus was still in the band; that's her on the finger cymbals and gull whistle. I wrote the song – like the others from this era – in the Sandymount Orphanage and I think I had been reading Joyce, hence the woman on the strand at the end. It was also in the time I met Johanna, so there is something of her in the song as well.' The Howson Phonofiddle, having recovered from its epic trek in Renchi's rucksack from Dalston to Allihies, makes another creaky, trippy appearance and adds to the dream-like vibe.

Ivan: 'Jove Was At Home is a hymn to the lovely Mary McSweeney, now Mary Pawle. Johanna was then visiting London and present at the recording, so some wags sang "Johanna is in Chelsea" instead of "Hosanna in excelsis," which fitted nicely. The choir on this track was led by that wonderful singer Heather Wood from The Young Tradition, who we knew through Jay Myrdal. Everyone played perfectly: Jay on glockenspiel, Linus on autoharp, Goulding on bass recorder, Booth on acoustic guitar.'

The band followed up the second recording session by playing a Les Cousins all-nighter the same evening, earning 15 quid.

After that it was another Dramamine-fuelled trip back on the boat to Dublin for a few gigs and an appearance on RTÉ's *Late Late Show*. The band made fairly regular appearances on this long-running programme – one of these, says Goulding, 'featured a stuffed fox beside the harmonium to signify our Strangeness.'

Booth: 'Later on, we did an RTÉ show with Status Quo. Goulding was fascinated with their keyboard player, who had his rack set at an angle so as he could strike an impossibly acute angle himself, leaning back with his shoulders almost on the floor, a sort of limboistic pose.'

December saw them back on the road in the UK for a few university gigs, one supporting Roy Harper in Salford, and an Implosion appearance at the Roundhouse, possibly with Skid Row. Goulding: 'A prospective groupie approached me after the show and gave me a present of a crucifix that I thought said PEACE but, on closer inspection, said PETE.'

After 50 years, any gig memories are mostly confined to dramatic highlights, so here is a collage of the band's imaginings of a 'typical' 1969 college gig. There's a full list of dates and venues in the Appendix.

Booth: 'Let's imagine we leave Renchi's Dalston gaff mid-morning because we're going to Exeter to play the University. We're in Gosport Lil, Gouldo driving as he's the only one insured, Ivan in the front seat, Linus beside me in the back, guitar cases between us and piled on the back window-ledge. It's a long journey and we are already knackered when we arrive. We find the place and after lots of enquiring and messing around, finally find the loading entrance to the hall where we are to perform. Gosport is diminished by Mott The Hoople's enormous

Transit van, but we press on regardless, lugging the hated harmonium up endless stairs and down dim corridors to the stage. Great heavy beast of a thing. If we were to count all the times we lugged the fucker into and out of gigs, it would amount to several miles' worth of carrying.

'There is a PA, so we don't have to set up our primitive sound system and – merciful hour – a sound man who is helpful. No time for a proper sound check, but we add our mics into the board and there are enough to go around, vocal and guitar mics for Ivan and myself, a harmonium and vocal set-up for Goulding and a mic for Linus, who seems a bit scared of it. Or maybe it's the size of the hall. We hover in the wings as the local folk duo do their thing and they're good... ish. Dexterous finger-picking and a serious Brit intent. A bit boring. We'll soon fix that. The audience applaud politely and we're on.

'It goes OK. Ivan has the usual tuning incident and succeeds in completely detuning his guitar. While he struggles manfully, Goulding and I tell stories of our trip down in Gosport Lil which go down really well. The audience is not used to being intimate with the performers. Back in tune, Ivan launches into Strangely Strange But Oddly Normal and to our astonishment the audience recognise the opening riff and become ecstatic. Sort of. We blunder on, trying out new songs such as Wasps and Ashling, which are well received. We tell the audience we need a place to stay. We finish with Donnybrook and get an encore. In the wings a puzzled Mott The Hoople shake their heads. Respect. After the gig we load out and even get help from some local hippies, who also offer us their floor. So, it's back into Gosport and a short drive following our new-found friends to their place where we are offered coffee, dope and floors and mattresses and cushions on which to lay out our sleeping bags and subsequently, late in the early morning, ourselves. Stir gently and repeat, more or less.'

Ivan: 'At the soundcheck, Goulding's mic-testing catchphrase was always "Two sweet teas." Then we'd go off, get a drink and make up a set list – usually two 40-minute sets. As Booth says, we would start with SSBON, and often end the first set with Goulding's Le Le Rockin' Sound. We would just hope the instruments stayed in tune and that fellow musicians remembered the most recently decided upon arrangement... Both Tims were good at chat between songs, and I would rely on them to tell an anecdote or two, preferably not one related the previous night! Audiences were generally well disposed.'

Goulding differs: 'There was no "typical" gig, as such, each being perfectly unique; there was our special charm. Nobody knew what was coming next, least of all ourselves!'

Goulding's Le Le Rockin' Sound was another live favourite. Not recorded by the band until 2007, it has a catchy chorus that runs: 'It's just that same old rockin' sound, running through my brain... Peter

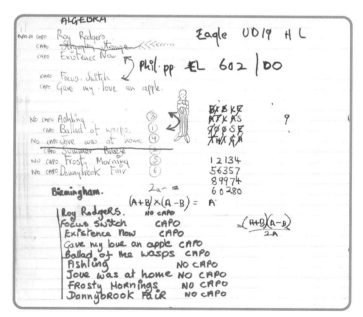

This setlist from late 1969 comes from Goulding's old maths exercise book, including a few previews of *Heavy Petting* songs. 'Focus Switch' was the working title of Mirror Mirror because, Tim Booth tells us, the song originally had an addition to Ivan's spoken bit at the end which went – dramatically – 'The Focus Switch - DON'T PULL IT!'

Pan wants Wendy to do that thing, to do that thing again.' It makes passing reference to an early Dublin graffiti artist named Lee, who would crop up again later in another Goulding song.

The holiday period saw the band back in Dublin for a few club gigs. Most Irish bands struggling to make it in the UK (like Granny's Intentions) would regularly head back home to try to get some decent gig income on the ballroom circuit. Strangelies, on the other hand, rarely played in Ireland outside their regular Dublin club venues, making their money on the UK college gigs. This seems a good point to introduce the man nicknamed 'Manager Pearce.'

## Steve Pearce

Towards the end of 1969, they acquired a dynamic manager in Stephen Pearce, the son of a potter from Co Cork. Booth had met him at school when they were both about thirteen. Booth: 'He had been sent to the school by his progressive parents, and was placed briefly in my class. He was, and is, smart, adventurous and wilful – a natural manager – and as Strangelies' career progressed he would turn up at gigs. He found us intriguing and enjoyable, so when it became clear that we needed management, he seemed a natural choice for all concerned. We never really discussed his fees or signed contracts, he just slipped into the role and was very good at it. Up to this time we had been travelling to gigs in Gosport Lil, the PA – such as it was – in a small trailer, the harmonium wrapped in plastic sheeting and lashed to the roof-rack. Mott the Hoople nearly had a hernia laughing at us when we pulled in beside them at the Exeter gig.

No photos of Steve from this period could be located, but here's one from 1979, with him towering over his first wife.

'Pearce was a whirlwind of ideas. He thought nothing of ringing up total strangers and setting up meetings. After Blackhill became our booking agents, gigs improved exponentially. He also met with Charlie Watkins of WEM and did a deal whereby we could buy gear direct from the factory, cutting out the middle man. So – suddenly – we had a state-of-the-art PA. He developed our relationship with Julia Creasey at Blackhill Enterprises and persuaded her over to our corner; she worked very well for us. So, Steve eventually got us a decent Transit van and PA, guitar amps, a dedicated booker and a roadie and generally made us look professional in a very competitive market. We needed to cut the band back to basics to pay for all this, which sadly led to Linus leaving.'

Ivan: 'I first met Steve when he came back to Ireland after a trip to New Zealand and Japan with his brother, Simon. Simon was to work in glass, and Steve was to follow in his father's footsteps as a master potter at Shanagarry Pottery, near Cork. They were both big young men, and I saw photos of him with his pottery teacher in Japan, totally dwarfing him. He was mighty at dealing with logistics and booking agents. He took up a lot of space when visiting the Witchseason office in Charlotte Street, almost like a friendly bull in a ceramic warehouse.'

Goulding: 'He was a very much larger-than-life character who would think nothing of whacking the attractive young secretaries off their stools in Julia's office with exuberant friendliness. He also mercilessly took the piss out of my vegetarianism and practice of yoga.'

The new year started without Linus. As Booth says, the band were still struggling to make a living at this point, and to save on costs, she had been asked to leave. Ivan: 'We sacked her in trying to streamline our operation, which was a pity, but economic factors prevailed at the time.' Goulding was closest to her, and was deputed to tell her the news. She was, predictably, very upset. Linus' role in the band had always been unclear – she'd only really performed with them on a few Dublin gigs, some of the later *Kip* recordings and at some of the late 1969 gigs. The ISB had led the way in incorporating women into psych-folk outfits, but whereas Rose and Likky had clearly defined, if secondary, roles, Linus remained peripheral. This may have been related to prevailing cultural attitudes to gender, but Linus herself appears to have been ambivalent about being part of the Strangelies.

Tim Booth: 'On stage she was a touch tentative. She knew her limitations. I don't think Joe thought much of her ability and he mixed her right back in the recordings. I really liked her, but she and I drifted apart as she drifted into the band. I really don't recall her on stage or in the car at all during our English gigs at that time.'

In October, the ISB and Stone Monkey had all moved to Glen Row, on the Glen Estate near Innerleithen, to live communally but separately in a row of cottages. One of these had originally been reserved for Ivan and for Marymac, who had decided to move from Dublin with Niamh to live there, with Ivan visiting in between gigs. Linus decided to join them for a while, and the three of them went over to Scotland at the end of January.

Marymac: 'Linus, Niamh and I took the train to Belfast and boarded the ferry from Larne to Stranraer. The band had decamped to London. We went to stay at The Row, where John and Ishy from Stone Monkey were warm and generous hosts. The ISB and Stone Monkey were in full rehearsal mode for their pantomime, U. Fabulously fantastic costumes were being created in one of the cottages by Jane Mock, and I was able to put some of my sewing skills to use by helping out on finishing them off. In April, when Jane had finished work and returned to the States, we moved into her cottage.

'The atmosphere at the Row was very friendly and people came and went from cottage to cottage. There were occasional get-togethers for some celebration or other and I remember a very happy Christmas day feast that we all shared in the little hall down in the farmyard. The ISB were often away but the rest of us lived a fairly regular life. Linus returned to Dublin after a month or two and I stayed for about 16 months. She and I hitched down to London one weekend to visit Strangelies who were staying at Joe Boyd's place. We got a lift in a lorry from Carlisle and had an unforgettable journey over Shap Fell in fierce snow and ice. I remember seeing some trucks that had gone off the road and another that had jack-knifed. I think that we got the train back!

'I attended some of the gigs but Niamh being a baby, and also the fact that I worked some of the time, kept me busy. I made a few trips down to visit Ivan in London, and later at the farmhouse they moved to in Essex, and he managed to get up to the Row at various intervals. For us, it all seemed like a normal lifestyle in the Dublin of the Sixties that we had inhabited.'

Back in London, a couple of days recording were slotted in at the turn of the month, the final Sound Techniques dates for the new album. In fact, only two of the songs from the sessions made it onto *Heavy Petting*. One was Ballad Of The Wasps. Goulding was aiming for a Country and Western feel and Dave Mattacks played drums, the first time the band had used a kit. Mattacks, at that point virtually the Witchseason house drummer, was the obvious choice. Roger Mayer, who engineered the session, says Mattacks tightened up their 'folk-oriented timing.' Sweeney's Man Johnny Moynihan, then visiting the band in London, added some filigree bouzouki. Goulding's acid hymn I Will Lift Up Mine Eyes was the other *Heavy Petting* song. Goulding: 'Lift Up Mine Eyes is the purest of acid visions, a pantheistic hymn even if dressed up in Church of Ireland vestments. After all, Pantheism was first named by the Irishman John Toland. The song exhorts us to see that time 'delivers a handstand' and the world that appears to be coming at us is actually a projection of the mind. The writer, perched "deep in a Latvian thicket," avows to leave a slough behind: shades of *The Pilgrim's Progress*. This refers to the Latvian hippy who was visiting The Orphanage and had managed to import LSD into Ireland in his socks. The last section is a quote from Leisure by W.H. Davies. Those under the influence of LSD had little option but to stop and stare.'

The other two songs recorded, Sweet Red Rape and Good Evening Mr Woods, were eventually dropped from the next album in favour of the newer material recorded later in Dublin. Again, it's hard to fathom Joe Boyd's choices, as they are both excellent. He's since gone on record to admit that compiling the LP was done during a 'frantic race to the wire' to get everything finished before he left London to work in LA.

Booth: 'On Sweet Red Rape, Goulding played percussion on my two Japanese table-tennis bats, which then seemed a good idea... Smoking materials were few and far between in Ireland at that time. One day Ivan came proudly back with a packet of birdseed, which he thought we could grind up and smoke, thereby saving lots of money. It was called "Sweet Red Rape" and it was awful – so the song took off from there. In the lyrics, I think a Chandelabra is a surreal mixture of a chandelier and candelabra, possibly solar powered. Ritalin was the brand name of a rather strong 1960s cough mixture which, if ingested in bulk, had interesting secondary side effects...' The band tried a different arrangement of the song, with Neil Hopwood on kit, during the final Witchseason sessions in late 1970, but sadly got no further than a backing track.

Ivan's Good Evening Mr Woods was originally titled 'Speak Of Tsao Tsao,' a Chinese saying which means something like 'speak of the devil' or 'serendipity.' Ivan thinks the name switch came after Sound Techniques boss John Wood suddenly appeared in the studio just as the band were talking about him. Ivan: 'The lyric "There you go" (Tat Tvam Asi, that art thou) was a phrase often used in those days. "Round and round we go" – reincarnation, anyone?' It's another great song and performance, tapping into the same vein of ennui as Mirror Mirror; it's second only to that in the Ivan Does Cosmic hall of fame. Booth provides some strong harmony vocals and Goulding adds some inventive contrapuntal bass lines on the piano. There might be a slight ISB influence here; they had used the same 'piano bass' idea on Ducks On A Pond (*Wee Tam & The Big Huge*).

An Exeter University gig from 6th February stands out in band memory, one of the few Ivan noted in his diary as '10/10.' Booth: 'Taste were headlining the first time we played Exeter; we had been booked to play twice in the Junior Common Room, before and after the main event in the University's concert hall where Taste were to perform. The JCR was a bit like a large suburban sitting room: couches, sofas, old newspapers and tasselled lamps. We set up in a corner, using our primitive PA. We did the first set to an empty room, using it as a sort of sound check, then went to see Taste on the big stage. They were fantastic, Gallagher stomping and careering around the stage, making sure no jam went unkicked, the rhythm section roaring behind him like cosmic surf, a superb feat of musical prowess and showmanship. Follow that.

'Back in the JCR, there was a definite buzz and we became part of it, dimly lit by the table lamps, the audience lounging around on the beaten-up sofas. Halfway through our set, I became aware of a check-shirted figure in the front sofa, smiling and nodding as we chugged on, an occasional frown, followed by a look of relief, long fingers brushing back his hair. When we finished, he came up and introduced himself, saying how he had really enjoyed our set and understood what we were attempting, but we needed to get some proper gear, PA and guitar pickups and... he knew a man who might help, fellow called Michael Crowley who ran a great music shop in Cork. Next time we were passing, drop in, say hello, tell them Rory sent you. Rory Gallagher was a very kind man – he only saw our good side.'

The following day the band played support to John Martyn at a Les Cousins gig, which was taped. The recording offers the only real chance we have now to listen in to a Strangelies club set

at one of their regular venues. Located in a basement in Greek Street, Soho, which had earlier served as a 1950s skiffle club, Les Cousins was owned by the Matheou family, whose son Andy Matheou ran the folk club. It was known for its all-night sessions and was favoured by the sort of left-field folkies who were less welcome in more purist places. Goulding: 'I remember hearing Nick Drake there and meeting him afterwards at a pub up the road. I told him how much I loved his music and the poor fellow just looked at his boots. He seemed to be highly sensitive and shy.'

This gig was actually bootlegged as an album called *Sitting Down Here In Greek Street*. It was also known as 'The Duffle Bag Tapes' as that's where the tape recorder was concealed by someone going by the name of Lagga. As one might imagine, the sound quality is fairly poor.

The set is a preview of much of what would be on the *Heavy Petting* album. It starts off with the then un-released Ashling – although Booth does have to stop in between verses to remind Goulding to get his recorder out, it's otherwise a good performance and the band is on pretty strong form throughout. Goulding follows with Ballad Of The Wasps, boasting a Country and Western feel, and then Ivan turns in a creditable version of Jove Was At Home – if anything, slightly less fey than the studio version. After this comes to an abrupt end, Booth sings Sweet Red Rape, on which Goulding appears to be playing percussion on the infamous table tennis bats. He might just be hitting a chair. Next is an embryonic version of Goulding's new song, The Piece Of Cod – though there are some strong harmonies, the arrangement feels unworked out, with a weird bluesy section in the middle. The song had not been firmed up in time for the final *Heavy Petting* sessions at Sound Techniques a week earlier, and didn't fit in with the Dublin electric folk-rock sessions held a couple of months later, so it fell between two stools. It finally turned up 30 years later on a Goulding solo CD from 2000 – fittingly, Booth and Ivan sang harmonies on it.

Riding On The West Cork Hack is next – it's from *Kip* and so the first song most of the audience would recognise, though this doesn't seem to have fazed them, going by their very positive response so far. The band have worked out a tacky ending with a quote from 'The Shadow Of Your Smile,' which they deployed on the later BBC *In Concert* session. Ivan's instrumental When Adam Delved is next, followed by Booth's Tennessee Waltz/Gave My Love An Apple. This is also still being worked out, and some of the transitions are bit wobbly. In the final line, 'I'm sitting down here in Sandymount' has become 'sitting down here in Greek Street.' The closing Strangely Strange But Oddly Normal feels as if it's a gesture towards playing 'the hit' which has perhaps out-stayed its welcome; cues are missed and Ivan's vocalising starts to run riot in a faintly disturbing manner. Good-night My Friends rounds off the set very well, and the duffle bag and Lagga shuffle off, contentedly we would guess, into the Soho night.

It's probably this gig that Booth remembers: 'A Cousins gig, parking around the corner by a strip club where the touts lauded their wares with the cry of "Positively no wax." Go figure. Down the stairs with Horace the Horribly Heavy Harmonium, and performing alternate sets with John Martyn, so a lot of funny cigarettes in circulation. During the second set, a tall blond-haired boyo sat down just in front of the stage, nodding and smiling as we struggled with our chords. He lit up, and passed a huge number up to the stage. We partook, the music changed subtly, and the Thor-like figure elevated his right hand, palm up as if hefting the weight of our musical intent, and a soft Norn Iron voice issued forth: "Nice one, babies..." Nice one Henry McCullough, a frequent visitor to both Orphanages, who went on to greater things with The Grease Band, Spooky Tooth and, later, Wings. Gone like Rory Gallagher and Gary Moore, way too soon.'

The new material was still bedding in. The Piece of Cod was one of the last few songs Goulding wrote and performed with the band, composed in the old School House in the autumn of 1969. Goulding: 'It developed in performance over a year or so, and was written as a traditional tune morphing into a ballad-type song and then punctuated by a sea shanty. From the window of the house you could almost see as far as America, the next land mass, 3,000 miles away. In the autumn you could see the lights of the herring trawlers at night in the bay. Those times had seen some tragic losses at sea of trawlermen going about their trade. The song is akin to a hymn for those that perished and the hills and sea where they lived. It is a song of praise and awe at the whole manifestation, the sacredness of which was clearly highlighted by lysergic acid. Living in Allihies for the last 50 years, I have witnessed many fishermen lose their lives in pursuit of their work, hence the lines:

**"Salty the brow of the mariner, bright were his eyes and bold his grin**
**Sour the reek of the seaweed, sweet was the smile that once ensnared him"**

We played this in Newcastle, at my final gig with the band, and I remember Steeleye Span shared the bill and commented favourably on it. I could imagine them doing a cover.'

A Kent University gig in a lecture theatre a few days later outstripped Ivan's ratings system with '10 ½ out of 10.' Booth: 'A lot of pot. So stoned were we, that Ivan lectured the capacity audience on the evils of ganja, pointing out that the very presence of so much weed in the air had caused his guitar to detune across all its strings by a semi-tone.'

Goulding: 'Ivan amused us and the audience immensely with his lecture, which was extensive and took up most of the second half of the gig. It was astrological in nature and correlated Mars in Uranus with the grant system and the fact that middle C in Canterbury was an octave lower than in London. He also told a porter at the dinner table that the tablet he was putting in his water was "only vitamin C." The poor man was only trying to serve him his dinner. Ivan was trying to come down.'

David Ambrose, one of the many Orphanage visitors, had stayed in touch with the Strangelies. He booked them to play at 'A Palimpseste of Erly Engle-Land,' an event he organised as part of Guildford Arts Lab's contribution to the local festival. David: 'It was an attempt to look at the Middle Ages from a twentieth-century perspective, so alongside the Strangelies we had jugglers, fire-eaters, readings from Chaucer, Morris dancers, a psychedelic light show and a hog roast. The hog roast caught fire and had to be sprayed with a fire extinguisher and then wiped down for consumption. There may have been a dancing bear, too.'

Filming in Battersea Park (still from Iain Sinclair's film).

When Adam Delved had been written specially for the Guildford event, for which the band worked up a mummers' play. In February Renchi and Iain shot some footage of them setting off from Dalston in Gosport Lil and rehearsing for the gig out in Battersea Park. Catman Andy Anderson is centre-stage in a dog's head mask, Ivan is doing a very odd robotic dance in a type of tabard, Goulding plays whistle and Booth is on fiddle. Lorraine Sufrin, also from the Orphanage days, makes a cameo appearance. The play may have fitted in very well at Guildford, somewhere between the light show and the Chaucer readings. The Strangelies did two sets, mumming erratically and then playing a short selection of their more baroque material, like Dark-Haired Lady, alongside When Adam Delved.

Until the final two months of the band's existence, they played no organised tours, and the string of university gigs was becoming enervating. They were the first of the new wave of Irish bands to play the college circuit, and logistics didn't enter into their gig list. The end of February, for example, saw them doing a performance at Hounslow Arts Lab with Annie Briggs and Humphrey Weightman, then driving to Preston, sleeping on fans' floors and then back to London, filming in Battersea, then driving to Southsea and back to London again the following day for another Cousins gig, then heading off to the Guildford Festival. Self-sufficient and ready to step in for Blackhill as a last-minute support act virtually anywhere in the UK, they foreshadowed the Robert Fripp concept of a 'small, independent, mobile and intelligent unit.' All this was draining, especially for Goulding.

# Tessie

On the road, the band would enliven the lengthy drives with their own variant of Knock Down Ginger, a game normally played by children which involves knocking on the front door of a victim, then running away before the door can be answered.

Booth: 'We used the version played by the Goulding brothers in Co Wicklow in the early 1960s. The rules were basic. A group of young people – extreme athleticism may be required – select the abode of a person or persons unknown to them. One of the group – the Tessie – must enter the vicinity of the abode and on encountering a resident must address them, using only the precise words delineated here-under. No other words or exclamations, including grunts or shouts of pain, are allowed expression by the Tessie during the round. The words are: "I'm sorry I'm here, I'll leave immediately. But – I may be back." The Tessie must now respond non-verbally to the resident's actions, watched by the other participants of the game. Points may be scored for valour at this juncture. A getaway car is an optional extra.

'At that time, we all travelled in Gosport Lil, with the old pig trailer and the harmonium on the roof-rack. We were returning to London from a gig and were somewhere east of Bournemouth when Goulding – who was driving – decided to "do a Tessie." Laughing sagely, he swung the car off the road and through an imposing set of entrance gates, ignoring the OHMS warning notices and the Strictly No Entrance signs. We proceeded up a narrow but well-maintained driveway, surrounded by deep vegetation, laurel bushes and hydrangeas under thickly planted trees. Rounding a corner, we were confronted by a red and white striped pole positioned horizontally from what appeared to be some sort of guardhouse. As we had considerable forward motion, he swung Gosport and trailer into the bushes and the weight of the combined package gave us traction and impetus. We ploughed on and emerged unscathed before a large Edwardian mansion on to a tarmac parade ground, surrounded by white-painted stones with a Union Jack on a tall flagpole. Here an armed squad of what appeared to be elite marines (but may well have been military cadets) were being drilled by a central casting sergeant. Ivan had been elected Tessie, but we allowed him to merely open the side window as we pulled up alongside the goggle-eyed ranks and the – now apoplectic – sergeant. He delivered the fateful line, and in the astonished silence, Goulding spotted a sign for the Exit and drove off at speed. We made it out to the main road and did not appear to have been followed.

'Our relief at not being either arrested or shot was intense. This was after all the late Sixties and we had an Irish registration, a suspicious trailer and a sinister plastic-wrapped object on the roof-rack, not to mention a considerable stash. Several miles down the road and by now almost frothing at the mouth with laughter, Goulding decided to try another round of Tessie.

'He pulled the car right and we entered a disturbingly narrow lane. Far too narrow to turn around. We had to keep going. The lane got narrower and the featureless brick walls on either side became higher, until we could go no further. Wedged like a cork in a bottle. We could not reverse as there was not sufficient width to allow the turning of the front wheels. We could not exit the vehicle, as the doors could not be opened in the confines of the walls. After careful thought and the consumption of a wacky baccy cigarillo, I managed to climb out of the rear boot door, uncouple the trailer and push it back down the lane. Ivan exited and we managed to pull the car a few yards backwards so that now it could be reversed. Back on the main road, we hitched up again and proceeded to London relatively uneventfully. Proud and unchastened. Needless to say, the game has not caught on.'

Goulding: 'Booth didn't mention Advanced Tessie, however. This comprises all the thrills of burglary without theft. It involves entering but not breaking and the aim of the game is to be able to draw a ground plan of the house. Not advisable in these times.'

When Steve Pearce got them a Transit van, 'dark green with three aircraft seats and dodgy remoulds on the front wheels,' Gosport Lil was largely retired, but not before one final adventure en route to a Leicester gig. Booth: 'As Linus was no longer in the band, there was room for Manager Pearce in the car. Just as well. We got snowed in on the M1 for many hours, stuck in a traffic jam looking at the legend "Drain Daily" on the brake pressure cylinder of a vast artic stuck in the drift alongside us. Pearce reconnoitred and said we could lift Lil – a relatively light car – over a gap designed for maintenance vehicles in the barrier between the motorway lanes. We did this with considerable effort, unhitching the trailer and unloading the harmonium, and proceeded down

The pig trailer, well into retirement in Co Kerry.

the empty London-bound lane until we could turn off. We found a phone box and rang to explain that we would not make the gig that evening. We drove back lanes and snowbound local roads and made it just before midnight. They put us up and we played at lunchtime the next day. Walking to our lodgings through the snow that night we passed an open window to a room full of students and heard the dulcet strains of Strangely Strange But Oddly Normal being beautifully played by a small group. On looking into the lamplit window, we realised it was being played by a single guitarist... both parts.'

After a gig at a regular 'prog night' organised by Bristol promoters Plastic Dog at Acker Bilk's club, The Granary, there was an Implosion concert at the Roundhouse with the Chris Spedding Band, Formerly Fat Harry and Sour Milk Sea. '10/10,' noted Ivan's diary. Touring was taking its toll on him too, and on the unpropitious date of Friday 13th he recorded glumly: 'Back on cigarettes.'

Finally, there was a break in dates; Ivan hitched up to Glen Row to see Mary and Niamh and the Tims went back to Dublin. All three reconvened at the Sandymount Orphanage at the end of March 1970 to hook up with Gary Moore for what became a new phase in their career.

# CHAPTER 4

# The Dublin sessions

The band arrived back in Dublin with some broad-ranging new material to record. Whereas Ivan was increasingly wearing his heart on his sleeve, Booth and Goulding wrote about love and relationships in a fairly oblique way, if at all. Booth's Gave My Love An Apple is a surreal look, through a lysergic prism, at his relationships with Linus and with Johanna. Booth: 'Just as, at that time, laden BOAC and TWA long-distance flights had jet propulsion bottles – known as JATO for Jet Assisted Take Off – strapped under their wings to assist jump-off, so too did your bog-standard Irish hippy songsmith require that vital extra lift. Sometimes it came from a bottle, but more usually a small white paper laminate of the windowpane variety.'

Flashback to Booth aged 17, ready to start roving.

Summer Breeze is more obviously personal, tapping into what Booth calls 'the Wild Rover tradition.' Booth: 'My younger brother Peter had recently died from Hodgkin's disease and I was feeling a touch fragile and defiant, so it is a bit autobiographical. Johnny Moynihan was originally down to play bouzouki or whistle on this, and we certainly rehearsed with him in Joe Boyd's flat, but Goulding got the gig.'

Ivan's Goodnight My Friends was also fairly recent: 'We used to have some lovely sessions in The Mangrove restaurant on All Saints Road, London, where there was a harmonium downstairs, and we would sing a "Negro Spiritual" which had about four chords. The lyrics were Amens with lots of harmony.' The Mangrove was a well-known meeting place for the Notting Hill black community, as well as for artists, musicians and white radicals.

Goulding in his local Marian grotto, 2008 (Photo: Adrian Whittaker)

History does not record what they all made of the possibly ill-advised fake spirituals emanating from the basement.

Goulding's new song, an appeal for assistance from above, had been started the previous year: 'Mary Malone Of Moscow originates from my stroll down Kingsland Road, Dalston in a new pair of pinching shoes. The rhythmical pain must have led to thoughts of Lee, the phantom sign writer in Dublin in the late Sixties. His chalk handwriting was unmistakable and his messages were pithy: "Greeks May Tax The North Pole...

Who Burns Wonderful Man To Death? … Forty Morris Nurses Murdered Each Week Fighting In The USSR… Prince Charles Are Nuts In The Head… I Fight Irish Airplanes" and so on. Near my home in Allihies is a Marian grotto with the message "O Mary Help Me" spelt out on the breeze-blocks. At the end of recording the song Tim Booth experienced some confusion about his suitcase, armchair and guitar. For the record, he never came down again.'

The band gradually worked up the Lee angle for the benefit of gullible journalists, claiming to a Dutch newspaper later that year that many of their lyrics were transmitted to them via his chalked messages, a sort of graffiti version of William Burroughs' cut-ups.

Years later, in 2010 *The Irish Times* traced the story of Lee Burns: 'These were not the artless daubs of latter-day graffiti merchants… This was more like some odd branch of literature, a story being told one line at a time on different surfaces around the city; the reader, in happening upon these lines, decided what order they came in… This was a time when the public domain, and what you might give to or derive from it, was worth attention; when wordplay and wit were priced above rubies.

'Usually there was a declaration about some person; the cast of characters was long, with references to people from history and from the present day. But their names shifted. LEE turned up frequently, as did ROY. LEE sometimes became LE and ROY became KING. Sometimes you had LEROY, the king. WHO BURNS WONDERFUL MAN TO DEATH? was the first of these plaintive messages spotted in late 1968 by two recent ex-schoolboys. In the year that followed they came upon more of them on their rambles at night through the capital on a trajectory from Gardiner Street to the Grand Canal.

'The identity of Lee Burns, if that's who he was, remained a mystery, though someone claimed to have seen him in action one night, and described a Schubert-like figure with plump face, ruddy cheeks, tiny spectacles and wild hair, and a long overcoat. It sounded like him all right.

'He continued his work for about a year, on ledges, walls, in plain view and down dark alleys. It became the sport of a select few to find each new message as it appeared; there were letters to *The Irish Times*, and a song by Dr Strangely Strange. Then, after more than 50 of his utterances had been noted, the writer stopped writing. Had he completed his work, or tired of it? Emigrated to the Bogside or Berkeley to join the revolution? Died? Been arrested? We may never know. But one of the last new messages to be sighted struck a new note, of serenity and forbearance: BIRD OF PREY FOR ME.'

## Two days in the Eamonn Andrews Studios

The two days of recording with Gary Moore and Dave Mattacks heralded a major change in direction, though it's debatable how much of this was planned out. To some extent, things just happened. One factor was a growing feeling the band needed to have a bigger sound: they'd encountered so many PA problems when playing support to rock bands, in larger venues than the small clubs they'd been used to previously. Booth

The Mighty Avons in the Henry Street studio.

remembers that once they'd decided to use Gary Moore, it was clear they would also need a drummer. What's more, recording Ballad Of The Wasps with Mattacks had showed the band that he could even out erratic tempos and give some definition to their transitions between song sections, often endearingly wobbly on earlier recordings. Andy Irvine, who added mandolin on one track, was a chance addition; he was around in Dublin at that point as he had left Sweeney's Men and was pursuing a solo career. Undeniably, the Dublin recordings had a much fuller – and tighter – sound, coupled with a rhythm section, and these sessions set the eventual tone of their second LP.

Joe Boyd seemed to be in favour of the shift, and Witchseason certainly shelled out to fly over folk-rock drummer of choice Dave Mattacks, along with engineer Roger Mayer.

Joe: 'I think I remember discussing using Gary Moore with them before the Dublin sessions. The mix of acoustic and electric was what was in the water in those days – the ISB were using electric bass.'

When veteran Irish broadcaster Eamonn Andrews opened his first recording studio in Dublin's Henry Street in the late Fifties, it was a small, unprepossessing place geared to the production of radio programmes. In the Sixties, use by showbands like Booth's nemesis, The Mighty Avon Showband, and early freakbeat merchants like Granny's Intentions necessitated a larger studio, which was opened in 1966 down the road at 4 Henry Street. By the time of the Strangelies' sessions, the Andrews empire had grown to include a new venture, The Television Club, housed in the former Four Provinces Ballroom (aka 'The 4 Ps') over the river in Harcourt Street. It was here that the band were booked in for two days' recording. Joe Boyd was too tied up to be present, but Sound Techniques staff engineer Roger Mayer effectively co-produced the sessions.

Booth: 'It was a ballroom by night, studio by day – sound baffle screens on little wheels, microphones cabled out, and the big live room with its sprung floor became a producer's nightmare.'

Roger Mayer: 'The four-track recording desk was also relatively primitive compared with what was now available at Sound Techniques – perhaps that was why Joe was reluctant to rely on the in-house engineer. My job, according to Joe, was to try and make sure that things stayed on course.'

Gary Moore: 'The studio was weird, cos it was on the ballroom floor and they'd bring out all these screens and put them around the instruments.' Perhaps surprisingly for the Strangelies, there was some advance preparation for the sessions, which were characterised by efficiency rather than the nervous hilarity of the *Kip Of The*

*Serenes* sessions. Of course, as a part-time resident of the Orphanage, Gary already knew all the songs and had often played along with them in rehearsals there.

Roger: 'They knew what they were in for so they'd done some rehearsing and some pre-recording strategies… it wasn't the deer-in-the-headlights routine they had on the first album.'

Gary: 'Yes it was planned – we had rehearsed, I just joined in with them and played.'

Booth behind his screens.

## Tuesday 31 March 1970

The first morning was spent setting up. Gary was known for playing at great volume, even in rehearsals, and there were some concerns about this.

Roger: 'Gary had wanted to play through a larger stack – we all agreed this was impracticable, so we used a practice amp. I remember trouble with that and numerous electronic problems during the sessions.'

Booth: 'At the time, Gary and his cohorts in Skid Row used enormous amps – 200 watts or more – and he didn't need that sort of volume to record with little old us. Previously to recording we had attended a party in the British Embassy where Tim Goulding introduced me to a petite blonde girl who had a guitar and a little amp. This amp we managed to borrow and whether Gary blew it whilst recording I am not sure – Ivan thinks so – but it did blow while in our care and led to all types of hassle getting it fixed. Poor girl – I think she subsequently died tragically by her own hand, but neither Ivan

nor I think the borrowing of the amp was in any way connected to this.'

Gary: 'I didn't turn up to the sessions with a huge amp! In those days, if you played loud you couldn't record anything – they would always get on your case about being too loud. But that's true about the tiny little practice amp – I just used that – they miked it up inside and added a bit of reverb and it sounded really good. And the amp didn't blow up – it held its own for the songs!'

Gary nearly didn't make the session: 'Skid Row had been in the studio the night before and I went home the next day and was listening to the tapes and then the police arrived. They were after these two guys who were living in my flat, Happy and Noel, that had been going out and raiding dispensaries. They took them away but they didn't do anything to me – they took me down to the station and then they let me go!'

Recording the first song, Goulding's Mary Malone Of Moscow, went very smoothly in one take, and the newly added rock elements of Mattacks and Moore blended well.

Dave Mattacks: 'It was the first time I'd met Gary. I had an enjoyable time – the Strangelies were musically eccentric, but not as far out as the ISB!'

Gary: 'It was a good session. Mattacks was a great drummer with a really nice feel – I really enjoyed playing with him… I think they wanted to do a bit more of a rock thing. It was all down pretty quickly.'

As the recordings were on four-track, tracks had to be 'bounced' to allow for vocal overdubs. On these sessions, the bass, drums, guitar and lead guitar were mixed from four tracks into stereo, thus freeing up two tracks for lead vocals etc.

Roger: 'Bouncing is a one-way street – you can't go back and fix anything once you've done that – it was a little disconcerting, to say the least. I couldn't hear what was going on in the monitors so I had to trust to luck.'

Gary: 'It was OK though, we got a good sound.'

When Andy Irvine dropped by, he was quickly lined up to play the following day. He noted in his diary of the time: 'I had met Dr SS in Bewley's before this & had been invited to go along to the 4 Ps where they were recording. They have Dave Mattacks with them from Fairport, a dapper, well-dressed man. He told me how Steeleye Span beat Fairport 8-3 in the football match.'

When Gary left, probably for a gig, Mattacks and the core band recorded the acoustic instrumental When Adam Delved, then had to pack up sharpish.

Roger: 'They never actually mentioned that to me or Joe until I got over there – it came as a shock to me! I'd set up everything up in the ballroom and then they said: "It'll all have to come down again tonight because there's a dance – you can set it all up again in the morning." I stayed the night at the Orphanage. I don't remember too much about that because once the session finished, we went to the pub and it got a little… vague.'

# Wednesday 1st April 1970

Gary was free that morning, and once the band was set up, Summer Breeze was nailed on the fifth take, which was then hurriedly bounced on to two tracks so piano and lead vocal could be overdubbed on the other two. Preserved for ever in the sub-mix was an overloud organ coming in in the second minute – you can hear it quickly being faded down. As Booth says, it's a defiant lyric, and there's a grit and edge to his vocal on this recording which was a new departure for him.

Ivan's Sign On My Mind needed a preparatory run-through, as the band had decided to incorporate a reluctant mandolin player. Ivan: 'We press-ganged Andy Irvine, who had never played the song before – but I think the timbre and texture is greatly enhanced by his playing.'

Andy's diary: 'After a couple of pints in O'Donoghue's, I rambled down to the recording studios & watched Dr SS recording. Dave Mattacks seems to be a great drummer & Gary totally stole the show with his guitar playing. I played some chords on the mandolin on one number. I thought it was brutal but it's hard to know what Dr SS thought. I got a bit uncomfortable with the whole thing and after they had done a number with Brush on bass – I split.'

On the first take of SOMM (released as a bonus track years later) you can hear Ivan trying to reassure Andy, and Gary trying out the various motifs he assembled to such powerful effect on the second and final take. Gary was just three days shy of his eighteenth birthday when he recorded his impressively mature and structured solo.

Joe: 'That's a very nice guitar solo!'

Booth: 'Dave and Gary seemed to us to know each other from some other universe we were not privy to, playing together as if they had always done so, and the results still speak clear and sharp across the years.'

It was early afternoon by now, and time was running out. SOMM was bounced so that Ivan's vocals, organ and whistle could be overdubbed. As the band were starting work on Booth's Gave My Love An Apple, another visitor arrived.

Booth: 'Brendan "The Brush" Shiels arrived and informed Gary that he had to go immediately, if not sooner, as they had a gig that night in Rockall or some such faraway spot. To facilitate departure, Brush took over the bass playing duties from me and after two takes the job was considered oxo [in Dublin, this means very good, as in 'it's all gravy'] and the boys belted off into the sunset, leaving a bemused Strangelies to wonder how he could learn the arrangement so quickly when it had taken us almost a lifetime.'

The Brush: 'I wasn't even supposed to be on the session, I'd just come to pick up Gary. But I was a fearless youth, I spent 24 hours a day playing, so I had this one-take-and-go approach.' On the two takes of Apple (the first was also later released as a bonus track) you can hear how Mattacks helps the band define the transitions between song parts and Shiels really drives the song along. In a later album review, *Melody Maker*'s Andrew Means was impressed: 'There's a lot of personality and plenty of surprises here. It's the kind of experimentation that

leads to something like Gave My Love An Apple, a song with a million tempo changes and stylistic shifts that just plain shouldn't work, but ends up being exhilarating.'

Apple was mixed into stereo so lead vocals and Goulding's fiddle could be added. The band nailed Kilmanoyadd Stomp in a couple of takes, with Mattacks improvising a shaker with some coffee beans for a percussion overdub. He packed up the drums while the Strangelies tackled the quasi-gospel harmonies of Goodnight My Friends, abetted by Annie Christmas and Johanna from the Sandymount Orphanage. The sessions over, the band trooped off for a pint in Toners, leaving Mattacks and Mayer to fly back to London with the recordings. The three four-track BASF tapes labelled 'Eamonn Andrews Studios' were still in the Witchseason vaults when the re-release of *Heavy Petting* was researched, forty years later.

After celebrating his 18th birthday on April 4th, Gary was reunited with the Strangelies at a gig in the 2,000-seater National Stadium in Dublin, a boxing venue with the central ring being the stage. John Peel was the MC for an evening at which the band were joined by Liverpool Scene and Skid Row. It did not go smoothly at first.

Goulding: 'Booth and I were struck by Ivan's singularly sparse playing and by the contorted expressions that went with it. Brave to the core, it turned out that every time he touched the strings, he got an electric shock.'

All went well in the end, and set the band up for some radio work back in the UK. Booth: 'Afterwards, Peel – who admitted that he had never played us on the radio because he didn't much like us – said that he now understood our appeal and would invite us on his show asap. We never looked back.

# Chapter 5

# 'We hope we won't get too heavy' – finding a drummer

Because of his impending departure for the States, Joe was anxious to start shopping the new Witchseason album to record companies. By mid-April the band were in London again, for three days of mixing the *Heavy Petting* tracks at Sound Techniques. The Dublin recordings, all approved by Joe, were enough to fill one side, but there wasn't enough material with Dave and Gary for a whole album in the new vein. Choices had to be made about which of the older recordings were to go on the album.

In the studio, even the ISB usually deferred to Joe, although Robin was no pushover. Similarly, the Strangelies were all fairly biddable, so some surprising selections were made – neither of Ivan's two great cosmic songs made it on, and Booth's Sweet Red Rape was also rejected. If Joe had just assembled the material recorded to date at Sound Techniques, you'd pretty much have a 'Kip Volume Two.' As it is, the album in its released form is very much a document of a band in transition from *Kip*'s acoustic pastoral musings into a fully-fledged folk-rock outfit. The Strangelies formed part of Joe's B-Team, formed with the aim, as he says, of releasing more records without spending a lot of money. To keep costs down he would fit the band's recording slots into unused studio time – as and when – and so, recorded over a very long period rather than in a discrete set of album sessions, the record as a whole is an uneasy mixture of approaches and lacks *Kip*'s unity. Interviewed by *Melody Maker* when the LP came out, Goulding hinted at this: 'Some of the tracks were recorded nearly a year ago... it would have been nice to have a little more time.' Ivan added: 'It's not perfect. There were one or two things that weren't too good.'

In hindsight, it might have been better to leave the release for a few months until the band had found their own drummer and worked up more material with a rhythm section, but Joe's hurry to get everything sorted before he left meant this was not possible.

Up at Glen Row, Marymac had been involved in the preparations for U, the ISB's ambitious multi-media show. As well as the flamboyant costumes Mary remembers making, it featured mime and dance by Stone Monkey. Malcolm and Rakis were the best of the dancers, but the others tended to lapse into what one reviewer called 'vacuous hand-waving.' Critically, U suffered from the newspaper reviewers judging it on the same level as West End musicals, when really it was the ISB's end-of-term play. Ivan, a thespian at heart since his Trinity

College drama production days, went along with Marymac to see one of the ten Roundhouse U shows that April, but failed to enthuse the two Tims. Booth, a big fan of the earlier ISB albums, had gone off them: 'I was allergic to the tweeness.' Ivan enjoyed much of U, though he found it 'just a bit too long, and a bit uneven in terms of pace.'

After the week in cabaret, the mummers' play at the Guildford Festival earlier in the year was the final time the Strangelies as a whole indulged any of Ivan's theatrical leanings. The Music and Poetry events in Dublin clubs were now just memories, and that Iain Sinclair 'moment when all of that underground activity may have felt it could go public' had passed. The Strangelies had become another of the bands playing their songs on the circuit – although reliably more quirky than almost all the others.

The band were becoming fairly well established on that circuit. After playing at a secondary school in Crawley (for inexplicable reasons), there was a particularly good concert at one of the Oxford colleges. Ivan awarded it a 10/10 rating in his gig diary, and Booth recalls 'some sort of May Ball with Chicken Shack and lots of Hooray Henrys. Very enjoyable.'

The next morning, they flew to Belfast for their first Northern Ireland gigs, organised by Roger Armstrong, a young student from the Queen's University Esoteric Music Society.

Booth: 'We were body searched by the Drug Squad on our way in. We flew in with just our instruments and a few tabs Ivan had stashed and forgotten about in his piccolo. Luckily, they were not sussed.'

Roger Armstrong: 'At the time I was a budding social sec at Queen's. The logistics were a nightmare, as they were playing in the UK the night before and we had to fly them in the next morning, so I had to hire a back line. I bent over backwards to do this as I had only booked local bands beforehand and I thought: This is the big time – a proper band with records and a manager! Anyway, between us, Steve Pearce and I made it happen.'

After another Norn Iron concert at the University of Ulster, there were three gigs in the Irish Republic. The Limerick event was where Goulding discovered their audience demographic: 'Some fans approached us before the gig with the unanswerable question: "Are ye Blues or Commercial?" a question akin to "Is it true you have stopped beating your wife?" They were schoolboys, mostly in their early teens.' Clearly, the boys had not read the local press ad for 'Ireland's First Contemporary Folk Group in their own kind of madness. Admission 5 Shillings.'

Cork University was next, and went down well. Booth: 'This gig has gone down in the annals. The audience watched from behind their collective sofa as Ivan took a wander about the stage between numbers, expounding on something or other and, not seeing our new guitar-to-acoustic-pickup leads, managed to step through them, yanking them off the guitars... crunch.'

After a late-night jam session with student folk band Raftery, the band struggled in the next morning to collect their equipment. Goulding: 'I bent down to pick up a bass bin, slipped a disc and had to be carried off.'

The students on campus, hearing the ambulance sirens, assumed it was a drugs raid by the Garda and panicked until they realised it was Goulding being carted off to hospital.

Ivan: 'So, l had to drive Gosport Lil. The Renault 4 had a gearshift l wasn't acquainted with, and l hadn't done a lot of car driving. l definitely wasn't insured, but that would not have been such a serious issue in those times. It was a good challenge, not the least the corner from Bridge Street into McCurtain Street with a bit of a hill on a corner, traffic lights, gears, brakes etc.'

Booth and Ivan played the final gig, back at Trinity, as a duo while Goulding recuperated in hospital. He recovered in time for Johanna's photoshoot for the new LP cover at Dargle Cottage later that month.

It was Dramamine Blues time again and back to the UK for the usual random selection of venues the length and breadth of England. A typical wodge of dates started at Hitchin, sharing a bill with Shirley Collins. Goulding's back was still not great, and so old mate Frank Murray roadied and drove them to a Southampton gig, followed by a Doncaster folk club appearance with a long-haired Christy Moore. Then it was straight down to Brighton University the following day.

Ivan: 'Andy Anderson the Catman came – it was a somewhat excruciating gig, with missed cues and tuning problems, but for him it was a memorable night's entertainment. "The key lies in the music – it could open their minds," was one of his regular comments.

## Dargle photoshoot

Some of Johanna's photos formed the basis of Roger Dean's *Heavy Petting* artwork, and those with the band hiding in bushes and half in shadow under a tree were the inspiration for his album cover cut-outs (q.v.).

'Dargle Cottage,' the building with the balcony and steps, is actually quite an imposing house. It was well-staffed, with three gardeners, a cook, a housekeeper and a butler. A few pictures were taken indoors in the Sun Room, including one with Ivan at the family's Bechstein Boudoir grand piano, once played by Louis Armstrong. The smaller building (BELOW LEFT) is the Gate Lodge where Tim's friends Mr and Mrs Willie Kerrigan lived. Willie, the former groom to Sir Basil's father, had become head gardener. The Mount Street Dodge, now looking rather less resplendent and seen in one photo, was garaged there.

## Peel session

In late May 1970, John Peel made good his promise of the month before and the band went into the BBC Maida Vale studios to do a session for *Top Gear*, their first on UK radio. Three new-ish songs were taped, presumably with the idea of promoting the forthcoming *Heavy Petting* LP on which they all appear. Jove Was At Home has not surfaced, but an off-air recording exists of the other two. Ashling is much like the album version, complete with Howson Phonofiddle and some very nice whistle from Goulding, who also provides an array of keyboard overdubs on Mary Malone Of Moscow: harmonium, organ and piano. Booth plays banjo on the intro and outro; he and Ivan add some impassioned backing vocals.

The session was broadcast on 6th June. Strangelies were playing the Clitheroe Castle Pop Festival, so missed their BBC debut. Booth: 'We had wanted to listen back after the recording but the jobsworth BBC sound engineer was going off shift and would not co-operate.'

Part of the band's growing tendency towards professionalism was that they now had their own homespun stationery. Booth knocked up a letterhead for them with an impressive list of three different phone numbers for 'telephonic communications' in both London and Dublin. There was also a poster and generic tickets, for use by promoters.

When they got back from Clitheroe, the band stayed in London for a week or so, doing some club gigs and running into a couple of young hopefuls at Witchseason.

'This ticket admits nothing,' Booth's all-purpose gig ticket.

## Fate & ferret

Andrew Greig and his friend George Boyter, huge Incredible String Band fans, had formed a duo in ISB wannabe mode called 'Fate & ferret.' (Note the carefully considered use of ampersand and case, which they felt would make all the difference to their prospects.) In June, when they were both 17, they hitched down from Scotland in a fish truck to visit Joe Boyd and play him their demo (it didn't go well). In the Witchseason office, Anthea Joseph introduced them to the Strangelies. In 2017, Andrew recalled the meeting in his book *You Know What You Could Be*:

'They did not look much older than us, but more authentically bohemian... They were chirpy, friendly and openly excited about their first LP. George and I looked at the cover. Three guys and a girl in weird clothes, one wearing a bird-beak mask, sitting on rocks in a mountain pool with assorted instruments. We could do that. We went to a pub and had a Guinness with the Strangelies. Mike and Robin appeared extra-terrestrial, but these lads were clearly pals who laughed and took the piss out of each other. They had no side, were fun and easy to be with.'

Booth's all-purpose gig poster.

Interviewed for this book, George remembers 'a feeling of kindred Celtic connection and in particular how nice they were. They didn't smell of fish – unlike Fate & ferret!' Andrew had a 'sense of fellow-feeling, buoyed up by their cheerfulness and achievement of actually having an album coming out with Joe. And their songs seemed, like ours, very localised. We grooved to that.'

Back in Fife, they bought *Kip Of The Serenes*. Both liked the humour and that it was 'full of digressions and whims.' 'The effect was charming, stoned and cheering,' recalled Andrew. 'They sounded like us, only better. This was encouraging. Give us a studio, we felt, some support and overdubbing and a bit of reverb on our voices, and we would sound like we did in our heads.'

F&f never did make any of their four planned albums and Andrew became a writer, not a musician. Decades later, though, they did get to share a stage with the Strangelies, adding backing vocals and, in Andrew's case, a spot of banjo. But that's a story for the Epilogue.

Clitheroe Castle Pop Festival was the Strangelies' first music festival, a one-day open-air event running on a Saturday from 2.30 - 11.00. Around 2,000 punters forked out 10 shillings each to see some of Blackhill Enterprises' best acts, making this one of the largest audiences the band had played to. Also on the bill were Kevin Ayers And The Whole World, Michael Chapman and the Third Ear Band. It rained.

Ivan (who awarded it 10/10) and Booth don't recall much of the gig, though Goulding does: 'I have a vivid memory of this festival, not least because, high up on a grassy bank above the stage, I spent some time trying to talk a young hippy out of committing suicide. I had some sympathy for him as the Third Ear Band were playing down below.'

In London, Joe had mastered the LP and found a record label to lease it to. Joe: 'My fundamental deal was that Island advanced money to Witchseason Productions. The original idea was that they would put out everything that I did, but it ended up that they had first option on everything. By 1970 I had come to understand the nature of the beast. Island was hugely successful at that time – Chris Blackwell loved Nick Drake and Fairport, but the truth is he didn't really get things like Vashti – I think it was after the first experience with Strangely Strange – this whimsical, rural aesthetic – the people at Island just didn't get it. So, I didn't even bother to play this stuff to them – I just said "You're not gonna like this," and took it away. I knew this guy at Phillips – I think he'd put out the Brotherhood of Breath for me when he was at RCA previously – which is how the Strangelies ended up with them. The same thing had happened with Vashti Bunyan's album.

'I finished about 16 LPs in 1970 – so I have to confess I have almost no memory of this album. It came out September 1970 when I was in the throes of leaving. I was so frantic – at first, just keep running fast enough to save Witchseason – then when I'd come up with the solution of selling the company to Island, I was tying up the loose ends as fast as I could because I had to turn up for work in LA in the first week of January 1971.'

A postcard to Glen Row from Iain Sinclair, with a 'heavy petting' newspaper cutting.

The album actually ended up on Phillips' progressive label, Vertigo, perhaps because someone there thought the Gary Moore rock aspects would fit in well on the Vertigo roster alongside Black Sabbath and Uriah Heep. Like *Kip Of The Serenes*, *Heavy Petting* was titled after a Goulding catchphrase, this time born out of his obsession with the 'problem pages' in the Irish press. The 'Heavy' in the title was also intended to reflect the transition towards a rockier sound.

The band were still getting lots of work on the college circuit, but June saw them play at three larger gigs, their appeal boosted by their John Peel appearance. They appeared at an event at the Garage Club, Barnet, with Trees, Quiver, Formerly Fat Harry and Peter Green, who had now left Fleetwood Mac, with plans for solo albums and free concerts 'with friends I like jamming with.' He didn't jam with the Strangelies, but they did let him use Goulding's harmonium. Booth: 'We played and my German friend Christl, in a black leather dress, a spiked dog collar round her neck, danced as if there might be no tomorrow. The acid kicked in, kicked in, kicked…' The sound was terrible, and Ivan awarded a rare 0/10.

A bigger concert, also in June, was supporting Santana at the Lyceum Ballroom, alongside James Litherland's Brotherhood and Elton John. Like many ballrooms of the era, the venue had a revolving stage which would

rotate through 90 degrees every 30 minutes. The Strangelies coped manfully with this. Roger Mayer: 'I was at the gig. It was all very bizarre – nobody quite knew what was going on and people were toppling over as the stage rotated.' Booth: 'Did we go around twice? Or is this just part of the Strangely legend, created and curated by Manager Pearce?' Ivan's diary recorded only that 'the gig went quite well.'

Towards the end of the month, they played at Implosion at the Roundhouse, with Liverpool Scene, Clark-Hutchinson, Patto and Skid Row. Gary joined them for Sign On My Mind.

Booth: 'After the Roundhouse gig, Lorraine Sufrin offered a bed on the floor of a flat she shared somewhere near Greenwich. The band and Manager Pearce retired to the pub across the road where copious ingestion of substances took place. Although Pearce and I attempted to find her place later on that night, I was by then so ripped on acid that we were unable to find her street – although we banged on several doors in the vicinity, including, as she later told me, hers. Such was our insistence, she and her friend thought we were Plod and would not open the door. I spent a few enjoyable hours wandering the foot passage beneath the Thames and contemplating the Cutty Sark before we retired to a friend's gaff in Hampstead for further psychedelic adventures... but those are other stories.'

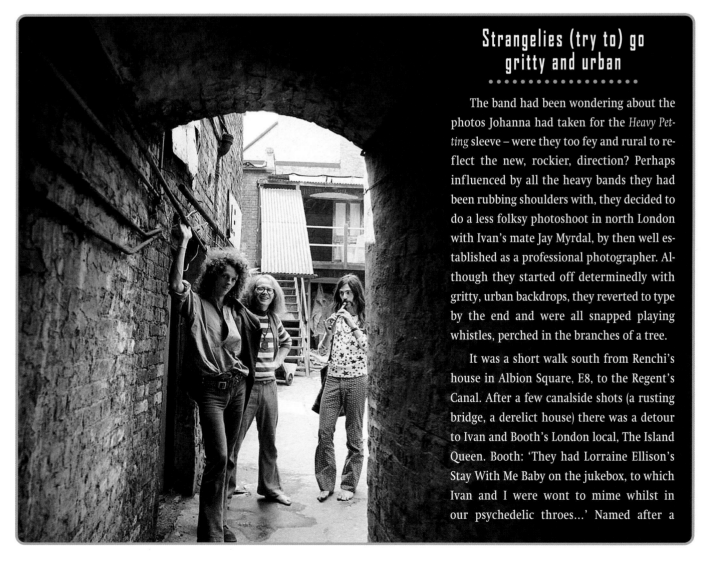

## Strangelies (try to) go gritty and urban

The band had been wondering about the photos Johanna had taken for the *Heavy Petting* sleeve – were they too fey and rural to reflect the new, rockier, direction? Perhaps influenced by all the heavy bands they had been rubbing shoulders with, they decided to do a less folksy photoshoot in north London with Ivan's mate Jay Myrdal, by then well established as a professional photographer. Although they started off determinedly with gritty, urban backdrops, they reverted to type by the end and were all snapped playing whistles, perched in the branches of a tree.

It was a short walk south from Renchi's house in Albion Square, E8, to the Regent's Canal. After a few canalside shots (a rusting bridge, a derelict house) there was a detour to Ivan and Booth's London local, The Island Queen. Booth: 'They had Lorraine Ellison's Stay With Me Baby on the jukebox, to which Ivan and I were wont to mime whilst in our psychedelic throes...' Named after a

Mississippi steamboat, the pub still enjoyed some notoriety as the place where Joe Orton and Kenneth Halliwell used to hold court with their admirers in the early Sixties. They had lived in the same street as the pub, Noel Road.

After attracting suspicious glances from a local (maybe it was the dirty bare feet) they continued along the canal until the section where it disappears into a tunnel at the Angel, Islington. It was time for tea (or Coke), followed by more gritty urban stuff on a nearby building site. After that was Hampstead Heath, and a series in a park shelter near the Hampstead Ponds, a sequence of 'keep on trucking' shots and then, inevitably, the old hippy elements prevailed and it was time to climb that tree. The final picture shows them heading off the Heath towards Gospel Oak station, with what looks suspiciously like Terry and Gay Woods trailing along behind them. Maybe they were there all along, just keeping out of shot. (All photos: Jay Myrdal )

In the end the stills were too late for the LP cover, but Booth knocked up a promotional flyer for it himself, with one of Jay's photos and some Letraset. Presumably there was nothing left in the Vertigo promotional budget once they'd paid for Roger Dean's horrendously expensive 'flaps' cover...

## Finding a drummer

Dr. Strangely Strange 'Heavy Petting' (Vertigo)

The transition to being a rock group of sorts continued. In June 1970, *Melody Maker*'s Karl Dallas interviewed the trio for a feature misleadingly titled 'Strangely Strange – a sort of Emerald String Band.' The comparison attracted the attention of many ISB fans, including a young drummer from Uttoxeter called Neil Hopwood. Dallas had a perceptive take on the band: 'Like the Incredibles, [their] music steals up on you rather than socking you over the head. There are soft nuances in the lyrics... and an almost religious sense of communion.' However, he was fairly unquestioning about the stories he was being fed; this was the interview containing Ivan's myth-building story that ex-member Brian Trench had 'split to make revolution in France.' Having just recorded *Heavy Petting* with Dave Mattacks, Strangelies informed Dallas they were now looking for a drummer. 'Dave would be too good for us,' Goulding told him, 'we'd have to get someone more on our own level. People don't come to hear music so much when they come to hear us. They come to hear the songs.' Ivan explained that 'they come for the whole thing. People really seem to groove on us having tuning problems.' Booth added: 'When it's all going well and you see the audience starting to grin, there's tremendous feedback. You get very turned on, and they get very turned on.'

In a later interview, Ivan explained that when they used Mattacks, it was 'the first time I'd ever listened to the drums and realised they could be a tasteful instrument, not just a noise.' Booth added that it now seemed logical to add a drummer, as the new album featured one, but hoped that 'we won't get too heavy.'

When the Strangelies announced a date in the Midlands, Neil decided to check them out. On 25th June he went along to their Burton-on-Trent Town Hall gig, where Bridget St John was supporting. Only Goulding has

A fresh-faced Neil Hopwood

any sort of memory of the events that evening: 'During the gig Ivan suddenly left the stage. Tim and I ad-libbed a radio play of some sort. Ivan returned and told the audience he'd had to go for a pee.'

The band had taken to asking every audience if they knew anyone who'd like to drum for them, so Neil felt encouraged to make a move: 'After witnessing their original, eclectic and interesting live set I was keen to join these three troubadours, so I approached them afterwards and found them most affable.' That did it. He was now in the band, more or less, and vague arrangements were made to 'have a session' back in Ireland after the band had had a break.

Before the Strangelies could pick up the rest of their lives again, there was an odd agricultural fair appearance in Bennettsbridge, Co Kilkenny. Goulding: 'In the afternoon animals were being weighed at the cattle booth and their weights announced on the tannoy. Then they did the same for the three of us. It was an agricultural fair, after all. That evening Pearce had booked us in for a concert in the parish hall, where we played to a nonplussed rural audience, who probably expected a showband rather than James Joyce poems. After the show I went to collect the money from the startled parish priest, who was lost for words: "I would just like to say, just like to say... Good Night." I think we had some sort of drunken party afterwards.' In his diary for that date, Ivan recorded the word 'Poteen' in bold letters.

## Bennettsbridge Mid - Summer Festival

### JUNE 26 TO JULY 12, 1970

**Other Festival Attractions :**

**OPEN-AIR CONCERT :** Dr Strangely Strange — Dungeare Mummers.

**DANCING** in Ireland's largest Marquee. Full catering facilities.

**£200 PONY RACING** with perpetual Waterford Glass trophy.

**£100 TALENT CONTEST.**

**£500 BINGO.** Buses from all centres.

**VINTAGE CAR RALLY.** Cars from all over Ireland.

**£50 DONKEY DERBY.**

**TUG-O'-WAR.**

**FEIS.**

**FANCY DRESS PARADES. BABY SHOWS. DOG SHOWS, etc.**

**MISS SUNLIGHT COMPETITION. 14-day Holiday for Two in Majorca, plus spending money.** Prize kindly presented by W. H. Mosse Ltd., Bennettsbridge.

SEE OUR OFFICIAL PROGRAMME FOR FULL DETAILS

After recovering, Ivan headed back to Glen Row, where he spent a tranquil summer hanging out with his family, the ISB and other Glen Rowers: there were barbecues, swimming in the loch, UFO sightings, a performance of *Jack And The Beanstalk* with Robin, Likky and others and a trip to the seaside with Stone Monkey.

(LEFT) Stone Monkey at the local village shop: (FROM LEFT) Ishy, Rakis, Malcolm, John, Mal (Photo: Iain Skinner)

(RIGHT) Booth as tree, 1970

(BELOW)
'Shore Leave' by Goulding, 1970

Goulding went back to painting in his Allihies studio, continuing to work on acid-enhanced hyper-real close-ups. Booth was amassing work for his first solo show in the Brown Thomas Gallery, Dublin. One painting, 'Portrait Of The Artist As A Young Tree,' was based on a black-and-white photo taken during the Eamonn Andrews sessions. It was bought by Goulding's father, Sir Basil.

After a month or so in Uttoxeter waiting to hear back from the band, Neil was starting to wonder if the invitation to join up had just been a flight of stoned fancy. His second letter to Goulding eventually produced a response:

*14 August 1970*

*Dear Neil*

*— a pox upon me for such a delay in answering your two really nice letters. I've been down in the South-West of Ireland miles from the noisy din of urban life and somehow one day seeps into another, not to mention the Atlantic Ocean and its soporific properties.*

*— am glad you are keen on getting out of the Kiln for some gentler clime because none of us are anxious to live in heavily permeated atmospheres. As to music we must have a session. The situation is much the same as when met you. That is we are all doing other things until the second week in September when we commence playing together again in preparation for the autumn tour that starts off on October 1 in England somewhere....At present we are all under orders to write some new songs... Ivan is in Scotland at the Stringband's cottages, Tim is in Dublin and I'm here in West Cork sitting by a long window that looks out towards America... it's pretty peaceful...*

*We'll get in touch soon, best wishes, Tim*

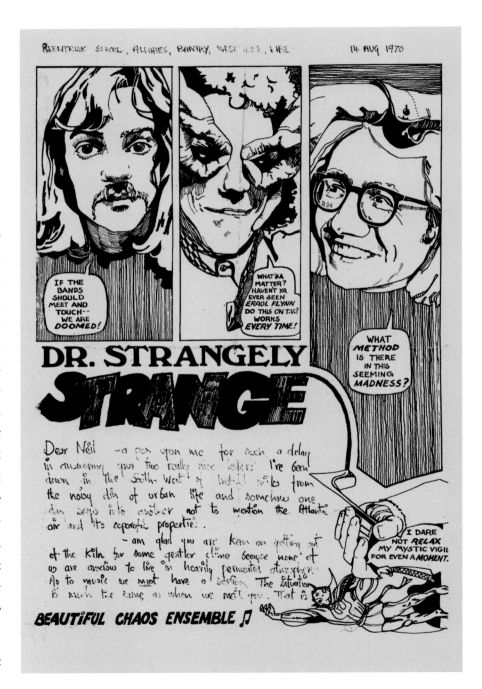

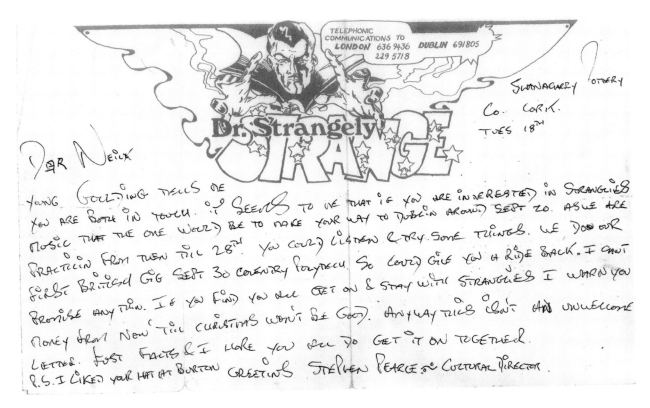

A few days later Steve Pearce wrote from Shanagarry with some managerial instructions:

DEAR NEILL

YOUNG GOULDING TELLS ME YOU ARE BOTH IN TOUCH. IT SEEMS TO ME THAT IF YOU ARE INTERESTED IN STRANGLIES MUSIC THAT THE ONE WOULD BE TO MAKE YOUR WAY TO DUBLIN AROUND SEPT 20 AS WE ARE PRACTICIN FROM THEN TILL 28TH. YOU COULD LISTEN & TRY SOME THINGS. WE DO OUR FIRST BRITISH GIG SEPT 30 COVENTRY POLYTECH SO COULD GIVE YOU A RIDE BACK. I CANT PROMISE ANYTHIN. IF YOU FIND YOU ALL GET ON AND STAY WITH STRANGLIES I WARN YOU MONEY FROM NOW 'TIL CHRISTMAS WON'T BE GOOD. ANYWAY THIS ISN'T AN UNWELCOME LETTER. JUST FACTS & I HOPE YOU ALL DO GET IT ON TOGETHER.

P.S. I LIKED YOUR HAT AT BURTON

GREETINS STEPHEN PEARCE – CULTURAL DIRECTOR

## 'Money from now 'til Christmas won't be good' – Neil joins up

Neil made his way to Dublin for 'a session' and soon found himself a band member:

'My name has caused some confusion. It is Neil Robert Hopwood. There's an old Cornish proverb that says "A dear child has many names" but, as with many other sayings, there's always the exception to the rule. Far from being dear, at Sunday school I caused a little consternation by telling the teacher my name was Bloody

Cowboy Hopwood. I had been nicknamed Fred since the age of four, owing to my habit jumping on to the horse-drawn milk-cart which stopped outside my Uttoxeter home to make deliveries. The owner was called Fred and so I got nicknamed Little Fred. I'm not sure why, but in my late teens I decided to call myself Neil Wood. The comedian Harry Worth had shortened his name from Illingsworth, after all. The band found out my full surname when I presented my passport for our Dutch gigs in December 1970, so from that point I was known as Hoppy.

'I was born in Lichfield and lived in Uttoxeter, where at the age of 13 I taught myself drums. I played in a few local rock'n'roll bands, including Johnny Saturn & The Asteroids and blues band Harley Street Blues, who supported Duster Bennett and Rory Gallagher's Taste at Henry's Blues House in Birmingham.'

'When first rehearsing with the band in Sandymount there was no kit available, so I learned the arrangements using bongos, the Japanese ping-pong bats and various bits of percussion borrowed from the front room at Tim Booth's Sandymount place. Most of the songs from *Kip*, which did not have bass on, seemed to work with these. Many of the songs from *Heavy Petting* had bass and drums, so we strove to keep a similar sort of mood whilst playing these songs live, although arrangements would change from time to time. Being the new boy, I was always open to any suggestions, but mostly felt that the band trusted my judgement in this. I was hoping that I could add something to their overall sound without destroying any of the band's slightly chaotic ethos, which had initially attracted me to them. My earlier experience of playing jazz and blues, I think, gave me the confidence to try and play more subtly, rather than just bang out a heavy beat. I was already a fan of early Pentangle, Eclection and Fairport etc, and I think this put me in good stead for my short but enjoyable stint with the band. As for vocals, the other band members were saved from that aural assault by my reluctance to join in.'

'I met Steve Pearce, their manager. I remember him as a big, caring and friendly man, and have fond memories of him lampooning your typical Irish showband Country and Western singer in overblown sentimentality mode. His strains of "Buckets full of tears, as I left me dear old mother, standing by the garden gate..." etc used to have us all in stitches.'

The band as a whole had some new songs to learn. Goulding's offering was Horse Of A Different Hue: 'A cannibal describes human flesh as tasting like "long pig." As for the shorter swine, they probably have as much notion as to what this ditty is about as the author has.' It was a song about love and relationships, actually, viewed through a similar surreal/lysergic prism to the one Booth had used in Gave My Love An Apple. Settling down in Allihies with Orphan Annie had a lot to do with it: 'Quite unexpectedly the grass turned green / Quite unlike anything I'd ever seen / And then I knew those storybooks ring true / Love's just a horse of a different hue.'

Ivan's Lady Of The Glen couldn't be more straight-ahead. His summer in Glen Row with Marymac and Niamh had strengthened his relationship with them both: 'This is a love song in a slightly Celtic rock mode, aimed at the person whose hand I later sought in marriage. Luckily my musical proficiency was not a prerequisite, (nor indeed my financial status, perhaps it was just my looks!). I'll stop now...'

Ivan had also added a final section to the old song Cock-A-Doodle-Doo, written in the Orphanage in 1968 and originally recorded for *Kip Of The Serenes*. After a couple of years on the road, the song had transcended its original 'Gonna leave this town behind' blues vibe and become a meditation on his childhood and subsequent life: 'Yonder stands the youngest son / Look, his life has just begun / Once I threw away a chance / Can't you teach him how to grasp.'

The band kitted themselves out for their new 'rock band' mode. Booth: 'Ivan – in one of our instrument-buying frenzies – purchased an electric guitar of dubious Japanese manufacture. A Kawai. He soon learned to produce fearsome distortion on this instrument and developed a stage persona to go with it. Actually, I think Goulding and I developed it for him.' Ivan noted that it cost him nine pounds ten shillings, with case.

Booth: 'Later on, for three pounds, I got hold of a Vox bass, which was very easy to play as it was much smaller than your standard Fender. My son Jesse still has it. I also bought a five-string banjo from a pawn shop in Manchester – it was a music-hall type of thing, all inlaid with ivory and mother of pearl and looked great, but the neck was a little suspect.'

When the band came back to England, they picked up Neil's drum kit up on the way to the first gig on the tour. Now they were ready to folk-rock.

# CHAPTER 6

# Heavy Petting and other activities

*Heavy Petting*, released on 11th September 1970, was already in the shops by the time the four-piece arrived back in the UK. Unlike the *Kip* release, this time round there were some gigs to promote the album. Calling these 'a tour' was stretching it a bit, though, as they were the usual random geographical distribution. The first one, in Coventry, was 'neither here nor there,' according to Ivan's diary, but the concerts improved rapidly as Neil settled in. The band dutifully slotted into a round of press interviews arranged by Vertigo, 'promoting the album' with *Beat Instrumental, Music Now, Record Mirror, Disc & Music Echo, Melody Maker* and others. Topics included the need for long 'rest periods' off, introducing their new drummer, and the difficulty of getting gigs in Ireland because of the showbands' stranglehold on the scene. Booth told *Melody Maker*: 'The only place we get the kind of audience we like is in England, but we don't want to come over here full-time,' adding that Irish audiences would get upset 'if you didn't play the Dubliners type of thing.' 'We like to do as much work as possible while we're over here,' added Ivan. The increasingly well-worn tale of Lee's chalked messages was trotted out, as well. Dave Mattacks got a few approving mentions, but not Gary Moore, still a complete unknown at this point.

Also feeling stifled by the Irish live music scene, Skid Row had relocated to London that summer to record their first album and play gigs. Their first LP came out the same month that *Heavy Petting* was released, but in his *NME* interview Gary didn't mention the Eamonn Andrews sessions and stuck to Skid Row topics. Like the Strangelies, the band had gone as far as they could in Ireland: 'The whole scene is dominated by showbands. It's a closed shop because the people who manage [them] have an interest in the ballrooms too.'

Photographer Barrie Wentzell shot a roll of film of the Strangelies posing on the flat roof of the *Melody Maker* office. No more wacky poses, capes, phonofiddles, bushes, reading a newspaper up a tree or parkland walks – here was a group of hard-faced young men staring blankly at the camera. This was a rock band.

Apart from fixing up the interviews, the new record label did little to promote *Heavy Petting* other than paying for one shared ad. It was deemed unimportant, sandwiched as it was between two of Vertigo's prog-rock classics, Uriah Heep's *Very 'Eavy Very 'Umble* (June 1970) and *Paranoid* by Black Sabbath (September 1970). There was no single to promote it, either, though Summer Breeze was included on an October sampler, *The Vertigo Annual 1970*. Despite Booth's hopes ('I thought this release would make me hideously rich') this failed to attain the huge sales of *Nice Enough To Eat*. And although that song was an appropriately rocky choice for the compilation, it was squeezed in on the double album where it could pass unnoticed, at the end of the second side of the second disc. There was a TV appearance, though: RTÉ remained a faithful supporter, so the band made a quick return trip to Dublin to mime to Mary Malone Of Moscow on the *Late Late Show*.

Photo: Barrie Wentzell

## Roger Dean's sleeve design

Unlike the *Kip* sleeve, an in-house production, the band had virtually nothing to do with the new LP sleeve and were, according to *MM*, 'not too pleased' with it. Ivan was upset: 'I was really broken up when I saw the cover. The guy who did it [had] seemed to do some good work.' Booth was a bit more philosophical: 'We said to Vertigo that all the words must be legible, but perhaps it wasn't their fault. But then it's the music that matters.' Goulding: 'Vertigo did go to great trouble over it, but it was just a pity how it turned out.'

Roger Dean provided *Heavy Petting* with what John Peel later called an 'auto-destructive sleeve' with complex folding flaps, one of the reasons an undamaged vinyl copy is so valuable now. It initially came as a bit of a shock to the band, who had provided Vertigo with a batch of ingredients for the album artwork, including song lyrics, Johanna's photos of them on the balcony of Dargle Cottage and another set of them hiding in some bushes. Booth: 'We wanted a simple fold-out with lots of pics and Strangely notes and clear typography.' Roger Dean actually wanted to base the front cover round a painting of a tree he had done, but Vertigo had other ideas.

Roger Dean: 'The art director at Vertigo, Mike Stamford, liked to commission projects. His ideas weren't particularly visual, but he had an enthusiasm for extravagant paper sculpture. I'd done the Ramases album *Space Hymns*, which was a three-foot by two-foot piece of card, folded, but my interest, to be honest, was to reproduce the imagery rather than the complexities of the cut and fold. The Strangelies were one of the bands I never met and I probably hadn't heard the music at that point either. The cut-outs were my way of accommodating the photos of them peering through gaps in the bushes. The idea of doing something very treelike was there already – it came from an idea for a painting that I didn't use for an album cover until 2007 [It can be found on page 28 of Dean's book, *Views*]. But that was much more complex than they wanted to go – so this was a simplified version of that. The cantilevered house photo is odd – it's nothing like my architecture, which is very curvilinear – but it's them, it's their place, so it wasn't a challenge.

'*Heavy Petting* was probably one of the first few covers where I hand-drew a font. I had got into hand-lettering by chance; I was under pressure to complete an album sleeve but my friend Jan who usually helped me with the graphics had left for India, and I hadn't a clue – so I just sketched in a layout where I hand-drew the title lettering as an indication of what it would look like when the typesetting was done. Of course, the record company liked it. Suddenly I was in a way of creating another world, painting another world, making a document that looked like it came from another world. Slowly at first, but I got more confident and efficient at doing that. Rick Griffin was a big inspiration – the Grateful Dead album cover for *Aoxomoxoa* was amazing, it looked like it came from a place no one had ever visited!

'I have to say that, whereas I admired Mike Stamford for pushing to experimentation, I don't think it ever really worked. I didn't like what I did, and I think my original idea with the tree would have been a way, way better cover. It would have been dead simple to print and looked stunning – but it didn't have the scope for doing the experiments he had in mind. It was conceived in layers – you could see the tree and you could see creatures in it, you could see a wooden staircase in it winding down below the foliage and I had an idea of how it would open up. I made some allowance for a cut-out, but it still worked as a painting – as opposed to what happened, which was we put all the emphasis on the cut-outs and the montage.

'You had to treat it very gently – you can't really slide it on a shelf next to other record covers without damaging the flaps – it's a real pain in the arse, though it's not like *Sticky Fingers*, which will do damage to other covers! It was an era of experimentation, but what killed this, surprisingly, wasn't the arrival of CDs, but a world-wide paper shortage in around 1973 or 1974; after that you didn't get these incredible experiments and the era of gatefolds ended.'

Ivan has now grown to like the design, though it caused some controversy in reviews: *Melody Maker* called it a 'weird, uncontrollable sleeve.' The Tims are unrepentant. Goulding: 'I still loathe it, as much for the flaps as the Aer Lingus Kelly green and illegible typography.' Booth: 'I hated the cover from first sight. This piece did not work as a vinyl storage system – the stupid flaps tore off when you slid it into a rack of LPs. This was justified by use of the flaps as props to display the album in shop windows – a self-supporting system – other bands must have been so jealous... It would have been good to meet Roger and discuss concepts, but the art director at Vertigo knew best and we were kept apart most cruelly, I think.'

These days, *Heavy Petting* is one of *Record Collector*'s 100 most collectable progressive albums; in theory, mint copies can fetch up to £1,000, though the usual rate looks to be around £300. It's now in danger of becoming one of those albums that is better known for its sleeve than the music contained on it.

When *Heavy Petting* was re-released by Hux, Booth did some new artwork for the digipack, featuring images of time delivering a handstand and many other lyrics.

## 'The counterculture is in our midst, my fellow Irishmen' – the album

Ballad Of The Wasps starts Side One, heralding the new, tighter approach; it endures in the Strangelies' repertoire to this day. Summer Breeze is the first electric track, its impact increased by the new defiance in Booth's vocal. Like Sign On My Mind, Ivan's Kilmanoyadd Stomp dates back to the *Kip Of The Serenes* era. Here, he manages to make his harmonium part swing, no mean feat. Though harking back to *Kip* in overall feel, Goulding's I Will Lift Up Mine Eyes showcases a level of polish in the massed harmony vocals which again demonstrates that, after more than a year on the road, the band had honed their act. Ivan's outstanding Sign On My Mind is distinguished by Gary Moore's guitar solo, which starts quietly and spirals into nirvana, with a beautiful sense of dynamics. Gave My Love An Apple starts with a brief quote from Tennessee Waltz, in Booth's view 'the acceptable face of schlock country.' It's another electric track and, as he says, 'it rocks a tad.' Ivan's ultra-fey Jove Was At Home and his When Adam Delved instrumental sit a little awkwardly in *Heavy Petting*'s new, edgier context. Booth's Ashling is also old-style acoustic Strangelies, even featuring Linus, but its haunting quality echoes Sign On My Mind, making it somehow work here. Goulding's Mary Malone Of Moscow brings the listener back into electric folk mode, with some strong Gary Moore acid guitar, and Goodnight My Friends provides a suitably valedictory close to the record.

Press reviews of the album were better than for *Kip*; it attracted a certain amount of acclaim in *Melody Maker*, who enthused that 'the band have added some much-needed bite into their barnyard folk' and declared it 'an excellent album for those with a little imagination.' *Record Mirror* judged it 'pretty and well-constructed,' while *Disc & Music Echo*'s verdict was: 'Interesting and entertaining. It holds your attention because you never know what's going to come next.' Music journalist Andrew Means engaged with the album in more detail: 'It adds drums and creates a wonderfully mad form of folk-rock, including vocals in an old-fashioned folk style and plenty of organic instrumentation (recorders, bouzouki, mandolin etc). But the real plus is the combination of quirky songwriting with genuine rock and blues strength. There's a lot of personality and plenty of surprises here. It's the kind of experimentation that leads to something like Gave My Love An Apple, a song with a million tempo changes and stylistic shifts that just plain shouldn't work, but ends up being exhilarating. I find this album more satisfying than anything by the Incredible String Band – and the long guitar solo and powerful drumming on Sign On My Mind are worthy of *Unhalfbricking*.'

Home in Dublin, much closer attention was paid to this new release by a local band. A review feature in *The Irish Times* starts by announcing grandly: 'The counterculture is in our midst, my fellow Irishmen.' The writer dismisses the tired old comparison with the ISB which the Strangelies often encountered, explaining that their songs had 'none of the weighty religious imagery' of the ISB and that the band worked 'in a much lighter vein.' Sign On My Mind's 'plangent penny whistle' and 'nicely built guitar solo' are singled out for praise. Goulding's 'whimsical hymn' (I Will Lift Up Mine Eyes) gets a mention, but Mary Malone is his 'main achievement, a celebration of the Dublin graffiti master which attains an apt musical equivalent to the cryptic lunacy of its subject and is surely the best song on the album.' Booth comes out less well, though. Despite a positive mention of Gave My Love An Apple, Ashling is 'rather dull and there is an uncertainty of tone in it.' The piece ends by commenting that the band are 'rather tentative about their humour as yet, like a shy person making a pun... Perhaps to cover this up they have given the album the wildly inappropriate title of *Heavy Petting*.'

So, with nearly 50 years of hindsight, where does *Heavy Petting* fit into the psych-folk panoply? With this album (and *Kip Of The Serenes* before it), *Electric Eden* author Rob Young considers that the Strangelies were presiding over the slightly belated birth of a psychedelic Ireland. No one else was really merging folk-based material with loud blues-based guitar solos, certainly not in Ireland; even the UK's Fairport Convention tended to opt for a more modal approach. The medieval and baroque elements echo the work Shirley and Dolly Collins did with David Munrow and the Early Music Consort on *Anthems In Eden,* as well as Dolly's flute organ arrangements on a couple of ISB tracks, notably God Dog. There are three songs with hymn-like qualities: Jove Was At Home and Lift Up Mine Eyes arguably mirror the Watersons' fondness for Vaughan Williams' revision of the English hymnal, while Goodnight My Friends shares a common affinity for spirituals with the ISB's covers of Bid You Goodnight (in A Very Cellular Song) and Take Your Burden To The Lord.

Finally, what better song to capture the 1970 zeitgeist than Sign On My Mind? In *Beautiful Day*, a 2005 book on Irish rock, writer Gerry Smyth picked Sign On My Mind as the song that encapsulated 1970, and made some very perceptive comments:

'Eight minutes and 45 seconds that communicate more about the late hippy period than volumes of scholarly research ever could. The lyric concerns... perception, its possibilities and, more insistently, its limitations... An extended penny whistle solo functions as a prelude to the track's true tragic voice, Gary Moore's weeping guitar solo... Growing in complexity with each passing bar, Moore's contribution perfectly complements the mood of regret and melancholy created by Pawle's lyric and the band's plaintive ensemble performance… [The song] stands as a fitting valediction to a decade of awakening and promise: it's been a blast, the lyrics seem to say, but now we have to come down, and that's always an odd trip, confused and nostalgic by turns.'

## Common Farm

As part of the increased consideration they were paying to the logistics of being a touring rock band, Strangelies (or Manager Pearce) had organised their own English base in the Essex countryside. Renchi was planning to sell his house in Dalston and it was becoming difficult for the four-piece to find accommodation in London. In October they moved into the attic at Common Farm, an eight-bedroom communal farmhouse in Kersey, north of Colchester. Kersey was a pretty village, well known in those days as home of the thriller writer Hammond Innes, who lived at Ayres End.

Booth: 'We had often stayed in Joe Boyd's place in World's End, but this was less than ideal, both for him and us, so this seemed like a reasonable idea. Which it was, a place to live and practise when not gigging.' Ivan: 'It was not far from the metropolis, handy enough for the Great North Road or whatever they had in those days…'

Moving in was dramatic. Ivan: 'The first night we stayed there, a (presumably disgruntled) neighbour fired a shot from a 12-bore straight at the house from near the perimeter of the front lawn. It was a somewhat unsettling experience.' Booth: 'The crack of the weapon and the smack of impact were almost simultaneous, so the shooter was close to hand. I don't think it was a shotgun, more like a .22 rifle or a powerful pellet gun. It bored through the glass but did not hit the opposite wall. Being dope-smoking hippies, we didn't involve the police. Welcome to Kersey, good Doctors. We never found out who done it, but I like to imagine it was ol' Hammond himself, disgruntled and disgusted at having his little English world invaded by the counterculture.' Neil, though, thinks 'the shot through the window was made by a farmer's son with an air rifle. He probably got bored with the usual rural pursuit of shooting at crows and magpies.'

The connection with the farmhouse was made by old friend Lorraine Sufrin, who was now living there with a large group of students from Essex University, some remembered as Polly, Dennis, Bardi and Zane. Ivan: 'We eventually lost touch with Lorraine, but I'd like to think she maintained the infectiously happy vibe that she always generated. She might have become a teacher, and if she did, she would have inspired her pupils.'

The household ran well on unwritten communal lines. There were regular supply trips to Community Foods, based in a house near the North Circular, and Neil says: 'The menu was brown rice with everything, from day one.' Booth recalls the kitchen: 'A large room with a range on one wall, dissolute presses and cupboards, perhaps a fridge. A sink and draining boards beneath a large window. The walls a frumpish yellow, peeling paint, damp patches and the steel-framed window a grid of small glass panes, one flowering a small bullet hole surrounded by a star of fracture lines.'

There was a living room with couches, and bedrooms upstairs. Strangelies, plus roadie Andy Barton, had 'The Boys' Dorm.' Booth: 'It was one large attic room, with our sleeping bags on the floor, clothes in duffle bags and suitcases. Guitars and amps stacked around the walls.' Neil: 'From autumn to spring The Dorm was not unlike a Scandinavian ice-hotel (albeit cheaper and less salubrious) but once I was warmly settled into my sleeping bag, that was it until late morning. Up at the crack of noon, no less!'

Polly Quick, living there at the time, kept a white rabbit which would occasionally hop about The Dorm. This played havoc with Goulding's mind, as he wasn't fully sure if it was corporeal or a type of *Alice In Wonderland* acid vision, and didn't dare to ask the residents if it was real. Eventually Ivan kindly enquired and confirmed that it was.

The same Boys' Dorm was a source of great hilarity, says Booth, 'when the Common Farm Rabbit crept into Ivan's sleeping bag and peed, leading to the possibility of the next album being titled *A Rabbit Wet My Sleeping Bag*, a Strangely homage to Zappa's *Weasels Ripped My Flesh*, which was to contain such Goulding gems as The Nostril Variations and Sparky Bought It In The Latrines.' Neil believes 'we finally honed the title to *Rabbits Wet My Sack*.' The pieces, believe it or not, were real. Ivan: 'The Nostril Variations and Sparky are both short instrumentals. Sparky came about from an amplifier making some frightening analogue noises at an inopportune moment, evoking the Somme. Nostril revolves around a bebop-type riff discovered by Goulding when we were still in London.' Goulding: 'The riff tapered off into some fake bass and vibraphone pastiche and lasted for a very short span as we couldn't keep it up... Well, Ivan could!'

Polly remembers little of the band's time there. Most of the farm inhabitants were students at Essex University, not really part of the then growing commune movement but 'just a bunch of students looking for a cheap place to live.' She, on the other hand, had a day job working as a primary school teacher some distance away. She would be up at six to walk to Kersey, hitch to Hadley and on by bus to Belchamp St Paul, then home by seven and early to bed. The band, in contrast, would often be coming in at three in the morning after getting back from a gig.

As a farmer's son, comparing it with the rich Kildare grasslands, Booth found the farm itself 'a depressing place, marooned in large fields which had been stripped of their hedgerows to facilitate modern crop farming methods. Acres of stubble in rolling waves. Autumnal burning. Smoke rolling across the abandoned farmyard, red pantiles missing from the barn roof, rusting machinery, clogged drains, the occasional walk across frosty rutted tracks, birds flying south across swollen enflamed sunsets.'

Common Farm vignette – Tim Booth, from memory

Neil: 'We often used to go into the village and local town for a pint or two, where I had a memorable 21st birthday session.' Finding Hammond Innes became a minor obsession. Booth: 'We were normally gigging at the weekends, so our down time was during the week. We used to go into Kersey, looking for The Hammond. A dark brooding presence, sitting at a corner window of a wainscoted village house – the whole place looked like a "ye olde England" film set – was our best bet.' Goulding: 'I remember him at the window of a building that fronts the street near The Splash, a small ford.' They never actually met him.

Though this book's acid consultant says the following tale is 'chemically impossible,' Booth vividly re-members one particular lysergic experience on the farm: 'Apart from practising, the rest of our downtime was curiously misspent. One day a sinister cap of acid was produced by a nameless and blameless personage. Quiv-ering with psychedelic anticipation, we carefully opened the capsule and divided the glittering contents into three, which we ingested. Those days – and perhaps even more so these days – street acid was cut with speed.' Speed was used mainly because it gave a bit of forward motion to pure acid, as otherwise it could stretch seconds into centuries, which not everyone liked.

Booth: 'The chemical formula was "hooked" on to strychnine molecules to hold the whole dodgy thing together for distribution. As luck would have it, I got the LSD and was soon gambolling about with the lambs, Ivan got the speed and began to tidy the kitchen, to the astonishment of the women, and Goulding – God be good to him – got the strychnine which manifested as severe stomach cramping. He took to his sleeping bag, curled foetally. Ivan swept the carpets before turning his attention to the windows, and I contemplated eternity with Frankie Lee, all of us watched incredulously by a bemused Neil. Next day we were on the road again. Ivan was not allowed to drive.'

The plan was to stay at the farm till Christmas, they told the music press in an October interview. 'After all,' said Goulding, 'the band rests for two-thirds of the year. You need that or you start writing songs about mo-torway cafes.' Baling out was already on his mind.

Life at Common Farm was nothing like that at the earlier Orphanages; probably, everyone involved had moved on too far individually for this to be possible, anyway. Though Goulding remembers this era as 'idyllic English country life with a seething den of hippies in a large farmhouse down the road,' Booth says that 'it was a brave experiment, but I was not sad to see the back of it. Kersey village was conservative, twee, as if lifted from a chocolate box lid, a place where we were unwelcome.' Ivan: 'It was a genial bunch at the farm, and it did suit as a place to sleep and eat and practise. However, of all the places the band was based, Kersey, despite the picturesque water splash and the gunfire, was quite bland; I found Rotterdam [in 1971] and Lots Road much more stimulating.'

# CHAPTER 7

# 'Let there be no panic' – Goulding bales out

After a few more warm-up gigs, including one at Les Cousins and a shared gig with Fotheringay in Southampton, the band were ready to move forward.

## In Concert

On 22nd October, they recorded an *In Concert* show for Radio One, hosted by John Peel at the Paris Theatre, Lower Regent Street. It was a double bill, with James Taylor headlining, and his then girlfriend Joni Mitchell was in the audience. The official BBC recording is yet to surface, but a much-bootlegged off-air 30-minute tape reveals a band at the top of their game, still quirky but with Neil Hopwood adding some authoritative percussion, plus some confident three-part harmonies from Ivan and the Tims.

Frosty Mornings is the opener, slightly revamped since the original recording. Neil adds some delicate brushes. A line from a Henry McCullough song is tacked on as a coda: 'There I go with you behind and I'm still following you.' The then unreleased Horse Of A Different Hue is very much like the studio recording which they made a few days later, complete with 'sock it to me' backing vocals by Ivan and Booth. It was for years known as 'Long Pig' (from a line in the lyrics) until its eventual release 37 years later cleared up the matter. Ivan plays electric guitar, Booth is on bass, there are some great backing vocals and Neil plays kit.

Neil: 'I don't remember a lot about the concert, although I would have had my trusty oyster-blue Trixon kit up on stage. At a later gig I vividly remember John Martyn incessantly banging away on it before a sound-check, and having to grab him round the neck to get him off it. We both ended up rolling on the stage floor in hysterical laughter, but that's another story.'

After a dodgy joke about Horse, Peel announces West Cork Hack as having first been performed to a local police sergeant in West Cork (he'd done his homework). The Howson Phonofiddle makes a live reappearance, Neil plays bongos and the Shadow Of Your Smile quote at the end, heard on the 1970 Les Cousins tape, has been retained. The harmonium and percussion combo give a swing to the song which was absent on the original recording. Peel introduces the band and mentions the 'amazing auto-destructive sleeve' of *Heavy Petting* as an intro to Ballad Of The Wasps. Goulding tells the listeners it's 'a cautionary tale, an anti-drugs song.' Some chance. Ivan is on mandolin and Neil is back on brushes for this, and again it flows along nicely. After another dodgy Peel joke (about American Indians), Sweet Red Rape, another song destined to remain unreleased till 2007, closes the set. Ivan plays some groovy electric lead guitar, Goulding piano and organ, and Neil is on bongos. There's an instrumental section towards the end where Goulding manages to quote from both Do Ye Ken John Peel (!) and Donnybrook Fair. Judging by the applause, the set goes down well with the audience. 'It's nice to have a group that laughs and smiles so much when they play,' says Peel.

The band gained an influential fan. Booth: 'When we came down to the stage to load out our gear after the show, Joni Mitchell was sitting at the harmonium, playing and singing Horse Of A Different Hue, following Goulding's chord chart but singing a completely different melody of her own. She thought it a great title for a song and told him the lyrics were "so quaint." She was lovely, but before we could really talk with her a strung-out, uptight Sweet Baby James dragged her away with a curt, "Joanie – we're outta here." Needless to say, I went off him. Bigly.'

The concert was broadcast by the BBC on 1ˢᵗ November.

A few days later there was a return to Sound Techniques, with Roger Mayer producing, recording four tracks for a projected third album – the so-called Rabbit sessions. By this point Witchseason was in some disarray and 'it was a very disorganised period; we were slotting into whatever time was available,' says Roger.

Neil: 'This was my first recording session at a proper studio! Excited indeed. This was the home of some of my favourite musicians: ISB, Fairport, John Martyn et al.' The addition of drums and percussion meant the band were tightening up their playing, and 'Horse From Rio,' as it was known at this point, now included a percussion-heavy 'Latin' intro, written after sharing the bill with Santana at the Lyceum Ballroom. Ivan's updated version of Cock-A-Doodle-Doo swings along pleasantly but his Lady Of The Glen is, frankly, uninspired; he was starting to lose his way as a songwriter. According to the music press at the time, they 'passionately' wanted a hit single, and so Roger mixed down an edited version of Lady for potential release and chart fame. At the end of the sessions, the band made another attempt at Sweet Red Rape, with drumkit and without pingpong bats. They ran out of time before Booth could add a definitive vocal track; recording approaches had changed as the studio developed use of their 8-track deck, and so now tended to start with guide vocals only. When Joe Boyd left for the States, the free use of studio time at Sound Techniques came to an abrupt end and the Rabbit sessions were forgotten about until they emerged from their burrow in 2007.

Around the same time, the band went to Olympic Studio to join Heather Wood on backing vocals for Spirit Beautiful, which Mike Heron was recording for his solo LP, *Smiling Men With Bad Reputations*. Neil: 'With a voice like mine, I volunteered to make the coffee, whilst the valiant trio laid down their part.'

Then it was back on tour, starting with Aberystwyth University. Goulding: 'We called this Aberwristwatch. Robert Plant was refused admission to our gig because he had no student card.' Booth: 'After that, we played Keele with the Edgar Broughton Band. They – in their revolutionary wisdom – decided that the newly refurbished common room where they were playing needed "liberating." To this end, they spray-painted the veneers with political slogans and generally trashed the room. Imagine their surprise when, on returning to their parked van after the gig to load out, they discovered that it had been "liberated" as well, the windscreen and side windows painted a revolutionary black with a tough enamel paint. Couldn't have happened to a nicer bunch of lads.'

Marymac, Johanna and Annie joined their respective partners for a string of three northern college gigs in Liverpool, Lancaster and Leeds, creating quite a stir in some quarters. Strangelies fan Nigel Cross was at the Lancaster University concert: 'Pretty good I recall, though the most memorable thing was the weird women that were hanging out with them. Scary feral beings, they were!'

The Leeds Polytechnic gig was another one for the annals. Booth: 'Once Ivan had purchased his Kawai guitar, he developed a stage persona to go with it as "The Jap." He took to wearing a short kimono-type garment on stage [Ivan says it was a Japanese happy coat] with a kamikaze headband, and liked to play barefoot just in case any random escapee bolts of electricity might chance to channel themselves down his legs. We took to introducing him to our audiences as The Jap and talked about him being a failed kamikaze pilot. As you do.' Ivan recalls that 'the organising student had some seriously strong hashish, either Afghan Black or red Lebanese.' This led to an interesting variant on audience participation.

Strangelies fan Nick Brown was in the audience at Leeds: 'I had an incredible experience at the Poly. They handed out small joints to those on the front row, where I was, and played a great set in which they managed to get their new drummer to drink three pints, which they then claimed improved his performance.' Neil: 'It's quite possible. After quitting drinking at the age of 18 I had a bit of a relapse on my first visit to Ireland. Led astray by a nice bunch of chaps, may I add!' Nick: 'I chatted to them in the bar at the interval. Great night. It was the only gig I ever remember dope being handed out! Ivan played the electric guitar with a bow during Sign On My Mind. The Poly was a small venue with cushions and often during breaks the audience threw the cushions at each other. Quite useful, I met one of my girlfriends through that.'

The mention of Ivan's pilot's licence had clearly been noted. Booth: 'After our performance a very intense American invited us back to his place for a chat and a toke. We could see he had something on his mind, but he was surrounded by amazingly nubile young women, so we took a chance. Alarm bells started to ring in my stoner head when I copped the posters on the walls of his gaff. One – an illustration of a young person wearing only a Kalashnikov and bearing the headline "Armed Love" – was particularly appealing. The American took Goulding and me aside for a chat. "Does Ivan still have his pilot's licence?" he enquired. We assured him he did. This was well received and our new friend spent a considerable time between joints with a world atlas and some Victorian dividers, plotting out flight paths and the route Ivan would take when he would fly in a considerable amount of Afghan Black to Leeds airport. We were very pleased to help him in this endeavour, pretending familiarity with both the loading and fuel capacity of the Cessna.' Ivan: 'The student seemed genuinely to believe the story about me having flying experience. The Tims did some fine embellishing and I ran with it as best I could!' Booth: 'In the end, Ivan gave the show away by being too honest with our gullible host and admitting to not ever having had a pilot's qualification. I can't remember how we got away that night, but we did.'

## Goulding decides to leave

On the way back to London, Goulding had some news for the other band members. Neil: 'Things seemed to be progressing well, good gigs, lots of fun, a new album on the way and then, out of the blue, Tim Goulding decided to leave.'

Goulding: 'From this distance in time, it is hard to pinpoint my reasons. The overriding one was that I was no longer enjoying the lifestyle and longed for a quieter life in the country in West Cork. Despite this, our career was, at least, not going downhill and we were becoming quite played in; one couldn't use the term "tight" because that would not be Strangely Strange. The gigs were nearly always exciting and surprising, but the in-between times were becoming tedious and non-productive. The long journeys in the Transit pounding up and down motorways were beginning to get to me and I found that touring was really a form of glorified nocturnal furniture removal.

'This led to the core realisation that I was called to progress my painting career. I always felt that I was a better painter than musician and could respond to the world in a more expansive way in that mode. Oddly enough I never possessed much painting technique but was challenged to seek it out. Never having attended art school, I learned a lot by sitting outside in the landscape painting in a very representational manner, nature being the ultimate master.

'I was also getting more and more into yoga. I used to do an hour of yoga in the morning most days, even on the mail boat, where I managed to stand on my head. Nowadays it's a matter of standing on my feet, preferably on dry land. I was also becoming increasingly interested in Zen Buddhism.

'I was still writing songs at this point, such as Piece Of Cod and Horse Of A Different Hue, but my musical skills were not expanding and I saw myself more as a songwriter than performer. To this day I would like other people to cover my songs, so it was a dream come true when Paula Gomez recorded my song Rivermouth in 2015.

'I had to decide whether to be a painter or musician. I intuited that I was better equipped to be a visual artist, and so decided to leave; since that time, I have ploughed that furrow, interspersed by making music and writing. These days, I am clear that painting, writing and making music all stem from the creative source, the mysterious urge to materialise something or, as Paul Klee said, "to make the invisible visible." My impending marriage to Annie may have had something to do with it, too.'

Goulding's announcement sent the rest of the band into a tailspin. The new line-up was really starting to gel. What's more, Irish and UK dates had already been booked for spring 1971 and an ambitious tour of northern Europe was at the planning stage, taking in Holland, Belgium and France. Ivan was determined to keep calm, though: 'When I was an extra on *Where's Jack?* out at Ardmore Studios, the head of Equity, a Kerryman named Dermot Dooley, used to say: "Let there be no panic." I enjoyed that Hiberno-English turn of phrase.'

Booth: 'When Goulding decided to swan off to do his bit for Art, Ivan and myself understood – in a con-fused kinda way – why he had so chosen. But we were not ready to stop. We had done quite a few gigs with Terry and Gay Woods in the Neptune and other Dublin venues and knew them across the years, or thought we did. We decided – for reasons that now escape me – that they might fit into our set-up.' Things were left fluid for a while, and it was decided that Goulding would stay on for the next batch of gigs.

The touring continued. Booth: 'We had a Lincoln gig where we played for an RAF social event in the squadron's clubroom, up some five flights of stairs with no lift. Somebody had booked us in to the gig as "Los Strangelies" and the pilots were under the impression we were a samba band. We soon put them right. Never in human history has so much been owed to so few by so many…' Goulding: 'On the way home we picked up a squaddie. Being a poverty-stricken outfit, it gave us the idea to be a sponsored band and make recruiting announcements between songs.' Then there was a 'South-West Tour,' probably the first time ever that Strangelies' gigs followed some kind of rational chronology and geographical distribution. At a Barnstaple double bill, according to the band, 'Blodwyn Pig had all their amps turned up to 11.'

Back in London, arrangements for Goulding's replacements were firmed up. Booth: 'Terry and Gay came to a December gig at Chelsea College to check us out. Terry overflowed with enthusiasm, comparing Goulding to Garth Hudson. It seemed to be working… Strangelies had a future. Phew.'

## Terry and Gay Woods agree to join

Following various ructions, Terry and Gay Woods had just left the first version of Steeleye Span which recorded *Hark! The Village Wait*. This album is considered by critics to be the best of all the Steeleye Span releases; Gay's melancholy harmonies and Terry's lamenting vocals and electric guitar are an important part of its strength. They were licking their wounds after an untimely departure, and were up for something different – for the time being, at least. A March 1971 *Melody Maker* interview with the Woods gave some background to their decision to join Ivan and Tim. Terry was hopeful: 'My own music is inclined to be somewhat serious so they can give me humour and wit, whereas their music was inclined to be all humour and wit. I think it will balance out.' He also explained that he and Gay had had hopes of getting their own band together, but first would be 'a Strangelies album [of] our own stuff with maybe one or two traditional things.' In fact, the departure of Joe Boyd and the closure of Witchseason meant a third Strangelies LP was very much up in the air; the Vertigo deal for *Heavy Petting* had been a one-off, and no more studio time could be funded without a record contract.

There was a tension built into the arrangements which was never fully articulated. Tim Booth and Ivan were very keen to develop a Strangelies Mark Two, whereas Gay and Terry's underlying assumption was that this was a temporary, stopgap arrangement. They were already contemplating their own album, as they told *Melody Maker*. Their friend Tony Reeves was in the process of setting up a new record label and had them in mind. At the time, though, it seemed like a good move for all concerned.

Terry Woods (LEFT) with Booth at his art exhibition, 1969

Ivan: 'When we decided to team up with the Woods it seemed a good idea, and pragmatically logical. We were keen to keep going, albeit missing that essential (Goulding) ingredient. Our live performances had changed. Neil Hopwood was as good as they get – good timekeeping, a nice sound, with imaginative fills. Drums needed bass, so that task fell to either Booth or Terry. I bought a small harmonium and electric piano, expecting to take over Tim Goulding's role in the overall sound. Easier said than done! My keyboard skills were in a rather embryonic state.'

Goulding agreed to stay on until January, when a batch of rehearsals was planned in Dublin. In fact, it took even longer than that for him to finally leave the band, perhaps an indication of his mixed feelings. Long-time supporter Steve Peacock was chosen as the band's mouthpiece for the imminent changes; tellingly, Terry and Gay did a separate interview with him before he met Ivan and Booth. Oddly, Steve's published piece in *Sounds* made no specific mention of the line-up plans, hinting only that 'the further development of Dr Strangely Strange will be interesting to watch' and noting the folk-rock transition: 'They've become more like a group, less like a family of wandering players, and their music has probably become easier for audiences to relate to.' Perhaps he'd picked up some underlying unease about the plans. There were clearly some mixed messages going on behind the scenes; in the same week, *Melody Maker* stated unequivocally that Goulding was leaving 'to concentrate on painting' and that Gay and Terry would replace him.

Meanwhile, it was still business as usual. After being stopped by the police seven times on the way back to Common Farm from another Implosion gig, the four-piece headed off to Holland and a further encounter with the law.

## Dutch mini-tour, December 1970

The band's first gigs abroad were down to an enterprising young Dutchman called Frank van der Meijden. In 1970, he'd left his job in education, and decided to become a booker and start a progressive rock club, Exit, in Rotterdam. Frank: 'They had nothing else really like it in Rotterdam then.' He ran it together with a friend called Berry Visser, who had a social work background, but had quickly moved into being a music promoter. Berry had put on Dutch gigs by The Flying Burrito Brothers, amongst others, but had then been declared bankrupt after running the first ever Dutch music festival in 1970. This was Holland Pop, later better known as Kralingen. Frank fronted up the promotion work as Berry couldn't operate under his own banner.

In summer 1970, Frank had come over to London and made some initial contacts with UK booking agencies, including Blackhill Enterprises; Spirogyra, a Blackhill act, was his first ever Dutch booking. He already owned and liked both Strangelies LPs, so when Julia Creasey offered him the chance to put them on in Holland, he was keen to set up some December Rotterdam and Amsterdam gigs as a try-out for a bigger tour.

The plan was to keep costs down by having the band to stay with him and his wife Jacqueline in their large flat on the ninth floor of a tower block at Prikkorf, in the Hoogvliet area of Rotterdam. It later became both famous and notorious as a stopover for bands on tour in Holland. Once the Strangelies had arrived via ferry from Harwich, they had to get to Frank's, but things didn't run to plan.

Booth: 'Exit was in the centre of the city in a maze of old twisty streets. Frank was going to meet us there and then guide us to his flat, but when we couldn't find the club it seemed like a sensible idea to pull over and ask a policeman. He didn't like the look of us and demanded to see our documents. Still not satisfied, he asked us to accompany him to the station. We had no choice and we were very thoroughly handled, searched, questioned and documented. The interview room had glass panels set into the top half of the walls,

# DR. STRANGELY STRANGE

Op woensdag 9 december komt de Ierse groep Dr. Strangely Strange in EXIT spelen. De formatie bestaat uit Ivan Pawle (gitaar-zang), Tim Booth (gitaar-zang), Tim Goulding (mondorgel-blokfluit) en Neil Wood (drums).

De groep, die in Ierse steden als Dublin en Cork behoorlijk populair is, is over het publiek daar niet zo best te spreken. Een verhuizing naar Londen (in navolging van Van Morrisons groep Them uit Belfast) lijkt voor de hand te liggen, maar de vier willen voorlopig liever in Ierland blijven wonen waar ze... teksten voor hun nummers ontlenen aan door een soort dorpsgek op Dublinse huizen met krijt aangebrachte kreten. In derdaad, heel Vreemd.

An odd little local newspaper article advertising the Exit gig, explaining how DSS lyrics were transmitted from Lee via chalked messages on Dublin walls and crediting Goulding as the band's 'harmonica' player.

of an almost Victorian design, the glass set into chipped and wounded white-painted wood. They did not find any drugs, but neither did they find any money – as Steve Pearce, who was travelling separately, had it all – so we were all arrested for vagrancy. Pearce had to do some fast talking to get us sprung in time for the gig.'

As fairly usual, the band remember nothing of the concert, but they were all struck by the unusual Paternoster lifts in the police station. Booth: 'They moved continuously, never stopping between floors, and you had to step on or off the moving platform which was contained by brown wood walls like a large coffin.' Frank was blissfully unaware of the whole drama and only found out about it later.

By this point, Goulding was seriously into the calming powers of meditation and yoga as he pondered his new future. This earned him much derision from Steve Pearce. Ivan: 'We were in Frank and Jacqui's flat when Steve said: "I'll show you how it goes." There followed a twenty-minute exhibition of proto-breakdancing: the living room was quite spacious and Steve treated us to an extraordinarily invigorating display of tumbling and turning, stretching and leaping, bounding and rebounding. It was a wonderfully creative performance which left us all agape.' Goulding: 'It put Groucho Marx in the shade!'

The following day, Frank and Berry were promoting a Frank Zappa and The Mothers gig at the De Doelen concert hall in Rotterdam, and invited the band along. Booth: 'We were front row seated, thanks to Berry. We had parked our wagon close to Zappa's tour bus on his instructions and when we emerged from an excellent gig (Flo and Eddie from The Turtles on immaculate backing vocals) the band had already pulled out, leaving a bunch of really strangely strange and oddly normally frustrated groupies in their wake. When they saw us climbing aboard our van, they descended upon us: "Look gurlz, anozer band!" The dictionary definition of a ravening horde... We were lucky to escape with our lives, although next morning both Goulding and Ivan appeared to have been cruelly bitten in the soft tissues of the lower neck...' Ivan contests this.

Goulding: 'One of the best gigs of my lifetime. Frank conducted his orchestra with an eagle eye. Key changes every twenty seconds. Harmonies to die for and totally zany content. Controlled hysteria.' Neil adds: 'Quite a cultural weekend as we also attended the Salvador Dalí exhibition in Rotterdam.'

After that there were two gigs at the legendary Paradiso, an old church turned hippy concert venue in Amsterdam. The first night was a shared bill with Spirogyra, the second with Sam Gopal's Cosmosis. Booth: 'It was a weird gig. The audience, most of them lying on mattresses on the floor, did not respond, but when we came off stage we were told over and over just how "far out man" we had been. They were way too cool or stoned to applaud; they were singularly zonked and stared open-mouthed and expressionlessly at us, or so we thought. In fact, they were watching a pornographic movie projected behind Ivan's head which featured a woman getting it on with a donkey.' Goulding: 'Ivan looked over his shoulder and quickly looked back to attend to a medieval riff he was attempting. Booth and I were in stitches.'

Booth: 'We went to the bar after the performance and were in the throes of negotiating a small drug deal – we were buying – when some loud and drunken American soldiers started giving everyone a hard time about the length of our hair. It was unpleasant as these guys were violent skin-headed fuckers. As the confrontation mounted, I noticed one of the Dutch dealers going to the wall phone and making a quick call. The cops arrived a moment later and my paranoia levels red-lined, but instead of arresting us peaceable drug-dealing hippies, they arrested the bigoted pinheaded military yo-yos. Dutch justice, Seventies style.'

They also acquired a new fan from Denmark. Booth: 'It was at the Paradiso gig where we first met Lars-Erik Ejlers. He spent the entire set with his elbows on the edge of the stage (which was at just the right height to allow this) gazing at us with complete devotion. He liked us so much he came back the following evening. Manager Pearce soon spotted him as a likely fan, and by the end of the performance, a Danish tour was in the offing.' Lars-Erik's proposition was simple: 'Just come to Denmark. I'll take care of everything.'

The band quickly built up a good relationship with Frank, who firmed up a full Dutch tour for the following spring. He too was given the ritual Strangelies nickname, conferred by Ivan: 'Met-Frank' – his phone greeting. Other new band nicknames had appeared: after having to provide his passport for Steve Pearce, Neil's secret was out, so he was immediately baptised 'Hoppy.' 'Ivan often amused himself by calling me Hotchkiss with a Japanese accent.' Ivan, meanwhile, had accumulated a whole string of nicknames, including Evans and Sven. Booth was The Beast.

After the Paradiso gigs, there was some hanging out in Amsterdam, where one night back at the hotel Ivan jammed on harmonium with Sam Gopal, and the whole band went to the TV studios to watch Jon Hiseman's Colosseum taping a show. Then it was back by ferry to Harwich, and the more mundane setting of The Boys' Dorm at Common Farm.

After the last gig of the year, at a Manchester FE college, the Tims went back to Ireland for a break. Ivan headed up to Edinburgh on the train and on to No 8, Glen Row to rejoin Marymac and Niamh. Ivan: 'I arrived late in Edinburgh and stayed at an authentic doss-house called "The People's Palace." It was cold and miserable and fairly degrading: loud snoring prevented me from falling asleep, so I headed off around dawn and hitched down to Innerleithen. There was a great creative vibe going on at the Row, but I didn't feel myself totally part of it all. I think it was mostly the Scientology that didn't suit.'

The Row was becoming increasingly permeated by Scientology beliefs and practices, and not all the residents were happy with this. Some just kept their heads down, and Rakis was never into it at all, but Rose Simpson in particular was contemplating leaving both the ISB and the Row. Ivan went to a couple of parties which took the edge off the new regime: one for Mike Heron's birthday, and one to celebrate Robin's marriage to Janet Shankman. Ivan: 'Robin and Janet's party was a joyous occasion in the community hall that was part of the estate. Finbar Furey, who was living near Innerleithen at the time, was invited, and he played the pipes and sang a couple of songs.' Ivan missed the annual new year bash at The Big House, where 'The Laird,' Colin Tennant, would get the Glen Rowers to put on a pantomime for his guests. Princess Margaret was an occasional visitor and one year, Rakis memorably took the floor with her for The Gay Gordons.

At some point between Christmas and new year, Rose made up her mind. Rose: 'By the end of what turned out to be my final US tour with the ISB, Mike, Robin and Licorice were absolutely committed to Scientology and, without actually confronting me about it, had made it clear that things couldn't go on as they were. I had to join them wholeheartedly in the Scientological endeavour, share their enthusiasm for it and embrace the lifestyle it demanded. We all went back to Scotland for Christmas together but I was miserable with the whole state of affairs, and tormented by the insecurity of a whole life now hanging on a belief system which I disliked. I couldn't see any way out of it except a whole change of life, so I walked out on all of it before a new year got going and carried me along with it. I don't think anyone, not even me, knew I was going to leave. In the same way I had drifted into the ISB, it just happened. I didn't discuss it or notify them, just went. If Joe Boyd had been around, I would have talked to him, but he wasn't... I tried to never look back and, in general, I succeeded.'

# CHAPTER 8

# Ivan gets a job offer: 'It was one of the hardest decisions I have ever had to make'

In early January 1971, the band met up in Dublin with Terry and Gay for ten days of rehearsals. To ease the transition, the plan was to play nine Irish dates as a six-piece.

Booth: 'Things seemed to go well. Through our old friend Jimmy Corrigan, who ran the Neptune, we hired the clubhouse to rehearse. This was good. We could set up the PA, the drums etc and just do it. On the second day, early in the morning, about eleven, Terry asked Ivan and myself to roll a joint as he thought it might go well with the coffee we were about to have in our mid-morning break. This was unusual, as Terry was not a big doper. However, as he was quite insistent, I obliged, and as I lit up, the door burst open and a huge motorcycle cop emerged into the room shouting, "This is a bust!" It wasn't. It was a T and G Woods joke. The cop was a real cop, but as he took off his armour, he became a normal human again, and once my heart had stopped its alarming, he turned out to be nice enough, and not about to bust us at all, rather to listen and comment on the rehearsals. Terry and Gay were greatly amused at the jape. I was not. But later on, at one of our first gigs as the new Strangelies, on the stage of Liberty Hall, I got my revenge.'

The Dublin journalist Terry O'Sullivan wrote for the *Evening Press*, then a hugely successful paper. He was known as the 'king of the social circuit' in Ireland and his gossip column, Dubliner's Diary, was required reading for many. Steve Pearce invited him along to the Neptune to report on one of the rehearsals. The published piece made only one, enigmatic, comment about the Strangelies' new musical direction: 'Gentle and delicate sounds, almost like Winnie The Pooh.' O'Sullivan was a serious alcoholic, notorious for getting through a bottle of whiskey a night, which may have had something to do with his perceptions.

EVENING PRESS THURSDAY, JANUARY 7 1971

Rehearsing for their tour are the "Dr. Strangely Strange" group, Neil Hopwood, Gay Woods, Terry Woods, Tim Booth and Ivan Pawle.

In the middle of all this, there came a brief point where the Strangelies could have been down to only one original member. The ISB had slowly realised that Rose wasn't going to come back, either to Glen Row or to the band. Rose: 'I don't quite know how the information got through to them, probably via their personal manager Susie Watson-Taylor who, like Joe, was someone I would talk to a bit.' The ISB had a spring tour lined up and, just like the Strangelies before them, desperately needed a replacement. Ivan, a friend of theirs for years and a good all-round musician, was the obvious choice. One evening at the Sandymount Orphanage, Ivan was called to the phone.

Ivan: 'After we had started rehearsing, I got a call – I think it was from Mike Heron – asking would I be interested in joining the ISB to replace Rose. I was seriously torn, but the fact was that I had already agreed to the Terry and Gay arrangement. So that's what decided me. I don't believe in what-ifs! It was a difficult choice, one of the hardest decisions I have ever had to make. But, there you go. In retrospect it was probably the right choice.'

The subsequent concert tour, in the north and south of the island of Ireland, seemed to go well. The reaction was good, Tim and Ivan told Steve Peacock, though 'a lot of people remembered Terry from Sweeney's Men, so [we] got the odd shout for Pretty Polly and other old Sweeney's numbers.' Cork rock band Gaslight played support, and bassist Bill O'Brien remembers: 'I think that we may have been a bit too rock for the situation, but we were big fans and thought that [the Strangelies] were great, although what Gay and Terry were doing there, I still don't know.' Goulding met his teenage fans in Limerick again, and Hoppy had an odd encounter at the Revolution Club in Galway: 'Whilst on stage and halfway through a ditty, someone beckoned me from the side of the stage. I went over to him and he asked me, "Do you like The Equals? They should have played here last week." I returned to the drum kit, and carried on playing, slightly bewildered.'

At the Dublin concert in Liberty Hall, Booth got his revenge for the fake bust incident: 'I got to watch as Hoppy pushed a custard pie into Terry's face – as a Laurel and Hardy type of thing. The custard went all over his Gibson SG. I think he appreciated it as much as I appreciated the false Neptune bust.' Booth told *Sounds* at the time: 'He was doing this idiot guitar solo, biting it with his teeth and getting a lot of feedback. The Irish audience were taking it really seriously, solemnly applauding at the end of it. Terry was dancing about saying, "Did you like it, did you, will I do it again?" when Hoppy got up from his drumkit with the custard pie. There was a sort of stunned silence from most of the people, who thought it was a gesture in the face of an ex-member of Sweeney's Men.' Hoppy: 'We had tried to get Terry to wear a dog's head (as no horses' heads were available at the time) but he was seriously concerned that Luke Kelly of The Dubliners might be in the audience, much to his embarrassment. To be fair, though, he was in on the custard pie jape, as was Gay, whose mum had made it the night before. I don't think he was expecting it to be thrown with such gusto.'

There were two more UK gigs as a six-piece before Goulding finally bowed out. Strangelies fan Raymond Greenoaken caught his final gig at Newcastle University on a bill that was headed by Steeleye Span. Raymond's verdict at the time was recorded in his diary: 'Predominantly electric but utterly excellent.'

Raymond: 'They played very little I was familiar with – Mary Malone, Summer Breeze, and they might also have done Gave My Love An Apple and Roy Rogers. As for the unfamiliar stuff, titles that stuck in my mind were Lady Of The Glen and Piece Of Cod. I recall they did Cruel Mother, an unaccompanied trad ballad: Gay stopped them a few bars in and made them start again. Other memories? As far as I can determine at this distance in time, Terry Woods was more or less sober throughout. Don't remember seeing the Woods around the place during the Steeleye set though, which would figure. Afterwards I corralled Goulding and grilled him on his future plans. I've no recollection what he said, other than that he spoke approvingly of my hand-drawn "Be Aware" lapel badge. Given his destination, it's no wonder he approved of it.'

After the Newcastle gig, Goulding headed straight off to a Scottish Tibetan Buddhist centre to get his head together, in the parlance of the times. He says: 'I remember feeling guilty about leaving the lads and really missed the musical interactions and the bizarre adventures that accompanied them. My harmonium lived on, though; it was eventually redeployed to Afro Celt Sound System and now lives in Iarla Ó Lionáird's studio. From this point on I rarely played piano, and for many years didn't have one, but continued to play the tin whistle, the instrument I find most expressive, despite not playing in the traditional mode.'

## Samye Ling

....................................................................................................

*'In the end my addiction to Dr Strangely Strange is rooted in the stretching of poetry into epiphany. Philosophy and "popular" music is a difficult marriage, but like all good Zen masters (one Strangely became a Zen monk!) humour illuminates as brightly as wisdom.'*

(Genesis Breyer P-Orridge, 2011)

Samye Ling, near Dumfries, was and is a monastery and international centre of Buddhist training, offering instruction in Tibetan Buddhist philosophy and meditation. It had been founded in 1967 by two monks, Akong Tulku Rinpoche and Chogyam Trungpa Rinpoche, both Tibetan refugees. The first Tibetan Buddhist centre to be established in the west, it was named after Samye monastery in Tibet.

In its early days, the monastery was a place of hippy pilgrimage. As Akong Rinpoche once said: 'We didn't have so much spiritual activity – we had hippies.' Quite a few celebrities passed through: as well as actresses Charlotte Rampling and Susan Hampshire, John Lennon, Yoko Ono and Robin Williamson all stopped by in the late Sixties. In 1969 Leonard Cohen studied there for several months while living at Garvald, a house near Samye Ling. He had complained to Chogyam about the broken shutters in his house, which would only open a few inches for ventilation, and was struck by the reply: 'The cracks, is how the light gets in.'

In the same year, David Bowie also spent a lot of time there and seriously considered becoming a thin white monk. He recalled: 'I was a terribly earnest Buddhist at the time... I had stayed in their monastery and was going through all their exams, and yet I had this feeling that it wasn't right for me. I suddenly realised how close it all was: another month and my head would have been shaved.' There were no superstars when Goulding was there, he told one interviewer: 'There was no one of note visiting, but there was a motley crew of serious students, people on a rest cure from a hectic social life in London and one or two burnt-out drugs casualties.'

Interviewed for this book, he says: 'I hardly attended the Tibetan rituals. I spent a month, five hours a day, learning Zazen sitting meditation with a 26-year-old Zen monk called Gendo, a Japanese man who had spent half his life in a monastery in Kyoto. He wore black robes and walked up the aisles between us cross-legged students (we were in agony). If one was to move, he would bow to us and whack us across the shoulders with a bamboo cane. No giggling. The technique was to count the breaths, one to ten, and occasionally we would chant the long Zen Heart Sutra. I managed to draw him outside and I remember persuading him to toboggan down the hill on a tea tray. His life had been very militaristic in the monastery back home and so a bit of tobogganing came as a relief, I think. He gave me a painting by his master in Japan which I still treasure today.

'There was also a wonderful elderly Tibetan monk and artist called Sherab who painted the most vivid Tangkas, in the tradition but brand new. [These are paintings on cotton or silk appliqué, usually depicting a Buddhist deity, scene or mandala.] His eyesight was failing and if not working on his latest Tangka, he was outside conducting ceremonies for feeding hungry ghosts. Pieces of cloth were burned to facilitate this. Apparently the ghosts have very long skinny necks and large tummies, so they are ever hungry. Poor sods.

'It was in the Samye Ling library that I first saw a picture of the great sage Ramana Maharshi (1879-1950). The loving look in his eye has inspired millions since, and I was one. It was maybe 30 years later that I realised the full significance of his teaching and presence: a silent man, who attracted people from all faiths and none, from all over the world, and also wild animals. Somerset Maugham was one of the first westerners to visit him and the last chapter of *The Razor's Edge* speaks of his visit to the master.

'Annie had joined me there and stayed for the full month. I think she attended the morning Tibetan ceremonies but not the stricter Zen sessions. She seemed to tolerate it well. We got married in the Register Office in Lockerbie, and then had a "belsing" on 16th March 1971 in a ceremony for new beginnings by Akong Rinpoche. It was a "belsing" as he could not pronounce "blessing," and took place in the shrine room with honking of horns, clashing of cymbals and the deep guttural muttering of chants interrupted by clearing of the voice, a Tibetan speciality. Sir Basil and Lady Valerie and a few friends and family joined us cross-legged on the floor.

'I came away with unshaven head, knowing very little about Tibetan Buddhism but a tiny bit more about Zen practice. Funnily enough, Polly Quick, from Common Farm, went there not long after me. She remembers staying for two months but not being very involved with the teachings. There was a lovely smiley Tibetan monk who brought her chocolate and said she was a very spiritual person but she hadn't realised it yet. She says she still hasn't.

'I did leave the Strangelies to become more conversant with Buddhism, but as to me becoming a monk, far from it. In fact, my life work has been my life – "a life unexamined is a life not lived." There is a youthful exuberance in our music, which is what Genesis P-Orridge responded to. It was definitely triggered by the sacrament of LSD (Strangelies might call that a Little Sit Down). The marriage of philosophy and popular music is an unlikely one, pioneered by The Incredible String Band; at times it became portentous and somewhat po-faced, but their lyrics also contained some timeless verities. Equally the Strangelies did plough this field, but with a twinkle in their eye. More irreverent. Some of Ivan's lyrics such as Mirror Mirror, Strangely Strange But Oddly

Normal and others allude to the wisdom of the Tao. Some of my lyrics are also in step: I Will Lift Up Mine Eyes, Existence Now and even parts of Ship Of Fools. I think Booth kept us in check with his brilliant lyrics, more socially and literarily aware. My path has been that of a householder but that does not preclude the path of a seeker after truth (whatever the hell that is).'

**A Zen poem**

**I'd like to
Offer something
But in the Zen School
We don't have a single thing**

*Ikkyu, 1394-1481*

# CHAPTER 9

# 'We really expect great things of this band'

After Goulding left, the new line-up kind of worked, for a while at least. The others enjoyed winding up interviewers with ever more fanciful reasons for his departure, including an alleged Goulding plan to travel overland to India by bicycle. Ivan told *Sounds*: 'He's going to do a warm-up lap by cycling around Ireland this summer. However, as yet, he doesn't have a bike, so that might not come off.'

The new line-up – publicity photo

The band started to take rehearsals more seriously: if there were mistakes, they would stop the song and try again. Booth told Steve Peacock: 'We used to just ignore that and... keep on playing though all the mistakes. No one would say anything.' Encouraged by Steve Pearce, Booth had even started having bass lessons from jazz-rock stalwart Tony Reeves, the friend of Terry's who was taking an interest in the revised Strangelies. Ivan commented

DR. STRANGLEY STRANGE     TERRY·GAY·TIM·NEIL·IVAN     FRANCES VAN STADEN PUBL. 01-624-3140

that 'it used to be serious acid music, but it's more serious drinking music now... [and] it's got a lot more Irish. Of course, having a chick singer has changed it a lot – she's very good.'

Booth remembers: 'Gay was – and is – a mighty singer. Rehearsing in the London Arts Lab, we used to send Terry off to score some fish and chips and as soon as he was out the door, launch into You Keep Me Hanging On, or Stay With Me Baby... I remember Terry coming back early, and being shocked by Gay's rock'n'roll wail. "Gay...? Gay...? How could you do this?"'

Ivan compiled a revised setlist for the five-piece. Band politics demanded that it was split fairly equally between the Strangelies and the Woods (see illustration from Ivan's diary). You can see that sometimes the songs were in odd keys like A-flat in order to fit with the concertina, which was half a tone out. Some of the Woods material emerged later on *The Woods Band* album, including Valentia Lament/Apples In Winter and January Snows. Hills of Greenmore was on *Hark! The Village Wait*.

In the new line-up, Ivan played various keyboards and some electric lead guitar, Tim and Terry alternated on bass depending whose song it was, Neil stuck mostly to kit and Terry added electric guitar, mandola, banjo and accordion. Gay sang some powerful harmonies and the occasional lead vocal, and played dulcimer, autoharp and concertina. This involved a lot of instrument-swapping, which could often mean a loss of momentum live. But, initially at least, it was all looking good. *Sounds* reported that Strangelies were 'confident they have finally found a band that will bring together all the threads that they have been spinning out over the past couple of years.' 'We really expect great things of this band,' they told Steve Peacock.

Ivan: 'I enjoyed playing on most of Terry and Gay's material. Gay had/has a beautiful voice. One of their few self-penned songs was Promises Promises which, despite its air of cynical regret (burnt by the music industry), had some good hooks and reminded me of *Volunteers*-era Jefferson Airplane. I admit that I fumbled around an amount trying to get the right chords in some of the traditional tunes – I blush and grimace when I look back.'

## 'For fuck's sake Reg, would you cop yourself on!'

Over the next few weeks, as the band got acclimatised to the new line-up, they shared bills with an intriguing range of acts. At a Dartford gig they played with Magician, who were psychedelic folkies, and Forever More, a precursor of the Average White Band. Bridget St John and Jo Ann Kelly were on the bill with them at Thames Polytechnic, Woolwich. One that stood out for Ivan and Tim was a concert in Stirling supporting Elton John, then still very much a cult figure. Over the years, they had played several gigs with him; at the first one, for a teacher training college in High Wycombe, he had the support slot. The Strangelies maliciously christened him 'Herr Commode.' Booth: 'Commode equals John, and Herr because he was not the easiest... We supported him a number of times as his fame and ego grew exponentially.'

Ivan: 'My most vivid memory of Elton John is the gig in Stirling University where we were probably equal-billed, but his star was in the ascendant while ours was on an opposite trajectory. One was immediately struck by his garb, which included high-heeled silvery boots, a Mr Freedom T-shirt (red stars on a white background) and a pair of hot pants of yellow satin.'

Booth: 'We nearly had to go on twice. Our Reg was obnoxiously late, the student audience were getting restless and a very worried social sec was attempting to negotiate a second appearance by the Doctors when Dwight and band came clumping in their stage gear into the dressing room. It wasn't really a dressing room, it was an old-fashioned lecture theatre with tiered seats, and it wasn't really their stage gear because Elton un-zipped his pale blue star-spangled jumpsuit from neck to crutch and stepped out in an excruciating set of tight leather lace-up thong-type undies, his flab bulging. It was too much for Gay, who was high up in the back of the theatre. "For fuck's sake Reg, would you cop yourself on!" It must have been the Dublin accent. He blushed from his belly up and the band went on stage rather faster than they had perhaps intended. We were gone when they re-emerged.'

There were a couple of gigs at the Traverse Theatre in Edinburgh. Strangelies fan Richard Dingwall was at one, and remembers: 'Robin Williamson (and perhaps Mike Heron) was in the audience. Terry Woods played concertina, which caused some difficulty for the band, since he claimed to have taught himself to play the wrong way round so he was in strange keys.' On the second night, perhaps as a welcome break from his Zazen sitting meditation, Goulding decided to make a surprise reappearance: 'I crept in incognito and got the sound engineer to sneak me a mic in the front row, then joined in on a chorus.'

But, after the first flush of enthusiasm, it wasn't working well with the Woods. These days, Terry Woods is a sober, easy-going elder statesman of Irish acoustic music. In his drinking days, though, he was not always easy company – what the Irish call 'a bollix,' argumentative and quarrelsome. In a later interview, he looked back on this era. By then he had quit alcohol, and told his interviewer that drinking so much had ultimately bored him. There was a time, he admitted, when he was afraid of himself: 'I was as bad and mad as everyone else, and wasn't an easy guy to be around when I was loaded.'

Tim Booth: 'We went on the road together and it occasionally worked. But it was – actually – way too much. Terry and Gay's marriage was breaking up, and this is the main reason Terry was drinking as much as he was, I think. Mind you, talking to him a few years ago, after he'd dried out, he said that his first years in the Pogues were much worse in terms of alcohol consumption: waking up behind a sofa in some New York loft, with no idea of how he got there or where he was, or what had happened in the last week, was an overdue wake-up call. I always liked Terry.' Ivan: 'There was a fair amount of acerbic bickering between them. I don't think too much emphasis should be laid on Terry's drinking, though obviously the mortifying Les Cousins recording is a palpable record of the nadir...'

Hoppy: 'The absorption of Terry and Gay into the band certainly had its ups and downs. That Dublin episode with the cop was disconcerting at first, but then I presumed it to be normal behaviour for jocular Dublin-ers. Although Terry was and is a serious musician, he could also be extremely funny, but I don't think he was really capable of adapting himself into the way that the band had previously worked. Gay's voice was uplifting at times, but the band's quirky and original material was being watered down somewhat. I tried to bridge the gap between the two factions but it was filled by a straggly rope-ladder leading to nowhere land!'

## 'Musical perfectionists - Stay Out!' - live at Les Cousins

The sole recorded evidence of the new alliance doesn't bear out the bright hopes of those involved. A February 1971 set at Les Cousins is a mix of Strangelies songs and later Woods Band material such as Van Diemen's Land. The set, though, is marred by an audibly drunk, rambling and out-of-tune Terry. Lagga was back in the club with his duffle bag and trusty Uher reel-to-reel. The note that accompanied his bootleg said: 'I often issue warnings of my tapes being of not so good sound-quality, but this time I say: musical perfectionists – Stay Out!'

Hoppy: 'We had to set up on an extremely small stage, with not enough room for my bass drum, so I used a suitcase instead.' The set starts well enough with Booth's Ashling. Terry plays mandola, Gay is playing dulcimer and Hoppy is playing bodhran. Lady Of The Glen is introduced by a nervous-sounding Ivan; there are some nice harmonies by Gay, but instruments are starting to go out of tune. Ivan plays electric guitar, with Tim on bass and Hoppy on drums; Terry plays mainly chords on his mandola, briefly leading the band into the traditional jig The Tenpenny Bit before returning to the original song.

Gay sings lead on Promises, later recorded on *The Woods Band*. The backing vocals are fairly raucous and it all sounds a bit Steeleye Span-ish. Ivan on piano, Terry on lead guitar. Summer Breeze is introduced by Booth – 'after the well-known count of four' – with Gay and Ivan on backing vocals. Ivan contributes a waltz-time electric piano solo and Gay plays some autoharp. Greenwood Side: Gay leads on this a cappella traditional song, which turned up later in the Gay and Terry repertoire. It works quite well initially, though some of the harmonies are badly off. Noisy Johnny is a reel by Terry Woods, played on his roundback tenor mandola. It also turned up on *The Woods Band*. Johnny was a Steeleye Span roadie with flatulence issues. 'A very boring song,' one of the band comments at the end. Piece Of Cod, Goulding's bequest, is a much more fully worked out arrangement than the previous live recording. Ivan leads, with Gay and Booth adding harmonies; Terry adds concertina. It works well and segues into a rock section at the end with Gay on lead vocals, plus kit and electric piano.

Time To Know is by Terry – things start to really fall apart here. It's preceded by a lot of embarrassed laughter, and features dreadful out of tune singing. 'It's too heavy to try to do seriously,' says Terry. Gay tells him to crack a few gags and go straight into it. Booth goes into Eurovision Song Contest mode, comments 'We're thinking of renaming the band Terry and The Wogans' and asks for three volunteers to sing with Terry. 'Ireland really needs you for this.' Gets worse. Band soldier on grimly. Gets even worse. 'How do you vote?' asks Booth. 'Terence Woods' song for Ireland has finished.' Much confusion about the next song. 'I Suppose,' says someone. 'We're going to do nothing now,' says Gay, 'cos everybody's too fucking pissed.' Terry is, for sure.

Booth introduces an instrumental as a Carolan tune; it turns out to be Tabhair Dom do Lámh (Give Me Your Hand) by Dall O'Citháin (Blind Roger O'Keane). Cue further embarrassed hesitation. Terry tells the audience: 'Gay is into movies, not music.' Ivan tells a non-story about trying to see the Woodstock movie in Liverpool but failing. Eventually it starts, an uninspired folk-rock treatment: Gay plays concertina, Terry mandola, Tim acoustic guitar, and Ivan harmonium.

Good Times Are Coming, Wait And See is a forgettable Ivan song ('a total failure' – Ivan) with harmonies by Gay; very wobbly. Then follows a rambling intro about tuning and the Marx Brothers by Terry; Ivan is Chico, Booth is Harpo. Van Diemen's Land (trad) has drunken, out of tune vocals by Terry. It turns up on Gay and Terry Woods' *Renowned* LP. You Are So Beautiful Free is another new Ivan song, another 'total failure.' He says: 'I had come up with a nice open (ish) guitar tuning, and it was written for my wife-to-be when I felt our paths might have irrevocably diverged.' Awful vocals by all bar Gay.

Roy Rogers is Booth's song. A creditable version to start with, but sadly Terry joins in at the end and either he or Ivan finishes with some appalling free-form electric guitar. This segues into The Farmer And The Cowman Should Be Friends (Rodgers & Hammerstein). It's kind of all right: Terry sings and plays electric guitar, Ivan is on electric piano, Hoppy on suitcase kit, Gay on autoharp, and Tim is on banjo. The set ends with Lowlands of Holland (trad) from *Hark! The Village Wait*, and then Show Me The Way To Go Home. Yes indeed.

This is probably the second set of the evening, which would have given Terry plenty of time in the bar. The Woods' contributions form about half the set, mainly try-outs of material which later became part of their own recorded repertoire. It is clear that the two factions haven't really melded; though Gay tries her best on some of the Strangelies' songs, Terry has little respect for them. You can see how it might have worked, and possibly did at some points on other nights, but what might have been endearingly ramshackle remains embarrassingly ramshackle. As Ivan says: 'The chemistry wasn't there and the constant changing of instruments meant a certain amount of to-ing and fro-ing, making it hard to establish a consistent overall rhythmic pattern to a gig. Our respective materials didn't gel as we had hoped they would.'

The Strangelies' allies in the music press struggled to come to terms with the new line-up. In a March gig review, Steve Peacock said the set had 'a sense of warmth and friendly enthusiasm' which transcended the sound problems at the event. 'They retain that air of amiable eccentricity that first attracted me to their music; they are tighter than before, and instrumentally and vocally they have a greater range… If their teething problems are sorted out during their current tour of the continent, this summer should see the Strangelies getting the recognition they deserve.' *Melody Maker* suspended judgement: 'Absorbing the varied talents [of the Woods] has left the band pregnant with potential, even though this will take time to develop.' It never did.

The gigs continued, the band sharing bills with such diverse acts as Principal Edwards Magic Theatre, The Kevin Ayers Band (with Mike Oldfield and Lol Coxhill), Curved Air, The Pretty Things, Magna Carta, John Martyn, Bridget St John, Michael Chapman, Steeleye Span and even Ian Whitcomb. There was a sort of Progfest at a Loughborough gig where the Strangelies played alongside High Tide, Egg and Titus Groan.

Towards the end of March there was a quick visit to Ireland for the Wexford Festival Of Living Music. John Peel introduced a folk-dominated bill including Fairport Convention, Tír na nÓg, Principal Edwards Magic

Theatre and The Chieftains. Mellow Candle, the Irish psych-folk successors to the Strangelies, made their second live appearance. They were soon to follow in the Strangelies' footsteps, gigging at Slattery's and becoming mates with Phil Lynott, Andy Irvine and Skid Row. Ted Carroll became their manager. Goulding: 'One word: fey.' DSS travelled from the hotel with the Fairports, and Hoppy remembers 'driving there in convoy, with Dave Mattacks mooning out of the Transit window.'

The reviews were a little muted. Steve Peacock wrote that they opened with 'a number of fine traditional airs… often lost in the anticipation for Fairports.' *Melody Maker*: 'The group is still digesting Terry and Gay Woods, but the improvement since they first joined is vast. Their marriage of traditional and self-composed material can hardly fail to prosper, though [it] still contains rough edges… Gay makes a valuable contribution, especially her dancing, which could well be converted into a solo spot.'

A revitalised Goulding turned up to watch their set. Booth: 'There was a lot of drinking in the hotel post gig. Next morning the night porter was a pale shadow of his former self.'

## Recording with Tony Reeves

Tony Reeves was a bass player who had worked with John Mayall, Colosseum and Greenslade. Booth's bass lessons with him hadn't worked out well, though: 'He laughed at my Vox bass. It was the only time I ever saw him laugh. I did not learn much from him and he learnt next to nothing from me. Which is as it should be.'

That autumn, Tony had announced plans for a new 'prog-oriented' project, a subsidiary of the Chapter One record label which was owned by songwriter Les Reed and licensed through Decca. By spring 1971, when he became more closely involved with the band, this was in active preparation. He was toying with the idea of producing an album with them, though Booth feels he had less interest in the Strangelies as a whole but was much keener on the Woods. In due course Tony did produce *The Woods Band* LP for the new (and short-lived) label, Greenwich Gramophone Co, for which he was 'Creative Director.'

Tony: 'The Strangelies were definitely one of a number of bands I was thinking of taking on to the new label. I can't really remember why it didn't happen, other than The Woods Band might have been a bit more commercial, even though the label was intended to be a bit cutting-edge, the opposite of Les Reed's label.'

Neither Ivan nor Tim got on with Tony particularly well ('I think he had had an empathy bypass,' says Booth) but he did get to produce one long-lost recording by the band, in March 1971. Lars-Erik Ejlers had just popped over to see them to sort out their Danish tour the following month, and the Strangelies had promised him a promotional tape which could be used on Danish radio. It was mostly recorded at their London base, the New Arts Lab, which was a large former factory premises in Robert Street, Camden. As well as being the HQ for John Hopkins' TVX video project, it had a large gallery, a cinema and various rehearsal rooms. Booth: 'We needed a place where we could set up the PA and come and go, and it was affordable.' The date meant that the Woods were away, possibly still in Ireland after playing the Wexford festival, so Reeves recorded a very unusual line-up playing Sign On My Mind: Booth on bass, Ivan on guitar, Hoppy on bongos and, on keyboards and backing vocals, Brian Trench! Brian was living in London at this point and was happy to embark on this very short-lived reformation of the 1968 line-up.

All concerned had completely forgotten about this until nearly 50 years later, when, in the course of researches for this book, Danish music historian Claus Rasmussen turned up a recording of the *Beat-Rapport* programme containing the session. This in turn engendered much band speculation about whether it was actually an original recording from 1968, until Ivan consulted his 1971 diary where all was revealed: 'Sunday 28 March 1971 – Tony Reeves recording + Brian Trench etc.'

Perhaps thankfully, the band eschew any mention of smørrebrød or *Danish Blue*, but start off with a rather sweet whistling version of Danny Kaye's Wonderful Copenhagen. Manager Steve Pearce adds a rambling disquisition on how the group started as 'an anti-group' until Trench pulls him up for logical inconsistency. After a well-executed Sign On My Mind, distinguished by a nifty organ part and some inventive harmonies from Brian, Ivan launches into a mock-academic lecture on the origins of the band's name ('adapted for radio by Ivan Pawle') and then it tails off. The tape, as played on the radio, ends with the album track of Strangely Strange But Oddly Normal. Listening back to the live track now, Tony is dismayed at the 'whimsical attitude towards tuning!' God only knows what the Danish listeners made of this 'Irish folk-beat group' when the clip was aired at the start of the Danish tour. Once the Woods had returned and the band had played a Stockton gig with Michael Chapman and Bridget St John, it was time to load up the Transit for a six-week European tour which finally broke up the band.

# CHAPTER 10

# Northern Europe Tour

The tour was a bold venture. Frank van der Meijden's network of progressive music clubs and venues and a well-developed freak scene in Holland meant the band were assured of a supportive Dutch audience, especially in Rotterdam and Amsterdam. There was no record company support, however, even though the Dutch company Philips owned Vertigo. *Heavy Petting* had only been released in Germany and Holland; *Kip*, as Frank's tour ad points out, was 'niet uit in Nederland.' France, Denmark and Belgium, where the albums were only available on import, if at all, and with no established rock club tour circuit, were pretty much unknown territory.

Goulding's departure and the addition of Terry and Gay had further confused matters, even for those who did know the band already. Very often the gigs were trailered as 'Irish folk-rock.' Frank: 'It was an easy label. We didn't know much about the music then!' Fairport Convention was a folk-rock band most people had heard of, and the revised Strangelies often were misleadingly linked to them. In Denmark they were known as an 'Irish folk-beat group.' A lot of the audience on the tour, then, would have been expecting some kind of sub-Fairports mix of jigs and reels, which played to the Woods' strengths at the expense of Tim and Ivan's songs.

## Holland

The band, plus Manager Pearce and roadie Paul Carter, arrived in early April, again basing themselves in Frank's Hoogvliet flat for the duration of the Dutch tour. On days off, Ivan took to hanging out by the river Maas, behind the flats. He became well known locally for wandering along the river dyke playing his instruments, followed by a gaggle of children, a bespectacled Pied Piper. Frank: 'Parents were concerned about their kids hanging out with this strange longhair – I had to calm them down!' Ivan: 'I preferred Rotterdam to Amsterdam, mostly because it seemed to be peopled by real "working" folk, whereas Amsterdam seemed so determinedly "alternative" to me at that time.'

After a concert in Maasluis at De Toverbal, they played in a tent in Rotterdam. Frank: 'Berry's social work

WEREWOLF
Management and Agency Limited
83 Charlotte Street London W.1
01 636 9436/7/8
Oonagh Karanjia
Anthea Joseph

An **Agreement** made the _____ 5th _____ day of _____ February _____ 197 1
BETWEEN _____ Ton Steenbergen _____ hereinafter called the
Management of the one part, and _____ Steven Pearce _____
hereinafter called the Artiste of the other part.
**Witnesseth** that the Management hereby engages the Artiste and the Artiste
accepts an engagement to present
_____ DR. STRANGELY STRANGE _____
(or in his usual entertainment) at the Dance Hall/Theatre and from the dates for
the periods and at the salaries stated in the schedule hereto.

**SCHEDULE**
The Artiste agrees to appear for _____ one _____ evening performance(s) at
a salary of _____ % of the gross Advance and Door takings.
The Management guarantees a minimum of £90

| VENUE | DATE |
|---|---|
| DE TOVERBAL, Rainastraat, Maassluis. | Sunday 4th April 1971 |

**ADDITIONAL CLAUSES**
1. The Artistes agree to arrive at the venue by 7.00 p.m. and to perform...
2. The management agree to provide suitable and adequate amplification including at least 2 microphones.
3. The management agree to provide suitable and adequate dressing room facilities.
4. Payment to be made to Werewolf Ltd. by cheque within 7 days of the completion of the engagement. artist cash on night

Signature _____

background was useful in getting government subsidies for cultural activities – it was easy then. This was a street gig, part of a demo in a shopping centre.' A benefit for the drug organisation Release in The Hague was followed by a performance at a Rotterdam youth rehabilitation centre, AMVJ. Ivan: 'Musicians from different bands would meet up here for jam sessions, which were often great fun, at least for the performers!' Booth: 'It was a hostel for junkies. I got held up on the stairs by a strung-out weirdo with a knife to my throat, looking for money, so I gave him an Irish pound and he ran off, bearing it aloft as if the fifth secret of Fatima.'

An appearance at the Diogenes student club in Nijmegen preceded a return to the Paradiso club, where they shared the bill with Zangeres Zonder Naam. It was an unusual billing and Frank has no idea how it came about. Maria Servaes-Beij (the real name of Zangeres…) had a camp and faintly kitsch appeal, with a strong gay following, and was somewhat of a Dutch institution.

Ivan: 'She had been like the Dutch Vera Lynn but, since Holland had been occupied by the Nazis, her status was quite different. Her performance was broadcast live, and we felt honoured to be on the same bill.'

The Haarlem Electric Centre gig is fondly remembered. Hoppy: 'Nice little venue... sort of alternative youth club. Lots of Asterix comics lying about for perusal.' Booth: 'We played at various clubs around the country, the best of which was

Frank's Dutch tour ad, featuring both old and new line-ups!

The Electric Centre in Haarlem, which had a restaurant, library and an upstairs smoking room. Good daze.' Several further club gigs were followed by a theatre appearance in Leiden, where the only extant review of the entire Dutch tour appeared in the local paper. The writer, Henk de Kat, was clearly a traddy at heart, regarding Gay and Terry as the musical focus. He was a bit flaky on the band history, too. Here's a translation:

'On their tour through Holland and Denmark the Irish folk band Dr Strangely Strange yesterday also visited Leiden. The Irish five-piece were excited about the intimate character of the Leidse Schouwburg, where this band, consisting of chamber musicians, immediately felt at home.

Until recently Dr Strangely Strange was an often-changing group of three. In that set-up two long-players were recorded. After a guitar-player left, drummer Neil Wood became a steady member, after which, not much later, the married couple Gay & Terry Woods  originally from Fairport Convention  also joined them.

Now a five-piece band, the Doctors have found their way since then. The connection to Fairport Convention is clear when listening to their music, which is light and friendly, but never too overtly cheerful or blatantly sentimental. Dr Strangely Strange has exactly the same credentials as Fairport, but is foremost also 'Irish.' Irish as in traditional material and Irish in their own songs. Even the cheerful songs are pervaded by the melancholy that is typical for that green island. Interestingly enough, and not in conflict with this, is the unexpected humour that is shared with the audience, as well as in the musical discoveries.

During the concert it became clear that Dr Strangely Strange consists of a few very likeable Irish, who on stage regularly took a delicious sip of that awful Dutch beer before playing further. In their playing virtuosity was not their main goal, but it has to be said that they performed extremely well on some instruments like the melancholy sounding concertina (a sort of a seaman's accordion), harmonium, lute [the mandola] and a sitar-like instrument [the dulcimer], all electrically enhanced.

For the Irishmen the hall was just the right agreeable combination between a rowdy bar and an atmospheric concert hall, so it became a very satisfying folk evening. Pity that there were only roughly about 100 people from the Leidse scene present. Although success should not be measured by attendance, the organisers will need more visitors to book more foreign concerts like this.'

After further concerts in Enschede (Theatre Concordia) and De Eland in Delft, there was a triumphant return to Frank and Berry's Exit Club, where they shared the bill with Lindisfarne. Booth: 'A great jam session after setting up, where Hoppy excelled himself on the kit, changing the tuning of his toms by blowing down a rubber tube and altering the internal pressure. Progressive or what?' Hoppy: 'That's right. I was experimenting after hearing some free-form jazz stuff. Terry once remarked that I should have been a plumber rather than a drummer. This may have been a more lucrative vocation in the long run...'

The Dutch tour appears to have been a success; the travelling was bearable and the interminable journeys with seven people crammed into a Transit, the Woods quarrelling in the back, were yet to come. Frank decided to extend the tour and set up some additional Dutch gigs for early May, after two scheduled concerts in Paris, at venues like the Electric Centre where the band had gone down especially well. The band cancelled five or so UK gigs to accommodate this, including a booking at the University of Kent alongside Spirogyra and Michael Chapman. Booth: 'Holland was a great earner for us because the clubs were government-sponsored and always paid up, even if the door was poor.'

After a final Dutch gig in Aalsmeer, there was a long drive up to Hamburg, where a last-minute gig had been fitted in on the way to Denmark. It didn't happen. Booth remembers it like this: 'We were booked to play the Kaiserkeller, a club just off the Reeperbahn in Große Freiheit. It used to be a Beatles hangout. We arrived in the early evening and went in to take a look. A tight and proficient English electric outfit were playing and the audience hated them: an audience composed largely of drunken American servicemen and their women who showed their lack of musical taste by throwing their beer bottles and the occasional chair at the band. Not our sort of place. Accompanied by Steve Pearce, we went backstage to the dressing room to negotiate with the manager. There was a notice in several languages on the wall: "Artists are advised to keep moving at all times while on stage."

'Manager Pearce must have won the cancellation debate, because we didn't play, yet he gave us all a few bob and sent us off into the night to score whatever took our fancy. There was a place called the Eros Centre just across the road, an upmarket bordello way beyond our means. In the underground car park attached to the emporium, Ivan was a big hit with a pretty Fräulein, who told him how she really liked hippies and attempted to entice him with some dope if he would only commission her services. By now he had come to his senses and refused her advances, unaware that Pearce and I were watching his every move from the shadows. And so on into the night. The next morning, I had steak tartare for breakfast. First and last time.'

## Denmark

On 20th April the band arrived in Copenhagen by ferry. The band's Danish admirer, Lars-Erik Ejlers, was a young Copenhagen artist and student of architecture, immersed in the left-field arts and literary scene there. It is easy to see why the anarchic Strangelies, always keen to break the barrier between band and audience, would have appealed to him. When he met the band, he was involved in several art projects. One was 'mail art.' The Fluxus movement, the starting point for artists such as John Cage, Christo and Yoko Ono, saw art as a process of communication. From this had developed mail art, a countercultural rebellion against art as something to be framed and marketed, a loose network of artists opposed to the commercialism and elitist nature of the mainstream art scene. Booth: 'He was involved with a convoluted postcard-sending piece where he would post out

images on cards. He was also a very early graffiti artist in and around Copenhagen, and used to leave a discreet "tag" to indicate his patch. No art on the walls, just a tag. I had a print of an oil painting he did, a crudely rendered but effective set of small images set into a grid, depicting in comic-book form a woman and a chair. It started top left with the woman seated on the chair and culminated bottom right with the woman and chair in ardent sexual congress.'

Lars-Erik (Photo: Hans Christian Poulsen)

Booth remembers Lars-Erik as a striking figure, 'very tall with shoulder-length blond hair and round steel-framed glasses that set off big lips. He gave me a pair of velvet trousers which were surplus to his requirements and I wore them proudly for years. They were pink.'

Lars-Erik had made good his promise at the Paradiso and been very active organising pre-publicity for the tour, with many Strangelies features in the Danish local papers. Unlike the Dutch publicity, these tended to have more of a psych-folk angle, with many comparisons with the ISB and mentions of the band's humour and lightness of touch. '[The band] is both spiritually and musically closely related to the Incredible String Band,' wrote *Aktuelt*, 'but their music is more outgoing. There is no doubt that the very strange Irish doctor will create good vibrations wherever he goes.' The journalist was looking forward to seeing Terry Woods' 'sister' Gay, who 'plays dulcimer, zither, concertina, Spanish goatskin drum, sings and dances jigs (Irish dance).' In the *Berlingske Tidende*, readers were informed that Strangelies 'can be both crazy and beautiful. The group prefer to avoid the ratrace of the heavy concert scene and a whole new pair of organisers have brought them over... They play completely spontaneous folk music, free, lacking constraints – and magical. They have released three [?] albums, but are known to go underground when the fat contracts are on offer... These are musicians who play for love of music, which can be amazing when they are accompanied by Terry and Gay Woods ("It's so nice to be married when you live this way").'

Lars-Erik also garnered a couple of slots on Danish radio's *Beat-Rapport* to promote the gigs. A month or so before the tour, he explained on air how he had come across the band in Amsterdam, really liked them, and had offered to set up some gigs. He had brought in a Danish musicians' co-op called Musik Og Lys [music and light] to help out and to avoid having to charge the high prices bigger agencies would set. If people were interested in putting the band on locally, they were to phone 120148 and ask for Simon. His next interview was a week before the tour, listing the concert dates and mentioning that there would be a couple of days off in between gigs in a Western Jutland summerhouse he'd borrowed for 'sun, time off and making a film.'

'Wonderful, wonderful Copenhagen,' though sunny, was actually a bit windy and cold when the band struggled off the ferry. Booth: 'When we arrived, Lars-Erik threw a great party for us and introduced me to a beautiful Japanese woman – Mariko – with flame hennaed hair and a revealing black and white optical print dress. A great start to our Danish adventures, despite a row between Terry and Gay about the nature of the ingredients in the spaghetti Bolognese on offer on board the ferry. Lars-Erik went out of his way to accommodate and look after us, organised the gigs impeccably and made what was a fairly gruelling schedule very enjoyable by offering the best in hospitality and entertainment on our days off. Denmark was particularly far out. Even Terry and Gay stopped bickering and enjoyed themselves.' The same evening, *Beat-Rapport* broadcast the 'live in the studio' session the band had actually pre-recorded in London.

Although a lot of hard work had gone into organising the tour, the underlying problem was that the band were virtually unknown, with no record out locally to boost attendance. In the course of an April week, Strangelies played virtually the length and breadth of the country, from Nykøbing Falster to Fredericia and Nyborg. A review of the first Danish gig, at the Nykøbing Falster Theatre, was clearly written by a fan: 'Gentle Irish folk music: Dr Strangely Strange Group deserved a more immediate reaction from the audience. Imagine a spring forest. The sun shines in the morning mist, maybe it sparkles in the dew of a spider's web. Gently, but melancholy. There you have Dr Strangely Strange's music in a nutshell. The group played traditional Irish folk music which flirted gently with electrified contemporary music. Beautiful is the only word that covers the experience. Each member of Dr Strangely Strange were virtuosos on their instruments... they interacted with each other. Wonderful.

'Their singing was pure. The voice of female member Gay Woods was youthful and yet powerful when she sang the often-sad songs. Small dance steps showed her engagement with the rocking background of the sometimes "rebellious" dance rhythms. They are not Irish for nothing. Just a shame that the group's words were often drowned in the awful acoustics. Countless calls from Dr Strangely Strange to the audience to dance, clap or just show joy got little response. But there was clapping. Politely. The musicians had deserved something else. A more immediate reaction.'

A 'tired but happy' Gay Woods reflected on the gig and on The Woods' plans for the band in an interview published the following day: 'It was a good audience. We were very excited about how we were received. But it doesn't matter whether we were happy with the audience, but whether the audience were happy with us. The only fly in the ointment was the noise from the rear rows when we played quieter melodies. Maybe the hall was too big, and the audience too few. Dr Strangely Strange is best in intimate surroundings. We've only played together since Christmas, so we were nervous. We're in the middle of a development, in the process of getting ourselves into the traditional Irish folk music scene, and now we have added electric instruments. It's part of our efforts to create tradition in our own way; traditional Irish music has stood still long enough – but we still need time. It's a shame that foreign audiences don't understand so much of our lyrics. There is a little rebellious undercurrent in many of them. I'm thinking here about the old Irish tunes; our own things are gentler. I hate, for example, loud music. The concert organisers took us for a small walk in the woods – it's good to find out where one really is and then relax a bit at the same time. We're not very excited about big cities.'

The next day there was a concert in Nyborg at Industrien, a craft workers' social club. Booth: 'Just down the road there was a big castle with a moat and a very simple interior. Large rooms with painted medieval op-arty tile designs on the walls and a vast table, sunlight streaming across the floorboards. Ivan and I took time off to pretend to divvy up Europe at this table in the style of the old warlords...' Somewhere along the line, Ivan had now acquired his Danish nickname,

'Svenson,' and Terry was known as Terry Dactyl. Gay missed out on a nickname. After a theatre gig in Fredericia, they played Odense at 5pm the following day and then a big gig in Copenhagen, the Dagmar Biografen, at midnight. 'Tiring,' remembers Booth.

MANDAG 26. APRIL 1971      Fyens Stiftstidende

**Uhøjtideligt**

AFSLAPPET humor og uhøjtide-lig selvironi kan ikke just på-stås at være det, der i første række kendetegner de fleste beatgrupper. Derfor var det ganske rart at møde disse kvaliteter hos den irske grup-pe Dr. Strangely Strange, som i weekenden spillede ved Ubberød Bru's-arrangement i Sanderum-hallen.

Dr. Strangely Strange, der ikke tidligere har besøgt Danmark, spil-ler elektrificeret irsk folkemusik, spændende fra egne kompositioner til gamle jigs og gæliske viser. Gruppens fem medlemmer, hvoraf den ene er en pige, behersker til-sammen flere end 20 instrumenter, og deres holdning til musikken er nok seriøs, men absolut uhøjtidelig. Visse numre har en lyrisk kvalitet, som kan lede tanken hen på Fair-port Convention, andre minder om Incredible String Band, og nogle er fornøjelige musikalske cirkusnum-re. Fælles for hele gruppens reper-toire ved koncerten i Sanderumhal-len var imidlertid, at musikken var velspillet, klangmæssigt afvekslen-de og rytmisk inciterende, og ikke mindst i erindring om Black Sab-baths voldsomme og aggressive koncert i Odense for nylig kunne man glæde sig over den irske gruppes uanmassende musik, hvis effekt lå i nuancerne og ikke i kompakt volumen.

Volumen fik man til gengæld hos koncertens to andre grupper, de danske Den flyvende Kuffert og Ache, men deres ganske udtryks-fulde og medrivende musik var dog værd at lytte til, selv om de ikke var nogen uforglemmelig oplevelse. Tilslutningen til arrangementet var pæn uden at være overvældende, stemningen var god, og det oden-seanske Pollach sørgede for kom-petent lysshow.

★      e-

Sangeren i Dr. Strangely Strange, Ivan Pawle. Han spiller bl. a. el-piano, orgel, mandolin, flageolet og guitar.

The Odense gig, in the Sanderum sports hall, got a fairly favourable write-up, but as with many of the European reviews, there was the feeling that the journalist didn't quite know what to make of it. Illustrated by a concert photo of an exhausted-looking Svenson, he wrote: 'Unpretentious! Relaxed humour and unpretentious self-irony cannot exactly be the first things that characterise most beat groups. Therefore, it was quite nice to meet these qualities in this Irish group. Dr Strangely Strange, who has not previously visited Denmark, plays elec-trified Irish folk music, spanning his own composi-tions and old jigs and Gaelic songs. The group's five members, one of whom is a girl, can play more than 20 instruments, and their attitude towards the music is probably serious, but absolutely unpretentious. Certain numbers have a lyrical quality that can make one think of Fairport Convention, others remind one of the Incredible String Band, and some are enjoyable musical circus numbers [hectic fanfare-type classic circus music].

'Common to the whole group's repertoire, however, was that the music was well-played, sonically varied and rhythmically inciting. Especially when considering Black Sabbath's violent and aggressive concert in Odense recently, one was delighted with the Irish group's unmatched music, whose effect is in the nuances and not in solid volume. The volume, on the other hand, was achieved by the other two groups on the bill, the Danish bands Flyvende Kuffert [The Flying Suitcases] and Ache… the atmosphere was good and local outfit Pollach pro-vided a competent light show.'

On Sunday 25th April, a day of 'Fis og Ballade' had been scheduled in Copenhagen. In Danish, this means 'larking about' or doing something crazy. The band actually ended up doing a low-key, unscheduled gig in a small harbour pub, the Havne Kro, in Kastrup, just south of Copenhagen. Lars-Erik's mate, the artist Hans Christian Poulsen, was in attendance and took a few snaps, including this one of Ivan and Gay. Booth is just out of shot on the left.

The two days off in Western Jutland had been scheduled for the following two days, but the film project didn't happen – perhaps they were running out of steam by this point. Concert attendances in general were small – Lars-Erik says it was a 'sophisticated audience' – and the tour lost money for Musik Og Lys: 'The tour with Dr Strangely Strange has been economically bad,' the Danish underground press reported afterwards.

In the meantime, it had got even colder and Hoppy had developed a major stomach bug. Right up to the morning of the final gig, a student hall in Aarhus, the band were still hoping to perform, but eventually had to cancel. They couldn't contemplate playing as a four-piece: 'We were somewhat fragile as a comprehensive unit,' says Ivan. 'Hoppy was a pretty good drummer and timekeeper and we relied upon him to hold us together. Without drums, a shambles might have ensued!' The next day's local paper printed an apology from the band, with talk of a return visit the following September.

The band headed straight off to Germany overnight. Ivan: 'I seldom got behind the wheel of the Transit, but it was I who drove us back from Denmark to Germany through Schleswig-Holstein in the middle of the night. I think everyone was asleep as we sped along the country roads, which seemed preternaturally quiet. As dawn broke, small birds started to wake up, and I hit quite a few of them as they tried to fly across the road. It felt as if they were unused to traffic at that hour. Eventually it was broad daylight and we drove into the centre of Hamburg, where we found a Schnellimbiß [fast-food outlet]. There was no seating, so we ate standing up. Schnell.' After a day or two recuperating in Rotterdam chez Frank, it was on to Belgium.

## Belgium

The two Belgian gigs were not part of Frank's tour, but had been set up from London by Julia Creasey. The first was just over the Dutch border, at a youth centre in Turnhout, Jeugdcentrum Kempen. Again, the band suffered from misleading pre-publicity, as in the *Gazet van Antwerpen* preview of the gig: 'One of today's best-known Anglo-Celtish bands will perform... Dr Strangely Strange consists of authentic Irish musicians who deliver authentic Irish folk music, with a twist. They alone will make this evening very interesting, but there is more...' Folk music historian Grahame Hood comments: 'Authentic Irish musicians' is an interesting phrase; it implies a lot of those bands, though playing Irish music, weren't really Irish. Sub-Dubliners type bands, rarely with Irish musicians in them, were very popular in northern Europe in the Seventies, especially in Germany. Bierkeller stuff.'

The audience were probably not prepared, then, for what unfolded once the 'authentic Irish musicians' took the stage. In the process of the tour, the emphatically English Ivan had been nurturing his rock guitarist persona. Inspired by seeing Stan Webb of Chicken Shack at a shared gig in York, he'd bought an extra-long guitar lead and a Crybaby wah-wah pedal, and developed a taste for wandering about the stage.

Booth: 'This was where Ivan – in his Japanese persona, kamikaze headband, kimono and Kawai electric guitar, the three Ks – decided to jump through a small trapdoor on the stage whilst playing a shredding guitar solo. Of course, he was barefoot and landed neatly on the crate of opened beer bottles the promoter had brought in for the after-show party. He now started to receive a series of considerable electric shocks, one of which propelled him out through another set of doors built into the front of the eight-foot-high stage. He proceeded down the hall with his long guitar lead, gesticulating wildly at Paul Carter – our roadie for this tour – his hair standing straight out from his head. He never missed a beat or a note and even his screams were in time with the piece. The audience took it in their stride, thinking it was all part of the act. It was a very good moment or two and once Paul unplugged him, he was none the worse. Indeed, there are some who say the experience improved his mental powers considerably.'

# Brussels

The band struggled on to Brussels where they had a gig on 1st May. Ivan: 'We went to the office of the record company when we arrived. Met a young country band there, Pendulum, who had just pressed their first single. They gave me a copy.' They were to play in Wemmel, a northern suburb of Brussels. Though all the band recall of Brussels is 'having a beer in the big square where all the civil servants reside' and 'eating some nice French onion soup' (Booth and Ivan respectively), some eyewitnesses have surfaced, 48 years later.

A young man called Jan Florizoone had booked the gig: 'I organised this little event with three artists on the bill. It took place in Familia, a local parish hall in Wemmel. We had Pendulum, a local country-rock / folk-rock band I happened to manage then. My friend Firmin Michiels was the band's guitar player. We also had Roland Van Campenhout, a Flemish blues singer/guitar player who is still around. At that time he played solo,

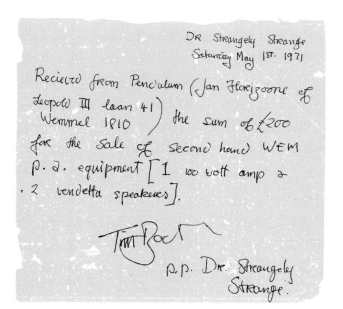

but a few years later he joined Rory Gallagher. After touring the world with Rory and his band, he continued on his own. He was a good friend of Rory and a great musician, and played with him on the album *Wheels Within Wheels*.

'Was the gig successful? I think so. When you're buzzy, organising, you don't have much time to watch the bands. But I remember the audience being very enthusiastic. The hall was filled to capacity, maximum 300. What else do I remember? The band stayed overnight at my place. My mum's place actually. I was just 20 then. That evening Pendulum also bought some of the Strangelies' PA, a couple of WEM speakers and an amp, as the band was considering splitting up.'

Jari Demeulemeester was there: 'The hall was a simple fancy and feast room, good for 300 people. The hall was filled with thirty Dr Strange fans, thirty who had heard the name before; the rest, sorry, came from filling seats from friend to neighbour. But it was an amazing show and it deserved a much better venue in the centre of the town. Unfortunately, there didn't exist one in that period. The concert was insanely good!'

As Jan (and Firmin) went on to become senior figures in the Belgian music business, Jan has a good insight into why so few concert-goers would have heard of the band. *Heavy Petting* wasn't actually released in France and Belgium, but available only via a very confusing system of imports: 'At the time an album could end up in the racks via exporters/importers or via the record company/distributor. But the local record company could also decide to import a certain quantity from the country of origin. They would do this to block parallel importation. This would also have been the case for albums with limited sales expectations, and in this particular case it could certainly have been the latter, also because the label/distributor was the same in both UK and the continent – Vertigo was a Philips-owned label. As far as the involvement of Philips was concerned, I don't recall having seen anyone from Philips at the gig, even though Philips was also Pendulum's record company.'

Despite the 'insanely good' gig, more serious discussions about the future were held in the Transit the following morning, on the way south to Paris. According to Ivan, they had just reached Waterloo when 'someone, maybe Tim Booth, said, "Look, lads, this just isn't working out: let's call it a day!" It was disappointing but inevitable.'

## Théâtre du Vieux Colombier, Paris: 'A good set of B-listers'

The Strangelies had a few days in Paris before their weekend dates on 7th and 8th May, and so the band was called on to find ways of passing the time. Booth: 'Ivan, mental powers improved by his 3K experience in Turnhout, liked to sit in the open sliding door of the Transit as I drove it around the Arc de Triomphe, a pair of huge plastic duelling cap pistols in his hands, which he would point at startled Deux Chevaux drivers. Different times.'

The gigs were in the Théâtre du Vieux Colombier, a 300-seater in the 6th Arrondissement, used these days by the Comédie Française. They formed part of 'Pop au Vieux Co,' an extended progressive music 'festival' organised over a two-month period by the theatre, which was looking to diversify and attract a different audience. There was very little advance publicity and attendances in general were poor; in a review of the first month of gigs, the French monthly *Rock et Folk* remarked sniffily: 'to use the label of Underground does not overstate matters, given the intimate nature of the events.' A scheduled appearance by Nucleus was actually cancelled as the organisers had not even sold enough tickets to cover the band's travel costs from the UK. Strangelies were cheaper and already at large in Europe, so their gigs went ahead.

Ivan's father had moved to live in Paris with his second wife Anne, so they hooked up with the band. Anne Pawle: 'The atmosphere in the theatre was very Belle Époque with all those plush, velvet seats and ornate golden awnings. The acoustics were perfect and very grand for the Strangely Strange troupe. One could have thought that they belonged to a National Theatre in Paris to be able to sing and play Irish music in such surroundings.'

The concerts were very sparsely attended. Anne: 'I wondered at the time why they hadn't asked me to publicise it in Paris. There was only a handful of people in the audience.' The band rose to the occasion. Booth: 'You could buy wine in plastic bottles in those days, and we used to toss full bottles into the audience and invite them to have a drink with us.' Hoppy: 'The artist John Napper and his wife Pauline were friends of the Woods and turned up at one of the gigs. John remarked that we were imbibing "bull's blood and pure alcohol." On reflection, it had the bouquet of a hardly claret!'

48 years on, Ivan revisits the scene of the crime

As usual, no one in the band remembers the gigs themselves, but progressive music fan Michel Polizzi was certainly present for one of them: 'I have precious few memories of that concert. I was familiar with the place and the area; there was a nightclub I patronised in the basement next door, and I had attended other events in the theatre. The image/feeling that comes up to my mind so many years later is one of a softly lit stage cluttered with instruments and things and musicians... I had only listened to the album once, maybe twice, so I didn't have any songs to recognise in concert. This is all very hazy. I was 18, and "that kind of music" had been cool in my Paris circles for a while: Incredible String Band, Fairport, Pentangle, Steeleye, acoustic Led Zep, acoustic Humble Pie... So, yes, I was there for sure, but that's about it.'

Michel Marchon, who reviewed the concert for *Rock et Folk*, was a jazz-rock aficionado. Lacking either a psych-folk or a folk-rock perspective, he seems baffled by his experience and goes for damning with faint praise. After the obligatory comments about the name (they were not 'strange' at all but possessing a 'charming beauty') he lists the line-up and says that the melodies often reminded him of Fairport Convention. 'The chanteuse who accompanies the group has quite a warm voice...' and, surprise surprise: 'Under the influence of "good old French vino," the guitarist was in an extremely good mood.' Terry Woods, we suspect. 'All this has a pleasant sound: a group of the kind you encounter by the score in England, a good set of B-listers.' And with that, he moves on to a much more detailed and perceptive review of French progressive jazz-rockers Total Issue.

The band stayed in a small hotel nearby. It had a plate glass door, and Tim Booth followed in Brian Trench's footsteps by walking into it one morning – he was stunned, briefly, but fortunately avoided a broken nose. He tells us the gig that night was also 'a stunner,' enlivened by a visit from some beautiful Danish women they had met previously in Copenhagen.

After the first night, Ivan's father and Anne took the band out for couscous in a North African restaurant nearby, where Gay was asked to sing. Anne: 'She was clearly too tired to do so. She had a wonderful voice that was very rich and powerful, but might have been too powerful for the smaller space of the restaurant.'

Ivan: 'I think that I may have drunk more than enough wine that evening. The next day we mooched around the Bois de Boulogne and the Jardin d'Acclimatation, played again that night, then drove back through

Belgium to Holland. I distinctly remember that, in those days, one had to have a carnet of the band equipment crossing the various borders; wherever it was we crossed back into Belgium there was no customs post, but I had my trusty plastic weapons to hand...' Booth recalls 'an infusion of paranoia,' as some of the PA equipment detailed on the list had already been sold off in Wemmel: 'We were driving on back roads once we reached the border so as to slip across an unmarked road incognito.'

After the Brussels gig, the band had decided to cut their losses and go home early. Julia Creasey had hurriedly arranged a support slot at a big Al Stewart gig on 16th May, which would be their farewell. Frank had been alerted, and cancelled three of the extra Dutch gigs, but there were still some Dutch commitments to fulfil. After a long and probably fairly grim drive back up to Holland, there were gigs in Haarlem (possibly a small festival), the Geleen Club, near Sittard (organised by Jan Smeets, who Frank tells us now runs the Pink Pop Festival), and Tilburg. The band arrived back in the UK on 15th May.

Frank: 'They had stayed with us for quite a long time altogether and we missed them when they left!'

Frank with Jacqui at The Manor Studios, 1973, whilst recording *Castle In Spain* with his first Dutch band, CCC Inc. Frank: 'Richard Branson did the deal and became very rich that same week, releasing Mike Oldfield's *Tubular Bells*!'

## 'The fusion of the two units was doomed to fail'

How does the band look back on the Woods era? Ivan: 'With the two Tims there had been great chemistry and, more often than not, the Strangelies project had been fun. Sure, it was a job, and sometimes hard work, with the travelling etc. There were occasional moments of joy, but this just wasn't working.'

Hoppy: 'Although the inclusion of Terry and Gay had a disappointing outcome, it at least gave me the chance of learning a few basic skills in playing Irish traditional music. I learned some tunes from Terry on harmonica, and Gay showed me the traditional way of bodhran playing. Ivan's whistle playing also encouraged me to take up the instrument, which I have featured in more recent recordings.'

Booth: 'We – Ivan, Hoppy and I – were serious about trying to make a tiny piece of Art... a little groove into the soft underbelly. Terry and Gay just wanted to play concertinas. Nothing wrong with that. The Lowlands Of Holland – how very lovely. But tell me about your needs first, before you get on our payroll. Think about it – we were very well set up, with a considerable and hard-earned reputation, musical integrity, a manager, an agent, a van and income, gigs, equipment and a musical ethos. So – as Gay once told me after the band had split – for her, joining Strangelies was a stopgap move. We had thought it was because they liked what we were attempting.

'The original Strangelies, Tim, Ivan and myself, had an appreciation of each other's talents and musical abilities – or lack of them – and had great patience and empathy for each other. We became a creative Gestalt. Whenever we inducted another musician into the act – for recording or performance – they understood this process and respected it. The Woods simply did not, so the fusion of the two units was doomed to fail. A pity, as they went on to make some very good music. As did we.'

The Woods, not unexpectedly, had a different take on the experience. They explained in a 1971 *Sounds* interview: 'We said that if the Strangelies hadn't gotten it together during the time we were on the continent then we would leave, because six weeks of gigging should pull a band tighter. Unfortunately, instead of getting together, they were getting looser.' Gay Woods says on her website: '[We] joined them to go on one tour… to Scandinavia. And it was great. They had a very hippy, surreal type of music but we introduced a bit of the Irish stuff and that was when I started playing the bodhran again. It was quite brief and I have to say I was very selfish at the time and I said to myself, what a great opportunity to go and look at Sweden [?] and Denmark. Their music was very strange. I actually had to play the keyboard at one gig – four notes. That was fun… It was a pity that it all fell apart but it was falling apart anyway when we joined. We did the tour and then everybody started breaking up again and we formed The Woods Band out of that.'

Terry was invited to look back on the period for this book, but didn't respond. He summed it up, though, in a 2001 interview for Colin Harper's book *Irish Folk, Trad and Blues*: 'It turned out to be the last real tour [Strangelies] were doing. Goulding was very much part of the whole Strangely Strange experience, so I didn't think anything was going to happen for them afterwards. Also, it was very obvious that it wasn't a vehicle for Gay and myself because, personality-wise, we weren't quite like them. But it was enjoyable and we had a fun time.'

# CHAPTER 11

# Final gig, final thoughts – and a period of retrenchment

## The last gig: Sunday 16 May 1971, Theatre Royal Drury Lane

The music press had been alerted to the split, and dutifully carried news articles explaining that the decision 'was taken in Brussels near the end of an extensive European tour.' The Woods were forming another group with added 'bass, steel guitar, percussion and Uilleann pipes, with the emphasis on traditional Irish music taken back to its roots.' *Sounds* added that the split was 'basically because Ivan and Tim were satisfied with the musical point that the group had reached and that Terry wanted to go somewhat further,' which sounds like a piece of PR spin. The brief news quotes from the three original members about their future plans reflect more of the reality: an underlying sense of disillusionment with the music business. Ivan wanted 'to play a gig every Christmas,' Hoppy planned to 'give up being a professional musician,' and Booth wanted 'time off for dreaming.'

The farewell concert itself seemed to go well, though there was a sombre undercurrent. Goulding and various old mates turned out to mourn their passing, and Karl Dallas wrote them an obituary in *Melody Maker* (see illustration). Booth: 'I wore tight red trousers as a mark of respect. And of course, it was not the end of the saga – not by a long shot. Just the end of our musical involvement with Terry and Gay, who went on to assail the heights in their particular spheres.'

**DR STRANGELY**

A LAMENT (Valentia's) was a sober finale to the career of Dr. Strangely Strange, who passed away in the early hours of Sunday night at the Theatre Royal, Drury Lane, London. Of volatile character, the deceased was always regarded with anticipation by those who followed his uncanny way of life. Indeed it is ironic that his friends and admirers should find themselves in mourning at a time when Strange seemed closer to harmonic creativity than at any time during his long and chequered programme.

Always one to work in a series of energetic outbursts intermingled with periods of fluidity and reflection, the Doctor began the year ambitiously, committing himself to research aimed at combining traditional and contemporary folk elements in one group identity. His death resulted from the breakdown of this machinery. Nevertheless his work has not been in vain. He has kindled musical imagination, and results should arise like the phoenix hereafter.

Steve Pearce lurks behind Terry Woods at the soundcheck.

Writing a concert review for *The Guardian*, Robin Denselow summed up the musical tensions well. Their set was 'an uneasy mixture, lacking in character, but including potentially excellent material. If they had all stuck to acoustic songs, and left out unfortunate attempts to ape the Fairports, they might have made a good band – too bad.' Jerry Gilbert bemoaned the split in *Sounds*: 'They really enjoy their music and on Sunday night they created their own little euphoria on stage through which they eventually disappeared... Their music and approach are thoroughly enjoyable, and technical appraisals just aren't called for. The musicianship of Terry Woods and Ivan Pawle stands out, not only because of its versatility but also its class. I've always enjoyed Gay Woods' singing and her final little jig all added to the excitement. Ex-member Tim Goulding was spotted in the audience just as the group embarked on one of his numbers, which was nice, and it's sad that we won't be seeing the antics of the group ... any more. But I wish they could have said cheerio in a more informal atmosphere.'

Paul Charles, then working on the Al Stewart tour for the Asgard agency, was impressed: 'It was the first time, only time, I'd seen them. They were great, they were a lot more together than they looked. I remember thinking: they're not going to get to the end of this song together. But they always did. I remember I loved the Irishness of their sound and voices, not in an Irish folk kind of way but in a more contemporary way. They certainly came across as if they were enjoying themselves. I also remember Al being very moved by the audience to the extent that he announced that he really wanted to take them (the audience) home with him.'

So how did the band feel when the concert was over? Ivan: 'A total non-event! There was no acrimony: it had been something we tried and it failed. Possibly not a complete waste of time... We probably went for a drink afterwards and then dispersed into the night.'

Hoppy: 'It was a sad occasion but inevitable, as the two factions had drifted apart somewhat, and I felt rather stuck in the middle. However, I think we all gave it the best shot we could have done on the night. I must have played well, as Al Stewart gave me his contact number after the gig. I never followed it up, as I didn't think I was ready to go to the States, where his next tour was planned for. I wasn't sure what I wanted to do next, but after our obituary appeared in the music press, I received the call-up from Ian and Gavin Sutherland, who had just been signed to Island.'

Booth: 'I think I was sad, but relieved to be getting out from under the Wooden influence. I felt – deep down – that we were not by any means finished or vanquished and would resurface further down the track, which turned out to be the case. The photos that Johanna took at the sound check show me in jubilant form, but that might only be because I'd managed to get the bass into tune...'

(FROM LEFT) Ivan, Terry, Booth at the soundcheck (Collage: Simon Ryan)

After the band dissolved, it fell to Steve Pearce to sell off the van and remaining equipment. He eventually returned home to run the family pottery, but the band felt bad about letting him down. Ivan: 'It was a pity that we were unable to reward Steve with commercial success after the amount of time, effort and money that he invested in the Strangely Strange project.' Booth: 'Steve was very likely out of pocket. We never saw accounts; the whole arrangement was based on mutual trust. He is a mighty man. A man of taste and deep subtlety and a very fine potter.'

# If only...

If the band had been able to regroup once the Woods had left, perhaps with a newly invigorated Goulding, the Strangelies could have continued touring fairly successfully for a few more years. Two years of headliners and support dates across the length and breadth of the country meant they already had a solid fanbase in the UK, and their Blackhill Enterprises booker, Julia Creasey, had just moved into band management (representing Al Stewart and other folk-rock acts).

Booth: 'Listening to the live recording from Les Cousins, it all comes back. Not in a good way. We were a good band prior to Goulding's departure. It's interesting to note that we were never again to feature on John Peel once Terry and Gay came aboard. In hindsight, we should have found another alternative to Goulding. Terry and Gay didn't cut it. Not for Dr Strangely Strange. But if we had waited a moment – been able to take a breath – we might have gone on to make a reasonable living out of our creativity...' Hoppy agrees: 'I think it could have continued to work very well if a more suitable replacement for Tim G could have been found.'

They could have been big in Europe. In Belgium they had three powerful allies. Firmin from Pendulum quickly moved into marketing for Barclay Records, then became Marketing Director for Polygram and eventually became Vice-President for Virgin/EMI Europe. Jan Florizoone also worked for years in the record industry, organising promotion at a senior level for EMI and Ariola-BMG and then running a big European awards festival, The Diamond Awards. Jari Demeulemeester, who had thought the band were 'insanely good' and was dreaming of a decent club venue in central Brussels, was soon running one, the Beursschouwburg. This was a multidisciplinary arts centre in the heart of the city with concerts, exhibitions, debates and films. After that he became director and programmer at Ancienne Belgique, a very successful Brussels rock club.

In Holland, Frank van der Meijden had built and nurtured a well organised circuit of rock venues round the country and was organising Dutch tours for many UK and American bands. Berry Visser was running the highly successful Mojo Concerts agency, responsible for around 85% of the foreign bookings in Holland for many years. He also had his finger in pies further afield, and, with Steve Pearce, had been making ambitious plans for the Strangelies. One was an American tour supporting The Flying Burrito Brothers, and another was some kind of eastern European gig. Berry can't now recall too much about this era, but thinks it's likely.

Booth: 'I never really knew the details of these mooted tours, but Berry represented Zappa and the Burritos, so the idea of touring America or eastern Europe was not so far-fetched. He had the connections and we would have been relatively cheap.' Frank: 'Berry had liked the Strangelies when they played at Exit. He was always very spontaneous so it is very well possible he promised to try to put them on other tours, but then they broke up.'

As it was, The Woods Band inherited some of these links instead. Later that year Julia Creasey became their manager, and Frank soon had them touring Holland again, though Paul Scully (who, aged 19, was tour manager) told Ivan he remembers Terry and Gay spending the whole tour bickering, both on and off stage… They did a return gig at the Leidse Schouwburg, and even played another concert with Pendulum supporting, at the University of Leuven summer school. And, of course, Booth's nemesis, Tony Reeves, signed them to his label and produced their first album.

## 'Use your mentality, face up to reality…'

Though Goulding has already set off on his inward journey, the other two founder-members definitely needed a period of decompression. By the time the band imploded, Ivan had morphed from studious beatnik to somewhat of a guitar hero, complete with long lead, wah-wah pedal and kamikaze alter ego. Booth had gradually abandoned all his folkie trappings for a hard-rocking persona, and it took him some time to come back to himself – in fact, he says now that he still hasn't.

The rest of 1971 was a period of retrenchment. After some winding-up work, Manager Pearce had moved on. Ivan: 'He went off to the States to attempt a songwriting career, doing a tour of campuses and clubs with John Prine and Philip Donnelly. On his return he devoted his formidable energy to his family's Shanagarry pottery, putting it firmly on the world map.'

Despite Hoppy's intention of giving up being a professional musician, he was back in action within a fortnight. Hoppy: 'After a couple of weeks back in Uttoxeter and not sure what I was going to do next, I was suddenly invited to play drums on the first album by The Sutherland Brothers, who were living not too far away in Blythe Bridge and had just been contracted to Island Records. On completion of the album, the four of us (Ian, Gavin, bass player Kim Ludman and me) were duly required to promote it with a heavy-ish touring schedule. We did support slots for other Island artists including Free, Amazing Blondel and Mott The Hoople at the major British town hall venues, which were always well attended and highly enjoyable in terms of fun and band camaraderie. Other occasional gigs with Brinsley Schwarz and Nick Lowe turned out to be a hoot, as enjoying the music was paramount to us and earning money for it was a bonus.

'In 1972 our manager had secured a slot for the band to support an upcoming singer/songwriter and his band for a short six-day tour, which is when I encountered David Bowie. I wasn't really a fan, though I was aware of Space Oddity and The Man Who Sold The World. I remember being on stage at the first gig, just after we had done our sound check; I was talking to Bowie's drummer Woody about his set-up when David walked in. Not speaking to either of us, he promptly moved towards the front microphone. I said something like, "How are you, alright?" but didn't get a reply, which was when he started blowing his saxophone into the mic and when I decided to go backstage for a beer. After the gig he didn't hang about, and I remember Woody saying he was quite shy and reserved despite his extrovert appearance. I didn't try to engage in conversation with him again, not realising at the time that this was the launch of Ziggy and The Spiders From Mars into the public eye and I was there witnessing it.'

## Ivan: 'I entered a brief period of freefall'

It was probably hardest for Ivan when the band came to an end. Goulding was already working successfully as a painter, and Booth was well on the way to being an established designer and graphic artist. But for Ivan more than anyone, Dr Strangely Strange had been his vocation. He was the most restless of the three, and the last to settle anywhere vaguely permanent, with something of the spirit of wandering British eccentrics like Laurie Lee or Patrick Leigh Fermor in him. Ivan: 'Although the band had run its course and it was inevitable, my self-confidence and self-esteem took a knock. I entered a brief period of freefall, half expecting to enter into fresh musical ventures with some like-minded souls. I had no long-term game plan. I went up to Glen Row to see Marymac and Niamh, then down to London to see about possibly exploring other musical avenues. I stayed at Haverstock Hill, where a contingent of Irish musicians was based – most of Granny's Intentions, plus Gary Moore and his partner Sylvia, with their little baby Saoirse. I stayed in Ted Carroll's room while he was breaking Thin Lizzy in the United States. I remember a great session one night at the Country Club on Haverstock Hill with Terry Woods and Gary Moore, playing Banish Misfortune.'

Marymac had decided to move on: 'In June 1971 Niamh and I went back to Dublin and briefly Co Wicklow, where Linus and I both bought barrel-top gipsy caravans and horses from the tinkers (or Travellers as we would now say). We parked up for a while and then set off across country to Co Clare. Linus had teamed up with Robin Birch, part of a set of pre-hippy beatniks including the likes of Clive Palmer, Rod Stewart and Robin's friend Brian Del Harding, who had travelled around some of the Scottish islands in the early and mid-Sixties, living fairly wild by all accounts, catching deer and fish and so on. Orphan Annie had stayed with them when she first went to Scotland.

Marymac's caravan on the road.

'Robin had a Scottish deerhound called Dirk, and Linus had rescued a borzoi she named Zelda. With pony Peggy pulling my wagon and Rosie, a cob, pulling Linus and Robin's, our entourage travelled across the centre of Ireland and landed down at Del's land, in the woods by the shore of Lough Derg. It was just down the road from the birthplace of Edna O'Brien. Del was a virtually self-sufficient fisherman whose main interest was in the pike of the Lough, and owned a tough little fox terrier answering to the name Dingo. We bought a trap and would go into Scarriff about once a week for provisions. We would swing by the abattoir to collect beef heads for the hounds – the cheeks would go into delicious hearty stews.'

Ivan eventually joined them: 'I soon tired of London as I was obviously getting nowhere. Blessings often arrive in disguise: I had left Marymac and our daughter Niamh up at the Row in rather unpropitious circumstances. I went down to West Cork, and then hitched up to Clare to reconnect with Mary and Niamh beside the lough. I had managed to pare my personal belongings down to a change of clothes, a couple of books, and my Kawai guitar. "Use your mentality, face up to reality..." in the words of Cole Porter's I've Got You Under My Skin. So, I hitchhiked to Tuamgraney, Co Clare and walked through the marshes along the lakeshore carrying my electric guitar with a rucksack on my back. Light was fading as I made my way through the ancient woods to stumble upon the encampment... Mary and I went off to Dublin to get married in December.'

Ivan and Mary just after their wedding.

# Tim Booth: 'I felt we actually had a lot more to give'

'When the band ended, Johanna scooped me up in her old green VW Beetle and whisked me back up to Glen Row, where I lived for most of the next year. I worked for the Glen Estate and drawing for DC Thomson's in Dundee. I made more money doing this than I had with Strangelies and this made up to a degree for the sadness I felt at the band's demise. Unlike Ivan I felt we actually had a lot more to give. It was a relief to have got free of the repressive Woods, but we should have regrouped with other more like-minded musicians. However, their continuous bickering had worn us out and we needed a break.

'At DC Thomson's, I did mostly illustrations and romance cartoon strips for *Jackie* magazine (LEFT). I also tried Desperate Dan and a few beefy commando-style boyos, but it seemed *Jackie* was my natural home. The last frame of the strip was difficult, as it usually featured boy and girl in a close-up passionate embrace, and the illustration commissioning editor – Mr Shortt – needed to see all four hands placed in a non-licentious manner within the frame.

'At the Glen Estate the factor, Alec, soon sussed that I had grown up on a farm and knew horses, scythes and sheep. I became a catcher for the spring shearing. There were thousands of sheep on the hills of Colin Tennant's estate and we used to round them up on horseback and bring them into the shearing paddock with dogs to help. Then we had to catch them and bring them to the professional shearers, one every two minutes or so. Back-breaking work and not for the Row's resident Scientologists, who never got their hands dirty in any way. There was music at the row, the String Band doing their thing, but at this stage in their career it was very Scientology based. I mostly jammed a bit with Malcolm Le Maistre and Stan Schnier, who had access to the Rolling Stones' equipment warehouse and produced Keith Richards' first serious guitar, which he no longer used. It was a wonderful Sunburst Epiphone Casino. It had that Keef sound and there was nothing I could do to make it sound all wimpy and Dr Strangely Strange.'

Stan Schnier had become the ISB roadie and latter-day bass player: 'Tim and I got into some funny antics. When the ISB was not working, they all headed down to the Scientology place in East Grinstead. I was not yet involved and stayed behind in this beautiful setting but with little to do. Tim lived next door and he was the first Gentleman Farmer I'd ever met. He knew his way around horses and was the first person I ever knew who wore a real riding mac… and it had years of hard-earned patina on it. And wellies! I wore cowboy boots, nothing practical for the muddy surfaces of rural Scotland. Tim and I would jam and hang out and on one particular occasion, risk life and limb. Tim was a true horse person, as was Johanna, and one day he appeared at the back fence with a gorgeous horse that the gamekeeper's son had acquired from some tinkers. He was wild as hell and Tim was determined to get him under control. I offered to assist, just like the good roadie I was.'

Booth: 'The horse was appropriately named Apache and had been rescued from the glue factory by the gamekeeper's son, Kenneth. A truly beautiful coloured gelding, but he had been mistreated and whipped and was completely petrified and contemptuous of humans. So Kenneth – who had a bit of Gypsy in him – did something called "couping" (pronounced kow-ping). This means – and only do this if you have balls of steel – you put a halter on the horse and turn his head away from your standing position, then pick up the fetlock of the leg on the turning side. The horse loses its balance and when he falls you jump across his neck and pin him down. Then he recognises you as stronger than him, his master if you like, and is – ipso facto – in a condition to be broken in again. Kenneth had done this with Apache and introduced him to a bridle and bit, but not yet a saddle. I used to ride him bareback, cantering him up the hill, then dismounting and leading him down, otherwise he would have run away with me, so we had got to know and understand each other.

'Then the Scientologists made their move. Robin's then wife, Janet, decided that she would ride Apache. With a saddle. Because there was nothing they, the followers of Ron, could not do. I advised against it, as he had not yet been reintroduced to the device. But I was overruled and the horse was saddled and brought to the gravel behind the cottages. A box was placed out to help Janet ascend, she being less than tall and Apache being some thirteen hands. There is a trick to putting a saddle on an unwilling horse. You have to give him a blow to the belly and wind him, so as he sucks in, you quickly cinch up the saddle. This had not been done with Apache.

He had blown out his belly and ribcage as the saddle was applied, so it was dangerously loose. I advised Janet of this and was told that as she was the horse's "Terminal" – a Scientology term for keeper – there would not be a problem. I stood back and observed. Sure enough, when the Scientologist foot was placed in the stirrup to mount, the saddle revolved downwards, depositing her on the floor, clattering the box in under the horse's hooves and causing him to bolt. I was more interested in rescuing the horse than comforting the terminally de-luded Janet, so I took off after him and after a while managed to catch him, cinch up the saddle girth and ride him up the hill, but when we reached the summit, before I could rein him in and dismount, he just took off!'

Stan: 'Without warning, the horse spun around and went into a full gallop towards the fence at the bottom of the hill. At the last second, he dug his two front hooves into the dirt, as if in a cartoon, and skidded to a stop directly in front of the fence.' Tim: 'I got the fright of my life and ended up staring into the horse's eyes, arms around his neck, clinging on for dear life.'

Eventually the time came to leave Glen Row. Booth: 'After some time of this, the Scientologists became too much to bear and I bid Johanna and the Row farewell and split back to London where I lived and worked doing illustration and animation for a number of years. Reunited with Humphrey Weightman, who had become a typographer in London, we backed the singer Carolanne Pegg in an outfit called The Bats. I played bass, Humphrey lead, Carolanne sang and played fiddle and harmonium, and Alan Eden was on drums. Our musical nadir was the Half Moon, Putney, but our zenith came when we played the 1972 Cambridge Folk Festival, where Humphrey says he "made grunting and howling noises on a Burns Black Bison guitar." The ensuing review in the local press was headed: "The day the roadies ruined the festival."

'But before that, an invitation to Ivan and Mary's wedding had led to some interesting developments…'

Ivan and Mary at the Register Office – (FROM LEFT): Pippa Scrivener, Ivan's sister; Gary Moore, and behind him muso friend Dave; friends Jeremy Black (with glasses) and George Farrow; Johnny Duhan and Pete Cummins from Granny's Intentions; Sue Bullock (at the front) was a witness, along with Tim Goulding. Mary says Tim looks like he is checking the racing results for the 4.30 at Fairyhouse, but actually the Banns had been published in *The Irish Times* and they probably needed to produce them. Tim Booth & Humphrey Weightman arrived late from London shortly after the ceremony.

# CHAPTER 12

# Frothy Swansdown and playing for The Boys: The Horsebox Tour

After a period of sorting out their housing, income and personal lives, the three original Strangelies were reunited at a gathering of the clans for Ivan's Dublin wedding to Marymac in December 1971. A decision to re-form and play a short university tour in both Northern Ireland and The Irish Republic was made. Roger Armstrong, whom readers will recall from the Queen's University Esoteric Music Society, was starting out as a promoter and agent, and he and Tim Goulding put eight or so dates together which met with approval; venues included Derry, Coleraine, Belfast, Galway, Dublin, Waterford, Kilkenny and Limerick.

Ivan says it struck them all 'as a good idea. We all missed various aspects of playing together.' For Tim Booth, 'This tour was a one-off, a chance to eradicate the Woods experience and do our own thing again. A mini vindication. We subsequently did many of this type of tour. No money, just a chance to get the music out there. I had moved from Glen Row to Fulham, where I was trying to freelance as an illustrator and quietly starving, so I hotfooted across for rehearsals.' Of the three, Goulding may possibly have had doubts about going back on the road, given his reasons for leaving in the past, but he can't now remember. Everyone certainly felt good about reaffirming their musical bond.

The trio did some rehearsing at Tim and Annie's place, the old School House near Allihies. Some of the new material had a more 'muso' feel; they started to explore a jazzy vein hinted at in the intro to their last recording with Goulding, Horse Of A Different Hue. The two short instrumental pieces from Common Farm, The Nostril Variations and Sparky Bought It In The Latrines, were exhumed; Nostril turned out to be a Goulding piano solo in Dave Brubeck mode.

'I think we pretty much took up where we had left off,' says Ivan. 'We had all been busy getting on with what we would have been doing if not gigging. It was good to play together again; we had established a common vocabulary, none of us attempting virtuoso solos or anything. I think vocal harmonies have always been our greatest strength, and that is probably the aspect I most enjoy about the Strangelies.'

'The old magic rekindled,' says Booth, 'and we augmented the line-up with Don Knox on fiddle and mandolin and old mate Steve Bullock ("El Tigre") on bass, sax and flute. Derek Boston, who had showband experience, was a good drummer and a great harmony singer.' The set included some trad hangovers from the Woods era, including the jig Banish Misfortune and Brian Boru's March, featuring Don Knox (another ex-Trinity College man), Steve on flute and Tim Goulding on tin whistle. An *Irish Times* tour review by the faithful Hoddy gives some of the flavour:

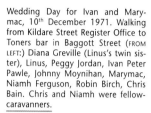

Wedding Day for Ivan and Mary-mac, 10th December 1971. Walking from Kildare Street Register Office to Toners bar in Baggott Street (FROM LEFT:) Diana Greville (Linus's twin sister), Linus, Peggy Jordan, Ivan Peter Pawle, Johnny Moynihan, Marymac, Niamh Ferguson, Robin Birch, Chris Bain. Chris and Niamh were fellow-caravanners.

'Their instrumentation includes alto sax, which leads one to expect a more Mayall-ish performance... and their jazzy introductory number leads one up the garden path further; their actual repertoire is an attractive mix of jigs, rock, sentiment and a recurring send-up strain that got into their work a few years ago when they were almost a revue-type outfit. Their earliest or "hippie" stage, playing free-form snake-charming music when the spirit moved them while clad in long purple robes, has unfortunately left no traces.'

There was also a newly composed Booth song of debatable merit, titled Living In The Jungle. The chorus went: 'Living in the jungle, it sure is hell / Living in the jungle, I just can't tell / You.'

Full band rehearsals took place in a garage near Steve's flat in Dublin. Steve, at that point still a student at Trinity College, borrowed a bass for the tour from Dónal Lunny. Steve: 'The only problem was that the key handle of the D string was snapped off, so I had to use a fork ("the tuning fork") to tune it, much to the merriment and bewilderment of the audience!'

Goulding's old friend Mark Davis, aka Dark Mavis, agreed to drive them in his Land Rover, the gear in a large horsebox towed behind. Mark tells us that the horsebox itself had a good pedigree; it was lent by Charley Keegan – at that time World Ploughing Champion.

On tour with them was also a light show by one Pete Downey; a Belfast acoustic duo, Keith and Spence, were the support act. Goulding: 'Great guys. In the Cork City Hall gig (a vast venue), they opened for us and got a tumultuous reception. On being called back on stage for an encore, one of them tripped over a prop and had to be removed to hospital with a broken leg. As this was going on, we played for time by drawing diagrams on a large blackboard that was on stage.'

Booth: 'We set off into the wide blue yonder, which turned out, once we crossed the border into Northern

Horsebox vignette by Tim Booth – note Goulding, Steve and Ivan in the front and Derek Boston with the sombrero.

Ireland – aka "Norn Iron" – to be more of a red, white and blue yonder with fringes of constipated orange and slashes of a bilious green.'

Band members dealt with the travelling in different ways. Goulding: 'Derek Boston told us of the show-band habit of "dropping a body," which was used for long-distance engagements. A form of speed; you stay awake for 24 hours.' Steve: 'This involved buying a Benzedrex asthma inhaler, cutting the top off and removing the contents, which consisted of a white coil of paper saturated with some kind of amphetamine-type stuff. Then you dropped it into a glass of Coca-Cola and allowed it to infuse for 15 minutes before gulping it down.' They intended to try this out before the Derry gig but unfortunately, the chemists were all closed, so they had to make do with Guinness, as usual. Given what happened there, probably just as well.

Some initial gigs in Cork, Dublin and Galway went very well, but the tour, quickly christened The Horsebox Tour, took the Strangelies out of their habitual milieu and right up against the North/South conflict. This, after all, was the very high-tension era of The Maze prison ('Long Kesh'), sectarian violence, bombings and covert paramilitary operations.

Booth: 'The gigs were fine, but getting to them... coarse. The Land Rover, although obviously an agricul-tural vehicle, was construed by some to be a military unit, perhaps containing undercover operatives wearing long-haired wigs. It was very uncomfortable to be in the front passenger seat and find we had somehow been subsumed into a convoy of British Army Land Rovers, our machine's bigger brothers, all mesh window grills, anti-bomb skirts and dark green paint. Would those trigger-happy republican marksmen be able to recognize our neutrality, maybe read the Southern number plate before squeezing off a round? Seems they were literate because we survived to tell the tale. The British army were a whole other thing.'

Steve: 'We were booked to play at Magee University in Derry for Monday 31st January. The day before, we packed all our gear into the horsebox and drove off to stay the night with Tim Goulding's parents. When we ar-rived, Lady Goulding was beside herself with rage. It was what became known as Bloody Sunday, when 13 civilians had been shot dead by the British Army during a peaceful protest march against internment. We watched in horror as it unfolded on the TV screen. She jumped up and said, "I'm going to call Heath!" This didn't bode well for the gig, but we were already booked, so what to do? Next morning, as we were all sitting down to breakfast, Sir Basil received a handwritten note saying: "British pigs, get out of Ireland." Sir Basil, a great collector of art, immediately sprang into action and said, "Right, I'm putting all the paintings on loan to the National Gallery of Ireland." This seemed like a good plan.

'We set off for Derry about 10.30 am with some trepidation. When we got to the border, at first the customs post seemed to be deserted, but eventually an officer nervously poked his head out of a hole in the wall and waved us on. We got to Derry at about four. The city streets seemed deserted of local inhabitants, but every vehicle we saw on the road was either an RUC or army Land Rover. As Tim says, ours was an unfortunate choice of vehicle, more so because it carried a Dublin registration. Eventually we found our hotel, checked in, then set off for the

Meet Mum and Dad – Sir Basil and Lady Valerie Goulding
in the Sun Room, Dargle Cottage

concert hall. This turned out to be a kind of overgrown Nissen hut with a capacity for maybe 500 people. The entrance consisted of two smallish doors but there were no signs of any emergency exits.

'There was a good turnout at the gig. We were greeted enthusiastically by the crowd and the first two numbers or so received rapturous applause. Suddenly, the punters in the front rows started pointing furiously in our direction and shouting. We surmised that this was a mass expression of joy and admiration, so those of us with volume controls turned the sound up. Then we realised they were shouting more loudly, "Look behind you!" We did and saw that the PA stacks, 15ft tall, were shaking as if to topple on to us. We moved to the front of the stage, all except Derek and his drum kit. At this point an "events manager" ran behind the stage and closed some large windows. The rest of the show carried on without incident, apart from the odd bum note. After it was all over and the hordes dispersed we asked what the hell had happened. We were told there had been two young gurriers [tearaways] at the windows with long poles, trying to push the speakers down on us. "That's nothing, last week the fokkers threw in canisters of CS gas!" Emergency exits would have been handy.

'We were starting to pack the gear into the horsebox when two scruffy young lads appeared out of the shadows and asked, "Hey mosters, youse there, will youse come down to the Bogside an' play fer the Boys?" We huddled together to figure out what to do. It was obvious that this was the same two who had tried to crush us with the speakers and that "the Boys" were the Provos, since the whole area of the Bogside was barricaded and under their control, as we had heard on the news for months. Derek chipped in that members of a Dublin band he knew had played in Derry some weeks before, had been asked the same, had graciously accepted the kind invitation and went on down. What you have to remember about Dublin showbands of this time (or perhaps for ever) is that they had a very rigid repertoire. You play all that week's top 20 numbers (or as many as you can, or can bear) then you finish by repeating the one you started with. Unfortunately, the mob, or audience, started to shout out various requests and they all joined with The Men Behind The Wire, which was by The Wolfe Tones and unknown to the band because the record had only got to 24 so far that week! The result was that all their gear and their bus was completely trashed and they narrowly avoided getting kneecapped too. Showbusiness!

'Fortunately, not being so prepared to die for our art, we all agreed that the best course of action was to fuck off as fast as possible. We told the little bastards that we had to leave to drive all the way to Cork, immediately, sorry. Rammed all the gear into the horsebox as fast as possible, any old way, then left at as much speed as the Land Rover could muster. We parked in what we had been told was a safe place then, as we walked back to the hotel, here came the squaddies. "Up against the wall – hands above your head!" they shouted, guns pointing at us. As they drew nearer, I could see that their uniform flashes said "Royal Gloucestershire Regiment." I had grown up on a farm in North Somerset and I knew that they were in fact a Bristol regiment. I muttered this to the rest of the band, and that it was a bit much to be harassed at gunpoint in a foreign country by soldiers from my own home town. One of the squaddies overheard this and said, "Yur, tha' roight then?" I confirmed it certainly was, in my best Bristol accent. He told the other squaddies we were not much of a threat, so they left us alone without shooting anybody. Back at the hotel drink was taken and I remember Tim Goulding giggling insanely about "frothy swansdown" with Booth and Ivan for some time, although what they were talking about, I can't say.'

Goulding: 'I don't remember the drama of this tour at all, except for the attempted toppling of the PA. But I do remember being in a Chinese restaurant where the waiter spent a lot of the time on the phone remonstrating with a dry cleaner who had "stolen his trousers." We were all in helpless hysterics.'

Steve: 'We eventually went to bed, all in a bad way. Next morning, we hit the road to Coleraine. However, we were told by a cop, as we stopped at an intersection just a few yards after we started off, that the connection to the brake lights on the horsebox wasn't working.'

Booth: 'While scratching our heads, a helpful passer-by, a youth of the mildest attitude, suggested we take ourselves and the troublesome connection to the army base just down the road as they had a new policy of being helpful to civilians and would doubtless be delighted to advise. "They'd luv t'see yez, so they would." This we innocently did, driving over speed bumps and through winding security chicanes to the very doors of an implacable steel and mesh fortress. As I was in the front left passenger seat it was my task to go and tell the squaddies of our predicament. I walked to the security gates, aware of ordnance swinging to train on me and the ratchet of weapons being cocked. Gulp. The sergeant didn't look happy, pasty-faced beneath a helmet that seemed uncomfortably big.'

Steve: 'The sergeant said, "Stay right there," and disappeared back inside. We seemed to be there for hours, waiting for him to return. Meanwhile we realised that, in the event of a drive-by shooting, we were in the direct line of fire. We considered just turning around and driving away, but then thought the better of it since the guards might shoot us in defence of the realm for loitering with intent in a vehicle and agricultural trailer, acting suspiciously, and having long hair for starters. Tricky!'

Booth: 'Arrival of officer. He's a mere child but has learnt to speak without moving his jaw. I stare at his clenched teeth. It seems, he explains, that the last vehicle to venture up here to the gates of Eden had opened fire with automatic weapons before driving away at speed, causing the teen squaddies to beshit themselves and the pimpled officers a deal of paranoia. We left, but not before His Imperial Darkness Mr Davis had had to perform painstakingly elaborate reversals of Rover and trailer. "You need to get those lights fixed mate, could cause an 'orrible incident," the sergeant shouted as we beat our retreat.'

Steve: 'Off we went without the brake lights being fixed but, given the general climate of terror and fear, it seemed unlikely that the cops were going to bust us for anything so trivial. We got to Coleraine late in the afternoon, just as it was getting dark. As we approached the university campus, we could see flames rising from various buildings. "The gig's cancelled, lads," someone observed, so we thought it best to carry on to Belfast, where we had the last gig in the North next day. I think Tim Goulding called Roger Armstrong, who sorted out some accommodation for us when we arrived there a day early.'

Roger was on hand to witness the Bingo Incident. Ivan: 'There was bingo paraphernalia on the stage. Tim Goulding had a habit of calling out numbers bingo-style, referencing a bingo caller on the seafront at Bray, Co Wicklow.' Tim: 'My brother and I used to visit to learn his techniques, such as "This is the last call, there'll be two more" and "It's a blue and the number is red 27."' Ivan: 'The audience was already arriving, and on this occasion, Tim couldn't resist using the equipment that was in situ: he spun the wheel, and the number 13 came up. He called out "Lucky for some, thirteen." I think we then all realised the awful Bloody Sunday resonance. True professionals, we carried on.' 'That didn't go down well,' remembers Roger.

After that, says Steve, 'the gig at Queen's went very well and the audience were greatly appreciative. Several encores, I believe. In the middle of a fairly rocky tune, Tim Goulding on piano and I played a movement in classical counterpoint, after I had worked out the riffs on the bass. Despite this it went down brilliantly.

'We had our overnight stuff in the horsebox already, and after the show we packed up all our gear and set off to find somewhere to eat as we had had nothing since breakfast. It was past 1 am so there was nothing open that we could find. We were driving along a very wide street – the Falls Road maybe – in the middle of the city and had to pull up at the traffic lights, right next to a large army truck. As I was sitting next to the window on the passenger side, the lads said to ask the squaddies if they knew anywhere open. As I slid open the window, about six young squaddies all pointed their rifles at me. They seemed to be about 17 years old, as scared as we were, shaking, and I could see their fingers whitening on the triggers as they aimed at a space between my eyes. A sergeant jumped out and came round to speak to me. "What is it?" he growled menacingly. "Do you know if there is a Chinese restaurant still open around here, sir?" "Piss off right now!" he shouted, most unhelpfully. Anyhow the young squaddies lowered their guns and we did indeed piss off smartish, since the lights had now changed to green.

'We drove around for a while, found no sign of any food anywhere, then we saw a sign pointing to the south and Dublin. "Let's just go now while we know where we are!" was the general consensus. Off we sped and soon found ourselves heading back to the border and home. Not far out of Belfast the country seemed to be pretty wild. There was little traffic but I guess it was now almost 3 am. Suddenly there were men with blackened faces in uniforms with guns and a chain with spikes dragged across the road, shining lights on our faces and forcing us to stop. They had their badges turned round the other way, so it was not possible to see who they were. They asked Mark who we were and where we were going at this time of night, etc. The officer in charge spoke on a walkie-talkie to someone further down the road, then told us to carry on.'

Back to Booth: 'Further down the road, we took a wrong turn, somewhere near Forkhill. Realising our mistake, we backtracked and found the main road again and, after a few miles, another checkpoint. All was not well, made worse by the realisation that the checkpoint was manned not by the army but by territorial style troops with no visible markings that I could see. [Members of the Miami Showband were killed at a similar checkpoint a few years later in 1975 by paramilitaries, see box.] Why were we late? Norn Iron accents. The nervous officer shone his torch at Dark's face. Weapons were pointed. "Everyone out!" We clambered down. The first checkpoint had radioed ahead with an ETA and we'd missed it, so where had we been? Simple. We had been up to something. Southern longhairs travelling together in an all-terrain vehicle with a trailer on the back? Elementary, my dear Watson. Line them up and search the vehicle and trailer and what's this... strange electrical boxes and wires? It took a while, but we eventually convinced them of our innocence and stupidity and they let us proceed. Luckily we were mostly too stoned to feel any real fear and the soldiers too stupid to think to search us for the substances causing our fearlessness.'

Steve: 'We got back to Dublin around seven in the morning and finally got something to eat.

## The Miami Showband Massacre

The band were right to be nervous at the border. Just three years later, The Miami Showband, an extremely popular Dublin-based cabaret-type band including both Catholic and Protestant musicians, was attacked on the way back home after a gig over the border in Banbridge. Halfway to Newry, their minibus was stopped at what appeared to be a military checkpoint, where gunmen in British Army uniforms ordered them to line up by the roadside. At least four of the gunmen were serving soldiers from the British Army's Ulster Defence Regiment but secretly members of the paramilitary Ulster Volunteer Force. While two of the gunmen (both soldiers) were hiding a time bomb on the minibus, it exploded prematurely and killed them. The other gunmen then panicked and opened fire on the dazed band members, killing three and wounding two. It is believed the bomb was meant to explode en route, killing the band and framing them as IRA bomb smugglers, and possibly leading to stricter security measures at the border.

Two serving British soldiers and one former British soldier were found guilty of the murders and received life sentences. Those responsible for the attack belonged to the Glenanne Gang, a secret alliance of loyalist militants, rogue police officers and British soldiers. There are also allegations that British military intelligence agents were involved. And in a poignant footnote, Goulding tells us that the father of Fran O'Toole, the Miami Showband vocalist who was one of those killed, was the bingo caller from Bray.

[For more information, there is an excellent Wikipedia entry on the incident, from which this piece has been adapted.]

Later that week, the British Embassy in Merrion Square was burnt down in the middle of the day. Hundreds of Gardai arrived to protect the building, but a bunch of about 20 men in balaclavas carrying beer crates full of Molotov cocktails arrived near the front door of the elegant Georgian mansion and lit and started to throw them over the heads of the cops at the door. The fire brigade showed up but refused to plug into the fire hydrants in solidarity with the people of Derry. Meanwhile two men climbed from an adjoining house on to a balcony above the front door and smashed all the windows they could reach. The door quickly burned through in the draught and within minutes there were flames roaring out of the roof and upper windows... Anyhow, I don't know about the rest of the band, but I haven't been back to Northern Ireland since.'

Goulding, Steve, Booth, Derek Boston and Ivan on the stage in the Trinity Exam Hall.

Booth: 'The final gig was in the Exam Hall of Trinity College where Ivan and I had been such diligent students. We had rehearsed carefully. The set up went like this: we were announced over the PA and the house lights went down. No stage lighting, just the glow of the standby lights on our amplifiers as we took our positions on stage. Ivan seemed to be having a problem with his guitar amp, lots of crackling and feedback squeals. Muffled comms between Ivan and TG, some of which is being picked up by the PA. "Can't get this thing to work!"

'I'm now at my microphone. I go, "Testing, testing 123," and the PA starts to feed back. By now the audience are getting restless as we've been at this malarkey for a few minutes now. Ivan appears to be having a hissy fit. The audience start to heckle. We let the confusion build on stage, shouting at Ivan to "Get it together, man!" I go to my mike and start to apologise to the audience, explaining that we are experiencing equipment failure of such magnitude that there is nothing for it but to cancel the gig. "I'm... afraid... we'll... have... to... call... the... whole... thing... off!" Spoken slow and deliberately as the lights came up with a snap to reveal us all at our stations, instruments ready and with a kick drum and snare intro from Derek we go into a specially written ditty called... "We've decided to call it all off." It only lasts a minute and at the end there is a stunned silence from the audience and then a roar of approving laughter.

'And now they are in the palm of our hand and the gig is amazing. Lovely, readers, it was lovely.'

# PART 4
# Epilogue

# CHAPTER 1

# 'Learning to integrate into society'

Ivan: 'On completion of the Horsebox gigs, we each set off once more to "do our own thing" as in raising children, learning to integrate into society etc – whatever you're having yourself.'

Booth and Ivan began to join Goulding in regarding Strangelies as just one aspect of various other things they were doing; the ambitions were much smaller-scale and gigs were extremely sporadic. It was a good move, long-term, and ensured the longevity of the band.

Goulding had already settled into what was to prove a very successful artistic career. In 1971 he had been chosen as one of three young artists to represent Ireland in the Paris Biennale that September, which he attended in person. Since then he has exhibited extensively, including solo and group shows in Ireland, England, Portugal and the USA. This is how Hilary Pyle summed up his work in *The Irish Times*, 1989: 'For many years Tim has worked in series, often spending three or four years on one subject. These collections can be radically different in both style and content but always stay true to a response to what appears in his life both visually and emotionally. The modus operandi remains "see and play." [He] has developed a compelling style which can rise with a swell into realism, and subside again into abstraction without losing its consistency. It can be seen as the natural succession in Irish Art to the work of George Russell in that it represents an inner landscape at the same time as being true to what is visible to the eye.'

Goulding was later made a member of Aosdána, established in 1981 as an Irish equivalent of the Académie Française to honour those artists whose work has made an outstanding contribution to the arts in Ireland. Membership of Aosdána is by peer nomination and election and is limited to 250 living artists who have produced a distinguished body of work that is original and creative.

Goulding: 'On the personal front, I became proud father of a daughter, Camille, in August 1985. She is a geographer and environmentalist, and married the musician Josh Hoisington in 2015. They live in Brooklyn, NY and he currently works with the band Sofitucker. Camille's mum Helen Strong died in 2003. She was the sister of Kevin Strong, an honorary Strangely who played and recorded with us in the Eighties. I married Georgina Lynch in 2005 at Castle Leslie in Co

Tim Goulding, recently

Monaghan, the site of Paul McCartney's nuptials.' Goulding still lives near Allihies, and occasionally guests at gigs organised by Georgie for Castletownbere's High Tide Club.

Ivan took longer to settle. 'Early in 1972 we left Del's encampment and trekked over the Slieve Aughty mountains to Dunally, near Peterswell, Co Galway. We were well received in those parts since emigration had been the norm for so many decades and fresh faces were greeted generously. We became known as "The Hipsies." Peterswell's famous son had been an accordion player, Joe Bourke, who had gone to New York. We went to the local pub, where some of his 78s were unearthed and we danced with our neighbours. In truth we were hardly ever in the pub at that juncture, mostly probably we had no spare cash! Around this time, Vashti Bunyan, her partner Robert and Rakis from Stone Monkey travelled over from Scotland down through the North in their gipsy-style caravan, and camped near us, by Kinvara. Robert got work fishing with a German who had a boat in Kinvara, but it was the time of Long Kesh prison and hunger strikes and there were some fairly heavy vibes in the island of Ireland, so they all headed back to Scotland.'

Marymac: 'We stayed near Kinvara until September, when Ivan and little Niamh and I headed off with Peggy (the mare) and Nonie (her foal) on the long and winding road to Allihies, where Goulding and Annie were living. We wintered there with some friends until finally moving to Kenmare on 14th February 1973, where we have lived ever since. We house-sat for some Australian friends who wanted to return to Oz for a few years, and stayed there for about three years while looking to buy our own place. Kenmare seemed like an ideal place, combining scenery, schools, and a very lively music scene. Our son Ivan Junior was born there in January 1977.

'It was a busy enough town with opportunity to work, and very soon we took on managing and running the unusual combination of a cafe and laundrette, The Pantry and The Wash Tub. The people who had opened the business had returned to the UK and we took it on for a few years until the building sold. Our friend Flicka Small bought the building and businesses; Ivan rented The Wash Tub and I continued to work with her in The Pantry. She developed The Pantry into a really vibrant and well-known cafe and restaurant and we all had a

very lively social and work scene there for several years. During this time we were both involved with the annual Cibeal Cincise arts festival. Initiated by Joe Thoma [q.v.], it was a remarkable festival for those times featuring an exciting and ambitious array of talents from the many artistic disciplines: music, visual art, film, poetry and dance.

'In the mid-Eighties, when Flicka sold the premises, we both started working for Munster Wholefoods, at that time in its infancy and set up by an old Trinity friend of Ivan's, Martin Benham. That grew and grew and turned into a nationwide affair. I left

Mary, Ivan and a vintner, recently

there at the end of 1996, and in May 1997 I started my own business, Mary Pawle Wines, importing organic wines from France and Spain. Ivan always devoted a huge amount of his "spare time" to helping me and since he left Munster Wholefoods in 2008, we have been working together.'

Ivan: 'I have kept up the music, playing more often than not for my own pleasure. I am jolly glad not to have become rich and famous; in fact, that never was an objective.'

Ivan and Mary's daughter Niamh now lives in Canada with her family. Young Ivan has been involved in many musical projects since starting a band at school with some friends; later bands included Sea Dog, based in Limerick, and Boys Of Summer in Dublin. He works as a full-time archaeologist and is living in Dublin. In 2013 he accompanied Ivan Senior at the Hunter's Moon Festival in Carrick-on-Shannon and also took part in a prestigious 2008 Strangelies gig in Dublin. He plays guitar, bass guitar, keyboards and theremin.

Tim Booth moved gradually back from music to work in animation, graphic design and painting. He married Andrea Lewis in 1976 (the Boomtown Rats played at their wedding). They had two children, Jesse in 1980 and Rayne in 1982. Booth: 'They both play music and are very considerable artists. For 12 years Rayne was artistic curator of the Temple Bar Gallery, Dublin's premier avant-garde gallery, and is currently studying in Lisbon for a Master's in illustration and drawing. Jesse plays bass and has his own band, The Suitcase Trio – they are shit hot. I got divorced in 1998, having lived apart for many years. I have been with my partner Doris Knöbel since then and we are happily seconded to a house near Clonakilty. I also have another wonderful daughter, the beautiful Alice, from a brief London relationship after I left Glen Row.'

These days, Tim makes a living as an artist and writer.

Tim Booth, 2018 (Photo: Dave Robinson)

# CHAPTER 2

# 1972 - 2005 – a whirlwind tour

After the Horsebox Tour Booth and Ivan continued with various musical activities, together and separately. Steve Bullock: 'After the tour I did some gigs with Tim Booth and a brilliant young guitarist from Granny's Intentions, Ed Deane, at weddings and so on. We also played at a 1976 gig in Phoenix Park as "Instant Whip" with Jonathan Kelly on drums and vocals.'

Booth: 'Ivan, myself and Rick Ward from the Cana Band were hired to play at a wedding by a Strangelies fan called Damian. Ivan and I played Strangely Strange But Oddly Normal on the church organ as the bride and groom came down the aisle, much to the disgust of the official organist who attempted to refuse to turn on the instrument, but we had sussed where the switch was positioned.

'The reception was held in the Neptune Rowing Club. The families of the bride and groom sat on opposite sides of the room – not a great omen. We played manfully. When asked for a waltz – the older women liked a good one two three – we played the Tennessee Waltz over and over as it was the only waltz we knew. Then the best man decided he would like to sing. We gave him a C major on the piano. But he could not pitch. The three of us were all seated at the piano by now, as it was the only instrument with the necessary volume to carry over the antagonistic noise of the wedding supper. We gave him an E – no, a G – no – still couldn't get in tune.

'We didn't really know the song. "Yousa know d' one by Tom Jones... Delighred." We tried once more but the best man had no idea how to sing in any given key. He came over to the piano and placed his pint carefully on the space beside the keyboard. "Ye's are not much of fuckin' piano players!" And before he could be stopped, Rick made reply: "And yer not much of a fuckin' singer!" Blam. I can still see the best man's fist as it sank in slow motion into the side of Rick's jaw. This blow triggered a chain reaction in the audience and in the melee that followed, Ivan and I managed to crawl out between the tables, the broken glass, the smashed teeth etc, dragging a bleeding and stunned Rick with us. Those were the days. And we got paid! After that, Strangelies met up every year or so to do another gig or two... or whatever was deemed cool.'

Ivan: 'About 1980, we decided to give another stab at the big time, suitably enhanced by Joe Thoma on fiddle, TJM Tutty on bass and the Two Ronnies on drums. We had a succession of drummers over the years: Tom Coady, Tel Tetrault, Fran Breen, Robbie Brennan, Earl Gill Jr, and Punka Khosa inter alia. The inaugural gig at the Project Arts Centre was an unmitigated disaster. One still wakes occasionally about 3 am in a cold sweat. The main problem lay in my inability to keep the bouzouki in tune, plus a liberal use of smoke bombs... the less said the better. From then on the only way was up... the Stragglers' Ball at Kenmare's Cibeal festival.'

## Joe Thoma

Joe has survived an ever-rotating succession and then abolition of rhythm sections for the last 38 years, and these days is very much the fourth Strangely, playing mandolin and fiddle. He grew up in Kenmare, but had left town to study at the Crawford School of Art in Cork, where he joined a folk/traditional band called Raftery. Though Joe had started off as a big Rolling Stones fan, by this point he was an admirer of psych-folk music – the Incredible String Band and Dr Strangely Strange in particular. After the Strangelies played a May 1970 Cork University gig, Joe and his mates went back to a mutual friend's house for a late-night music session with Goulding, Booth and Ivan. After that, Raftery would sometimes visit and play music with Goulding, then living in Allihies, but by the time Ivan came to live in Kenmare in 1973, Joe was living in Dublin playing profes-sionally, having taken a year out of art school to pursue a music career.

Joe: 'Raftery did regular gigs around the Dublin and Cork folk clubs and various venues around the country, from Donegal and Derry to Galway and Kerry. We didn't try any Strangelies covers, though we did do the ISB's Log Cabin Home In The Sky. We played support to the Chieftains in Trinity College on several occasions, and we busked on Grafton Street. We were signed to Release Records, based in Dublin, and had started to record an album when one of the band discovered The Divine Light Mission and left to marry a girl in Brighton. The rest of us went back to college!

Joe Thoma with Tim Goulding, High Tide Club, Castletownbere

'The following year, 1975, I got a gig in the local Kenmare secondary school, teaching art... so I was now back. Tim Booth, a regular visitor to town, was very good at singing folk ballads and backing traditional tunes so with Ivan living in Kenmare and Tim Goulding in Allihies, we ended up playing sessions together at various gatherings. During those years, Ivan and myself started doing some gigs locally and it progressed from there. Every now and then the idea of reforming the Good Doctor would crop up and eventually that happened in 1980, when I was invited to join. It was already clear that it was going to be a very sporadic gig, though!'

Booth: 'In 1982-3 I was making a short animated film, *The Prisoner*, based around a WB Yeats poem, and decided to use some of the budget to record a music track with Strangelies. Once I'd returned to Ireland, I saw less of Phil Lynott, whose career was sky-hawking. I asked Phil if he would produce it for me, but he was either too busy or just not interested and suggested I get his pal Jerome Rimson as producer. Phil was then playing with his solo outfit The Soul Band, which predominantly used black musicians, and Rimson played bass. He was a lovely man, but I often regret not having Phil produce, as I think he might have been more in sympathy with the project. We recorded the tracks in Dublin with a view to perhaps making it part of some future album. Frank Murray persuaded Gary that he might become involved, which he kindly did, overdubbing the tracks in London, enhancing our music yet again. And all he wanted was a credit on the end title for his record company.' Extracts from the soundtrack appear on the Hux Records reissue of *Heavy Petting*.

'The tracks were made with the animated image in mind and, as it was the very first Irish film to have a Dolby Stereo soundtrack, had great impact when shown in a Dolby cinema. However, when it went on distribution in Ireland, the Idiot Distributors were unable or too incompetent to supply the Dolby prints to Dolby cinemas, so mono prints were shown in Dolby cinemas and vice versa. This did not help its audience perception and, as Dolby cost an arm and a leg back then, gave me a few grey hairs. The film was invited to the Annecy Animation Festival and also the Berlin Film Festival where – I found out later – it was a contender for a prize and because of German love of technology, looked and sounded amazing for its time. It gets shown on TV now and then.'

Ivan: 'At this juncture, we had a real doctor playing saxophone, namely Kevin Strong, who went on to save lives while we manfully strove to blow minds. Starting out as a quasi-acoustic outfit, we had mutated – through a series of hybrid crossovers and implants – into a fun party band people could dance to (in the old-fashioned pre-E way).' This was one of the Strangelies' periodic, usually ill-fated, attempts to update themselves – see also Strange Lee Strange, below.

The CD age saw an infamous 1992 Island Records reissue of *Kip*, mastered from the original stereo master tapes with the tape deck left running at the wrong speed by a somnolent tape op. The resultant release was therefore slower, and pitched a whole tone down the scale from the original, making the band sound old before their time. Despite numerous complaints (and promises) this has never been rectified, and so, even now, if you buy an MP3 download, or listen to the album on Spotify, it is the appalling 1992 version.

Goulding: 'In 1994 the Doctors did a mini tour in Cork and Kerry (the Pray For Us tour or The Pork And Sherry tour). At each venue there was a Camilla Parker-Bowles lookalike contest, won at one gig by Paul Scully, later producer of our *Alternative Medicine* CD.'

The Incredible String Band fanzine *Be Glad* had devoted a lot of page space to the Strangelies, and in 1994 the band also resurfaced in the UK to

play a 'Tea Dance' at the magazine's ISB convention in Leeds. This was the Strange Lee Strange era, with the crack rhythm section of Punka Khosa and TJM Tutty. The show featured a weird, staccato 'Dance Version' of Sign On My Mind, a great Ballad Of The Wasps and new songs from what would become *Alternative Medicine*, as well as sympathetic versions of old favourites like Donnybrook Fair. An 'Official Bootleg' cassette on sale at the event featured a range of demo recordings from over the recent years.

## Alternative Medicine

Ivan: 'Having played together steadily but with irregularity over the past while, in 1996 it was deemed time to tackle that "Difficult Third Album" before another century was on us.' Booth: 'We put our own money up, with the additional financial help of Strangelies fan Roland Bokius, who currently runs a bar in Mainz called Sixties. Paul Scully produced the recordings in Ballyvourney Studios, situated between Kenmare and Cork. Gary's generosity reasserted itself and he flew over from London and laid down his usual mind-boggling guitar on three tracks; the laughter and sheer joy of being all together once more was just the best drug. Again he would not accept a fee, saying we could not have afforded him anyway – which was true – so it was better he do it for nothing. He was a kind and generous man, always willing to record with us or add in to something we were attempting. There were other times across the years: his kindness and interest in my son's band after they had performed a slightly shaky set in Whelan's – which Gary had insisted on attending. After the gig, he bought them pints and talked intensely to these young lads about music. And that band is still together.'

*Alternative Medicine* was released in 1997 via Ace Records, run by old mates Roger Armstrong and Ted Carroll, and is a bit of a curate's egg. There are some very good tracks and Goulding's piano and Hammond parts (he finally got his hands on one!) are outstanding. Ivan's Lilty's is an idiosyncratic instrumental which mixes Russian and Scottish motifs, and Hames And Traces, a lovely song, harks back to his horse-drawn caravan days of 1972. Booth's The James Gang adroitly continues one of his cowboy themes. The Heat Came Down, also by Booth, alludes to the pre-heroin, more innocent days of Notting Hill dope dealers and boasts lead guitar by Gary Moore. Darksome Burn is Goulding's heartfelt piano-based setting of a Gerard Manley Hopkins poem, but his best song is Whatever Happened To The Blues, a slow-burn rocker which also features fiery guitar by Gary. Goulding says they had 'three great days' in the studio when the lead guitar parts were added. Moore was particularly impressed by Whatever Happened To The Blues. 'He invited me to sing and play it with him the next time he played Glastonbury. It never happened,' says Goulding.

As a whole, the album feels overproduced and suffers from an overdose of democracy – all the songs are credited to everyone, even Paul Scully, the producer, and TJM Tutty, the bass player, gets two tracks. It ends up dissipating that unique Strangelies ethos. We won't even mention the elements of Ill-Advised Reggae. The strongest track is Epilog, Booth's unadorned requiem for Phil Lynott: just the three original band members on vocals, guitars and harmonium. 'Played live, in the studio. One take, like it always used to be,' says Booth's sleeve note.

Booth has another Gary story from this time: 'Doris and I were living that time in Dundrum where she ran a super-efficient ironing service. One of her customers was Mark, who owned the local chemist's and as I had taken lots of photos of our recording session in Ballyvourney, I took these to Mark to have them developed. I had been shooting with available light, trusting the exposure meter, but the photos were glitched. Mark, a pretty decent guitar player himself, recognised Gary from the ghosted image and expressed his admiration. When Gary came by the house a little later, Doris asked Gary if – as a great favour – he would deliver Mark's recently ironed shirts down to the chemist's shop. He loved the notion and did so, walking into the shop unannounced, the goods held out before him, straight-armed in rustling plastic. "Your ironing, sir." Gary got as much fun and joy from this simple act of generosity as did the recipient and once Mark had got over his surprise, the two talked that intense music talk, Gary signing a CD Mark happened to have in his car.'

On its release, the album received scant press attention. Eamonn Carr of Tara Telephone, now working for the Dublin-based *Evening Herald*, wrote a sympathetic feature outlining the band's history and celebrating their 'buoyancy of spirit.' However, there was little in the music magazines, apart from an odd review in Q magazine which concluded that their 'honour was just about rescued' but urged them to 'ditch the wobbly vocals,' preferring two of the instrumental tracks. The Irish distribution was a real disaster, says Goulding: 'The record company gave us 1,000 copies which we gave to Mulligan Records, who went bankrupt and threw them out.'

With The Bairns, Scottish tour. Note Joe Thoma far left, with stylish moustache

Perversely and typically, the band decided only to promote the new album with a brief 'World Tour Of Scotland.' Goulding: 'Joe Thoma played fiddle, and we had the Sweeney brothers from Kenmare on board, Dan on bass and Niall on drums. We called them "The Bairns" as they were so young and brought the average age of the band down to about 50. We did about eight gigs, one in Traquair, south of Edinburgh, with our honorary member Davy McFarlane who is an ace blues harp player. He featured on *Alternative Medicine* and also on my solo effort *Midnight Fry*. Ishy from Stone Monkey lives in Traquair, near Glen Row, and put that gig on. Mainly we played in the north of Scotland, including the Highland music festival based out of Inverness. We played a really good gig at the Blue Lamp, Ullapool and in Nairn, Fraserburgh, Stirling and a remote West Coast town called Plockton. We also recorded a live BBC Radio spot at the Lemon Tree in Aberdeen.'

Though audience numbers were not always that great, the band enjoyed the outing. In a *Hot Press* article about the tour, Booth wrote: 'We'll have to do this again, only next time we'll pre-plan a bit more and get the itinerary into some kind of shape. 2,500 miles in 10 days is pushing it a bit, but as Joe Thoma says, "I enjoyed 95% of that, and 75% of it… I enjoyed hugely!" Our audiences seem to have felt the same way, which – for old men like us, these days – is as good as it gets.'

Joyce's desktop – a still from the film

In 1998 Booth received Arts Council and Film Board funding to make another animated film, for which Tim Goulding recorded the piano soundtrack, variations on Strings In The Earth And Air. The film, *Ulys*, was a five-minute condensed version of Joyce's *Ulysses*, which you can find on Vimeo. In the journal *Animation*, academic Thomas Walsh wrote that 'Booth uses the structural affinity of linguistics and animation to clarify Joyce's more obscure image-schemas, thereby demonstrating not a transformative form of adaptation but an archaeology that digs through the strata of a symbolic order to disinter a real, material body, that lies underneath.'

There you go. It's a very creative piece, using animation particularly successfully to re-enact some of the metamorphoses in the novel and looking, as Joyce did, at national identity.

## Midnight Fry

Goulding's solo CD, *Midnight Fry*, was recorded in 1999 at home in Allihies and Dublin and released in 2000. Goulding: 'There were four months of recording days and the Strangelies and many other musician friends featured. With a seven-piece band, The Cooks, I did a seven-date tour around Ireland, including the Blue Moon Club at Cork Opera House and Whelan's of Dublin.' In the UK, *fROOTS* magazine was impressed: 'Goulding has

created his own ambient soundscape, one that pulses and resounds in aural delights and images, truly unique.'

Goulding was pushing the boundaries with this album, using loops, drum programming, synths and sequencing. There's even some Goulding rap by 'The Timmi G Project.' Andrew Philpott, later a collaborator with Depeche Mode, provided a whizzy remix of one Celtic-tinged track, O-Mané. The standout recording is Piece Of Cod, which finally realises the arrangement which the Strangelies had been groping towards thirty years earlier. Booth and Ivan add backing vocals and Goulding contributes some funky electric and acoustic piano. A wonderful version.

The mid-Nineties 'Celtic Tiger' boom in the Irish economy, and all the corruption and greed that went with it, had returned Booth to some of the preoccupations he had explored in Donnybrook Fair. He had been working on a novel in which the 'creative outsider' was no longer the unicorn but Misha, a young female crusty. *Altergeist*, published by Fish Publishing in 1999, is a dyspeptic, dystopian piece of what you might call cyber-punk. Here's an extract from the blurb:

'If your name's Misha Ploughman, and you're just trying to get along, then the last thing you need is heat. But that's what you've got, because you've got the only copy of something called a Simulated Alternative Mimetic Memory Induction programme wired into your skull, and even though you don't want it, everybody else does, and when you run, it's tough to know who to trust. You only know who you can't trust. You can't trust the law, because there's none in New Ireland. You can't trust the Church, because they think they're the law. And you can't trust the State, because they think they're the Church. And most of all, you can't trust your friends, because you can't remember who they were anymore. All you can do is trust yourself and Ripper the SkateKing. And that gets you deeper into trouble, because nobody warned you about the Altergeist Effect.'

Since 2006 Booth has also written and drawn Dan Dare strips for *Spaceship Away*, an illustrated fanzine which is largely based round the space hero Dan Dare, of the Fifties/Sixties boys' illustrated magazine *Eagle*.

In 2003 Goulding released another solo CD, *Big Red / Old Yalla*, 'a set of ambient grooves for Maurice Henderson's paintings.' Goulding: 'Big Red and Old Yalla are aural interpretations of two 6 foot by 8 foot abstract colour field paintings by my great friend, the late Maurice Henderson, who lived near me in West Cork. One painting is singing dripping variations of red and the other is sizzling yellows and oranges. Both tracks feature vocals by American musician Ross Peacock, who never uses whole words but plays the voice like a synthesizer, something akin to Sprechgesang. Ivan Pawle features on guitar and Joe Thoma on fiddle. Old Yalla includes recorded bumble bees to reflect the sizzling yellows. There are a host of percussive and vocal samples mixed with grand and electric piano, and organ. These were the first fruits of my Sweet Ticket Music home studio, using Logic audio. Also included on the CD is an unused track originally recorded for a film made at the Burning Man festival.'

After the Scottish tour, all went fairly quiet on the music front, though in 2005 the band did reconvene to play an acoustic gig at the wake for Annie Christmas, who had sadly died of leukaemia in May that year.

# CHAPTER 3

# A Strangelies Renaissance

The last decade has seen something of a Strangely Strange rehabilitation and renaissance. Once a small footnote in psych-folk history, they have been the subject of two film documentaries, won an award at the Cork Indie Festival, seen all their old recordings remastered and re-released to great critical acclaim and four-star reviews, been featured on an Olivier Assayas film soundtrack, played at London's Barbican Concert Hall and at a triumphant homecoming gig in Dublin, and been celebrated in Rob Young's groundbreaking *Electric Eden*.

2007 was the year things kicked off, with an unreleased archive compilation CD and a London gig. I had started occasional work for Brian O'Reilly's Hux Records, and persuaded him that there might be a small market for a compilation of the Strangelies' BBC sessions. It turned out that the only tapes still in existence, recorded on my old reel-to-reel, were slightly distorted versions of two songs from the band's John Peel session and 15 minutes in reasonable quality of the 1970 *In Concert* broadcast. Aware that this might not provide very good value, I suggested we could supplement these with the two muffled tapes of the band live at Les Cousins which had been recorded inside Lagga's duffle-bag. Brian sensibly pointed out the shortcomings of this selection and suggested I should find out if there was any other archive stuff.

This is the point in the book where the biographer steps out from the shadowy margins of impersonal passive constructions. I got in touch with the band, who vaguely remembered some unreleased 1970 Sound Techniques recording sessions for a couple of songs, with which we thought we might augment the mix. After interminable delays and with some help from Joe Boyd, we finally got the go-ahead from Island/Universal. I was eventually given a tape list of Dr SS recordings which included a lot of titles I didn't recognise and even more intriguingly, several reels marked 'unknown.'

Inside the Universal Music Tape Facility, there was an archive playback and mixing studio equipped with ancient 4- and 8-track reel-to-reel machines looking a bit like old-fashioned gas cookers. Audio engineer Ben Wiseman and I got to work on the pile of dusty old Witchseason Productions tapes I'd ordered in from storage. Playing the first reel we picked was like being in a time machine – suddenly it was 1969 and we were eavesdropping on a Strangely Strange recording session, complete with muttered imprecations,

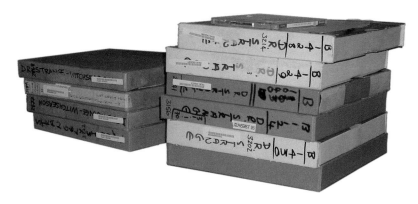

dropped guitars, a lot of muffled giggling and authoritative-sounding instructions from Joe. And that's how we 'discovered' a whole album's worth of unreleased material, *Halcyon Days*, with brilliant songs such as Mirror Mirror, Sweet Red Rape and Horse Of A Different Hue.

By now the Strangelies had settled back into being a predominantly acoustic four-piece, with the ever-faithful Joe Thoma on fiddle and mandolin. Goulding told writer Rob Young: 'We're not trying to be a band in any ambitious way, more like three pals speeding towards geezerhood. That gives us carte blanche.' They added three newly recorded tracks in *Kip* vein to the album: Booth's Invisible Kid, Ivan's Halcyon Days and Goulding's Le Le Rockin' Sound, a new take on the 1969 live favourite.

On 16 June 2007, Bloomsday, we launched the CD with a sold-out show at Denmark Street's 12-Bar Club. There was a real buzz about the event, and *The Times* had made it one of their gigs of the week: 'With a CD of hitherto unreleased songs just out, the celebrated 1960s emissaries of Irish psych-folk reform...'

It was the Strangelies' first London gig in 36 years, and there was a great celebratory atmosphere. A host of figures from their history turned out to cheer them on – Joe Boyd, Frank van der Meijden, the Ace Records crew, Sylvia Keogh, Jay Myrdal and many other friends and hardcore fans.

Before the set, we showed Booth's *Ulys* animation, and there was a premiere for *Strangelies in Dalston*, Iain Sinclair's (silent) film diary, now set to an audio track of Tom Barwood's inspired mash-up of *Kip Of The Serenes*. Later that year, Iain set up a limited DVD release for the film, which is now sold out.

Press reviews of the album were universally positive: there were 4-star reviews in *Uncut*, *Rock'n'Reel*, and *Mojo*, where Sylvie Simmons dubbed it 'a wonderful piece of archaeology.'

In March 2008 Booth's daughter Rayne used her considerable organisational skills to set up a triumphant 'homecoming gig' at the swish Sugar Club in Dublin. It sold out, of course, and Joe Thoma remembers it as one of their best gigs. It was a joyful family affair, with Ivan Pawle Junior guesting on lead guitar in the finale, and sister Niamh in the audience. Goulding's nephew Barnes Goulding played drums and Booth's son Jesse played bass. Old mates who turned up included Frank Murray, latter-day Strangelies sax player Dr Kevin Strong and guitarist Ed Deane from Booth's Seventies band.

2009 was a busy year for the reinvigorated band. Encouraged by all the positive responses, in February Hux had remastered and reissued *Kip Of The Serenes*. This is one of very few re-releases to be marketed as being 'at the correct speed.' Extras included an early version of Mirror Mirror, and there were alternate takes of SSBON and of West Cork Hack, where you could eavesdrop on Joe Boyd's problems remembering the title, which gradually morphed into West Coast Hack! At the end of one take, Booth had led the band into an a cappella sea shanty, Ranzo, so we left that on too.

The four-piece Strangelies came over to London that month for three 'playing the album' gigs, in what was quickly dubbed the North London Tour. For my role in setting this up reasonably patiently (it was like herding cats), I was duly awarded the honour of a Strangelies' Nickname, 'Ado.' Up there now with Garo and Philo, I thought. After a secret warm-up event at The Plough, Walthamstow, the biggest gig was on February 21st at The Gaff, a curious Goth club in Holloway Road. What the audience didn't know was that, behind the scenes, plans had been carefully laid for Gary Moore to ap-

Live at The Plough

pear as a surprise guest. Despite his superstar status, Gary was up for sitting in; two years previously he had appeared unannounced with Nine Below Zero in a tiny Berkshire pub. He was due to play on the final part of the show, when the band were joined by a scratch rhythm section to perform Piece Of Cod, Horse Of A Different Hue, James Gang and, of course, Sign On My Mind. Gary was due back from France with his daughter Lily early that evening on the Eurostar and had planned to dump his luggage, leave Lily with a babysitter and get a cab over to the venue. A spare amp was set up in readiness onstage and a bottle of Sancerre (his favourite wine) was cooling in the dressing-room fridge, but an increasingly frantic series of phone calls revealed firstly that the train had been delayed, and then that Gary had not been able to find anyone he trusted to look after Lily. Oh well, there'll be another opportunity, we figured.

The Gaff gig went very well, surviving a few missed cues and a brief Ivan melt-down caused by a squeaky air-conditioning unit. There was a memorable introduction to Ship Of Fools, not one of Booth's or Ivan's favourites. Goulding: 'We have not played this song for 38 years, and, after tomorrow, will probably never play it again.' Post Celtic Tiger, Booth had updated Donnybrook Fair. Deirdre Of The Sorrows was now 'selling off her real estate' and the final verse went:

**'I used to sing this song back in 1969
About the fair in Donnybrook where the water turned to wine
But all the old excuses, they can leave you in no doubt
The Tiger ate the Unicorn, chewed him up and spat him out'**

The final gig, at the Green Note in Camden, was as a trio; Joe Thoma had to go back to work in Kenmare. The support act was Iain Sinclair, reading from his Hackney book and the section from his *Kodak Mantra Diaries* which deals with Ivan's ill-fated acid trip. The sold-out performance attracted guests from as guests from as far afield as Hungary, France and Germany.

The revised *Kip* also attracted strong reviews. Writing a four-star review for *Uncut*, Rob Young described it as 'pastoral folk at its most psychedelic... the definitive package of this late-60s Albion dreamtime oddity.' *Mojo* also awarded four stars, but the best review of all came from the band's standard-bearer in the popular press, *The Sun*'s Simon Cosyns, who gave it five stars: 'A thing of joy.'

Back in Ireland, indie director Conor Heffernan produced a thirty-minute documentary film about the band, using some contemporary interviews and rehearsals coupled with some of Iain Sinclair's 1969 footage. The Irish Gaelic TV channel, TG4, broadcast another documentary about the band, based around preparations for an April art exhibition at the Carnegie Arts Centre, Kenmare alongside a gig at the same venue which Joe Thoma and Ivan remember as a stand-out performance.

The band were back in London in July to appear at the Barbican in Joe Boyd's Witchseason Weekender. The first night, An All-Star Fairport Convention, involved just about everyone who'd ever played in that band. The second night, The Music of the Incredible String Band, involved Clive Palmer and Mike Heron but no Robin Williamson, and many special guests. Encouraged by what he'd seen at the 12-Bar Club, Joe had added the Strangelies to the line-up. They were paid £750 plus expenses, by far the most they'd got for a gig in their entire career!

Other guests included Trembling Bells, Alasdair Roberts, Richard Thompson and his daughter Kami, blue-grass banjoist Abigail Washburn, and fairly late in the proceedings I persuaded Scritti Politti's Green Gartside to also offer his services. There were three days of intense rehearsals with Joe, who ruled with 'a rod of iron,' and MD Robyn Hitchcock. Robyn was duly awarded his own Strangelies Nickname. On the Friday the band did another unannounced warm-up gig at The Plough Folk Club, followed by a 45-minute solo concert at the Barbican Freestage on the Sunday afternoon.

There was a mix and match approach to the ISB show, which saw Goulding playing the whistle solo alongside Clive Palmer on his Empty Pocket Blues and Green joining the Strangelies for Mike Heron's Air in the first half; after the break they returned to play Cousin Caterpillar, along with Trembling Bells and Richard Thompson on guitar. Joe Thoma added virtuoso fiddle on Log Cabin Home In The Sky, joining vocalists Richard Thompson and Abigail Washburn, and also on Chinese White, with Robyn Hitchcock and Mike Heron. Joe really came into his own that evening. After the show, there was a protracted late-night jam session in their hotel bar which saw the two Tims and Ivan venturing their own take on gospel and Joe sitting in with virtually everyone. He got on especially well with Abigail Washburn, who'd decided to stay up all night to catch an early flight, and at 6 am, when she left for Heathrow, they were the last two standing.

Over the course of the rehearsals and gig, the gregarious Strangelies befriended most of their fellow performers and Green Gartside, in those days still anxious about performing live, was taken under their wing. Rose Simpson from the ISB was there for the Sunday show. Though there was to be an 'everyone on stage' mass finale for the 'May the long time sun shine' ending of Cellular Song, Joe Boyd had ruled against inviting her up to join in. We hatched a disobedient plot in which, at the last minute, Rose jumped up out of the audience and ran on stage right, into the Strangelies' welcoming arms.

The weighty book *Electric Eden*, published in 2010, provided an authoritative and definitive survey of psychedelic folk and its antecedents, and celebrated the Strangelies' contribution to the genre. Author Rob Young had already had some very tangential involvement with the band when, the year before, he lent them his gong to use on the 'sound the foghorn' bit of Ship Of Fools at The Gaff. His section on the band summed them up very nicely: 'Their two albums… were lysergic pageants of waking dreams summoning an Ireland of wonders, populated with a gallery of eccentric characters drawn from history, mythology, fiction and the recesses of their own imaginations – a kind of *Ulysses* in pantaloons.'

Booth had recently returned to the 'Ireland of wonders' theme with a new lysergic pageant, Hy Brasil. Irish myths talk of a phantom island to the west of Ireland in the Atlantic. Normally shrouded in mist, Hy Brasil becomes visible one day in every seven years. For the 'artists and writers and poets' who'd like to take a trip, Booth provides a suggestion:

**'How do we find this old Isle of the Blessed?**
**Well a tab of White Lightning is probably best**
**For that high definition reception'**

*Heavy Petting* was being prepared for re-release by Hux in late 2011, and I had interviewed Gary Moore by phone as part of the research for the booklet. Would he be up for guesting on 'his' songs at a big London Strangelies gig, I asked him: 'You let me know when you wanna do the *Heavy Petting* gig and I'll try and do it! It's no problem.'

In February 2011, I was in the process of booking the Jazz Café in Camden, and talking to Dave Mattacks and Andy Irvine about joining the line-up, when we heard the shocking news that Gary had died suddenly while on holiday in Spain. In the end, we went ahead on a rather smaller scale than originally planned, using guitarist Paul Simmons from The Bevis Frond, who steeped himself in the essence of Moore for the gig. The event became a sort of Strangelies memorial for Gary.

Booth summed up Moore's great talent in his *Hot Press* article: 'Imagine a great spindle in among the stars of heaven, a huge rotating driveshaft, lathing at the heart of the cosmos, everything known orbiting around this central gearing, galaxies spiralling out and away, star systems revolving, space and time peeling out around the revolving core and there is music playing, mind-altering celestial riffs to illustrate and illuminate the turning of this, the greatest wheel. Gary Moore knew this music, this life-sustaining calm in the centre of things and could reach out and capture it and had the sublime ability to bring it down to earth – decode it, lay it out in a priori sequences – for us lesser mortals to hear, understand, marvel at and appreciate. Thank you Gary.'

The *Heavy Petting And Other Proclivities* CD remaster posed a small dilemma – what to do about the legendary Roger Dean cutout sleeve? In 2005, Repertoire Records had tried a miniature version, but we all felt this was expensive to do and didn't really work small scale, so an 'alternate take' was created using some of Johanna's other stills from the original sessions. We needed some more Dean-style letters to spell '...and other proclivities,' which design ace Mychael Gerstenberger ran up for us and were deemed up to scratch by the man himself. Extras featured Gary Moore, including the first take of Sign On My Mind from the Dublin sessions and a short medley taken from Booth's *The Prisoner* soundtrack. And three live 1970 tracks with Hoppy, taken from an old reel-to-reel tape, very much like the 1970 *In Concert* broadcast, also finally saw the light of day...

## Heavy Petting launch

The second North London Tour, in October 2011, was even more tightly delineated than the first – one gig in Dalston and two in the same Camden street. It was still like herding cats, but I had some invaluable logistical help from my partner Deena (known in some quarters as 'the electric landlady') – together, we lived and breathed Strangelies for four packed and hilarious days.

I had lined up some additional musicians for the electric section of the Jazz Café gig. The plan was for lead guitarist Paul Simmons to join Sgt Buzfuz record producer Jon Clayton on bass and Paul Dufour, the original drummer in the Libertines. All three had rehearsed to the original record (Ivan was under strict instructions not to change any arrangements), so the first time the augmented band actually played together was at the warm-up gig the day before. Paul Simmons: 'I'd spent quite a few weeks going through the Gary Moore tracks and had got a handle on the general feel of them. No rehearsals with the band themselves but it worked fine. We got on amazingly well and continue to stay in touch to this day.'

Unfortunately, The Plough had since closed down, so I had prevailed on Resonance FM's Ed Baxter, programmer of our Dr Strangely Strange radio documentaries and a covert member of the psych-folk brotherhood, to book us an undercover slot at Dalston's Café Oto as support to Kinnie The Explorer, a four-piece neo-psychedelic band from Brighton. The *Time Out* listing referred to 'psychedelic folk-rock from Mountains Of The Mind.' Mountains Of The Mind acquitted themselves well, though they did slot in a fairly extended Jazz Café soundcheck the next day, along with another guest. Mike Heron was in town and had kindly agreed to do a song with the band, so the Strangelies revived their arrangement of Air from the Barbican gig. Also present at the soundcheck was a slightly nervous banjo player. I'd asked author Andrew Greig, once half of Fate & ferret, if he would like to play the banjo intro on Mary Malone Of Moscow – 'You bloody bet I would,' was his response. This is how he remembers his guest spot. It's an edited version of material originally written for a F&f work in progress:

Andrew: 'I locate the Jazz Café. George is there, already talking to the three Strangelies. It is as though we had just left them in the pub in 1969, walked round the block and come back in again. Still a bunch of old hippies, basically – goofy, generous, good company. Hair has turned grey or disappeared, but the essential levity and spark remain. The years have aged but not soured them...

'For tonight the Strangelies have added a rhythm section, plus their fiddler, Joe Thoma, a reserved, sardonic Irish man in a tweed jacket. Joe brings a certain steadiness to the band, and plays a heart-melting solo air. Someone is missing: Gary Moore sprinkled rock magic over *Heavy Petting*, one of the great guitarists. But he has died of a heart attack a few months earlier, and this concert is in part a memorial to him.

'His youthful stand-in is Paul Simmons, who plays crunching, fluent lead guitar. At such moments, the Strangelies sound like a rock band in a way the ISB never did – then they cut to whistle and organ, some spacey harmonies, fiddle, a bit of baroque, then rock out again.

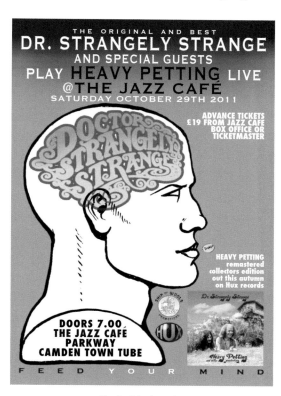

Tim Booth's gig poster

'Time to run through Mary Malone. I start the lead-in on banjo, which opens weirdly on the third beat of the bar. Pesky hippy musicians! I stumble, lose it... I try it again, get through it and the band take the song away.

'The audience stream in, mostly grey haired or no-haired, happy, buzzing. Lots of hugs, handshakes and reunions, introduction of grown-up children. A familiar herby smell clings to some sweaters and beards.

Laughter, beer, red wine. Missing faces, present by their painful absence. We're getting to that point in life when every celebration has an element of wake, and every wake is a celebration of still being here. Adrian introduces the band to cheers and laughter as they sort themselves out. They start Ballad Of The Wasps at more or less the same time, and the evening takes off.

'Mike Heron is going to sing Air. There he is, just appeared in the wings. Forty plus years on but the wide grin, beaky nose and stocky build are unmistakable. Mike comes onstage to be greeted with great enthusiasm by the standing audience. He looks pleased and surprised. A Hawaiian melody ripples off the keyboard. My skin begins to prickle, I haven't heard this in years. Mike takes his hands from his pockets and steps to the microphone. He leans in close and, fractionally anticipating the beat, sings "Breathing, all creatures are…"

'Time for Mary Malone. Banjo neck slippery with sweat, I squeeze onto the stage, trying not to trip over the cables. Tim at the keyboards gives me a wink. I can only hope the banjo is still in tune because I can't hear much over the crowd noise.

'I count myself in, past the two missed beats, then begin. It's fun, loads of fun being with an amplified band, carried up in the net of bass, drums, keyboards. I come back in at the right place, then it's plain sailing though I must keep counting bars. Always that balancing act of enjoying the moment while anticipating what comes next. What comes next is the pause, the cut out, the end. Applause and I'm off, flushed and heady, still concentrating on not tripping up.'

The enhanced band at the Jazz Café (Photo: Sean Kelly)

The gig went brilliantly. The audience included writer and comedian Stewart Lee and his mate Richard Herring, as well as *The Sun*'s Simon Cosyns. They didn't meet… Genesis Breyer P-Orridge was also on the list, but had to send last-minute apologies owing to flight delays. In what I considered a fantastic PR coup, Stephen Fry had tweeted his eight million followers about the gig. None of them showed, though we did have an impressive Norwegian posse, all wearing the T-shirts Tim Booth had designed for the gig.

There were some strong versions of the *Heavy Petting* tracks, Paul Simmons played a blinder, and Ivan was actually seen grinning and even dancing on stage! There was a sense of circles being completed. Many of Strangelies' friends and family were there, as well as the Ace Records crew, Gary's ex-partner Sylvia Keogh and their daughter Saoirse.

Booth: 'I really enjoyed that gig and felt we played well despite a few missed cues, which we managed to cover up. Roger Armstrong and Ted Carroll were impressed.'

Ted: 'I can't believe it... Strangelies were actually tight.'

Roger: 'I think they discovered their inner showband...'

Paul Simmons: 'The gig was pretty nerve-racking, considering Ivan told me thirty seconds before I went on that Thin Lizzy's old manager and Gary Moore's daughter were in the audience. But – it was a fantastic success, with a great vibe on stage. I remember being approached after the gig by members of an Eastern European Gary Moore Fanclub (Hungary possibly) who had travelled over for the show and asked me for autographs!'

Goulding: 'Joe Thoma and I agree that this was one of our best gigs. Some of the acoustic numbers from *Heavy Petting* stood out for me and of course the addition of bass and drums, with the inimitable Paul Simmons, really let the rockier ones rock. It was an especial delight for me to have use of the Jazz Café's acoustic grand (in tune) to intersperse with my trusty Yamaha P120.

'I remember jumping up in the middle of one song and doing a rather advanced dance on the edge of the stage. Luckily a fellow sufferer spotted this and gave me instructions how to relieve the pain. It was cramp in the toes, though the rest of the audience presumed it was part of the show. After the gig, I remember giving the MONDO STRANGE T-shirt off my back to a Norwegian Strangelies fan.'

Ivan: 'The gig was highly enjoyable, and virtually stress-free; the house PA team was among the best ever. We were quite well rehearsed (comparatively, for us!) and hugely enhanced by Paul's lead guitar work. It was a great honour to have Mike Heron on stage with us at one point. We met so many friends there: there was a sizeable contingent from my East Suffolk family of cousins and siblings, always a joy to see, and Mary and I met lots of friends like Jay Myrdal and Renchi, whom we

Fate & ferret onstage with the Strangelies at the Green Note (Photo: Sean Kelly)

hadn't seen for ages. There was a celebratory atmosphere in the place. I seem to remember there were even sur-titles for the lyrics, but this I may have simply hallucinated in the sheer exhilaration of the night.' He had.

The final gig was at The Green Note, Camden. Andrew Greig had the support role, and read a poem about driving south in the fish truck to meet Joe Boyd, plus some Fate & ferret memories 'which may form the basis of a book.' These he eventually worked up more fully for the Greig/Heron co-authored *You Know What You Could Be*, which was born out of meeting with Mike again after the Jazz Café gig.

In the main set, the Dr SS four-piece played mainly acoustic material, including *Kip* songs and the newish Booth number, Hy Brasil. Andrew was impressed: 'Tonight they're in great form… Donnybrook Fair reminds me how Irish they are, in the way loss and heartbreak, history, piss-taking and death are all incorporated, ac-cepted, celebrated. They are ramshackle then tight, erudite and innocent. When Ivan sings he must adjust his sense of timing, the rest of the band crack up.'

Andrew and George stepped up from the audience to join the band for the encore, making this the second London Fate & ferret London appearance in around forty years.

The reissued CD again got some great reviews, including 4 stars from both *Uncut* and *The Sun*. Stewart Lee, still under the spell of the Jazz Café gig, reviewed the album for the *Sunday Times*: '*Heavy Petting* featured the psychedelic blues licks of guitarist Gary Moore, making for a cautious but compelling hybrid of fragile folk forms and more muscular rock moves. The lengthy Sign On My Mind, with both a tentative first effort and the strident second take included here, is a slowly uncoiling acid-folk classic, rivalling Fairport's A Sailor's Life and Trees' Sally Free And Easy.'

Over in New York, Genesis Breyer P-Orridge wrote an 'Epiphany' piece on the Strangelies originally in-tended for *The Wire* magazine, calling *Heavy Petting* 'a treasure trove of acid folk extraordinaire… The Strangelies blend absurdism with lyrical poetry, emotion with coarse pub humour, and sudden melodic changes with in-congruous soloing. Unlike the ISB, the albums don't hold together as a whole narrative set into a stylistic struc-ture that remains consistent within an album. The Strangelies' songs swerve and dodge all over the place. Where the ISB is essentially pastoral, the Strangelies are more Chaucerian, bawdy in a noisy medieval Irish Inn. Far more surprising and bizarre is the appearance of Gary Moore on Sign On My Mind. And a blistering, perfectly interlocking performance it is. In fact a cover of this, complete with solo, is still on the Psychic TV/PTV3 "to do" list.

'Dr Strangely Strange albums… are that rarity of items, music that can uplift the most dour and maudlin moment. A warning to unadventurous "folkies," acid, dark, Goth or whatnot, *Heavy Petting* is the odd one out and is a contradictory, more rockist approach than the others (they even boogie at one point!) but there are enough gems and intricate, intelligent lyrics to make up for the loss of acoustic weirdness.

'In the end my addiction to Dr Strangely Strange is rooted in the stretching of poetry into epiphany. Phi-losophy and "popular" music is a difficult marriage, but like all good Zen masters (one Strangely became a Zen monk!) humour illuminates as brightly as wisdom. I cannot imagine not having the twisting turning contradic-tions and malapropisms that litter this wonderful, wonder-full music with diamonds of hope. Dr Strangely Strange smiles at you and if you cannot smile back, oh goodness, we are lost…'

In *The Guardian*, long-time fan Robin Denselow assessed both album and gig:

'Thanks to the alt-folk revival, even lesser-known 70s psychedelic folk-rockers are back in fashion. Dr Strangely Strange were Ireland's answer to the Incredible String Band, a delightfully quirky outfit whose vinyl releases have become collectors' items – and rightly so. Now digitally remastered, and with out-takes and live tracks added in, this set... includes fine, fluid early guitar solos from the great Gary Moore, then a teenager. The songs match surreal lyrics against an engagingly bizarre kaleidoscope of styles; Moore's blues-rock is intercut with ragtime, country (including a burst of the Patti Page favourite, Tennessee Waltz), acoustic traditional and medieval styles, along with church music and carols, with Jove Was at Home suddenly segueing into a triumphant Gloria, Hosanna in Excelis. There is also inventive vocal harmony work – which sounded particularly impressive when the now-expanded trio relaunched the album in London this week.'

In 2012, word reached Ivan from his music publisher that Olivier Assayas, director of films such as *Irma Vep* and *Personal Shopper*, was planning to use Strings In The Earth And Air for his semi-autobiographical film about the early Seventies, *Something In The Air*. Alarm bells rang, and we managed to get to Assayas just in time to prevent him from using the version supplied to him by Island/Universal which was – surprise surprise – still at the wrong speed. The Strangelies were in good company on the soundtrack, Assayas' very personal choice which included Syd Barrett, Soft Machine's Why Are We Sleeping, Kevin Ayers' Decadence, Nick Drake and the Incredible String Band. Assayas had bought *Kip* when it first came out, his attention originally drawn by the LP cover. At a London screening of his film, he told me he loved the LP and had always been surprised it wasn't a really well-known album. He had faithfully hung on to his vinyl copy through the years – though he kept it hidden from the view of his friends during the punk era!

The film is really good, too. *Sight and Sound*: '*Something In The Air* looks back to the early Seventies as, if not a lost paradise, at least a lost hotbed of infinite possibilities. Assayas depicts a culturally and politically vibrant era made and lived through by intelligent, sensitive beings taking full advantage of their moment.'

Late 2016 saw a brief run of Irish gigs. In September, after a warm-up gig at The High Tide Club in Castletownbere, Dr Strangely Strange played their first festival for over forty years, on the Salty Dog Stage at The Electric Picnic festival, Co Laois. Booth: 'The festival gig was fine. We played at lunch/breakfast time to a bunch of entitled millennials and the few DSS fans who had made it out of their sleeping bags. The sound crew could not do enough and we were well looked after. But the event itself was not so great. My prevailing memory now is one of the stench of overflowing toilets, the rumble of continuous sub-bass, littered camping grounds and zombied spectators. I would not really like to go back...'

After an October Cork Indie Festival screening of Conor Heffernan's documentary, the band did their first Cork gig since 1972. It was a strange one: the band was augmented by a few guests, including Paul Simmons, but Ivan had lost his voice. At the last minute Mary Greene, who had sung backing vocals on *Alternative Medicine*, had to step in on his songs.

The Indie Festival honoured the band's career with the Award for Pioneering Musical Practices. The citation read: 'Ireland, and particularly "Rebel" Cork, has a reputation for welcoming musical innovation and experimentation. This award is made in recognition of the ground-breaking work of Dr Strangely Strange, a group that has blended folk, rock and "psychedelic lounge music" from the late 1960s to the present day. Their contribution to, and influence upon, each of those musical genres in Ireland has been significant. Their pioneering creativity remains inspirational for a new generation of musicians, and the spirit that IndieCork aspires to foster.' More recently, *Kip* was celebrated as one of Richard Morton Jack's *101 Iconic Underground Rock Albums, 1966-1970*.

On they go. Joe Thoma plays with local musicians from Kenmare. Tim Booth is still writing and creating all kinds of visual art, Tim Goulding still paints and records in his home studio, most recently with Terry Woods, and Ivan is still busily composing new songs and obsessively reworking his old ones.

The Strangelies continue to 'meet up every year or so to do another gig or two.'

The Strangelies hit seventy (Tim Booth)

## Strangelies renaissance photos

Our friend Sean Kelly took some great live photos at the 12-Bar Club, the Sugar Club, the Gaff and the Jazz Café. Here is a selection. You can see more, in colour, on his website: *www.seankellyphotos.com/Strangely.*

# Appendix
To be taken twice at night

# Song Lyrics

## *Kip Of The Serenes* lyrics

**Strangely Strange But Oddly Normal** (Ivan Pawle)

Friends greet you on the way, say 'There you go!'
You may wonder where you're supposed to be going
I have often thought of the youngest daughter
And the joyous overflowing

When dark clouds pall the sky I have cast my eye
To the path where we are treading
Oh, I could rack my brain trying to explain
Where it is I think that we are heading

Strangely strange but oddly normal...

Why only the other day I was making hay
For I supposed the sun was shining
But when I looked up, by harsh neon I was struck
Must adjust my sense of timing
Must be just my sense of timing...

Well I've had some things on my mind and they're mostly all the time
Like cardboard scarecrows on the seesaw
And were I to impart those things I held to heart
Why – **fitting pieces to the jigsaw**

**Dr Dim And Dr Strange** (Tim Goulding)

*A baker in Ferrara thought he was composed of butter and durst not sit in the sun or come near the fire for fear of being melted. He was one of those who do talk with you and seem to be otherwise employed, and to your thinking very intent and busy. Still that toy runs in their mind –*

That fear, that suspicion
That abuse, that jealousy
That agony, that vexation
That fiction, that pleasant waking dream

Catman the minotaur
You'd better lick your lips
The film's almost over
They're only showing clips

The prelate's on the pig's back
And he's running down the hill
The swans turned to sailing ships
The honey's on the windowsill
The projectionist's Zhivago
He promptly blows his cool
He muddles up the spools
There's a pike in every pool
And that's for gospel

*And this is what Dr Dim has to say:*
Keep your eyes peeled, nerves steeled
Well-healed in the field

Adage after aeon
And proverb after life
Sugar-daddy introduce
The world and his wife
While revolution's rife in the graveyards

*Dr Strange has this to say don't you know:*
Dry throat, hard stool
Bitter pill as a rule
Dry brains, hard mind
Worse you couldn't find.

He's a stoker on the mad March steamer
She's a county chemist and an antique dealer
Dr Strange astride the astral tram
Speeds to cure the melancholy man
With a placebo from Desperate Dan
And sound advice to jettison the fever
He cites a saline purgative
For chronic paranoia
Keep a cleaner nose than usual
Get in touch with Martin's lawyer
The crux of my proposal is that notice in the corner
*And this is how it reads, folks:*
Keep your eyes peeled...

To be taken twice at night, the emetic for the blight
To be taken night and day on an aluminium tray
A pudding with the proof inside the eating
*And this is what Dr Strange has to say – God bless him*
Dry throat...

The strangest cure of all, the writing on the wall
To hear the prophets call from Eden to the fall
There's nothing there at all, at all...

## Roy Rogers (Tim Booth)

I asked Roy Rogers would he lend me his horse
And he said, 'Yes of course, I can lend you my horse.'
And galloping heroically over the plain
You know that I was never seen again

I asked Jesse James would he lend me his chaps
And he said, 'Well yes, perhaps.'
And his brother Frank who was meaner than hell
He threw me down a wishing well

I asked Bethsheba to take off her clothes
And find some repose from her labours
She smiled as she slipped right out of her zips
Saying, 'Why, thank you good neighbour.'

And she asked me if I'd like to come back again
And she'd tell me exactly what her name was
She asked me if I'd like to come back again
And she'd tell me exactly where the blame was

I asked Lloyd George if he'd lend me his hat
And he said, 'Mmm hmm – but keep a straight bat.'
He put his arms round my shoulders and he taught me how to sing
Fol-da-diddle-dee – he taught me everything

I asked Rupert Bear just what should I do
With all this folding paper
He said, 'Better late than dead,
Do it now, not later.'

And he kissed fair Jane she was the Queen of the May
And smiling through his face he blew the afternoon away
And he kissed fair Jane she was the Queen of the May
And grinning through his teeth he blew the afternoon away

I wrote this song on my bank overdraft
A noble piece of craft – oh, a thinly burning shaft
And the sub-manager says that I owe lots of bread
Hey hey, that's no way to treat your friend...


## Dark-haired Lady (Ivan Pawle)

Dark-haired lady I would love thee
I would fain put thee above me
I would gather shells for
Weaving magic spells to
Bind thee to me
Blindly woo thee

Dark-eyed lady pray abide me
I would only stay beside thee
I would show you reasons
For the changing seasons
Make the sun shine
If you'd be mine

Dark-eyed lady art so cold
I could win thee were I bold
I shall take my pledge and
Leave thee on the ledge and
Care for someone so much fairer
Fair-haired lady I shall love thee

'Lean out of the window, Goldenhair,
I heard you singing a merry air.
I have left my book
I have left my room
For I heard you singing
Through the gloom'

*(Goldenhair lyric from Chamber Music by James Joyce)*

## On The West Cork Hack (Tim Goulding)

Sucking and blowing
Winter wind snowing
The ghastly film the frozen buds
I grasped a straw and stoned a crow
MY PIPE WAS TRULY BURNING

It's easy it's easy it's easy to forecast
It's easy it's easy it's easy to visualise
But when you have to live it

Waiting and wailing
Cracked up and failing
The stubborn tiles crack and laugh
The copper rock the purple milk
Blind the lame and deafen the unwary

You wouldn't think a sergeant could bolster the adrenaline
You wouldn't live to see the day when licences for breathing
ARE ISSUED TO THE ANGELS

Riding on a paperback to good-time music
The jungle birds the Kerry snails
Slipped between the yellow score
Of starlight rhythm

Love was just a bitten nail littering the seashore
You knew you'd hit the paper crux
You'd seen me on the Metro
IN A WAKING DREAM

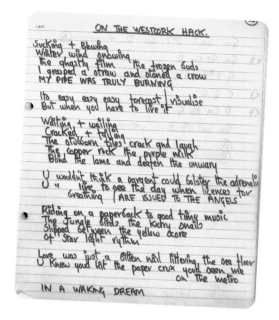

## A Tale Of Two Orphanages (Tim Booth)

Mistress Mouse and Mister Puppup sit outside the bar-room door
Their youngest son's in Jerusalem reporting on the war
And three blind master plumbers have just got back from the moon
And Harvey and the Grease Band singing words that have no tune

Hogarth's on the beach-head looking for another home
Leaving naught behind him but a photograph of Rome
The Egyptians hanging on my wall have nothing more to fear
And Harvey and his brass band singing words they learnt by ear

Orpheus the rambler was seen last night in France
By the orphans of the lighthouse at a Pentecostal dance
And meanwhile back on Mount Street oh the sun comes shining down
And Harvey and his pretties singing words which have no sound

Cloud bringers and go-getters get and bring what you can find
And nobody shouts or stumbles or has any axe to grind
Oh the priestly rent collector says his mind is on the bend
And Harvey and his brass band make their song come to its end
Well there ain't no point in kicking up a row,
There's nobody here but me…


**Strings In The Earth And Air** (Music: Ivan Pawle, words: James Joyce)

Strings in the earth and air
Make music sweet
Strings by the river
Where the willows meet

There's music along the river
For Love wanders there
Pale flowers on his mantle
Dark leaves on his hair

All softly playing
With head to the music bent
And fingers straying
Upon an instrument

The twilight turns from amethyst
To deep and deeper blue
The lamp fills with a pale green glow
The trees of the avenue

The old piano plays an air
Sedate and slow and gay
She bends upon the yellow keys
Her head inclines this way

Shy thoughts and grave wide eyes
And hands that wander as they list
The twilight turns to darker blue
With lights of amethyst

## Ship Of Fools (Tim Goulding)

The way of an eagle in the air
The way of a serpent upon a rock
The way of a ship in the midst of the sea
The way of a man with a maid

Chains of strength, chains of fear
Mocking words in Satan's ear
The manger whips, the nursemaid lies
Chains that launch the ship of sighs

Child sun baby moon
Cast a faint hope or fail too soon
Windward burning boats, slitting throats
Hopeless I'm gazing

Child head, baby brain
On the slipway blocked again
Your tide is out your blinds are drawn
Sailor fools are born

Sound the foghorn horns
Screaming siren scorns
Petrifies the human pawns

Child deranged, galactic fault
The arc lights burn, the squadrons halt
Baby breathes the gale and tastes the salt
Alarmed and cowering

Child tenor, baby crooner
Tripping double time on board the schooner
Blows the whistle and sucks the crisis pipe
For a lifelong passage
Sound the foghorn horns…

Child skipper, baby mate
Ship of fools becomes the ship of fate
While gospel singers cool the panic-struck
Force Ten, bitter luck

Child cry, baby sleep
My cavern is yesterday, my crater deep
On deck the captain scans the X-ray card
We need a metal surgeon
Sound the foghorn horns...

Child steals, baby seeks
Travels miles in lifeless weeks
Then turns the coverlet and shakes the sheets
They're only learning

Child chokes, baby dies
Fetid rumours, human cries
Transparent fighters fly the transient skies
A hard coming we had
And a harder going


## Frosty Mornings (Ivan Pawle)

Frosty mornings stay at home
Think about the time that's gone
Trying to reason what went wrong
Then you start to write a song

Running in the street, bumping into those you meet
Heading over heels, scratch your head see how it feels
Jumping on a bus, jumping off again because
There's nowhere to go and it's going to snow
Think it's going to snow, think it's going to snow

There's no point in coming down
Just because you're in the town
See the way a winter breeze
Weaves a pattern through the leaves

I'm looking at a scene – everything is coloured green
Standing on your head, finding things beneath the bed
Sitting on a floor, waiting for a friend to score
Climbing up a tree to see if it is he
See if it is he, see if it is he

Makes no difference where you've been
Whirlpool chasms suck you in
Round about you swirl and glide
Now you're floating on the tide

No matter what you do
Don't forget it isn't you
Nothing you can hide
Nothing lives that hasn't died

Shoo be do wah
Shoo be do wah
Shoo be do wah shooby do wah wah


## Donnybrook Fair (Tim Booth)

Muircheartach the leather cloakéd king
Plugged in his amplifier and began to sing
And Henry Grattan standing in the rain again
Down on Dawson Street waiting for a number Ten
To take him to Donnybrook Fair
He's got some business to do there
Oh it is possible to do anything
Dance among the Queens
Or play chess with the High King

Thomas Wentworth standing underneath the silken sail
Turns to the Unicorn and asks him how he's failed
And Deidre Of The Sorrows catching crabs on the sea-shore
Turns to the Unicorn and asks him what he's for
Well I'm for Donnybrook Fair
When I get the time I'll see you there
Pick a golden apple from the heart of the sun
I can assure you it is very easily done

Joseph Mary Plunkett with a sword in his right hand
Walking to the GPO to play with the band
And Patrick Pearse comes squinting through 1916
Turns to the Unicorn and asks him how he's been
Well I've been down in Donnybrook Fair
How come I didn't see you there?

Oh it is possible to do anything
Dance among the Queens
Or play chess with the High King

The Mighty Cretin Showband lead the pikemen from the rear
And nobody sees the Unicorn quietly standing there
And the long-faced leading singer tries to imitate Jim Reeves
The Unicorn just shakes his head, bows from the waist and leaves
And he's gone, gone to Donnybrook Fair
When I get the time I'll see him there
Pick a golden apple from the heart of the sun
I can assure you it is very easily done

But the monkey and me in cloud-stepping shoes
We danced away wherever we choose
All good people you must stay together
Rainbow skirt and a cloak of feathers
Stay down in Donnybrook Fair
When I get the time I'll see you there
The mocking bird has come to say
He wants to blow your heads away

'The king of love my shepherd is
Whose goodness faileth never
I nothing lack if I am his
And he is mine forever
Where streams of living waters flow
My ransomed soul he leadeth
And where the verdant pastures grow
With food celestial feedeth'

What will yer have, will yer have a pint?
I'll have a pint with you sir
And if somebody doesn't order soon
We'll be thrown out of the boozer

'And so through all the length of days
Thy goodness faileth never
Good shepherd may I sing thy praise
Within thy house forever'
Amen

# 1969-1970 song lyrics

## HMS Avenger (Booth/Goulding/Pawle/Greville)

See the *Kip Of The Serenes* chapter for some background to this.

## Existence Now (Tim Goulding)

You sir in your happy dream
Lucky man to wander unafraid and unaware of
You girl, lucky too
Blind to every flash of nature's quaking change around you.

When all pretence's playing cards are down
Your wounds are clear to see beneath your gown
Your hair no longer hides an anxious frown
Your smile can't always fool the cosmic town
Ambition can't disguise his hollow crown

For men will ignore or delay it by tricks and illusions
The river flows forever and this is what it says
Existence now... now

The river flows forever, it murmurs and it spits this song:
'We are all who were or will be, we are never right or wrong
You are only shy observers crying on the shores of change
Impermanent performers playing notes so strange.'

You sir in your happy dream
Caged in a city or sitting by a poisoned stream
You girl lucky too
We ply the selfsame waters
The boat rocks me, the boat rocks you

## Going To Poulaphouca (Tim Booth)

Going to Poulaphouca,
Going to see my girl,
She's the one with the long black curl
And she certainly looks good to me,
She certainly looks good to me.

Riding on a moonspoon,
Thought I'd take a peek,
Hello earth, you look so very deep
And I certainly look up at you
And you certainly look down at me.

Standing on the surface,
Standing looking up,
Just to think if gravity should stop...
Well I'd certainly look high to you
And I'd certainly look high to you.

Swimming in a river,
With a seal friend,
Something or other she forgot to defend
And she certainly looks bruised to me
She certainly looks spruce to me.

Going back to Dublin,
Me and Gosport Lil,
Get a little food in Sammy's Bar and Grill
And it certainly feels good to me,
It certainly feels good to me.

## Mirror Mirror (Ivan Pawle)

The equable tenor of time
Constantly gliding by
Luminaries revolving sigh
Seeking neither sense nor rhyme.
Migratory illusions fly
Planet travellers time defy
Turn the cartwheel in the sky
Kissing Mother Earth goodbye.

I had to make it back to my ship
my planet was drifting, stars eliding, images colliding
in the nebulous beyond
devoid of pabulum, the meter reads:
Turn back
Turn back dear mortal
Catch the scattered seeds
Back to the riverbeds
Back to the planet earth
Back to the elements
      the place of birth
Back to the colour it green beams
      silent street-scene screen dreams
Back to 1943 BC

Mirror mirror in the sky tell me is it He or I?
'How immense then does this universe appear.
Indeed it must be either infinity, or infinitely near it'


## Le Le Rockin' Sound (Tim Goulding)

Early in the morning, in the garden,
It's told
They rolled the stone.
Can that condone the years of hate,
Or compensate for famine and fear?
O those truant words, words on a city door
Well I'm now so sure

*It's just that same old rockin' sound,*
*Running through my brain*
*Peter Pan wants Wendy*
*To do that thing, to do that thing again,*
*To do that thing, to do that thing again*

Lee in his waistcoat on le crater's edge,
He saw the winner take all.
Like a loser's friends like a godsend
To Ringsend culture and crime
Oh those truant words, words on a city door
Well I'm now so sure

Rock in his Stetson, down on the Udson,
See how he mangles his lines.
Like a fat boy winning at see-saw
He stars but seldom shines
O that dog, he won't walk, walk where the cat has been
Bathes in the kerosene, howls at Halloween

## Piece Of Cod (Tim Goulding)

Listen to the ocean's song that weaveth mighty music
That quells the beast within the man
That the darkest fevers sootheth
Dispelling awkward hours
Happy as flowers

See the herring fleets that trawl the waves of many a bay
Join the vapour, ride the summits,
With the wild wild winds play
At scooping the naked air
Nothing can lie to you there
Holy the highest mountains
Rosy the dawn that licks their sides
Holy the drownded sailor
Crushed by the wrath of the ceaseless tide
Time takes all away...

Salty the brow of the mariner
Bright were his eyes and bold his grin
Sour the reek of the seaweed
Sweet was the smile that once ensnared him
All like lightning gone...

*Shanty:*
They that reel both to and fro
Staggering about like drunken men
They that calleth from the deep
At the end of a rusty tether

# Heavy Petting lyrics

## Ballad Of The Wasps (Tim Goulding)

Down in the Dargle valley
Not a mile from the Lover's Leap
Where two bold men and a girl of iron
Lay down to take some sleep

Their minds flew way above them
Like birds in the clear blue sky
While below in the shady clearings
Their bodies heaved a sigh

Where in the woody country
Would they leave us all behind
'Twas here by the mountain river
They tried to prove us blind

Rain hail sleet snow
It's hard to understand
Rain hail sleet snow
But this lot beats the band

When the day was over
And night was drawing nigh
Jeffa Mole and Dave woke up
They swore that they could fly

So climbing to the valley's height
They launched out into space
And as their bodies left the ground
Giant wasps did take their place

And to this day on the Lover's Leap
When the sun is on the wane
You can see three wasps just a-flying there
They beat their wings in vain

Rain hail sleet snow
It's hard to have some fun
Rain hail sleet snow
But this lot takes the bun.

## Summer Breeze (Tim Booth)

Yes, I'm like a summer breeze upon the highway
O my slowly moving feet
Yes I do believe that they're going my way
And I don't believe that you will control me
And I don't believe you can console me

Like a summer breeze, you know I'm lost in winter
I'm living and I'm dying and
I don't know what I am into
And I don't believe that you will abhor me
And I don't believe that you can cure me

Yes I am a feckless man and that's the way that I like to be
Well I have not many friends and those I have
They're all very very dear to me
And I don't believe that you will console me
And I don't believe you can control me

You can console me.

## Kilmanoyadd Stomp (Ivan Pawle)

See Miss Niamh so clean and bright
Trying to put me on
She don't fool me, then she might
When she's heard my song

Custom-building alibis
Yesterday's the big surprise
Slowly you may realise
There's no sense in being wise

Trucks are trundling down the road
Everybody's got a big load
All across the frozen waste
Everybody hides their face

Take a good look at Cousin Kate
Standing by the garden gate
Wondering where the trucks all go
And I suppose she once did know

There's just one thing left to say
Before I go off on my way
There's no meaning to this song and
If you found one you'd be wrong.


## I Will Lift Up Mine Eyes (Tim Goulding)

*(Spoken: The upkeep tonight*
*is for the collection of the harmonium)*

I will lift up mine eyes unto the heavens
Garden of earthly delight
Where time delivers a handstand
And the colours are ever so bright

And I'll worship the seas and rivers
Mountains plains and skies
And I'll travel with time and tide to sing you
Sing you this advice

I will lift up mine eyes unto the mountains
Mountains of the mind
Deep in a Latvian thicket
There's a slough I'll leave behind

But I'll worship those seas and rivers
Mountains plains and skies
And I'll travel with time and tide to sing you
Sing you this advice:

'What is this life so full of care
We have no time to stand and stare
No time to stand beneath the boughs
And stare as long as sheep –
Or cows.'


## Sign On My Mind (Ivan Pawle)

There's a sign on my mind
'I have gone away'
If you read it, do not grieve

It is not aimed your way
Tired of thinking
I'd been sinking into a dream
Things just aren't the way they seem
Not what they appear

Things aren't what they would appear

Out of time, finding rhyme
Dance into the sky
Missing boats, keeping notes
Please don't ask me why
Reading signs, moving lines
Walking on my toes
Coming through, passing queues
Following my nose

Things aren't what they would appear.


## Gave My Love An Apple (Tim Booth)

'I was waltzing with my darling
To the Tennesee Waltz
When an old friend I happened to see
I introduced him to my sweetheart
And while they were dancing
My friend stole my darling from me'

I gave my love an apple, Lord, she never said a thing
I gave her a string of rifle ammunition
And I hung it on a brass key ring
I gave her lots of this and that
And a playpen for her son...
But she only said 'Get out of here
The dance has only just begun'

I never been to Harlem, or stood near the Golden Gate
But I walk up and down Londonbridge Road
And I'm trying to get my head straight
I gave her lots of this and that
And a cookbook on how to get it done...
But she only said 'Don't hit me on the hump'
And beat me up with her sponge

I gave my love an aeroplane, Lord, she never even blinked
So I swum the Irish Sea again
I was following some blind instinct
I gave her lots of this and that
And a 37-barrel Gatling gun...
But she only said 'Why don't you give up
You know I gotta step along'

*(Spoken: 'Yeah step along Garibaldi Moorhen,
if it's the last thing you ever do')*

I think I'll go to Nashville or maybe then again I won't
I think sometimes I'll make out
And I know that there'll be times when I don't
And I never even said to her
About the time I thought I loved a nun...
I'm sitting down here in Sandymount
And I'm waiting for another one to come

Maybe she will come along – I don't know –
Maybe she won't
It's all right.


## Jove Was At Home (Ivan Pawle)

Jove was at home when Marymac
Saw the world for the very first time
I could have sworn Hermes brought the word
To the house that is mine

The moon bore her scion
To the home of the Lion
With lanterns of amber and jade
The sun swung below
Beaming aglow
And the fish swam away with a swoon

Jove was at home when Marymac
saw the World for the very first time

GLORIA, GLORIA
HOSANNA IN EXCELSIS!

## When Adam Delved (Ivan Pawle)

*Instrumental*

## Ashling (Tim Booth)

As I walked out one old lady dog-walking day
I spied a thin young woman
She was tightly laced in grey
I removed my hat, straightened my back
And to her I did say

Pray tell to me, pray tell it plainly
But who exactly are you?

She hung down her head and she raised up her eyes
This thin young girl with the wizened hand
And she said to my surprise
I'm only here to pass the time until my fancy dies

Pray tell me sir are you the kind
Who would mistreat me
Or are you only coming in
Across the fields to greet me?

O no, I said, I'm here to stay
But I may leave next week
I know you are a seagull girl
I can tell it by your beak
And worse than that
There are things that I still seek

What's that, she said from behind her veil
This dried up lemon lady
Who looked not unlike a grey-backed gull

I search, said I, both night and day
For those who talk my talk
In some far place not too far removed
Where I may gladly walk
And sing my song, though my heart be mostly chalk

At this she cried, threw up her arms
And suddenly grew wings
Not unlike those you might find
Upon a grey-backed gull

It's over now, she's far and gone
Leaving me with my load
The hedges grow, the beetles work
And the garden's not been mowed
I sit and think and I play at cards
And I wonder why she goed
Or did she fly, or was it I
To whom this thing was showed
The sands are bare, no seagulls
And I think I should have knowed

She did not say it to my face
But now I see my lot
For now I know that where my place is
There I can be not.

## Mary Malone Of Moscow (Tim Goulding)

My new shoes are pinching
I guess they'll soon wear in
Once I went so high
That I never came down again.

Won't you tell me what goes wrong
When it's coming on so strong
Can't digest
Cattle uneasy
Air of unrest

Greek may tax the North Pole
Jews the hemisphere
But Lee the King of Kings
Has put them in the clear

He can be heavy with his chalk
And his emancipated talk
Cast off
Royal stones
Massacres, bones

Mary Malone of Moscow
E for electric dead
Caught forty Morris Nurses
Feeding the birds in her head

I can't believe this cosmic joke
I tried to break the news, it broke
Well's bone dry
Friends gone away
No supply

Mary won't you help me
The going's gotten heavy again
The sacred Bo is the place for me
And the furze the place for the wren

My old heart is aching
Aching for some sign
Sign of the wonderful man
Who tries to rate your mind

I'll show him where he can unload
The gospel of the city road
Right here
Guaranteed
No fear

O Mary won't you help me
The going's gotten heavy again
The sacred Bo is the place for me
And the furze the place for the wren

My new shoes are pinching
I guess they'll soon wear in
Once I went so high
That I never came down again.

## Goodnight My Friends (Ivan Pawle)

Goodnight my friends, do not you cry
The Lord is coming for my soul
People get ready
The Lord is coming for your soul
Amen.

# 1970 songs

## Cock-A-Doodle-Doo (Ivan Pawle)

Gonna leave this town behind
Before my body leaves my mind
Gonna rise up before the dawning
And leave it with the morning sun
(come come)

Sure I've met some gentle people
But I do see the cock crowing from the steeple
And I'm bound to go
Wheresoe'er the wind doth blow... (go go go)

Cock-a-doodle-doo!

Yonder stands the youngest son
Look, his life has just begun
Once I threw away a chance
Can't you teach him how to grasp
Can't you sing your song to me
Can't you teach him what to be
Can't you sing to me your song
Wonder where I might go wrong

Teach him what tomorrow brings
Bring my sorrow joy
Bring his spirit on home to Thee
Bring my spirit on home

Bring his spirit back on home

## Good Evening Mr Woods (aka Speak Of Tsao Tsao) (Ivan Pawle)

The path exists but not the traveller on it
Trapped in time we turn and stumble off it
The word exists but not the man to play it
Lost in space we lack the skill to play it
And there is a way

There you go!
Speak of Tsao Tsao and Tsao Tsao appears,
Breathing air
Round and round and round we go
And round we go

La La La

Now you see it, now you don't
Now you'll be it
Now you won't

## Sweet Red Rape (Tim Booth)

With a nod to the most direct and effective action,
It's been decided to ignore a woman's blue tears,
We know you, you blonde flamboyant female attraction,
Believing in God you've been a coward now for years.

Believing in God you've been a coward now for years.
Those who sleep uneasily all day long,
Those who prepare water for troubled fish,
Take heart now and depart now from the throng,
Or ignore the manifesto if you so wish.

Ignore the manifesto if you so wish.
A winter's day in old downtown Belmullet,
Streetmen and the withered girls going to man the de-mob truck
And I just sit here, waiting for one final silver bullet
And I'll fall back into all those things, goodbye, won't you wish me luck.

O throw the old retainer to the wolves
Pass the bread and praise the chandelabra
Yesterday, at the Bureau of Inquiries, I found out my Ritalin name...

Who's going to feed my canary when I'm gone?
Who's going to feed my canary when I have passed on?
Can you tell me Mary
Who's going to feed my canary
Sweet Red Rape?

O was he not a thinker kindly spinster?
O good God sir, he was sir, yes he was, sir.
Good God sir, yes he was.

Sweet Red Rape

*(Repeat until cured)*

## Horse Of A Different Hue (Tim Goulding)

If any man might indulge a pain
Take a chance, and then just chuck it down the drain
That's when the water turns to wine
Long pig to shorter swine

Grab that pig don't delay
For the cool cool light,
The cool cool light of day
Save that soul, feed that foal
When love prevails long pig tells no tales

Quite unexpectedly the grass turned green
Quite unlike anything I'd ever seen
And then I knew those storybooks ring true
Love's just a horse of a different hue

If any man might file a claim
Lose his nerve
And then die of shame
That's when the water turns to wine…

Quite inadvertently we made Cape Clear
Quite undeniably we had no fear
And then I knew those storybooks ring true
Love's just a horse of a different hue

## Lady Of The Glen (Ivan Pawle)

She's a lady that knows how to love
And she's been gazing through her windowpanes
She's been watching the rain through her sun
And turning the days in her mind.

She's got ways to be happy
But she's not looking for the key
She moves through the months like a meadow
And she flows through my life like a river.

Seed planting lady, wading through this world
Sweet and shady lakeside lady
Let me light my beacon on your hill.

## Halcyon Days (2007) (Ivan Pawle)

Here in the autumn sun,
Looking over what we've done
And it's mostly been great fun:
In the long hot days of summer,
Playing music in the sun,
Sharing our dreams and yarns that we'd spun.

*Halcyon days, deep deep blue*
*Halcyon days, deep deep blue*

Back in the Orphanage
Down by the Mount Street Bridge
Sure we never had a care:
And in the long dark nights of winter
Playing music round the fire,
Chasing our dreams and learning to share.

## The Invisible Kid (2007) (Tim Booth)

The Invisible Kid came by today, least I think he did.

And I'd like to say he was looking well,

But with a kid like that, it's really hard to tell...

He took off his hat and pulled up a chair and I could clearly see

He was hardly there – a shadow boy

On the edge of the night, or a trick of the light...

He dusted his boots and hitched up his pants and said:

'I've just come in from Paris, France. They're eating snails there,

It's a heck of a thing – how you been?'

I said: 'I'm fine – how about you?' He said:

'What am I supposed to do? They see right through me

Everywhere I go, don't you know?'

The Invisible Kid, you can see him too

And he wants to know what you're going to do,

When the chips are down and the die is cast

And the future roams into the past,

The Invisible Kid, he's the last of his line and I'd like to feel

He's doing fine, but that fatal flicker

On the edge of night, it just might...

Be the Kid coming around for a social call

*All lyrics © the songwriters.*

# Dr Strangely Strange Gigography:
# January 1969 – May 1971

Many thanks to Ivan for most of this information, largely taken from his gig diaries. There were almost no real 'tours' in 1969 and 1970 – the UK gigs tended to be scattered across the length and breadth of the country with no discernible pattern, whereas almost all the Irish gigs were in Dublin.

## 1969

| | |
|---|---|
| January 4 & 5 | Recording at Sound Techniques |
| January 4 | Les Cousins, London with John Martyn |

### Ireland

| | |
|---|---|
| February 12 | Famine Relief Concert, Dublin |
| February 13 | Dublin University Folk Society |
| February 16 | Slattery's, Dublin |
| February 18 | Ghetto Club, Dublin |
| February 20 | Sinnott's, Dublin |
| February 21 | Neptune Rowing Club, Dublin |
| February 23 | Slattery's, Dublin |
| February 26 | University College Dublin |
| February 27 | Interview with B.P. Fallon, RTÉ Radio: *Like It Is* |
| March 2 | Slattery's |
| March 3 | Interview, *Spotlight* music magazine |
| March 4 | # 5 Club (Ghetto), Dublin |
| March 6 | Teilifís Éireann (TV recording) |
| March 9 | Slattery's |
| March 12 | Teilifís Éireann (TV recording) |
| March 14 | Neptune Club, Dublin |

### UK

| | |
|---|---|
| March 20 | West Ham College, London E15: Release Benefit presented by John Peel with The Occasional Word Ensemble, Mike Hart and Bridget St John |
| March 21 | Les Cousins |
| March 22 | Les Cousins |

| | |
|---|---|
| March 25 | Ivor Cutler Audition |
| March 28 | Electric Cinema, Portobello Road, 11 pm |
| March 29 | Peeler's Club, Bishopsgate, London |
| March 31 | Recording at Sound Techniques |
| April 1 | Recording at Sound Techniques |

## Ireland

| | |
|---|---|
| April 10 | Photo session in Dargle Valley for *Kip Of The Serenes* cover |
| April 18 | Neptune Club Dublin |
| April 25 | Neptune Club |
| April 27 | Slattery's: afternoon and evening gigs |
| May 2 | Neptune Club |
| May 5 | Chariot Inn, Ranelagh, Dublin |
| May 10 | Trinity Art Society |
| May 16 | Dublin University Folk Society |
| May 24 | Trinity Art Society |
| May 25 | Slattery's |
| May 28 | Adelphi Cinema Dublin, supporting Fleetwood Mac |
| May 29 | Sinnott's |
| June 28 | Mansion House, Dublin |
| July 4 | *Kip Of The Serenes* released |
| July 13 | Slattery's |
| June 18 | Neptune Club |
| June 19 | # 5 Club |
| September 22-26 | 'One Over The Eight' Revue, The Gate Theatre, Dublin |
| October 6 | Project Gallery, Dublin (poetry and music gig) |

## UK

| | |
|---|---|
| October 17 | Sheffield |
| October 18 | Essex University Folk and Blues club with Joanne Kelly, Brett Marvin and the Thunderbolts, Michael Chapman |
| October 20 | Cardiff Institute of Science and Technology |
| October 26 | Birmingham University |
| October 28 | Mother's Club Birmingham CANCELLED |
| October 30 | St John's Church, Redhill with Egg and Moonglum light show |
| October 31 | Les Cousins with Mick Softley and film/slides by Renchi |
| November 7 & 8 | Recording at Sound Techniques |
| November 8 | Les Cousins, allnighter |
| November | *Nice Enough To Eat*, Island sampler released |

## Ireland

| | |
|---|---|
| November 23 | Slattery's |
| November 27 | Dublin University Folk Society |
| November 28 | Teilifís Éireann (TV) *Late Late Show* |
| November 30 | Slattery's |

## UK

| | |
|---|---|
| December 4 | Salford University with Roy Harper |
| December 5 | Merton College, Oxford |
| December 7 | Roundhouse, London |
| December 12 | Hendon Tech (possibly the last gig with Linus) |

## 1970

## Ireland

| | |
|---|---|
| January 1 | Sinnott's |
| January 18 | Slattery's |

## UK

| | |
|---|---|
| January 30 | Kingston-on-Thames, unknown venue |
| January 31 | Recording at Sound Techniques |
| February 2 | Recording at Sound Techniques |
| February 3 | Mixing at Sound Techniques |
| February 6 | Exeter University, possibly supporting Taste |
| February 7 | Les Cousins, supporting John Martyn |
| February 11 | Kent University |
| February 12 | Portsmouth Polytechnic |
| February 14 | Finchley Town Hall with Daddy Longlegs |
| February 15 | Electric Cinema, Portobello Rd |
| February 17 | Hounslow Arts Lab with Annie Briggs and Humphrey Weightman |
| February 18 | Preston, unknown venue |
| February 24 | Filming mumming, Battersea Park |
| February 27 | Southsea, unknown venue |
| February 28 | Les Cousins. An audience recording is in circulation. |
| March 3 | Palimpsest event, Guilford Festival |
| March 4 | Leicester University (postponed) |
| March 5 | Leicester: lunchtime gig, venue unknown |
| March 7 | Implosion: Roundhouse, Camden with Chris Spedding Band, Formerly Fat Harry & Sour Milk Sea |

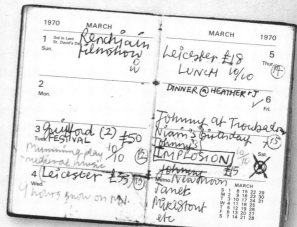

| | |
|---|---|
| March 9 | Granary, Bristol |
| April 1 | Recording at Eamonn Andrews Studio, Dublin |
| April 4 | Gary Moore's 18th birthday |
| April 9 | National Stadium, Dublin with John Peel, Liverpool Scene & Skid Row |
| April 13 & 14 | Sound Techniques: mixing *Heavy Petting* |
| April 19 | Thomas Bennet School, Crawley, Sussex |
| April 22 | Hull, unknown venue |
| April 24 | Norwich, unknown venue |
| April 25 | Oxford, unknown venue. College Ball with Chicken Shack |

## UK - Norn Iron

| | |
|---|---|
| April 26 | Queen's University, Belfast |
| April 29 | University of Ulster, Coleraine |

## Ireland

| | |
|---|---|
| May 2 | Confraternity Hall, Limerick |
| May 3 | University College, Cork |
| May 4 | Trinity College, Dixon Hall. Ivan and Booth duo gig |
| May 12 | *Heavy Petting* photo session, Dargle Cottage |

## UK

| | |
|---|---|
| May 15 | Hitchin, with Shirley Collins & Trevor Crozier |
| May 16 | Southampton, venue unknown |
| May 19 | Doncaster Folk Club with Christy Moore |
| May 20 | Brighton University |
| May 26 | BBC studios, Maida Vale: *Top Gear* session |
| May 29 | Les Cousins |
| May 30 | Electric Cinema |
| June 3 | The Crypt, possibly in Portobello Road |
| June 4 | Karl Dallas interview |
| June 6 | Clitheroe Festival with Third Ear Band & Kevin Ayers & Mike Chapman |
| June 14 | Barnet, Garage Club, with Peter Green, Trees, Quiver & Formerly Fat Harry |
| June 15 | The Phonograph, Finchley with Stefan Grossman & The Amazing Band, featuring Robert Wyatt |
| June 16 | Guildford University |
| June 17 | Lyceum, London supporting Santana with James Litherland's Brotherhood & Elton John |
| June 19 | Leicester University supporting Taste |
| June 21 | Implosion: Roundhouse with Liverpool Scene, Clark-Hutchinson, Skid Row & Patto |
| June 22 | Mercury Theatre, Ladbroke Grove: BIT Benefit |
| June 23 | Bradford (University?) with Mike Chapman & Mythica, an acoustic trio featuring guitarist Peter Dobson |

| | |
|---|---|
| June 24 | York University: all-night ball with Fairports, Chicken Shack and many others |
| June 25 | Burton-on-Trent Town Hall with Bridget St John. Hoppy makes contact |

## Ireland

| | |
|---|---|
| June 28 | Slattery's |
| July 2 | Bennettsbridge Festival, Co Kilkenny |
| September 11 | *Heavy Petting* released |
| Sept 20 - 28 | Dublin, rehearsals with Hoppy |

## UK

| | |
|---|---|
| September 30 | Coventry Polytechnic. Hoppy's first gig with the band |
| October 2 | Shoreditch, venue unknown |
| October 5 | Canterbury, venue unknown |
| October 7 | Barrie Wentzell photo session of four-piece for *Melody Maker* |

## Ireland

| | |
|---|---|
| October 9 | Teilifís Éireann, *Late Late Show*. Mimed Mary Malone Of Moscow |

## UK

| | |
|---|---|
| October 16 | Les Cousins. *Vertigo Annual* released featuring Summer Breeze |
| October 17 | Southampton, venue unknown with Fotheringay |
| October 22 | Paris Theatre, London. BBC Radio John Peel *In Concert* show, with James Taylor |
| October 24 | Les Cousins |
| October 28 | High Wycombe, venue unknown, with John Martyn |
| October 30 | Recording at Sound Techniques |
| November 1 | Recording at Sound Techniques |
| November2 | Recording at Olympic Studio: Mike Heron session for Spirit Beautiful |
| November 5 | Aberystwyth University |
| November 6 | Keele University |
| November 7 | Nottingham (University?) |
| November 13 | Liverpool University with Jackson Heights and Spirogyra, featuring Barbara Gaskin |
| November 14 | Lancaster University |
| November 15 | Leeds Polytechnic. Tim Goulding told the band he was leaving |
| November 18 | Portsmouth |
| November 19 | Lincoln RAF Base |
| November 20 | Leicester University (lunchtime); Essex University (evening) |
| November 21 | Les Cousins |

## South-West tour

| | |
|---|---|
| November 23 | Bournemouth |
| November 24 | Room At The Top Club, Redruth |

| | |
|---|---|
| November 26 | Camborne, free concert at Cornwall Tech |
| November 27 | Queens Hall, Barnstable with Blodwyn Pig |
| November 28 | Van Dyke Club, Plymouth |
| November 29 | Surrey University, Guildford |
| | *South-West tour ended* |

| | |
|---|---|
| December 1 | Chelsea College |
| December 2 | Oxford Polytechnic |
| December 3 | Chelmsford Polytechnic CANCELLED |
| December 4 | Westminster Polytechnic |
| December 5 | Sussex University CANCELLED |
| December 6 | Roundhouse: Implosion, with Sam Apple Pie |
| December 7 | Interviews with Steve Peacock, introducing Terry and Gay |

## Dutch tour

| | |
|---|---|
| December 9 | Exit Club, Rotterdam |
| December 11 | Paradiso, Amsterdam with Spirogyra |
| December 12 | Paradiso, Amsterdam with Sam Gopal's Cosmosis |

## UK

| | |
|---|---|
| December 18 | North Cheshire College of Further Education, Manchester |

---

## 1971

---

## Irish tour
### Gigs with Goulding and Terry & Gay Woods in the band

| | |
|---|---|
| January 15 | Franciscan Hall, Limerick |
| January 16 | Revolution Club, Galway |
| January 17 | City Hall, Cork with Gaslight |
| January 19 | Connolly Hall, Waterford |
| January 20 | Liberty Hall, Dublin |

## UK - Norn Iron tour

| | |
|---|---|
| January 21 | Coleraine University |
| January 22 | Queen's Hotel, Bangor |
| January 23 | Guildhall, Derry |
| January 24 | Queen's University, Belfast |

## UK

| | |
|---|---|
| January 27 | Aberystwyth University |
| January 28 | Newcastle Polytechnic supporting Steeleye Span |

**Tim Goulding's last gig with the band**

| | |
|---|---|
| January 30 | Dartford, venue unknown, with Magician (psychedelic folkies) & Forever More (precursors of the Average White Band) |
| February 5 | Thames Polytechnic, Woolwich, with Bridget St John & Joanne Kelly |
| February 6 | Youth Centre, Guildford with Egypt |
| February 12 | Stirling University supporting Elton John |
| February 13 | Traverse Theatre, Edinburgh |
| February 14 | Traverse Theatre. Tim Goulding guests |
| February 16 | Dundee |
| February 17 | Big Apple, Brighton |
| February 19 | Borough Road College, Osterley with Principal Edwards Magic Theatre |
| February 20 | Durham University with Kevin Ayers & Gringo (progsters) |
| February 23 | Manchester University Rag Ball with Curved Air & Brett Marvin |
| February 25 | Hypnotique club, York |
| February 27 | Les Cousins. An audience recording is in circulation |
| February 28 | Cloud Nine, Peterborough |
| March 6 | Southampton with Keith Christmas |
| March 8 | Bournemouth Polytechnic |
| March 11 | Loughborough, with High Tide, Egg, Titus Groan & Indian Summer |
| March 12 | Fairfield Hall, Croydon. Lunchtime show |
| March 12 | Queen's College, Oxford. Ball with The Pretty Things & Kevin Ayers |
| March 13 | Roundhouse, Dagenham supporting Skid Row |
| March 20 | Bedford University with Magna Carta |
| March 21 | Eire, Wexford Festival with Fairport Convention & Mellow Candle |
| March 26 | Roehampton, venue unknown, with Ian Whitcomb |
| March 28 | Arts Lab, Camden. Recording with Tony Reeves |
| April 2 | Stockton, venue unknown, with Mike Chapman & Bridget St John |

# European tour

## Holland

| | |
|---|---|
| April 4 | De Toverbal, Maasluis |
| April 5 | Manifestatientent, Rotterdam. A street gig |
| April 6 | Release benefit, The Hague |
| April 7 | AMVJ hostel, Rotterdam |

| | |
|---|---|
| April 8 | Diogenes club, Nijmegen |
| April 9 | Paradiso, Amsterdam with Zangeres Zonder Naam |
| April 10 | Electric Centre, Haarlem |
| April 11 | De Villa, Rotterdam (lunchtime) and Moksha, Gorkum (evening) |
| April 12 | Don Kiesjot Youth Centre, Sittard |
| April 13 | Leidse Schowburg, Leiden |
| April 15 | Theatre Concordia, Enschede |
| April 16 | Eland club, Delft |
| April 17 | Exit Club, Rotterdam, with Lindisfarne |
| April 18 | Club Willidan, Aalsmeer |

## Denmark

| | |
|---|---|
| April 20 | Arrive in Copenhagen. Pre-recorded radio appearance |
| April 21 | Nykøbing Falster Teater with Molly & Camelius Mørks, Dynamostråle lightshow |
| April 22 | Industrien, Nyborg with lights by Potlach |
| April 23 | Theatre, Fredericia |
| April 24 | Sanderumhallen, Odense (5.00) with Flyvende Kuffert, Ache and lights by Potlach |
| April 24 | Dagmar Biografen, Copenhagen (midnight). See poster for bill |
| April 25 | Fis og Ballade (larking about) in Copenhagen. Pop-up gig in Kastrup bar, Havne Kro |
| April 26/27 | Western Jutland film project – *CANCELLED owing to illness* |
| April 28 | Stakladen, Aarhus – *CANCELLED owing to illness* |

## Belgium

| | |
|---|---|
| April 30 | Jeugdcentrum Kempen, Turnhout |
| May 1 | Familia Parish Hall, Wemmel near Brussels with Pendulum and Roland Van Campenhout |
| May 2 | Decide on dissolution of band in Waterloo |
| May 7/8 | Théatre du Vieux Colombier, Paris |

## Holland

| | |
|---|---|
| May 10 | Electric Centre, Haarlem |
| May 11 | Geleen Club, near Sittard |
| May 12 | Tilburg, venue unknown |
| May 15 | Return to UK |

## UK

| | |
|---|---|
| May 16 | Theatre Royal, Drury Lane supporting Al Stewart |

**Final gig**

# Where are they now: a selective list

Arranged by first name

## Andy Anderson, the Catman

Jenny Richardson writes: Andy left Brighton in the early Seventies and moved to Edinburgh, where he ran an 'Emporium' for a while. I remember buying some picture frames and a rainbow-coloured enamel cooking pot there. I think he also did a bit of street performance. In his later years he actually looked like a wizard, with very long white hair and minus teeth. His flat was jammed full of a collection of toy cars, books and various ephemera. He's still in Edinburgh, as far as I know.

## Anthea Joseph

Andrew Greig writes: After Witchseason ended, Anthea moved to Artist Relations at CBS, 'making sure my friends ate and drank properly, and if possible went to bed before dawn.' She remained devoted to music and musicians, shared their outlook and lifestyle, and defended them to the record company. Dylan continued to phone her up at unpredictable times. Once he complained his fiftieth birthday was coming and he didn't know what to do. 'It's simple, Bobby – you have a party and ask your friends.' 'Uh, right. Yeah.' Pause. 'You do have friends, Bobby?' Giggle. 'Maybe.'

To have more time with her mother as her health declined, Anthea became a 'roving personal assistant' to Maurice Oberstein of Polygram. When Elizabeth (like Anthea, a committed smoker) died of a heart attack, their cottage at Friston was badly damaged by fire. Anthea was shaken, lost and destitute – the cottage, her principal asset, had not been insured. She never fully recovered and continued to live amid the partial ruin, going to London only on special occasions. She wrote: 'I garden sporadically, read Georgette Hayer novels, and drink gin.' One of her later stories was of leaving a Rolling Stones party in the 90s with Dylan because they'd decided it was boring. They walked the streets for hours in the rain, talking of old times and lost friends...

She died suddenly in 1997 at the cottage in Friston, dressed up to go out to a local Christmas party. The surviving Fairports, at the improbable funeral in the village church, packed with music luminaries, sang Meet On The Ledge. She was at once a one-off, a convent-educated bohemian, and emblematic of those times.

## Annie Christmas

Annie remained working as a TV producer in South Africa. Sadly, she died of leukaemia at a comparatively young age, in May 2005, and the Strangelies regrouped to play an acoustic gig at her wake.

## Ashtar (Gregory Brown)

Nothing is known of Ashtar after 1974, when he headed off to South America.

## Berry Visser

After decades spent running Mojo Concerts booking agency in Holland, Berry now has an alter ego as 'Madame de Berry.' In this guise he runs and performs at the museum Huize de Berry, a sort of temple to kitsch located in an old warehouse in Delft. He says: 'The building is a composition alive with colour, tactile fabrics, dolls, clocks and paintings, a magical world. Golden statues, flamboyant lamps, flowers, dozens of chairs, soft wallpaper and above all else: colour. Lighting plans for the rooms took two years to complete. Enter the dream world of an imaginative man.'

## Brian Trench

In 1982 Brian began writing for *Gralton*, an Irish political magazine named after James Gralton, a leading Irish communist/socialist, who in 1933 had become the only Irishman ever to be deported from Ireland for his views. Trench was a full-time journalist for 20 years, working on politics, foreign affairs, industrial relations, music (especially jazz), industry, technology (especially IT) and the media.

He later founded the Masters in Science Communication at Dublin City University and, as a Senior Lecturer there, pursued research interests that focussed on science on the internet and science journalism. He retired in 2010.

## Dave Robinson

After touring across America with The Jimi Hendrix Experience and other major bands, Dave returned to London and managed Brinsley Schwarz, Graham Parker, Nick Lowe, Dave Edmunds, Ian Dury and Elvis Costello.

In London, he created a network of pub venues where bands could play what they liked, paving the way for punk. He built a recording studio above the Hope and Anchor pub in Islington and, with Jake Riviera, started Stiff Records. After Stiff, Dave became president of Island Records, where he oversaw the careers of U2, Robert Palmer, Stevie Winwood and Frankie Goes to Hollywood. Dave then ran the Blue Note Club in Hoxton as well as the Acid Jazz Label, which helped to launch the acid house and drum'n'bass dance movements.

Booth: 'These days Dave Robinson is to be found on a Sunday noon doing a two-hour stint on Boogaloo Radio under the 'Free Yourself' banner. Here he talks about his many and varied adventures in the music business, the characters and artists he has worked with, often introducing some of them live and illustrating his reminiscences with pertinent platters. He is still as funny and sharp as he was when we first met him.'

## Del Harding

Still owns land at Bealkelly Woods, Ivan and Mary's former gypsy caravan campsite in Tuamgraney, Co Clare, where he helps organise traditional skills demonstrations and promotes information about woodland and wetland ecology and biodiversity.

## Don Knox

Don went on to form Spud, the first foray into management by later U2 manager Paul McGuinness. Spud were a 1970s folk-rock group who were heavily influenced by the likes of Sweeney's Men, Fairport Convention and Steeleye Span. Don says: 'Spud discovered Paul McGuinness, not the other way around. We had already released two albums before I asked Paul (an old Trinity friend) to manage the band.' Don has been a specialist painter and artist for the last 30 years.

## Frank Murray

A friend of Phil Lynott and – thanks to Ted Carroll – occasional roadie for the Strangelies, Frank worked as a tour manager for Thin Lizzy and others, and later became manager of The Pogues. He went on to work in the US theatre and film industries. He died in 2016.

## Frank van der Meijden

After many years as a manager in the Dutch music business, Frank is now a fulltime artist, producing some remarkable work with found objects. See his latest collages/paintings at *www.frankvandermeijden.com*

## Gay and Terry Woods

Grahame Hood writes: After the Strangelies, Gay and Terry formed The Woods Band. Their projected line-up of a pedal steel guitarist and a Uileann piper might have changed the future of Irish folk-rock, but the piper they wanted, Paddy Keenan (later in The Bothy Band) was deemed too young by his parents and forbidden to join. The album itself, drawing on the repertoire the Woods had used with DSS, was a blend of traditional Irish with a tinge of American folk-rock influences. Much of their live work was carried out in Europe, and the band line-up changed frequently. Gay: 'We had various people playing with us every now and then but it never worked out. It always got back down to the two of us, which I didn't really like.' The Woods recorded four more albums as a duo, plus a compilation of sessions recorded for the BBC, before calling it a day in 1979 and divorcing in 1980.

Gay joined a new wave band called Auto Da Fé: 'It was so liberating for me to stand up and not be a folkie any more.' The band split in 1986, and after a few years out of music Gay agreed to rejoin Steeleye Span in 1994, singing with Maddy Prior until 1997, then as sole female lead until she left in 2001. Maddy rejoined the following year. Gay still intends to issue a solo album one day.

Terry got involved in music management before being persuaded to join The Pogues in 1986, staying until 1993 and appearing on *Top Of The Pops* as part of the Fairytale Of New York line-up. He also joined the reformed Pogues from 2001 to 2004. In 1994 he formed The Bucks with Ron Kavana, and then a new Woods Band, which still exists.

## Humphrey Weightman

In London, Humphrey worked on underground publications and designed many LP covers for Topic and CBS, including the first two Anne Briggs albums, *Anne Briggs* and *The Time Has Come*. Alongside his typography work, he played soul and funk with American blues singer and harmonica player Major Wiley (circa 1973). In 1972 he worked with singer Carolanne Pegg, whom he had met in April that year through Anthea Joseph: 'We worked together for some eight months – a mix of the usual clubs, a tour of Holland (replacing Annie Briggs) together with the Cambridge Folk Festival with Booth et al.'

Anthea, Carolanne and Humphrey, Highgate Cemetery, 1972

In the mid-Seventies he moved back to Ireland, working with Planxty for a while as their sound engineer during the Christy Moore/Andy Irvine era. Working as a chef at Armstrong's Barn in County Wicklow, Humphrey achieved some fame: in the 1974 *Good Food Guide*, Armstrong's Barn was awarded the highest possible rating for a restaurant, and earned a star in the *Egon Ronay Guide*; in 1977 it was awarded a star in the UK and Ireland *Michelin Guide*. Humphrey disappeared from the band's day-to-day lives for years but, from time to time, would suddenly pop up out of the blue; The Invisible Kid, a Booth story-song from 2007 which shares a Western theme with Roy Rogers, is loosely based on him. The Kid character 'is a bit like someone from a William Burroughs novel,' says Booth.

Eventually Humphrey tired of being a master chef and returned to the UK. He currently lives near Berwick-upon-Tweed, where he still works as a typographer and is, he says, 'simply a Forrest Gump on the sidelines.' He also plays guitar in Eimar Woolf and her Foul Weather Alternatives, 'a scratch band playing country/soul and swamp/funk.'

Humphrey in The Foul Weather Alternatives, 2018 (Photo: Thom Sandberg)

Humphrey: 'Annie Briggs – to my mind the finest singer in the past 60 years, without whom there would've been no June Tabor, Maddy

Prior or Sandy Denny – remains a true friend, and we talk about gardening occasionally (she lives some three hours north of me).'

Iain at the Green Note showing Tim Booth's cover for *Icarus* (Photo: Sean Kelly)

## Iain Sinclair

After running a small publishing company, Albion Village Press, in the early Seventies, Iain has been a full-time writer, film-maker and psychogeographer ever since. He still lives in the same house in Dalston where some of his Strangelies film was shot. There's not room here to detail all his activities, but *www.iainsinclair.org.uk* is the place to go.

In 2009 he appeared with the Strangelies at the Green Note, Camden, reading from his *Kodak Mantra Diaries*. Renchi's walk from Dalston to Allihies, which Iain recalled for this book, reminds him now of Van Gogh's walk from Ramsgate to Canterbury, Chatham, Lewisham and Welwyn, about which he is currently writing.

## Jay Myrdal

Jay Myrdal studied at the University of Montana and became a professional photographer in January 1968. Ten years into his career, he photographed Kate Bush for the cover of her debut album *The Kick Inside*. He also photographed album covers for Toyah and Classix Nouveaux. Jay has now retired from photography, but has become the harmonica player in the Oxfordshire/Wiltshire-based blues-rock band The Wirebirds.

## Jeffa Gill

In the early 1970s Jeffa bought a small farm on the hillside valley of Coomkeen, just above Durrus village in West Cork. In 1979 she became a cheesemaker. Now approaching its fourth decade, Durrus Cheese is still handmade by her, her daughter Sarah Hennessy and others. Her cheeses continue to win awards at both national and international level, most recently winning 2 and 3 Gold Stars at the Great Taste Awards in the UK.

## Jenny Richardson

Has lived and worked as an artist in Scotland and Ireland and is currently living on the Beara peninsula, where she has stayed since 1998. She still exhibits in Dublin, Beara and Edinburgh. It was her idea to get Brian Trench to join the band: 'I was living with Tim Booth in Waterloo Road and I was friends with the Incredible String Band, who were becoming famous at that time. As we were heading to Toners I said to Mr Booth, "What about you and Brian getting a band going?" Into the bar we sashayed. "I've had a great idea," says he. I said nothing about my ownership of this great idea.'

## Johanna

Johanna lives a quiet rural life in the UK.

## Julia Creasey

When she first met the Strangelies, Julia was working as a booker for folk music promoter Roy Guest, but soon moved to Blackhill Enterprises, taking most of her roster with her. In February 1971 she set up her own management agency, based near Bond Street in an office shared with the Asgard agency. She represented Al Stewart and, from September 1971, The Woods Band. We tried to trace her as part of the research for this book, but failed.

## Lars-Erik Ejlers

In the Seventies LEE ran a Danish music booking agency, Good Music. He went on to work as an architect in Copenhagen and is now retired.

## Linus (Caroline Greville)

Ivan: 'Linus has been living and working in Co Galway, raising her family and gardening. There are quite a few musicians in the area, and she has been seen singing and playing at informal sessions.'

## Neil Hopwood

Hoppy: 'I left the Sutherland Brothers shortly after that Bowie tour, as they had decided to go totally acoustic. After that I played in Jimmy Powell's Dimensions and also with folk duo Leonard and Squire, occasionally backing folk singer and comedian Tony Capstick and a young Julie Matthews, later with The Albion Band. In the Eighties I joined Britain's premier Cajun Band, R. Cajun & The Zydeco Brothers, with whom I recorded seven albums as well as recording briefly with Paul McCartney, a song for his daughter Mary and new husband Alistair (the band had played at their wedding). In the late Eighties I also joined local songwriter Kevin

Hand's folk influenced band, Yeah Jazz, who previously had singles and album success in the Indie charts. By the mid-Nineties I had got fed up of sitting in vans for hours on the motorway, so decided to concentrate on recording and playing locally. Myself and Dave Blant from The Zydeco Brothers and Yeah Jazz renamed ourselves The Vice-Bishops of Uttoxeter for a recording project, acquiring the name from a TV skit by Messrs Fry and Laurie; for live gigs we joined up with guitarists Pod Malkin and Dave Faulkner, forming the Vice-Bishops' Blues Band. The band has two album releases, and continues to play regularly at our resident venue near Uttoxeter. Recent guests there over the last two years have included members of Climax Blues Band, Gavin Sutherland and others.' Details and more info can be found on *www.facebook.com/thevice-bishops*

Hoppy, 2016

## 'Orphan' Annie Mohan

After Annie and Goulding split up, she remained living and working in the old School House in Allihies. Goulding: 'She was an inspired weaver of rugs and wall hangings in the Navajo tradition and used a 180-year-old Norwegian loom. Her work is in several artists' collections.'

As well as being a talented photographer, she was a professional chef. She served on the sail training vessel The Asgard for many years as cook, befriending many of the young cadets. She was also chef in the ground-breaking restaurant The Blue Bull in Sneem, Co Kerry and The Lime Tree restaurant in Kenmare, Co Kerry. In later life she was the leading light of a circle of friends and musicians based at O'Neill's Bar in Allihies village. She died in 2017.

## Paul Scully

After surviving an early job as tour manager for The Woods Band, Scully later became live sound engineer for The Pogues and producer of the Strangelies' third album in 1997. He is currently sound engineer for Luka Bloom.

## Renchi Bicknell

Tim Goulding writes: My old schoolmate and lifelong friend Renchi moved from London in the Seventies and lived for some years at Theddon Grange, a large country house bought by seven families and run on a loosely communal basis. While there, he ran a bookshop, The Little Green Dragon, in the nearby town of Alton. He then moved to Glastonbury where he and his wife Vanessa ran a very popular guest house, The Flying Dragon. Renchi continues to paint and make films in his inimitable style. He is a true original.

## Robin Birch

Robin separated from Linus after having two children with her, and now divides his time between Ireland and Spain.

## Roger Armstrong

Former Queens University social sec Roger Armstrong was persuaded to take early retirement from a brief career in band management and moved in behind the counter at Ted Carroll's Rock On Soho stall. He then achieved greatness by joining Ace Records, (see the entry for Ted Carroll) of which he is now MD.

## Roger Mayer

Roger went on to engineer or co-produce many of the Incredible String Band's later albums and solo projects. After the closure of Sound Techniques, he moved to the States and worked with the likes of David Gates and Bonnie Raitt. He left audio engineering in 1984 and now works in the film and video areas. The Hendrix wah-wah pedal bloke was a *different* Roger Mayer.

## Stan Schnier

After moving back to the States, Stan worked as a manager for Janis Ian and then Art Garfunkel. Since 1992, he has been a freelance photographer in Manhattan, where he lives and works. He is Professor of Photography at Wagner College on Staten Island, where they still use 'old-fashioned' film as well as Smartphones. He starts every week with a boat ride across New York Harbour, and has been building a portfolio of images of the bustling port. You can see them at *www.stanschnier.com*

## Steve Bullock

Steve: 'I live in Jimena de la Frontera, near Algeciras and La Linea, the border with Gibraltar, where I work as a barrister. I'm getting too old to put up with the profession and the judiciary any longer; of course, as a result of the knuckle-draggers and racists who gained a marginal majority in the referendum, the border may even be closed. It may be necessary for me to get Spanish nationality in order to continue living here, as I have for the last 30 years.

'Why my nickname of "El Tigre?" Maybe because I was more ferocious in those days but I don't remember any acts of violence... I even went to San Francisco in 1968 and saw the Grateful Dead in Winterland and Big Brother and the Holding Company at the Fillmore and lots of Black Panthers in Oakland and New York, which was mostly a war zone in those days. I suppose one picks up certain attitudes as a result of being exposed to this sort of shit, not necessarily consciously. Now it's more "El Pussycat," unless you're a client or adversary!'

## Steve Peacock

Moved out of music journalism fairly early in his career and became an agricultural journalist. Until recently he was editor of the BBC *Farming Today* programme and agricultural advisor to *The Archers*, but is now retired and very active in the Birmingham choral scene.

## Steve Pearce

Ivan: 'Steve devoted his formidable energy to the family Shanagarry Pottery, expanding it greatly and putting it firmly on the world map.' The business was badly affected by the 'Celtic Tiger' crash of the Noughties, and though the pottery still operates, albeit on a smaller scale, Steve is currently living in Italy, where he remains uncontactable.

## Ted Carroll

Ted commissioned Tim Booth to design the original Thin Lizzy logo, several promotional comic strips and other devices, and stayed on as manager of Thin Lizzy until 1974, when they were on the verge of superstardom. He then set up the Rock On stall in Soho market with Gary Moore's friend Sylvia Keogh, later a Camden Rock On shop, and then Chiswick Records. When Chiswick was licensed to EMI in 1978, they had enough back catalogue of their own, so he formed Ace Records, originally for his own reissues. Ace now issues a formidable catalogue of old and new recordings, including of course the third Strangelies album. Ted is now retired.

## Tony Lowes

After spending a couple of years travelling in North Africa, Afghanistan and India, Tony moved to the Beara peninsula, near Goulding, and continued to work as a writer. In 1971, Iain Sinclair published his *Elephant Book (or, How the Elephant Made It through the Psychedelic Symbol)*, with illustrations by Tim. Lowes lived a simple rural life in Allihies, fishing, gardening and growing. Christa Jo, Annie Mohan's weaving teacher from Edinburgh, came to live with him and they had five children together. The Strangelies gradually lost touch with him, though. Tony rubbed people up the wrong way, first when he wrote *The Tim And Annie Diaries*, an outré manuscript about a nominally fictional West Cork life, and then when he formally objected to the design and colour of Tim's house.

Tony is currently a well-known ecology campaigner, a director of Friends Of The Irish Environment.

## Tony Reeves

Went on to join Greenslade, recording three albums with them in the Seventies. Subsequently he played with Curved Air and in jazz band Big Chief, then including saxophonist Dick Heckstall-Smith. For the last 30 years Tony has been running MTR Ltd, a manufacturer and distributor of professional audio products. He still gigs regularly, with Big Chief and others.

# Strangely Strange But Oddly Normal

Here is Ivan's lead sheet so you can sing and play along.

There is, on YouTube, an appalling live version of SSBON by comedian Nigel Planer (where he actually displays surprising familiarity with Ivan's phrasing). Otherwise, no-one apart from Robin Williamson ever recorded any Strangelies' covers. Nevertheless, SSBON was undoubtedly the 'hit,' continuing from its placement on *Nice Enough To Eat* to star on at least eight different compilation albums. In 2005, a whole Island Records box set was named after it.

## VERSE TWO

When dark clouds pall the sky, I have cast my eye
to the path where we are treading,
Oh! I could rack my brains, trying to explain
where it is I think we're heading .....

(Strangely strange chant for x bars !! )

## VERSE THREE

Why, only the other day I was making hay
For I supposed the sun was shining.
Ah, but when I looked up by harsh Neon
I was struck — Must be just my sense of timing
must adjust my sense of timing

(INTRO)

## VERSE FOUR

Well I'd had some things on my mind, mostly all the time,
Like cardboard scarecrows on a see saw,
And, were I to impart those things I held to heart,
Why! Fitting pieces to the jigsaw . . .

(OUTRO)

Ⓒ Ivan Pawle

# Interviewees

Huge thanks to all those who gave up their time to help fit pieces to the jigsaw:

| | |
|---|---|
| David Ambrose | Jay Myrdal |
| Roger Armstrong | Mary Pawle (Marymac) |
| Olivier Assayas | Steve Peacock |
| Steve Bullock | Michel Polizzi |
| Joe Boyd | Hans Christian Poulsen |
| George Boyter | Polly Quick (now James) |
| Paul Charles | Tony Reeves |
| Roger Dean | Jenny Richardson |
| Lars-Erik Ejlers | Dave Robinson |
| Jeffa Gill | Paul Scully (via Tim G) |
| Raymond Greenoaken | Rose Simpson |
| Andrew Greig | Brendan 'The Brush' Shiels |
| Neil Hopwood | Paul Simmons |
| Andy Irvine | Iain Sinclair |
| Johanna | Joe Thoma |
| Tony Lowes | Brian Trench |
| Dave Mattacks | Frank van der Meijden |
| Roger Mayer (Sound Techniques) | Berry Visser |
| Gary Moore | Humphrey Weightman |

A rare 1969 Australian edition of *Kip* on cheapo/reissue label Calendar Records, housed in a laminated picture sleeve. The strange back cover features some fairly prosaic liner notes, as opposed to Booth's artwork.

The legendary American record collector, the late Ron Kane, turned up a very rare Island Records cassette release of *Kip*. The plain cover used only Booth's Letraset Blippo titles, and the inlay photo, featuring Linus, was from an early Orphan Annie Dublin photoshoot.

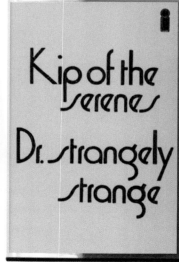

# Thanks

Design, layout and services above and beyond
by the inimitable Mychael Gerstenberger of Malbuch, Berlin. Vielen Dank!

**Special thanks to my research assistants:**

Grahame Hood: musicology and music history

Claus Rasmussen and L-P Anderson: Danish research

Riemer Sijens: Dutch research

**Critical readers:** Debbie Cole, Andrew Greig, Grahame Hood, Deena Benjamin Omar
and Iain Sinclair plus, of course, the band. Special thanks to Molloy Woodcraft!

**Help with web stuff:** Norman Lamont

**And thanks to:**

Olivier Assayas for his piece on *Kip*

Nick Brown for memories of the Leeds Poly gig

Simon Cosyns – standard-bearer in the popular press

Pit Dafis at Gomer Press

Phine Dahle – Danish translator

Jari Demeulemeester – Wemmel gig info

Robin Denselow for staying the pace

Lars-Erik Ejlers – Denmark tour info

Mark Ellen – for sensible advice

Flanders Arts Institute (Belgian gigs): Lobke Aelbrecht, Quinten Van Wichelen

Jan Florizoone and Firmin Michiels – memories of Wemmel

Evelyne Gerstenberger for extra-intensive proofreading

Raymond Greenoaken – cuttings and memories

Andrew Greig and his book *You Know What You Could Be* (co-written with Mike Heron)

Colin Harper and his book *Irish Folk, Trad And Blues* (early Dublin music scene)

Paul Hunter for proofreading

Bob Johnston at The Gutter Bookshop, Dublin

Matthew Karas for a decade of harmonium support

Stewart Lee for his piece on *Heavy Petting*

Tony Lowes for permission to use his *Kip* in the desert tale

Médiathèque Musicale de Paris

Jon Mills and Andy Morten at *Shindig!*

Deena Benjamin Omar for the Dublin map, author photo and for seeing the book through to its birth

Brian O'Reilly for permission to use some Hux material originally written as liner notes

Genesis Breyer P-Orridge for permission to quote from his Epiphany piece

Anne Pawle for Paris gig memories

Ivan Pawle for loan of his diaries, 1969-1971

Michel Polizzi for memories of the Paris gig and archive help

Steve Potter, late of Wordery, for help above and beyond

Hans Christian Poulsen – Denmark photos

Niall Reddy for Dublin library research

Andy Roberts and his book *Albion Dreaming: A popular history of LSD in Britain*

Beatrix Roudet and Norman Ellis for French translation help

Simon Ryan for graphics help

Bart Sas – Turnhout town library archivist, Belgium

Daniel Scott of Allison and Busby, for sensible advice

Michael Sexton's book *The Yeti Society* for Samye Ling background

Harry Shapiro and his book *I Can't Wait Until Tomorrow* for Gary Moore material

Sylvie Simmons for encouragement

Iain Sinclair for his photos, film clips, memorabilia and his books *The Kodak Mantra Diaries* and *Hackney, That Rose-Red Empire.*

Gerry Smyth for permission to quote from *Beautiful Day – Forty Years Of Irish Rock*, by S. Campbell and G. Smyth

Graeme Thomson and his book *Cowboy Song* for Phil Lynott material

Geoff Travis and Rough Trade for support

Jim Wirth at *Uncut*

Molloy Woodcraft for considerable amounts of ~~proofreadign~~ proofreading

**Background reads**

John Banville – *Time Pieces – a Dublin memoir*

Jill Drower – *99 Balls Pond Road: The Story of the Exploding Galaxy*

Robert Graves – *Adam's Rib*

Howard Marks – *Mr Nice*

Rob Young – *Electric Eden*

Ian Whitcomb – *Rock Odyssey*

Various – *Trinity Tales*

**Websites:**

The site *irishrock.org* was invaluable. Where else could you find a detailed history of Granny's Intentions? The 'Marmalade Skies' site also provided a lot of handy background on British psychedelia of the 1960s. The *Irish Times* online archive was very useful, despite boasting an extremely creaky search engine. Support Wikipedia!

**Finally…**

Thanks to you, the reader, for buying the book and getting this far. I hope you enjoyed it. I'd love to get some feedback, and if you feel like letting me know your thoughts about the book, please mail me via the Contact page on my website:

*www.drstrangelystrange.co.uk*

Adrian Whittaker, January 2019

# The Albums

### Halcyon Days
*HUX Records HUX 092 • includes 32-page booklet*

COCK-A-DOODLE-DOO • EXISTENCE NOW • GOOD EVENING MR WOODS • GOING TO POULAPHOUCA • MIRROR MIRROR • SWEET RED RAPE • HORSE OF A DIFFERENT HUE • LADY OF THE GLEN • HMS AVENGER • HALCYON DAYS (2006) • THE INVISIBLE KID (2006) • LE LE ROCKIN SOUND (2006) • COCK-A-DOODLE-DOO (Kip version)

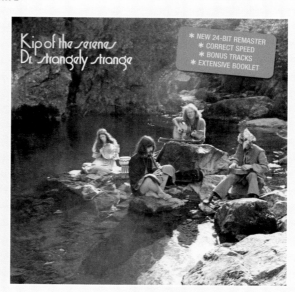

### Kip Of The Serenes
*HUX Records HUX 104 • Remastered at correct speed • includes 32-page booklet*

STRANGELY STRANGE BUT ODDLY NORMAL • DR DIM AND DR STRANGE • ROY ROGERS • DARK-HAIRED LADY • ON THE WEST CORK HACK • A TALE OF TWO ORPHANAGES • STRINGS IN THE EARTH AND AIR • SHIP OF FOOLS • FROSTY MORNINGS • DONNYBROOK FAIR + **BONUS TRACKS:** MIRROR MIRROR (Kip version) • WEST CORK HACK (alternate take) • STRINGS IN THE EARTH AND AIR (instrumental edit) • STRANGELY STRANGE BUT ODDLY NORMAL (alternate take)

### Heavy Petting And Other Proclivities
*HUX Records HUX 127 • Band-approved remaster • includes 36-page booklet*

BALLAD OF THE WASPS • SUMMER BREEZE • KILMANOYADD STOMP • I WILL LIFT UP MINE EYES • SIGN ON MY MIND • GAVE MY LOVE AN APPLE • JOVE WAS AT HOME • WHEN ADAM DELVED • ASHLING • MARY MALONE OF MOSCOW • GOODNIGHT MY FRIENDS + **BONUS TRACKS:** SIGN ON MY MIND (Take1) • GAVE MY LOVE AN APPLE (Take1) • HORSE OF A DIFFERENT HUE (Live) • BALLAD OF THE WASPS (Live) • SWEET RED RAPE (Live) • LADY OF THE GLEN (Single edit) • THE PRISONER (Medley)

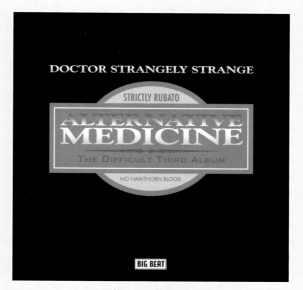

### Alternative Medicine
*ACE Records CDWIKD 177*

LILTY'S • DARKSOME BURN • THE HEAT CAME DOWN • THE JAMES GANG • HALE BOPP / JIG FOR JACK • HAMES AND TRACES • WISHING • WHATEVER HAPPENED TO THE BLUES • TOO MUCH OF A GOOD THING • HARD AS NAILS • PLANXTY ROLAND • EPILOG • STRANGE WORLD • PULP KAYAK

These CDs are available from your favourite record shop and online retailers.

Alternative Medicine can be obtained directly from ACE RECORDS: *www.acerecords.co.uk*